Substantial Justice

SUBSTANTIAL JUSTICE
An Anthropology Of Village Courts in Papua New Guinea

Michael Goddard

Berghahn Books
New York • Oxford

First published in 2009 by

Berghahn Books
www.berghahnbooks.com

©2009 Michael Goddard

All rights reserved. Except for the quotation of short passages for the purposes of criticism and review, no part of this book may be reproduced in any form or by any means, electronic or mechanical, including photocopying, recording, or any information storage and retrieval system now known or to be invented, without written permission of the publisher.

Library of Congress Cataloging-in-Publication Data
Goddard, Michael (Michael Bruce)
  Substantial justice : an anthropology of village courts in Papua New Guinea / Michael Goddard.
    p. cm.
  Includes bibliographical references and index.
  ISBN 978-1-84545-561-3 (alk. paper)
  1. District courts--Papua New Guinea. I. Title.
KWH334.G63 2009
347.953'02—dc22   2008053752

British Library Cataloguing in Publication Data
A catalogue record for this book is available from the British Library
Printed in the United States on acid-free paper

978-1-84545-561-3 hardback

A society beyond justice is impossible and undesirable. A completely just society is possible but undesirable.

Agnes Heller, *Beyond Justice*

Contents

List of Illustrations	ix
List of Abbreviations	xi
Preface and Acknowledgments	xiii
Introduction	1
1. Colonial Law: An Extended Prelude to the Village Courts	27
2. The Administration of Village Courts	53
3. Village Courts on Trial	77
4. Three Village Courts and Their Social Environments	113
5. Village Court Politics	145
6. Pari Village Court in Action	169
7. Konedobu Village Court in Action	195
8. Erima Village Court in Action	217
9. Between Groups and Individuals	241
Conclusion: The Local and the Global	267
Appendix: The Official Range of Offences Heard by Village Courts	281
References	285
Index	303

Illustrations

Maps

1. Papua New Guinea, showing provincial boundaries   xviii
2. Port Moresby area, showing locations mentioned in this book   xix

Figures

9.1. Natal relationship between Mary, Janet and Anna   248
9.2. Adoption of Janet and Anna   249
9.3 Marriages of Janet, Mary and Anna   250

Tables

6.1. Offences and disputes as officially designated in Pari village court during two periods of eighteen weekly hearings   172

7.1. Offences and disputes as officially designated in Konedobu village court during two periods of eighteen weekly hearings   197

8.1. Offences and disputes as officially designated in Erima village court during two periods of eighteen weekly hearings   220

9.1. Dispute outcomes by sex of plaintiffs and respondents in 185 cases monitored at Erima Village Court, 1994 and 1999   259

9.2. Dispute outcomes by sex of plaintiffs and respondents in thirty-six cases monitored at Konedobu Village Court, 1994 and 1999   260

9.3. Dispute outcomes by sex of plaintiffs and respondents in fifty cases monitored at Pari Village Court, 1994 and 1999   261

ABBREVIATIONS

AAA	American Anthropological Association
ADR	Alternative Dispute Resolution
AGD	Attorney General's Department
AGDISP	Attorney General's Department Institutional Strengthening Project
AIDAB	Australian International Aid and Development Bureau
AusAID	Australian Agency for International Development
CCAU	Community Courts Administration Unit
DJ&AG	Department of Justice and Attorney General
DPA	Department of Provincial Affairs
DSM	District Senior Magistrate
K	Kina (Papua New Guinea currency)
LMS	London Missionary Society
MS	Magisterial Service
MSC	Magisterial Services Commission
NCD	National Capital District
NCDC	National Capital District Commission

PNG	Papua New Guinea
UN	United Nations
UNESCO	United Nations Educational, Scientific and Cultural Organisation
UPNG	University of Papua New Guinea
VCO	Village Courts Officer
VCS	Village Court Secretariat

Preface and Acknowledgments

Papua New Guinea's village courts are not 'traditional'. The village court system was introduced in 1974 after a long period of debate, planning and finally the passing of a legislative act in the twilight of colonial rule. I had given village courts little thought during my first substantial period of anthropological fieldwork in the country, in the Western Highlands Province in 1985–86, which was not at all concerned with the anthropology of law. During that period I attended—with a sense of ethnographic duty rather than a legalist interest—a number of moots or disputes presided over by various mature men of status. Some of these men were ex-*kaunsel* (Tokpisin: councillors), originally installed under colonial community governance strategies, whose authority was still acknowledged by virtue of their age and past performance. Others were 'village court magistrates'. Sometimes they were men who served in both roles. Unlike many communities around the country, the people of the upper Kaugel Valley (my fieldwork site) had not built semi-permanent courtrooms in which to conduct the 'village courts', neither were the village courts conducted according to a timetable. Many other communities had, by the mid 1980s, moulded their village court to fit a model of the colonial formal courts, with a magistrates' bench, prayers to begin sessions, a national flag, and so on. But in the Kaugel Valley village courts followed the ideal of informality embedded in the legislation: they were held 'from time to time' and 'from place to place' as required when specific disputes arose. The difference between an informal moot—or a dispute settlement—or a village court hearing did not strike me as particularly significant, preoccupied as I was at the time with an unrelated PhD research topic.

In 1990 I returned to Papua New Guinea (PNG), taking up a lecturing position at the national university in Port Moresby. I lectured a variety of courses in social anthropology, among them the anthropology of law. I had hoped that residency in the country would enable me to make return visits to the Kaugel Valley for further research. However, I was prevented in the first place by the politics of a war which had occurred there since my fieldwork. My attempt to re-enter the valley ended at its head, as further access was controlled by the clans who were the enemies of the group who had been my fieldwork hosts and with whom I was consequently identified in local perceptions. Meanwhile, I had developed friendships in Port Moresby which were taking me into local communities, where the possibilities of urban research were evident, particularly in the so-called settlements which were being simplistically portrayed and unfairly maligned in local and overseas media.

My fieldwork interests were, then, being re-oriented by social circumstance rather than by systematic planning, but they did not include village courts until I was cajoled into a small cross-disciplinary team of academics recruited by the university's consultancy arm in 1991 to review the village court system for the Attorney General's Department (AGD). Thinking the exercise might provide me with some material for my anthropology of law lectures, I became the 'anthropological' consultant, alongside educationists and legal specialists. We travelled the country for a few weeks, attending village court hearings, talking to village court officers and disputants, and discussing the system's administrative problems with members of the Village Court Secretariat (VCS) and regional administrators. The consultancy awakened me to the importance and value of village courts in local communities and to the state. I also saw their potential value to a researcher in the urban environment, where the co-existence of groups from every region of PNG, with their specific micro-ethnic sensibilities, was fraught with everyday tensions and conflicts.

I fielded the idea of ongoing research in village courts with the village court secretary, Peni Keris, who not only gave me access to his staff and documentary resources at the Secretariat, but also approved my scheme to monitor some village courts on an ongoing basis. I picked three courts, two in Port Moresby itself and another in a village at the city's edge, and asked the magistrates if they would countenance my regular attendance. They were agreeable, and so began the project resulting in this book. My research was relatively intensive until 1995, when I left the University of Papua New Guinea (UPNG) and moved to Australia. It has continued intermittently since then, by virtue of several return visits and overall it has spanned about sixteen years.

Village court magistrates are recruited from their own communities, and each village court reflects the sociality of the particular community it serves. Therefore the study of an individual village court is, or should be, to a large extent conventionally ethnographic. To observe hearings without an anthropological understanding of the society from which disputants or officers come is likely to result in an inadequate understanding not only of the court proceedings and decisions one is witnessing, but of the background of any case before the court. At the same time, village courts are not organic products of particular societies in the way that we conceive 'traditional' moots or dispute-settling procedures to have been. The village court system was inaugurated legislatively, and is thus a state institution, bound by law and bureaucracy. Therefore conventional fieldwork is not enough in itself to produce a properly informed anthropology. Village courts and their officers are significantly affected and burdened in their procedure and dispute-settling practice by institutional forces beyond their control, and these need to be analytically understood. This book therefore combines localised ethnography with a larger, historical examination of the village court system, including an account of the century-long colonial administrative background to the introduction of the system in the mid 1970s. It further contextualises the courts in international processes involving legal and human rights concerns.

I have incorporated some previously published material here. Chapters 2 and 3 draw in part from 'Of Handcuffs and Foodbaskets: Theory and Practice in Papua New Guinea's Village Courts', which originally appeared in *Research in Melanesia* 16: 79–94, in 1992. A 2004 discussion paper titled 'Women in Papua New Guinea's Village Courts', originally published by the State, Society and Governance in Melanesia Project at the Australian National University (discussion paper 2004/3), was expanded into an article entitled 'Research and Rhetoric on Women in PNG's Village Courts' and published in *Oceania* 75(3): 247–67, in 2005. The latter is substantially reproduced in a section of chapter 9. A section of chapter 3 reproduces 'The Snake Bone Case: Law, Custom and Justice in a PNG Village Court', originally published in 1996 in *Oceania* 67(1): 50–63. A section of chapter 5 and another in the conclusion draw on 'Reto's Chance: State and Status in an Urban Papua New Guinea Settlement', which appeared originally in 2002 as an article in *Oceania* 73(1): 1–16, and subsequently as a chapter in my book *The Unseen City: Anthropological perspectives on Port Moresby*, published in 2005 by Pandanus Books (whose affairs are now administered by the University of New South Wales Press). I thank all the above-mentioned publishing organisations for permission to re-use this material. The map of Papua

New Guinea was kindly contributed by Don Niles, of the Institute of PNG Studies, Port Moresby.

I am indebted to a great many people, and several institutions, for support and assistance on the road to this book. At UPNG in the early 1990s, Colin Filer persuaded me to take part in the consultancy that spawned my research interest in the village courts, and Jonathan Aleck was a valuable resource so far as legal questions were concerned in the immediate aftermath of that exercise. I am grateful to the National Research Institute of Papua New Guinea for the affiliation status which made my 1999 fieldwork visit possible. Village Court Secretary Peni Keris has continued to facilitate my access to courts and resources. Other staff at the VCS from 1991 to the present time who have been most accommodating include John Takuna, Bruce Didimas, Darius Dorke, Tamo Mai, Kimson Kimeto, Stephen Seta, Robert Kandege, Perpetua Hau, Bonnie Tau, Tony Cameron, Ken Skews. Tony Pryke and Bob Welsh, who were involved in the Secretariat in its earliest days, provided valuable historical information.

The three village courts I have monitored at length are Erima, Konedobu and Pari. In those courts and the communities they serve I am indebted to a large number of individuals who showed infinite patience simply with my presence, let alone my endless petty questions, and who demonstrated more concern for my welfare than I deserved.

In respect of Erima I must specifically thank the following: Andrew Kadeullo, Tagube Epi, John Kameku, Clement Magula, Palipe Homoka, Peter Kunz, Simon Toni, Dai Andrew, Mege Baru, Otto Sul, Margaret Ule, Anton Nu, Ariel Nun, Kerai Alumo, Michael Du, Kaupa Konia, Robert James, 'Sanglas' Matiu, Oksy Tumbi, Kauliso Kasowa, Tom Nupu, Pepa Hin, Iteape Anebo, Maik Yobale, Agibe Nambi, Bob Omea.

At Konedobu and nearby settlements: Josephine Maniti, Molly Vani, the late Tati Marai, Dirona Lohia, Ben Aravape, Andrew Moiri, David Kemi, Rosa Harry, Avosa Tu'u, Geua Kisa, Maki Evera, the late Ume Sari, Jerry Max, Jack Marai, Andrew Wii, Joe Maniti, Dauri Kisu, James Mumurae, Idau Vagi, Jack Warebi.

At Pari village: the late Gaba Gaudi, Sisia Baeau, Puka Vagi, Oala Igo, Morea Hekoi, Lohia Daure, Sibona Gaudi, Lady Carol Kidu, Gaudi Kidu, Professor Sir Isi Kevau. Assistance with transcription and translation from the Motu language used at Pari village was provided by Doris Cassar and Janet Jovellanos of UPNG.

For practical support during fieldwork trips to PNG I am grateful to Denis Crowdy, Gima Rupa, Mau and Violet Vali and David and Helen Lawrence. For valuable anthropological and historical discussions and commentaries over the years I thank the late Nigel Oram, the late

Dawn Ryan, the late Bill Epstein, Keith Barber, Jadran Mimica, Michael Monsell-Davis and Ian Maddocks. Laura Nader and Rik Pinxten offered valuable criticisms and comments on an early draft of this book. The patience and support of my partner and intellectual companion Deborah Van Heekeren was vital to the completion of this project.

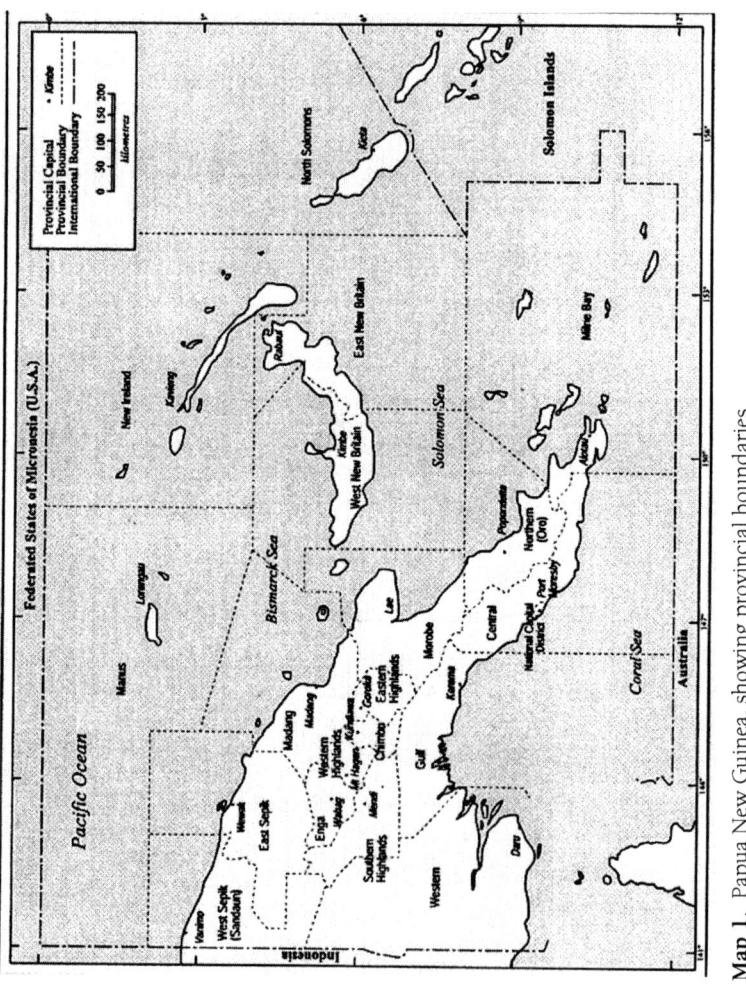

Map 1. Papua New Guinea, showing provincial boundaries

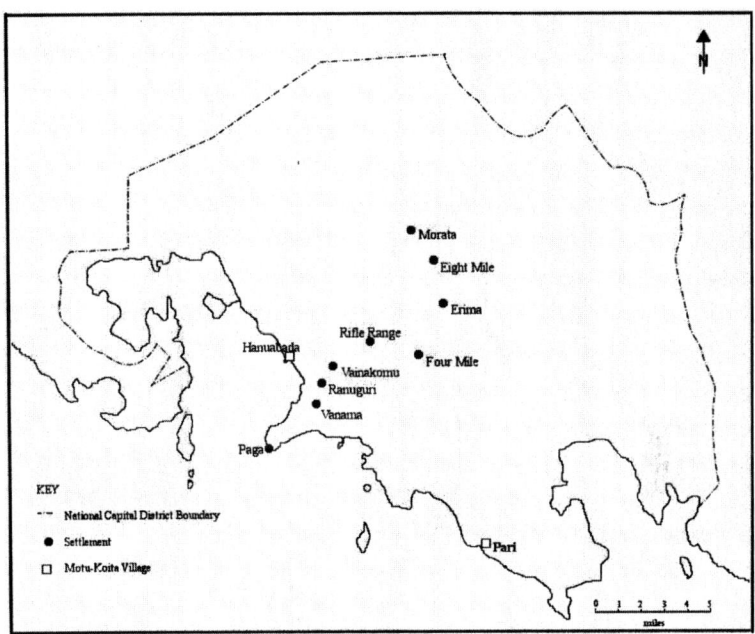

Map 2. Port Moresby area, showing locations mentioned in this book

INTRODUCTION

A person coming before a village court is stripped of every safeguard which he would enjoy before any other court, including legal representation, and left with only a presumption of innocence and an assurance that 'substantial justice' must be done, whatever that means.
—Justice Pratt, 1980

Like many jurists before him and since, Justice Pratt of the National Court took a dim view of Papua New Guinea's 'village courts'. The village court system had been introduced legislatively in 1974 partly to overcome the legal, geographical and social distance between village societies and the country's formal courts. Informality was an intended feature of village courts, and while they were subject to law their legally untrained magistrates were supposed to follow 'custom', and the courts were to be free of legal technicalities, including those manifest in the presence of lawyers. These features in themselves were enough to cause concern among conservative jurists at the time, when colonial rule was about to be replaced (in 1975) by political independence. In addition, the village courts were encouraged to decide all matters in accordance with 'substantial justice'. The concept of substantial justice is ill-defined in legal discourse, as Justice Pratt implied. It refers to the administration of justice in a way that satisfies a community's sense of fairness while not necessarily adhering strictly to legal technicalities. For jurists suspicious of Melanesian attitudes regarding social regulation, justice, punishment and retribution, any recourse to 'substantial justice' was especially worrying.

Conversely, the ambiguity which disturbed Justice Pratt makes village courts particularly attractive to a fieldworking anthropologist like myself. Village courts are positioned in the nexus of introduced law and a local community's sense of what is fair and just. They are therefore well placed to allow us insights into the conflicts, concerns and values of Melanesian societies inescapably engaged with capitalism, Christianity and the political legacy of the colonial presence. I do not share Justice Pratt's misgivings: a long period of involvement with village courts in general, and with three in particular, has convinced me of their importance and value to the communities they serve. I have developed a great admiration for the commitment of village court officers overall, and a deep respect for their collective wisdom, to a degree which puts me at odds with a body of critics who echo, in a more recent discourse of human rights, the discomfort of jurists like Justice Pratt. It is of course not unusual for anthropologists, working intimately with local communities and their institutions, to become advocates for their subject groups. But countering the opinions of (some) legalists and human rights advocates is not the only purpose of this book.

The fundamental work of village courts is to deal with disputes, which might at first sight seem a parochial matter, and of limited scope anthropologically. But as Pat Caplan has remarked, the study of disputes does not deserve to be narrowly categorised as a concern only of the sub-discipline known as the anthropology of law, for it 'leads us straight to key issues in anthropology—norms and ideology, power, rhetoric and oratory, personhood and agency, morality, meaning and interpretation—and enables us not only to see social relations in action but also to understand cultural systems' (1995: 1). The purview can be extended, towards the understanding of even wider, national and international, processes. Consequently, the attitudes of Justice Pratt and more recent critics take on a broader relevance, for the context of negative criticism of institutions like the village courts goes beyond legal or social concern for the immediate rights of the disputants, to the influence of the world political economy on village society in PNG, particularly through the medium of development aid.

In recent years development-aid agencies in Australia have shown a renewed interest in the village court system, which was inaugurated in the twilight of Australia's colonial administration of PNG. Guided by assessments that PNG is either a 'failing' state (see, for example, Hughes 2004) or at least a 'weak' one (see, for example, Dinnen 2001a), their concern is to develop the village courts into an efficient grassroots legal resource contributing to the control of the country's fabled 'law and order' problems and the advancement of human rights. The broader international processes behind these kinds of regional concerns are nicely summarised by Laura Nader in a review of law and development internationally:

> The rule-of-law enterprise is now big business, responsible for billions of dollars of investments. Legal connections are being established between national legal systems and transnational legal power brokers, interwoven with western ideas of democracy and international (read western) approaches to such issues as national human rights, women's rights (paving the way toward more strident, holier-than-thou rhetoric), guarantees of property rights, contracts, and minimal regulation—the purpose being to attract foreign investors. (2006: 104)

The Global Context

The history of village courts in PNG exemplifies a number of the themes traversed by Nader, and an anthropological study of the courts, while necessarily grounded in localised fieldwork, must acknowledge their articulation with wider legal and political processes. As Sally Falk Moore observed in a review of developments in anthropology over the second half of the twentieth century, contemporary anthropologists of law should have a wide vision of 'the political milieu in which law is imbricated. . . . It is evident that nothing is merely local in its formation or in its repercussions' (2001: 109–10). The need to understand the relationship between the global and the local is a *sine qua non* in anthropology in the new century. In respect of 'globalisation' and law (or perhaps we mean the increasing universalisation of Western concepts of the law), moreover, we cannot assume that globalising processes create simple uniformity among the local communities into which they reach.

Richard Wilson, who thinks we should not necessarily equate globalisation with Westernisation or standardisation, argues that the globalisation of political values may generate distinct political and social identities, and diverse legal and moral codes, created out of interaction and relationality (2007: 238). Within globalisation theory, he says, it is still possible to ask micro-social research questions about local notions of justice and how they relate to transnational codes of human rights (239). The possibility becomes an imperative in the case of village courts in a nation as socially diverse as PNG, which contains more than 750 language groups who regard themselves as ethnically distinct from one another. A significant theme of this book is that each of the approximately one thousand village courts in the country reflects, in its workings and decisions, the sociality of the particular community it serves. The variation persists in the face of recent systematic attempts to standardise the practice of the courts in line with the juridical views informing the interventions of development-aid organisations.

Consequently, the international processes described by Nader above have not yet homogenised local notions of justice in PNG. Parochial disputes, and personal conflicts and antagonisms, are endemic among 'grassroots' Papua New Guineans, and nowadays a number of options for solving, or at least managing, them are theoretically available. But villagers are often unable—or prefer not—to take minor offences or disputes to district or higher courts because of the costs and legal technicalities involved and the distance they might have to travel, among other reasons. At the same time, attempts to resolve matters through customary meetings or moots, or neo-customary channels such as local church-based counselling and mediation or community self-help committees often prove unsatisfactory. Village courts, staffed by local community members knowledgeable of local issues and the social context of minor disputes, yet representing the country's 'law' in a manner which is relatively easy for villagers to comprehend, have become enormously popular. Their accountability on the one hand to Western legal principles by virtue of their origins in legislation (the 'Village Courts Act'), and on the other hand to local notions of just outcomes, has resulted in an enormous variety of 'styles' of practice among them.

Globalising 'Harmony'

Two international themes which are particularly relevant to studying PNG's village courts are human rights issues and what Nader (1990) has called 'harmony ideology'. The latter is historically prior, and Nader has been its principal anthropological examiner and discussant (see, for example, 1990, 2002). Drawing on her research among the Talean Zapotec of Mexico, Nader elaborated the historical use of an ideology of harmony as a means of social control by colonisers and their governmental successors. The Talean subscription to harmony was a tradition stemming from Spanish and Christian origin, indicating the political nature of the uses of harmony. 'Legal styles are a component of political ideology that link harmony with autonomy or harmony with control' (Nader 1990: 2). She extended her argument to a recognition that harmony could come in many forms. It might be part of a local tradition or part of a system of pacification spread across the world along with Western colonialism, Christian missions and other macro-scale systems of cultural control (2): 'What is needed is an unpacking of ideas of harmony (and controversy), particularly as they relate to disputing processes. Harmony ideologies may be used to suppress peoples by socializing them toward conformity in colonial contexts, or they may be used to resist external control, as the Talean Zapotec do' (291).

In a discussion of disputing in Zambia and the 'myth of the harmonious community', Elizabeth Colson acutely comments that Westerners and anthropologists may value harmony more than the local communities they study, as anthropologists come from societies where there is relatively little sense of community and where quarrels threaten the social fabric 'in ways incomprehensible to those who do not think that social relationships are based upon good feeling' (1995: 67–68). Colson's comment is particularly relevant to the consideration of PNG societies, where there is evidence that 'good feeling' was not everywhere the traditional cement of social relationships and where antagonism and violence were often accepted as part of everyday life. Reciprocity and obligation have been enshrined in the anthropological literature as fundamental principles of human interaction in Melanesian societies since the publication in 1922 of Bronislaw Malinowski's ground-breaking research on the Trobriand Islanders (1966). They are manifest not only in the ubiquitous so-called 'gift economy', but also in violent retribution—as the longstanding and ambiguous use of the English term *payback* as a noun in popular discourse around PNG[1] implies.

Colson's point about the values of Westerners was exemplified in the tenor of the voice-over commentary of Robert Gardner's classic 1964 documentary *Dead Birds*,[2] about the Dani of Western New Guinea (which has a different colonial history to PNG, the eastern half of the land mass). The Dani were proving recalcitrant to the message of peace brought by missionaries, and engaged in chronic warfare to placate the spirits of their cosmos. Not far away from the Dani, the Jalé studied by Klaus-Friedrich Koch in the mid 1960s were still settling disputes in an unharmonious way despite a recent mission presence. People who felt wronged would frequently resort to taking matters into their own hands (often through violence), without attempting negotiation, and distinctions such as intent, negligence, inadvertence or accident were not part of their considerations in matters of restitution (Koch 1975). In the twenty-first century there is still evidence that 'good feeling' is not a preoccupation of all societies in PNG. In the case of the eastern highland Yagwoia, for example, Jadran Mimica emphatically states, 'The self-consciousness of these people in respect of their own violence makes no recourse to a gospel of peaceful coexistence', and goes on to distinguish the Yagwoia view of humanness from 'those partial and idealized qualities that inform the Western civic image of humanity focussed on "goodness", "dignity", "freedom", "negotiation"' (2003: 261).

Nevertheless, some societies in PNG do subscribe to harmony ideology. Given that a degree of missionary and/or colonial influence preceded anthropological enquiry in most of the country, it is difficult to ascertain the extent of pre-colonial 'harmony' ideas among Melanesian societies. Certainly, though, harmony ideology was introduced by missionaries in many areas. Missionary influence is a fundamental part of Nader's model of the historical spread of harmony ideology (1990: 2), and has been explored by a number of anthropologists, indicating the extent to which an essentially Western concept has been internationalised. Nader herself draws on the African examples from Malawi and Zambia provided by Martin Chanock (1998), one of the first people (his book was originally published in 1985) to examine the relationship between law and colonialism in depth. Chanock showed, among other things, that the 'customary law' which was codified during the colonial period was not a survival from the past but was a product of the colonial encounter consequently used for different ends by the rulers and the ruled. The colonial creation of 'customary law' has since become a common theme in anthropology, and we will return to it later herein. Chanock also indicated the influence of missionary justice in Malawi and Zambia. From the 1830s missionaries were legally active, combining Biblical law with English legal procedures (79), and sometimes administering harsh punishments, including flogging. The combined effects of missionaries, colonial courts and the responses of indigenous peoples generated what became 'customary law' which (to return to Nader's terminology) emphasised conciliation and compromise 'operating on the principles of Christian harmony ideology' (Nader 1990: 298).

It would be unwise to offer generalisations about missionary influence on dispute settlement in PNG, given the variations in the type and time of missionary contact in different parts of the country. On the southern coast, for example, the London Missionary Society (LMS) was active from the 1870s, while in the highlands some societies were still uncontacted by the mid twentieth century. Anthropological studies specifically addressing the influence, reception and adaptation of Christianity have exposed variety rather than uniformity (cf., for example, Eriksen 2005; Otto and Borsboom 1997; Robbins 2004; Tuzin 1997; Van Heekeren 2004). In some coastal areas local groups had similar experiences to those described by Chanock for parts of Africa. The LMS extended its influence quickly along the south coast, strategically embedding church activities in the existing social structure of local villages, recruiting and training villagers as pastors, and installing villager-run 'deacon's courts' (Oram n.d.: 6). As with the mission-operated courts of Africa, there was a contradictory aspect to these courts: they were guided by harmony ideology (the Christian message) while at the same time they penalised offenders by excluding them from church activities, and thus from village activities (11). The long-term effect of this early missionary intervention can be seen in the village court at Pari village, which is one of the three courts examined in depth in this book. Having absorbed Christian morality over many decades into their village identity, Pari people have come to see the adjacent PNG capital city, Port Moresby, as having a negative influence on their integrity as a community. In recent years their attempts to maintain their communality have included the promotion of harmony through their village court proceedings.

The example of Pari contains thematic similarities with that of the Talean Zapotec where, Nader says, harmony ideology has become a strategy for resisting the state's political and cultural hegemony and promotes local solidarity (1990: 2-3). In other parts of PNG evidence of missionary or colonial ideas of harmony being successful embedded in local dispute settlement in former times is less clear. In an ethnography which was controversial in its day, Ronald Berndt (1962) described the mimicking of colonial court procedure among an eastern highland group who went on to punish offences with corporal methods which would have horrified any Western jurist or missionary of the time. In contrast, Marie Reay (1974) described the discernible mission influence on 'councillors' appointed by colonial authorities to hear local disputes among the Minj (a western highlands group), where an emphasis on the restoration of friendly relations was underpinned by Christian ideation.

Harmony ideology was less clearly discernable when I conducted fieldwork in the 1980s (not focused on village courts) among the Kakoli, who lived in a high-altitude valley in PNG's western highlands. Missionaries had established themselves there only in the 1950s, and while the majority of Kakoli were nominally Christian three decades later, the degree to which they had absorbed idealised Christian attitudes was hard to gauge. They remained prone to inter-clan conflict, driven partly by very longstanding territorial rivalries (see Bowers 1968). Truces—these issues could never be realistically considered resolvable—were maintained in the colonial period and afterwards partly through the intervention of state agencies (mostly the police) and missions. For lesser disputes the Kakoli employed various colonially introduced dispute-settlement procedures, including forums presided over by senior males (some of whom had been colonially appointed as 'councillors' in former times), and village courts. Nevertheless, people who felt aggrieved were often likely to take direct action against offending parties. There was only a small degree of similarity with the situation in Minj described by Reay, inasmuch as some councillors displayed Christian piety, while many did not. In general, co-operation and reciprocal obligations among the Kakoli were still driven by the imperatives of communal subsistence production (see, for example, Goddard 1998), more than by harmony ideology.

More directly and more generally applicable to a study of PNG's village courts is a later development which Nader includes in her critique of harmony ideology: 'alternative dispute resolution' (ADR), which arose in the United States in the 1970s and was exported to other parts of the world over subsequent decades (Nader 1999, 2002). Initially, ADR was promoted as an alternative to adversorial forms of conflict resolution, a more civilised resource than litigation, and 'took hold and became institutionalised with such speed that many lawyers and social scientists were caught off guard' (2002: 53). Within a few years ADR had been introduced to Native Americans with the argument that it was more compatible than litigation with native culture and society (58). However, critical examinations of ADR began to raise questions about the way it was being justified to users: 'When disputes are framed as "communication problems", disputes about facts and legal rights become disputes about feelings and relationships. A therapeutic model replaces the legal one, and justice is measured by implicit standards of conformity' (145).

The ADR model was extended to other parts of the world in subsequent decades, and became an instrument of what Nader called 'coercive harmony', involving a movement away from justice towards harmony and efficiency models. The political concerns of the left and the right had converged 'to transform dispute resolution from the rule of law to the rule of coercion by economists and therapists' (Nader 2002: 164). Robert Gordon (2007) has expressed a similar view. The popularity of ADR in the USA, he writes, was due in part to its seeming potential to provide inexpensive mechanisms for dealing with conflicts that might clog up the court system. But in the hands of development experts it was exported as part of the US effort to promote 'democratization' and 'human rights' (355). However, Gordon claims ADR has had limited success outside the United States, mostly serving aboriginal enclaves whose needs could not be properly met by the encompassing state. While they provide a degree of automony for communities in dispute resolution, they may be as inflexible as the state 'and they are often unable to prevent the intrusion of state power into decision-making' (356).

ADR arrived in PNG in the late 1990s via Australia. Gordon's assessment (above) is certainly applicable to the use of ADR in Australia, where it had been promoted among local communities and Aboriginal peoples to overcome the putative inappropriateness of the conventional legal system to local disputes, manifest for example in delays and costs (see Buck 2005: 49–50). Indeed, the history of its spread in Australia is not dissimiliar to that outlined in relation to the US (see Buck 2005 and cf. Nader 2002: 136–49). In PNG, meanwhile, development-aid agencies were developing an interest in the village court system which had been in operation for more than two decades but which was suffering from the inadequacy of state support (see chapter 2 herein). Village courts seemed an appropriate vehicle for spreading ADR and providing an accessible and cheap alternative to the expensive, complex and formal legal system which was still inaccessible to local communities. So enthusiastically was it promoted that ADR courses were provided for judges and magistrates at all levels of the formal judiciary. Senior PNG jurists even travelled to Australia to learn ADR, which was promoted as an alternative to the 'Western adversorial' legal court system, and linked to putative 'traditional' ways of solving disputes through negotiation.

In the year 2000 I attended a conference in Port Vila, Vanuatu, on 'restorative justice in the Pacific Islands'. The concept of 'restorative justice' reinforced ADR discourse and extended its parameters beyond minor disputes in local communities. It could now be applied to major conflicts in the region such as the long-running conflict on PNG's Bougainville Island which had been triggered by local revolt against a copper mine in the 1980s (see May and Spriggs 1990). The discourse of restorative justice distinctly emphasised 'healing' and the restoration of 'social harmony' in preference to punitive responses to crime (see, for example, Braithwaite 1999; Strang and Braithwaite 2001). Ideally, in the restorative process, all the 'stakeholders' would meet and come to an agreement on what should be done (Strang and Braithwaite 2001: 1). The Vanuatu conference was attended by academics, politicians, police representatives and social workers from Australia and several Western Pacific nations, and 'restorative justice' quickly became a buzzword in PNG, at least. The government absorbed it into its ADR initiatives and, with encouragement from development-aid groups, attempted to draw community-level institutions including the village courts into its ongoing efforts to solve its 'law and order' problem (and assuage the reservations of potential international investors). The advent of restorative justice in PNG arguably reinforces Nader's assessment of ADR as a 'soft technology' of control (1999).

Globalising Human Rights

The other major international theme which an anthropology of PNG village courts must address is that of human rights. Kirsten Hastrup commented in 2001 that 'the intense discussion of human rights over the past decade is not necessarily a symptom of a high moral profile worldwide.... Rather it is a symptom of the malaise of the times. Evidently it is also a sign of the will to confront this malaise by way of an antidote in the shape of new international laws' (7). Richard Wilson (2007) has usefully reviewed the effects of human rights discourse on anthropology since the United Nations began the project which resulted in the Declaration of Human Rights of 1948. An early response to the UN's emphasis on individual human rights was a published statement by the American Anthropological Association (AAA) appealing to cultural relativism and objecting to assumptions about the autonomous and freely acting individual. The AAA statement was a 'communitarian riposte to the growing international emphasis on the universal rights of the individual, regardless of social, historical, and cultural context' (Wilson 2007: 233). Subsequently, though, influences such as Marxism, feminism, the disclosure of Vietnam war atrocities, ongoing political violence and the globalisation of networks of terror and conflict cast equivocation on the 'certainties of cultural relativism' (236).

In recent times changing global politics and a shift towards global justice have affected anthropologists' approaches towards rights, and rights discourse has also expanded into other areas: 'Long-standing concerns over gender inequality became reconceptualised as "women's human rights" at international conferences, such as the UN Conference on Women at Beijing in 1995. In the world of economic development, agencies such as the World Bank and government development ministries became converts to a "rights-based" approach to development' (Wilson 2007: 237). Moreover, Wilson says human rights talk performs a vital hegemonic role in the 'democratizing' countries of Africa and Latin America, compelling the population away from punitive retribution by characterising the latter as illegitimate 'mob justice' (245). A degree of articulation of human rights discourse and harmony ideology is visible in this kind of rhetoric.

Human rights discourse, particularly in the form driven by the UN, has become increasingly sophisticated during the past half century. It attempts to recognise that views of personhood and humanity vary around the world and that the complex relationship between individual and collective rights is differently understood among societies and states (see, for example, Messer 2002: 322–30). But it has not escaped the essentialism that underlaid the 1948 declaration. The Vienna Declaration on Human Rights of 1993 stated: 'While the significance of national and regional particularities and various historical, cultural and religious backgrounds must be borne in mind, it is the duty of States, regardless of their political, economic and cultural systems, to promote and protect all human rights and fundamental freedoms.' (United Nations 1993: 4). However, critics such as Thomas Eriksen (2001) and Sally Merry (2003) argue that recourse to an outdated notion of 'culture' has hampered progress in developing universally workable models of human rights. A Westernised concept of the individualised person continues to underlie UN policy (see United Nations 1993: 1). Further, the 'rule of law' (i.e. of internationalised Western law) is a repetitive phrase in UN statements on human rights.

Inasmuch as notions of self, sociality and agency are constructed in a particular way in contemporary international human rights discourse, the discourse itself has been described as a 'culture' which is individualistic, has recourse to a legal/technical framework for addressing suffering and emphasises individual rights over individual duties or needs (Cowan, Dembour and Wilson 2001: 12). The 'culture' is elaborated through the production of documents articulating normative visions of a just society and law-like documents such as resolutions and conventions, which are incorporated into state legal systems (Merry 2003: 70). Also, as Merry points out, human rights lawyers and activists are 'ideologically committed to implementing universal standards rather than appreciating local differences' (68), which enforces conformity rather than acknowledging diversity among the 170 countries under the UN's watch.

The dissemination of human rights discourse to PNG has been manifest particularly in a concern for women's rights. Given the social diversity of the country, and the similar diversity in values and notions of rights, this should be a cautious exercise. Nuanced anthropological studies of gender relationships in Melanesia have produced, overall, a complex picture inviting the inference that Western assumptions about Melanesian women's subordination (based mostly on superficial observations of the sexual divison of labour) have involved hasty generalisation.[3] While development-oriented literature lacks detailed examination of local conceptualisations of gender, there has been some acknowledgement of the detrimental effects of colonial attitudes and interventions on traditional gender relations and the status of women in PNG (see, for example, Brouwer, Harris and Tanaka 1998). Human rights commentaries on the status of women in PNG, however, are premised on current international rationalities of 'development' rather than on the hermeneutics of anthropological enquiry, and they rely heavily on empirical observation. Their judgments about relative inequality focus on what they find to be the most tangible evidence: physical violence against women, and (applying a conventional capitalist understanding of economics) women's lack of 'economic' equality.

Male attitudes and male actions have become a significant target of women's rights commentary and activism, in the effort to pursue 'development' in PNG. Males are positioned in this discourse as women's competitors, hindering women's equal participation in the modern state by political strategies which maintain the dominant position males are assumed to have traditionally enjoyed. The strategies are said to be rationalised by appeals to 'custom' or tradition (see, for example, Bradley 1998; Macintyre 1998, 2005). Moreover, some 'tradition' is regarded as having been recently invented. The 'invention of tradition' is a theme which came to prominence in literature of the 1980s (Keesing and Tonkinson 1982; Hobsbawm and Ranger 1983), which examined the political and social use of so-called 'traditions' which were actually recent constructions, inventions or manipulations of collective memory. A considerable amount of analytic modification and refinement of the 'invention of tradition' notion in relation to Pacific Island societies has occurred subsequently in anthropological discussion (see, for example, Otto and Pedersen 2005; Turner 1997) without affecting the way it is applied in human rights discourse about women's inequality.

The focus on male hindrance of women's equal participation in socio-economic life in contemporary PNG, and the connected tendency to see 'custom'—invented or otherwise—as an obstacle to the progress of women's rights is a local manifestation of a wider concern among human rights organisations who take culture to be static tradition, in which social behaviour is justified by a set of beliefs and values. Concerns about the invocation, or invention, of cultural traditions (these are commonly called *kastom* [custom] in Pacific Island countries) to the detriment of women contribute to what Merry has called the 'demonization of culture' in human rights discourse. The demonisation accompanies human rights assessments globally—paradoxically at the same time as cultural difference is positively acknowledged—and is embedded in international policy documents addressing the rights of women (2003: 60–64).

In relation to PNG village courts, whose officials are predominantly male, human rights concerns have been driven, since the courts came into existence in the 1970s, by a rhetoric that because the magistrates draw on (real or invented) 'custom' and are relatively ignorant of law, they discriminate against women. As I show in the course of this book the rhetoric is not grounded in rigorous research, and anthropological fieldwork has found that women overall fare no worse in village courts than men. District courts and the National courts (also predominently male-run) have not come under the same scrutiny from women's rights advocates, as they are assumed to rigorously implement the Western system of law in which internationalised concepts of human rights are embedded.

Recent initiatives in the implementation of human rights policies in PNG have resulted in new interventions in village courts. Originally, when the village courts were legislated for, their magistrates were intended to be knowledgeable of 'custom' and untrained in law. Nationalistic criticism of the colonial legal system on the eve of political independence in the early 1970s had fuelled calls from indigenous national politicians that these community-based courts should be free from 'European technicalities' (Chalmers 1978a: 267), and would represent a return of power to local communities. A quarter of a century later this natavistic view of village courts had been superceded by a legalistic preoccupation with (UN defined) human rights, reflecting state policy and practice rather than diverse community-defined values and rights. UNESCO has seen potential in the village courts to raise awareness of human rights issues, and village court officials now attend training sessions incorporating human rights awareness, particularly in relation to the rights of women, and basic legal training (see chapter 9).

The foregoing review shows how an anthropological study of village courts can be contextualised in an international political economy encompassing legal and human rights projects which penetrate state borders and reach into grassroots communities. Yet village courts are, at the same time, local institutions staffed by local community members and answerable to local attitudes and locally defined needs. 'Substantial justice' may be an imprecise notion in jurisprudence, but it is an appropriate description of what is sought by disputants in hundreds of societies in PNG who know little of the international processes described above. Their concepts of justice are conditioned by complex moral understandings derived historically from the imperatives of kin-ordered subsistence production, as well as by their observation and experience of colonially introduced laws, rules and punitive procedures. An anthropology of village courts requires an understanding of their sociality, and thus returns us to traditional themes in the anthropology of law.

Village Courts and the Anthropology of Law

The social embeddedness of PNG's village courts makes them thematically relevant particularly to the study of disputes and the effects of colonialism on traditional juridical institutions. Despite the wishes of development-aid and human rights agencies, village court magistrates are not trained in law. They deal almost exclusively with localised disputes and the expressions of aggrievement which arise from them, such as insults, property damage and personal violence. Their work combines official and unofficial aspects, and their mediation, arbitration and adjudication is significantly informed by, and affected by, the attitudes and values of the communities to which they are intimately related. They are a contemporary variety of the kinds of dispute-settling institutions that have been the focus of legal anthropologists in the past.

The study of dispute-settlement procedures was not a foundational part of anthropologists' early interest in non-Western law. A more pressing preoccupation for law-oriented anthropologists in the first half of the twentieth century was the question of whether law, as Westerners understand the concept, could be found in non-Western societies. The philosophical context of the question was the polar contrast between the Hobbesian argument that the laws of a society are the formal commands of the governing authority of that society and Locke's argument that the laws of a society are the minimal rules of conduct acknowledged by the members of that society. Adherents to the Hobbesian position would argue that since not all societies have governing authorities, not all societies have laws. On the other hand, the Lockean position implies that all societies have laws.

An anthropological position arguably closer to the Hobbesian view than to that of Locke was taken in A. R. Radcliffe-Brown's declaration—borrowing from the jurist Roscoe Pound—that 'law is social control through the systematic application of the force of politically organised society' (1952: 212). He qualified his view with a distinction between customary obligations and law, whereby 'some simple societies have no law, although all have customs which are supported by sanctions' (212). Alternatively, on the basis of fieldwork findings in the Trobriand Islands, Bronislaw Malinowski defined civil law, 'the positive law governing all the phases of tribal life', in a more Lockean fashion as a body of binding obligations 'regarded as a right by one party and acknowledged as a duty by the other' (1959: 58). He reinforced his definition with an appeal to the force of reciprocity: 'There must be in all societies a class of rules too practical to be backed up by religious sanctions, too burdensome to be left to mere goodwill, too personally vital to individuals to be enforced by any abstract agency. This is the domain of legal rules, and I venture to foretell that reciprocity, systematic incidence, publicity and ambition will be found to be the main factors in the binding machinery of primitive law' (67–68).

Malinowski's definition offered little in the way of guidance for legal anthropologists (as distinct from economic anthropologists) looking for tangible examples to observe in fieldwork, but direction began to emerge with E. A. Hoebel's emphasis on the systematic study of 'trouble-cases', derived from studies of Cheyenne 'law-ways' in the 1930s (Llewellyn and Hoebel 1941). Hoebel's contribution to the project of defining non-Western law was the argument that patterns of learned behaviour (understood by him to be 'culture') became norms, whose breach could be punished in accordance with community disapproval. Norms were laws if socially authorised physical force was regularly applied in fact or in threat when they were breached. 'Primitive' law could accordingly be researched, and even typologised, with the study of 'trouble-cases' (Hoebel 1968: 35–45).

The attempt to identify law in a manner which would be universally applicable and analytically useful to anthropologists continued to be contentious for some time, as evidenced in a disagreement between Max Gluckman and Paul Bohannan in the 1950s. Gluckman argued that whatever social norms pertained in non-Western (particularly African) societies, the same processes of judicial rationality were applied as in Western societies. He accordingly applied Western legal categories in a study of Barotse judicial processes (1955). Bohannan (1957), studying the Tiv, argued that juridical aspects of any society were shaped by that society's culture, and therefore Western legal categories (shaped by Western culture) should not be applied to non-Western societies. Questions of definition, and of how to analytically relate legal aspects to other aspects of society continued to be unresolved after the Gluckman-Bohannan clash, as a historical review of legal anthropology by Nader indicated. She began by declaring a belief that 'we are just now on the growing edge of an anthropological understanding of law in its various manifestations' (1965: 3) and concluded later that 'aspects of law assumed to be universal by eighteenth-century intellectuals remain a matter of search for twentieth-century scholars' (25).

The preoccupation of anthropologists of the 1950s and '60s with identifying law in non-Western societies was more than an abstract project. The idea of 'legal pluralism' had not yet gained currency, and in colonial territories like PNG jurists were reluctant to consider the possibility that alternative forms of law might exist. Long-serving judges were particularly recalcitrant, as indicated by the views of Justice Gore, who arrived in PNG (or, more precisely at the time, the Territory of Papua[4]) in 1924, and published a memoir of his long service there in 1965. He commented:

> Some anthropologists will perhaps argue that there was some system of criminal jurisprudence existing, but these freakish customs could not impress practical lawyers in the consideration of the imposition of a criminal system upon the indigenous population. There were no fundamental rules of conduct upon

which to build a criminal system, so there was no alternative but to apply the criminal system of the white settlers. . . . It was indeed fortunate that no primitive legal system, a system with some basic principles of worth, existed because it was easier and more in accord with the idea of a civilizing process to apply the system under which the white settlers lived. (1965: 75)

Among anthropologists, meanwhile, while definitions remained contentious, the substance of the studies by both Gluckman and Bohannan was evidence of a fruitful ethnographic turn. The study of disputes was providing a wealth of comparative data on conflict and order in small-scale societies (see, for example, Beals 1964; Berndt 1962; Bohannan 1957; Gibbs 1963; Gluckman 1955; Gulliver 1963; Pospisil 1958; Srinivas 1962).

In the developing study of disputing processes in the 1950s and '60s, disputes themselves were seen as something more than 'trouble-cases' illustrating 'law-ways'. Ethnographers contextualised them in wider issues of politics, kinship and religion in society, revealing layers of meaning beyond what immediately impressed observers as disputes between two parties. In a study of a Chagga (Mt Kilimanjaro, Tanzania) dispute, for example, Sally Falk Moore (1977) showed how the attempted settlement of a disagreement between two individuals became a public issue and the ceremonies involved in the dispute, articulating between different levels and types of social organisation, effected situational transformations. They were 'events on which various durable organisational interests impinged, and in which they competed for effectiveness' (186). Moore's work was an example of what John L. Comaroff and Simon Roberts later called the 'processual' paradigm, in contrast to the 'rule-centered' paradigm. According to the processual paradigm, they said, conflict was treated as endemic in social life and should be analysed in the context of extended social processes, hence the analysis of order should ultimately be grounded in social processes, not institutions (1986: 12–13). Citing Elizabeth Colson's (1953) study of social control and vengeance among the Tonga of Africa and Victor Turner's (1957) work on conflict among the Ndembu as earlier examples of the processual paradigm, Comaroff and Roberts argued: 'An adequate account of a dispute therefore requires a description of its total social context—its genesis, successive efforts to manage it, and the subsequent history of the relationship between the parties. . . . This relatively wider definition of scope also involves a shift in focus *away* from judge- (and judgment-) oriented accounts of the character and function of dispute settlement' (1986: 13–14).

The processual view of dispute is vital to an understanding of PNG's village courts, which are problematically situated in a legislatively *imagined* relationship between Western law and 'customary law', and in a *real*, practical, relationship between Western law and the extended social processes which are the context of the conflicts manifest in the disputes the courts deal with. Critics of the village court system are inclined to a legal centralist perspective (as will be seen in later chapters of this book), congruent with their preference that the courts be governed by Western law. Further, as can be inferred from Justice Pratt's comments about 'substantial justice' above, they also apply what Comaroff and Roberts call the 'rule-centered paradigm', imagining 'customary law' as a set of rules which are applied to given cases, and which are likely to be oppressive. In contrast, according to the processual paradigm, indigenous rules are not seen *a priori* as laws which can straightforwardly determine dispute outcomes. 'It is recognized, rather, that the rules themselves may be the object of negotiation and may sometimes be a resource to be managed strategically' (Comaroff and Roberts 1986: 14).

By the time village courts were being legislatively planned in the early 1970s, the effect of colonial legal processes on indigenous dispute-solving and social control practices was being acknowledged in Melanesianist ethnography to a much greater extent than had been the case for most of the colonial era. Elsewhere, the work of anthropologists such as Ian Schapera (1943) and later J. A. Barnes (1954) had portended a turn of this nature, but it was not until the mid 1960s that a significant body of ethnographies of colonised peoples began to address the way indigenous groups adapted, or reacted to, colonial influences in their own dispute-settlement procedures (see, for example, Cohn 1965, 1967; Collier 1973; Colson 1971; Fallers 1969; Van Velsen 1964). In PNG Ronald Berndt (1962) and Marilyn Strathern (1972) were among those who had specifically addressed the way unofficial 'courts' incorporated quasi-legal practices which local groups had experienced in their interactions with colonial *kiaps* (Tokpisin: patrol officers).

A Melanesia-oriented volume edited by A. L. Epstein (1974a) and prepared while the village court system was being legislatively planned, encapsulated the transitions the anthropology of law was undergoing during the period. Epstein's introduction to the largely dispute-focussed volume included a Malinowskian conception of Melanesian civil law: 'Melanesian societies do recognise a body of rules of binding obligation governing family relations, the acquisition, use and disposition of land and other forms of property, inheritance, succession and so on (1974b: 5).' At the same time, he and other contributors were using the term 'customary law' unproblematically (for example, Epstein 1974b: 39), in the fashion of the time.

Justice Gore's attitudes (see above) towards the idea of indigenous law-ways had been officially superceded by 1975, when PNG achieved political independence, and indigenous traditions became valorised in the nation-building endeavour. The 'freakish customs' were now re-classified as 'customary law', and legalists set about 'developing a legal system that would take far greater account of the customs and the perceptions of the people than was taken before Independence' (Law Reform Commission 1977: 9).

Customary law, however, would prove to be a slippery object for the legal profession to grasp. To begin with, the working definition of *customary law* in post-colonial PNG was the same as that for *custom*—'the customs and usages of indigenous inhabitants . . . regardless of whether or not the custom or usage has existed from time immemorial' (Law Reform Commission 1977: 17). PNG's Law Reform Commission noted that customary law was 'a flexible system of law which may be different from place to place and from time to time' and should be applied as the country's underlying law in a flexible way (1977: 17fn). Acknowledging that customary law was unwritten, the Commission characterised unwritten law as being determined by changing socio-economic characteristics and consequently changing to reflect the changes in society:

> It is the socio-economic characteristics, and in particular the level of the technology the community employs, that have a decisive influence on the law. Many of the features of the customary law of the communities in Papua New Guinea arise from the nature of the economies of these communities, and the relationships of dependence, co-operation or hostility among its [sic] members vis-a-vis members of other communities are in significant ways influenced by economic factors. (19fn)

While the concept of 'customary law' was being used unproblematically in the Epstein volume of 1974, some authors in it (A. Strathern 1974; M. Strathern 1974; Reay 1974) explicitly acknowledged the influence of colonially introduced institutions on local dispute-settling procedures. The juxtaposition of these themes—the Malinowskian referents of 'civil law', the idea of 'customary law', and colonial influences on local dispute settling—configures paradoxes which were to become manifest with the introduction of the village court system and the courts' consequent attempts to satisfy the legislative conditions they were burdened with.

The concept of legal pluralism was being cautiously adopted into the discursive field of the anthropology of law in the 1980s. Legal pluralism—in contrast to legal centralism—entailed the acknowledgement that multiple regulatory systems, including formal law and informal normative regimes, co-exist in many societies. Sally Merry defined it at the time simply as 'a situation in which two or more legal systems coexist in the same social field' (1988: 870; cf. Griffiths 1986: 2). The advent of legal pluralism involved a broadening of the anthropology of law, subsequent to the recognition of colonial influences (particularly that of colonially introduced Western law) which anthropologists had previously largely bracketed from ethnography. An acceptance of legal pluralism also produced a significant broadening of legal studies (in the hands of jurists less conservative than justices Gore and Pratt) beyond a traditionally narrow preoccupation with formal, national law. A broad understanding of the idea of a legal system implied, as Merry remarked, that 'virtually every society is legally plural, whether or not it has a colonial past. Legal pluralism is a central theme in the reconceptualization of the law/society relation' (1988: 869).

At the same time, the relatively unpolitical formulation of legal pluralism proved inadequate in the attempt to engage with 'customary law' as conceived by legalists in PNG. Merry's succinct query about legal pluralism in general seems particularly apt: 'Where do we stop speaking of law and find ourselves simply describing social life?' (1988: 878). In the same era, though, an anthropological critique of the notion of 'customary law' was developing which would lead to more political formulations of pluralism. A body of writings on colonial law and the creation of customary law in Africa (for example, Chanock 1998; Moore 1986; Snyder 1981, 1988; von Benda-Beckmann 1984) constituted an important turn. Chanock, for instance, showed that law was central to the colonial project, and that customary law was not a survival from the past, but was made by conflicts and changes involving missionaries, colonial officials and Africans. Customary law could not be understood outside of 'the impact of the new economy on African communities . . . [or] . . . outside of the peculiar institutional setting in which its creation takes place' (Chanock 1998: 4). Where previously anthropologists had been inclined to bracket colonial processes in the search for underlying customary law, studies like Chanock's showed the way it had been developed historically through those very processes and African reactions to them.

The investigation of these historical and political themes has continued in more recent legal anthropological literature, such as Nader's above-mentioned work on the Zapotec (1990), and Merry's (1999) study of transnational influences on Hawaiian legal culture from colonial times, and the transformations of traditional Hawaiian governance through missionary-supported religious law to a secular legal order. Compared to the legal pluralism of the 1980s, this kind of literature represents a critical turn which obviates Merry's earlier query about the difference between describing local law and social life (1988: 878). For critical anthropologists of law concerned with the relationship between the local and the global, *pluralism* can no longer simply refer to the existence of more than one legal system in a social field. In the light of the internationalisation of Western systems of law, combined with human rights discourse which impacts on states' implementation of transnational policies, a new kind of legal anthropology is necessary. Indeed, the label *legal anthropology* itself may be inadequate, considering the kinds of issues now addressed by anthropologists concerned at the uses of law in global, political contexts. The saga of the Ok Tedi copper and gold mine in PNG is a case in point.

The environmental damage, land loss and culture loss suffered by indigenous people in proximity to the open-cast Ok Tedi mine, and to peoples living more distantly along the Ok and Fly Rivers, and the legal actions brought by the latter, have been extensively reported and explored in depth (see, for example, Banks and Ballard 1997; Hyndman 1988, 1994, 2001; Kirsch 2001, 2004, 2006). Anthropologists who had been working in the geographical area found themselves engaged with issues of advocacy, activism, legal struggles and political conflict, which became reflected in publications which cannot easily be classified in relation to traditional subfields such as the anthropology of law (see, for example, Hyndman 1994, 2001; Kirsch 2006). The Ok Tedi case indicates the need for, and value of, an anthropological engagement with global processes, and perversely (since the political odds were clearly stacked against the legal efforts of the indigenous groups; see Banks and Ballard 1997) exemplifies Nader's previously cited point that the rule-of-law enterprise is international big business (2006: 104). Richard Wilson's formulation is handy:

> In order to understand the impact of human rights on conceptions of justice, the question to be answered is how social actors (encompassing both individuals and collectivities) have contested the direction of social change in the area of justice, and what the effects of this are for state formation and the legitimation of new forms of authority. This is a legal anthropology of action, transformation, and interaction between legal orders in the wider context of state hegemonic projects. (2007: 243–44)

An anthropology of village courts fits squarely in Wilson's formulation. Village courts were themselves colonially conceived and introduced to deal with colonially created problems. For example, in the 1960s the old colonial practice of appointing and using individual authority figures in villages, such as 'village constables', as mechanisms of indirect law maintenance was being phased out. A gap was consequently created between 'the law'—represented in rural areas by patrol officers—and local communities. Further, most of PNG's population was not using the formal system of justice (to which villagers had no realistic access if they did not live close to towns), and unofficial 'courts', some of which attempted to mimic the procedure of formal courts, were widespread. Not only were village courts a colonial creation, but they were supposed to bring into their judicial considerations another colonial creation, 'customary law'. Moreover, most of the communities they served had experienced colonially introduced law one way or another, and had been adapting what they understood to be its procedure into their dispute settling before the introduction of village courts. At the same time, however, the communities retained the rationales of traditional dispute-settling methods—rationales governed to a significant extent by the rules and obligations to which Malinowski, and later Epstein, referred. The latter factor influenced the way local communities interpreted the role of village courts, and village court magistrates were obliged to negotiate this interpretation while fulfilling their state-imposed juridical obligations. And as we shall see in the later chapters of this book, in practice village court magistrates give far more thought to the real complexities of local sociality than to 'customary law'.

We see here the extent to which traditional and contemporary legal anthropological issues are encapsulated in a study of the village court system of PNG. The fruitless search for 'customary law', as conceived by the system's planners and by subsequent jurists, evokes the early preoccupation of anthropologists, and challenges anthropologists to continue to consider the nature of law beyond its Western forms. The main work of the courts, the settling of disputes, puts them squarely in the realm of what has arguably been the most rewarding enterprise in legal anthropology, the study of disputing. Their colonial heritage, and their engagement with the effects of colonialism on local community interpretations of legal process, obliges the researching anthropologist to explicitly consider the historical colonial context of contemporary, post-colonial, dispute settling. Their struggle to negotiate the demands of state law, human rights issues defined by globalising institutions and Melanesian conceptions of substantial justice situates them in the purview of the critical anthropological perspective which has supplanted legal pluralism.

An Anthropology of Village Courts

My own research on village courts, on which this book is largely based, began in 1991 and is ongoing at the time of writing. In the first instance I was approached by the consultancy arm of UPNG—where

I was employed as a lecturer—to be involved in a review of the village court system for the PNG Attorney General's Department. I accepted hesitantly: I was wary of the compromises involved in consultancy work, but conceded that my lecturing in the anthropology of law might benefit from the experience. In the event, I came to understand the importance of village courts both to local communities and to the state legal system. I had already shifted my fieldwork focus from the Upper Kaugel Valley in the Western Highlands Province to urban Port Moresby, and I realised that the study of 'urban' village courts would be a handy focus for grasping the everyday problems of the grassroots people I was moving among. Consequently, I selected three village courts in the Port Moresby area for the purposes of ongoing comparative research. Two of the courts were in so-called 'settlements' in different suburbs of the town, and the third was in a village on the edge of town inhabited by Motu-Koita (a collective name for the two, intermarried, peoples on whose traditional territory the city of Port Moresby has grown).

My research at these three courts has continued to the present, though intermittently. It includes two periods of concentrated monitoring in 1994 and 1999, during which I attended each weekly meeting of the three courts for four months of each year. I recorded hundreds of cases on tape and in notebooks, with the added advantage of being able to discuss the cases and the magistrates' decisions with the magistrates themselves and, where appropriate, with disputants. Contextualising these studies in more general fieldwork in the communities served by the courts, I was able to come to a broader understanding of cases than I would have if I had been a casual observer of intermittent cases. In addition to these periods of concentrated monitoring I spent a considerable amount of time in the communities themselves during the period from 1991 until 1995, during which I was working at UPNG, and had easy access to my research sites. Since leaving UPNG and moving to Australia I have returned five times thus far to observe the same courts and the developments in their practice and in the administration of the system overall. In addition to the concentrated study of these three courts, I have attended courts and talked with village court officers and disputants in the Eastern Highlands, Simbu, Western Highlands, Enga, East New Britain, Madang, Milne Bay and Central Provinces at different times during the past sixteen years.

My fieldwork research findings provide much of the substance of this book. I have also drawn on the findings of a handful of other anthropologists who have done field research in the past on village courts in areas which I have not myself visited. In addition to ethnographic work I have examined the history of the village court system in both its administrative and practical aspects, as well as the greater historical colonial and post-colonial context in which its conception, introduction and development needs to be understood. To this end, the first chapter of the book is an account of the colonial period, concentrating on the political and legal attitudes of the colonisers from the late nineteenth century until the end of colonialism. During this period indigenous involvement in the local administration of colonially introduced law was a contentious issue, but it will be seen that courts akin to the modern village courts were mooted more than once, unsuccessfully. The problems encountered by the village court system since the end of colonialism can be understood to a significant degree as the legacy of the attitudes and practice of successive colonial administrations (in advance of recent interventions by development-aid agencies). Oddly though, the eventual model of village courts developed in the early 1970s—the twilight of Australian colonial rule—contained echoes of the model of 'native' courts proposed by German Administrator Albert Hahl almost a century earlier, and rejected by the Australian Administration which replaced his after the First World War.

Chapter 2 examines the introduction of the village courts and the subsequent administration of the system. The three decades of the system's operations can be understood as a dialectic between ideals and practice. On the one hand are the discursive ideals of informality, wise mediation and pastoral judgment informed by the integrity of 'customary law' (implying that the practical activities of village courts would be largely determined by the needs of their communities). On the other hand are the practical effects of legislative and bureaucratic impositions. The courts are governed by legislation which places them at the bottom of a hierarchy of legal courts and thus makes them answerable to fundamental demands of state law. Further, their position in the hierarchy has burdened them with the effects of equivocation over which branches of government are responsible for their maintenance.

Chapter 3 examines the practical problems encountered by village court officers on the ground. It does this partly by commentary on the periodic criticisms of village courts by legalists and the media, who have accused the courts variously of being overzealous in their application of the law, of being oppressive in their application of 'customs', and of being misogynistic. The chapter contextualises the criticism in the problematic legislative positioning of village courts in relation to state law and 'custom' referred to earlier in this introduction. Chapter 4 introduces the three village courts I have specifically researched and monitored, and gives an account of the social settings in which they operate. Each court reflects the sociality of the particular local community it serves, and applies a complex integration of introduced law and local convention in its dispute management procedures. Each court has its own distinctive characteristics, as do village courts across the country. The social context is reflected in the predominant types of cases which come to each court, and in the 'style' of the courts.

Chapter 5 is about the politics of being a village court official. Drawing on examples from the three studied courts, I show that as magistrates and other officials are chosen from the particular communities they serve, they are inescapably enmeshed in local politics. Local social dynamics and attitudes not only play a large part in determining who becomes a village court official but also affect the way they conduct themselves and the cases they hear. Chapters 6, 7 and 8 present the three courts in action. Using transcripts of some of the cases heard in each court, I demonstrate further the point made in chapter 4 that each court is distinctive, and its practice is shaped by the sociality of the particular community it serves. Thus one court favours a distinctly reintegrative approach to dispute settlement, in keeping with the sense of communal integrity in the village it serves, the second court is preoccupied with reconciliation and the amelioration of inevitable conflicts in the community, and the third court takes a more 'legalistic' approach, though it remains sensitive to the social and political exigencies of life in urban settlements.

Chapter 9 addresses a practical problem which is presaged by the discussion in chapters 2 and 3 and exemplified by the three chapters describing courts in action. There is a perpetual tension between the village courts' embeddedness in their community—in which *group* dynamics are dominant considerations in dispute settlement—and the courts' role as legal institutions governed by rules which ostensibly oblige them to treat disputants as legally responsible *individuals*. The discussion of individualism and group dynamics leads to a commentary on the incorporation of village courts into development aid programs and of the Western social concepts implicit in such projects. Subesquently, the conclusion draws together the ethnography of the village courts with the universal themes traversed in this introduction—and we return to the notion of substantial justice, which among grass-roots Melanesians is arguably contextualised in non-individualistic sociality, while Western legalist perspectives (conservatively exemplified by the comments of Justice Pratt above) view it in terms of individualised human rights.

Notes

1. So common is this term, with its 'eye-for-an-eye' connotations, that Garry Trompf used it as the title of a book intensively surveying retributive ideas and practice around Melanesia (see Trompf 1994).

2. Filmed and produced by Robert Gardner for the Peabody Museum. Distributed by Contemporary Films, New York. Gardner also wrote the book *Gardens of War: Life and Death in the New Guinea Stone Age* (1968). An interesting comparative perspective is provided by Karl Heider (1979), as the title of his ethnography, *Grand Valley Dani: Peaceful Warriors*, implies.
3. The anthropological literature on this topic is vast. Some sense of the developments in the way anthropologists have tried to understand gender relations in PNG can be gained from comparing earlier works such as Mead (1963), Meggitt (1964), and Brown and Buchbinder (1976) with later discussions such as Herdt and Poole (1982), Strathern (1988), Kyakas and Weissner (1992), Kelly (1994) and Bonnemère (2004).
4. Britain officially laid claim to the southern part of the eastern half of the New Guinea land mass in 1884, at the same time as Germany claimed the northern part. 'British New Guinea' became 'The Territory of Papua' in 1906, with responsibility for its administration transferred to Australia. After the First World War Australia took over the administration of the former German possession, known as 'New Guinea', as a 'Mandated Territory' on behalf of the League of Nations. After the Second World War Australia administered Papua as its own territory and New Guinea as a 'UN Trust Territory'. The collective name for the area became 'The Territory of Papua and New Guinea'. At Independence in 1975 'Papua New Guinea' became the name of the new nation. See chapter 1 for more detail.

1

Colonial Law

An Extended Prelude to
the Village Courts

The growth and spread of the village courts from 1975 to the present day could be interpreted as a success, testimony to their value to local communities throughout PNG, and to the dedication of their poorly remunerated magistrates. Later chapters will elaborate these aspects of their practice. However, they have also been targets of criticism, mostly by legalists, but occasionally by proponents of human rights, and particularly women's rights. These criticisms are discussed in later chapters in some detail, but the issues raised in them were largely a legacy of the attitudes and practice of successive colonial administrations, with which this chapter is concerned. The changing colonial attitudes to 'custom' and to participation by Melanesians in the judiciary gave rise to a politico-juridical climate at the end of the colonial period in which particular rhetorical and legal idealisations of the village courts were consolidated. These idealisations would prove to be far more burdensome than the disputes which the courts were expected to mediate or adjudicate.

The long prelude to the village courts began in 1884, when German and British administrations established themselves in the eastern part and nearby islands of the landmass known to Europeans as New Guinea. Europeans in Melanesia had previously consisted of explorers, traders, golddiggers and missionaries, negotiating their presence with whatever strategies were most expedient to their various intentions, and with variable results. In 1884 colonial political administration began and with it the imposition of legal systems by the British on the southern coast and eastern islands and the Germans in the islands off the northern coast. The German-held territory was administered initially through the ill-fated Neu Guinea Kompagnie, but within a few years by the Imperial Government. The imposition of European-derived juridical models set the ground for an ongoing debate on the merits of a single formal legal system, which was the context in which the idea of the village court system eventually developed.

German and British Juridical Policies

The Germans incorporated indigenous officers into their legal system at a grassroots level through the empowerment of men putatively elected, or ascribed power, by their local community to hear a limited range of disputes and grievances. The indigenous involvement was an initiative of Albert Hahl, who was originally installed as an Imperial Judge by the German Chancellor to be the Reich's official representative in the area over which the privately owned Neu Guinea Kompagnie had—by authority of the German Government—sovereign power. Hahl, a lawyer by profession, wrote later that his position manifested the independence of the administration of justice from the Neu Guinea Kompagnie's sovereignty (Hahl 1980: 3), although in fact he served also as the administrative head of the area of his jurisdiction for the company.[1] His double role foreshadowed an executive involvement in judicial affairs which lasted for most of the colonial period.

Hahl began to organise a system of 'native administration' shortly after his arrival in 1896, recruiting local men of high status in the vicinity of Kokopo (which the Germans called Herbertshohe) in East New Britain (Neu Pommern):

> It was not difficult to persuade the inhabitants of the nearest villages to choose one of the clan elders of their district as their *luluai* or acknowledged chief, responsible to me. The natives were to submit their disputes to him and the *luluai* was to report important matters to me immediately, or at the major court sittings, which took place in public from time to time. This meant that the chief with the assistance of some respected clan elders could regulate all family affairs and minor disputes peacefully at his discretion, without troubling me in the matter. (1980: 18)

To assist the *luluai*[2] the Germans appointed a *tultul* (also a term denoting high status in local indigenous groups) to act simultaneously as a liaison officer, a translator into Tokpisin, a quasi-police constable and in some cases a medical orderly (Rowley 1965: 84).

In 1903, discovering a degree both of misunderstanding and of exploitation of their position by *luluais*, Hahl went so far as to specify by proclamation what kinds of offences and disputes 'Native Magistrates' (as they were formally designated) could and could not hear. They were not allowed to grant divorces, hear land disputes or disputes about territorial boundaries, or deal with 'tribal' wars, murders, burglaries, damage to houses or gardens, incest, rape or adultery. Officially, they were limited to hearing petty disputes over money, garden produce or domestic animals, and to punishing people with cash fines which were to be passed on to Administration officers (Jinks, Biskup and Nelson 1973: 188–90). Their other function was to keep order in their villages and to oversee community implementation of Administration programmes such as roading, disease control, and intensification of village agriculture (to avoid famine), reporting breaches and problems to the Administration. They also collected the head tax, of which they were allowed to keep 10 per cent. In view of this, it could be argued that their judicial role was a limited condition of their executive role, rather than a manifestation of a specific intention by the Germans to develop an indigenous involvement in the formal legal system. The Native Magistrate system, using '*Luluai*' as a general term, was spread systematically through German-occupied areas until the First World War, although Hahl's subordinates beyond East New Britain placed less faith in the judicial abilities of *luluais* than Hahl himself and severely limited the types of cases they could hear, in favour of using them to enforce Administration orders (Firth 1986: 73–74).

In British New Guinea, which had become a protectorate at the same time as the German annexation, Administrator William MacGregor arrived in 1888 under instruction from the British Colonial Office to introduce a juridical system which was, as far as possible, 'summary in its operation and free from technicalities of procedure' (Joyce 1971: 182). He instigated a combination of Queensland (Australia) laws, some special ordinances for the colony and, beginning in 1889, a body of simplified 'Native Board Regulations'. The latter, drawn up by a Native Regulations Board which included MacGregor himself, were aimed at expediting the spread of British control and 'civilization'. Sorcery, adultery, some mortuary practices, assault, theft, spreading of 'lying reports' and destruction of 'valuable' trees were among behaviour outlawed by the Board in regulations specifically applied to indigenes and reinforced through 'Native Magistrates Courts'. MacGregor's Administration was particularly concerned to control the incidence of killings which it classified as murder and MacGregor saw, in the motives for murder (sorcery, intertribal warfare, sexual offences, revenge for stealing), 'the customs which he would need to eradicate in order to reform native society' (Joyce 1971: 185). Ironically, the 'customs' which MacGregor interpreted as motivating murder were often transgressions in Melanesian societies, which regarded them as seriously as did the Administration and imposed a range of punishments (see, for example, Chinnery 1925: 31, 133; Landtman 1927: 170).

Funding for the administration of British New Guinea was provided by Australia, with the State of Queensland guiding funding policy conservatively. MacGregor, as Healy put it, 'had to rely on a ragtag staff of local drifters made necessary by the miniscule Australian financial grants' (1986: 4). His field staff, nominally resident magistrates and assistant resident magistrates but mostly with no legal background, served simultaneously as explorers, punitive expedition leaders, *de facto* police commanders and general policy implementers. The financial constraints obliged MacGregor to make serious efforts to use indigenes in simple administrative roles. His attempts to include them in the system of justice involved in the first instance the development of a Papuan constabulary, which was used in a paramilitary capacity, but he also hoped to use local leaders to deal with crime (in terms of the Native Regulations) at village level. British administrators and missionaries in the few years before MacGregor's arrival had had difficulty in perceiving indigenes with visible authority over local groups and had come to the general view that the protectorate lacked 'chiefs' (Healy 1967: 20). Previous administrative experience in Fiji, where *ratu* (senior ranking chiefs) were used to advantage by the colonial Administration, may have predisposed MacGregor himself to look for the equivalent of 'high' chiefs. In Papua, despite the existence of various types of leadership including hereditary lineage heads, clan heads and village heads and elders in the British occupied area, he was unable to find any individuals who he felt could be classified as real 'chiefs'.[3]

MacGregor initially intended that European magistrates would train indigenes to preside over Native Magistrates Courts, but events in the Kiwai area of the Western Division (now the Western Province) discouraged the idea. A resident magistrate gave judicial authority to two Kiwai leaders, only to dismiss them within two years for alleged malpractice, fuelling official claims that natives were incapable of impartial judgment (Healy 1967: 21). MacGregor's solution was to introduce a system of village constables, which he said was 'the best substitute that can be created in the place of the tribal chiefs that do not exist in British New Guinea' (Joyce 1971: 165). His concept of village constables, like his concept of chiefs, was probably influenced by his experience of them in Fiji, where he had served as chief medical officer[4] and receiver-general (treasurer). In the late nineteenth century, colonial Fiji had indigenous magistrates, an armed indigenous constabulary, town and civil police, and village constables (Howard 1991: 32–33). MacGregor transposed two of these categories to British New Guinea in his introduction of armed police and village constables. The village constables, in contrast to Hahl's *luluais*, had no official magisterial functions: MacGregor's object was 'to create a force of rural policemen to deal with cases in their own villages, principally coming under the native regulations. . . . They are not provided with arms, and of course require to be watched closely and to be taught by magistrates, but they already form one of the most important institutions in the colony' (MacGregor 1894–95, cited in Jinks, Biskup and Nelson 1973: 61).

Individuals recruited as village constables were not necessarily local leaders or respected elders, and their recruitment sometimes created a social distance between them and their fellow villagers, which administration officers perceived as advantageous. C. A. W. Monckton, a resident magistrate who produced several memoirs of his turn-of-the-century service in British New Guinea, provides an ingenuous account of a recruitment at Cape Nelson (in what is now the Northern Province) resulting from a series of incidents generated by Monckton striking a villager. After the water supply of Monckton and his patrol team was poisoned in an act of retaliation, the magistrate captured a villager and strung him up by the neck, tightening the rope until the captive gave the name of the poisoner.[5] Monckton then enlisted the man to help capture his fellow villager, promising to pay him two tomahawks and to make him village constable, a position in which Monckton says the man subsequently gave good service (Monckton n.d.: 25–28).

The early *luluais* and village constables cannot, however, retrospectively be viewed simply as lackeys of the German and British colonial administrations or men of authority who used their new offices to become petty tyrants (cf. Epstein 1969: 251–52). As Rowley has observed, they could sometimes be men without high status who were pushed forward and used subversively by those with genuine power in local communities:

> The village official was on the one hand entirely necessary for the government, which had to have the assurance (or at least the illusion) that its authority extended into the village. On the other hand he was equally essential for the village, which required someone . . . able to judge just how far an order must be taken seriously, to specialise in keeping the people out of 'trouble'; and, when he failed to 'manage' the government, to be its scapegoat. (1965: 84)

The dual agency of *luluais* and village constables, as an executive instrument of the administrations of German and British New Guinea respectively, and as 'an instrument of adaptation by the villagers to irresistible power' (85), served to articulate administrative concern for the rule of law with administrative attitudes towards 'custom', that is, the range of indigenous social behaviour which was considered to be significantly at variance with Anglo-Australian and German norms. Custom, at this early stage of the colonial period, was defined operationally by the political intentions of the colonisers (both secular and religious), rather than by anthropological or legal-historical reflection.

Hahl saw his main task in New Guinea as 'bringing the natives under a well-regulated system of administration and encouraging them to work for the good of the country and thereby for their own good' (Hahl 1980: 10). Before his arrival the Neu Guinea Kompagnie had been a brutal administrative force but, more concerned with its financial affairs than with the social life of local people (Wolfers 1975: 63–64), it had no systematic policy or attitude towards matters of custom. In comparison to many settlers and missionaries of the period, Hahl showed a reasonable tolerance of indigenous social practice and he made an effort to develop some understanding of indigenous social organisation and political structures. This sometimes proved to be administratively useful. For instance, observing the Tolai practice of working for family heads for food and to repay brideprice contributions, Hahl turned the custom to his advantage by paying the Tolai in food and shell-money to build roads for him (Firth 1986: 63). His main intention, so far as 'custom' was concerned, was to eradicate warfare and he felt, by 1913, that his Administration had been reasonably efficient in this respect (Hahl 1980: 146–47). He also directly attacked the practice of slavery (26–27). He was aware that an abolition of 'blood feuds' (as he called them) and an insistence on the settlement of disputes by peaceful means would have further social effects: 'The influence of the clan elders was shaken and the power of the soothsayers and sorcerers diminished; a new concept of morality began to gain ground' (23). However his overt sanctions were directed at acts which involved immediate and visible personal harm or affected the infrastructure which he was developing. He showed little sympathy for concern by missionary organisations about other practices which they considered barbaric (Firth 1986: 136–60 passim), and had little interest in their spiritual endeavours, preferring them to put their efforts into Germany's programs of economic development (Hahl 1980: 154).

Hahl appears to have tolerated what he referred to as 'secret societies' (probably the male *dukduk* cult of the local Tolai, which was not particularly secret but involved masked dancers), and was prepared to defend them against attacks from missionaries (Firth 1986: 151). He was less concerned about their ritual or ideational content than about whether they interfered with 'freedom of movement'. He complained, for instance, that 'whenever they held their festivities, by special order of their leaders or chiefs the roads were blocked or opened to travellers only on payment of special dues in shell-money' (Hahl 1980: 38). Hahl dealt severely with the blocking of free movement on one occasion by making the offending *dukduk* dancers take off their masks and costumes, which he ordered to be burnt. 'These measures had far-reaching effects. The secret societies never gave serious trouble, even after I had restricted their ceremonies to particular times of the year. It soon transpired that these regulations were also welcomed by the natives themselves' (38).

In general, although his anthropological understanding of New Guineans in general was fairly crude,[6] he saw no reason to interfere with common institutions such as brideprice and the worship of spirits or ancestors. Of the differences between local traditions and the 'new order' introduced through colonial rule he wrote: 'There was a need to establish a plainly visible authority in order to allow the forces at play to undergo a process of mutual adaptation. . . . The old and the new could be blended in such a way that these people just emerging from a stone age culture could fit into a new environment' (Hahl 1980: 54). His development of the *luluai* system, exploiting a traditional institution both as an executive agent and as an Administration-sanctioned settler of customary disputes, was consistent with his political sentiment. Harsh as German rule was, driven by the imperatives of policies aimed almost exclusively at economic gain, the legal system it developed remained simple and, where village affairs and traditional 'customs' were concerned, did not involve large-scale direct intervention (Wolfers 1975: 71).

In British New Guinea MacGregor showed more concern to interfere with custom—his zeal on one occasion was checked by the British Colonial Office. In 1897 he wanted to introduce a marriage ordinance, banning the practice of brideprice payment on the ground that marriage should be an act involving the free will of the two individuals involved. The Colonial Office, under advice from missionary organisations who argued that Papuans did not have sufficient knowledge of Christianity to adapt to a new marriage system, thwarted the idea. Disappointed, the anthropologically naïve MacGregor 'did not agree that brideprice was so important to native culture that it should be retained' (Joyce 1971: 189). Despite this clash of opinions, MacGregor was more sympathetic in general to the spiritual endeavours of the missions than Hahl, reflecting a difference of emphasis between British and German principles of colonialism.

Through the Native Board Regulations the British intervened in a range of practices thought to be hindrances to civilisation. For some of these, such as sorcery and non-Christian mortuary practices, the inexact gloss 'native custom' could sensibly mean only that they were not experienced in contemporary Western societies, for they certainly were not peculiar to Melanesia. As we have already noted, they were predominantly practices which MacGregor regarded as causing mortal violence, but in terms of overall colonial policy the selection was governed by the prevailing concept of the civilising mission which included economic, religious and public health components.

MacGregor's attempts to involve Papuans in Administration programmes differed strategically from Hahl's in that, instead of exploiting the political embeddedness of agents in their own community and social institutions (as in the case of *luluais*), he sought to alienate his indigenous agents from customary practice. Hence his police constables and village constables were often ex-prisoners (Healy 1967: 22; Dutton 1985: 78; Jinks, Biskup and Nelson 1973: 61), based on a reasoning that their period in gaol (prison) would have weaned them off the more unacceptable of their native customs. His intention that indigenous magistrates should eventually be involved in the judiciary (Joyce 1971: 183) was qualified by a belief in the need to distance them from customary practice first: he did not share Hahl's interest in facilitating a 'process of mutual adaptation' through the colonial authority structure. When MacGregor left British New Guinea (whose colonial status he had changed from a Protectorate to a Possession), the Court system consisted of a Central Court, Courts of Petty Sessions, Small Debts Courts, Wardens Courts (dealing with land claims in relation to mining) and Native Magistrates Courts, the latter dealing with cases arising from the Native Board Regulations by imposing penalties of fines up to £25 or imprisonment for up to six months.

MacGregor resigned in 1898 and was replaced by Sir George Le Hunte, whose continued mention in histories of the colony is not due to his administrative policy as the last British lieutenant-governor but to his having led a punitive raid in 1901 on the Goaribi in the Gulf of Papua, killers of the missionary James Chalmers, and having returned the following year to retrieve Chalmers' skull (Jinks, Biskup and Nelson 1973: 74–76). It was an unstable period when administrative responsibility for the colony was being shuffled between Britain and the newly established Australian Commonwealth and the achievements of MacGregor appeared likely to come to nought. Le Hunte left after his encounters with the Goaribi, and the chief judicial officer, Sir Francis Winters, became acting administrator, leaving shortly after—and perhaps because of—acrimony among Europeans over his handling of trials of Europeans accused of murders and rapes of Papuans (see, for example, Wetherell 1996: 61–64). Winters was succeeded in turn by the new chief judicial officer, C. S. Robinson, who had a harsh attitude towards Papuans. The missionary Charles Abel recorded an incident in 1903 at Samarai when a trial witness was experiencing translation difficulties and speaking slightly out of turn. Robinson, as judge, told him to 'shut up' and instructed a constable, 'If he speaks again smack him across the mouth' (cited in Wetherell 1996: 67–68). Robinson travelled to the Gulf of Papua in 1904, a trip ending in controversy when he was involved in a scuffle in which eight Goaribi were killed. The Chalmers affair and its aftermath became a scandal. Robinson's intentions in visiting the Goaribi were viewed with suspicion, and his armed involvement in a scuffle added to the furore. Robinson took his own life with a pistol under the flagstaff at Government House in June 1904 (Jinks, Biskup and Nelson 1973: 76–80; Wetherell 1996: 68–69).

Hubert Murray and Australian Juridical Policy

In 1906, British New Guinea became the Territory of Papua, to be administered from Australia. Administrative stability returned when Hubert Murray, a lawyer who first came to the area in 1904 as chief judicial officer, was appointed lieutenant-governor in 1908. Murray shared MacGregor's view that there were no real chiefs in Papua, and commented: 'Had a class of chiefs existed with real powers we should have worked through them so far as possible' (1926: 6). He said (wrongly) of references to chiefs in contemporary accounts that 'the name is apt to be misleading; for in Papua their power is commonly personal to themselves and has nothing to do with any recognised position in the community. . . . Their influence is commonly very limited and often very short lived' (1928: 3). Murray also believed that Papuans had nothing which could be glossed as a justice system: 'So far as I am aware there is but scanty evidence of anything in the nature of a public administration of justice, or a communal punishment of crime, before the arrival of the white man' (1925: 57). Murray's Administration retained the village constable system and added a system of village councils to cooperate with European magistrates and village constables, explain Administration policies to villagers and assist locally in their implementation (1928: 6–7). MacGregor's 'Native Board Regulations' were supplanted by a Native Regulations Ordinance (1908) and Native Magistrates Courts became 'Courts for Native Matters' (Chalmers 1978a: 92).

The new Administration was unwilling to allow Papuans to have any real control over juridical procedures, and continued to see them as regrettably governed by uncivilised customs. Murray felt, for example, that fear of sorcery was a major obstacle to competence in indigenous magistrates (Jinks, Biskup and Nelson 1973: 136). Sorcery (the term was used in the widest and most unspecific sense) was a major concern for the Administration during this period. Murray regarded Papuans as living in 'constant terror of witchcraft' (1925: 67), and a resident magistrate of the period substantiated his own later reminiscences about the problem of sorcery beliefs by citing a comment by Murray that the elimination of sorcery beliefs would minimise serious crime in the territory (Griffin n.d.: 214). Forbidden under the Native Regulations, sorcery earned its alleged practitioners a six-month gaol sentence if they were found guilty. Notions of sorcery had no credibility as far as Murray was concerned—'We know of course that sorcery is all rubbish' (1926: 12)—and his cryptic comment on the gaol sentence, that sorcerers could not be put to death for an imaginary offence (1925: 66), reflected the ontological dilemma sorcery beliefs presented for the Administration. Magistrates regarded it as a major cause of crime (Griffin n.d.: 214–17) and were anxious that Papuans be disabused of their belief in it, yet the prosecution of alleged sorcerers suggested to Papuans that the Administration shared the belief.

Murray was adamant that the European criminal code would prevail over any customary equivalent which may have existed. In particular, he contrasted a preferred European concept of individual responsibility for crime with what he thought were Papuan notions of collective responsibility (1928: 10). A practical effect of this distrustful attitude was that it limited any potential which village constables may have had to fulfil MacGregor's earlier objective that they would 'deal with cases in their own villages' under supervision and teaching by magistrates (Jinks, Biskup and Nelson 1973: 61). Indeed, Murray's resident magistrates appeared ambivalent, at best, about the usefulness of village constables: 'These men are generally selected because they have a (more or less imperfect) knowledge of the Motu language.[7] Some of these men become very valuable servants; others are at the bottom of every outrage and crime committed in their district, and use their position to blackmail the villagers. But it is hard to think out any more satisfactory system' (Griffin n.d.: 195).

Whatever the idealised role of village constables was, the real relationship between village constables and their supervisors was more accurately depicted, perhaps, in a play which villagers at Fyfe Bay (in what is now Milne Bay Province) presented to entertain Hubert Murray during one of his patrols. The play was about the murder of an elderly village woman, and the characters included a village constable and a European, the assistant resident magistrate, who sent the village constable to arrest the culprit. The village constable brought the suspect in on the end of a rope. A later scene in the play was a trial, conducted by the European: the village constable's role in this was to be told to 'shut up' by the magistrate (West 1970: 124–25).

The Negation of Hahl's Juridical Project

The German administration of New Guinea came to an end at the outbreak of the First World War, when Australia began military occupation of the territory. After the war Australia took over the administration of New Guinea as a Mandated Territory on behalf of the League of Nations. Murray wanted the new territory to be amalgamated with Papua, but was in the minority on the three-person Royal Commission considering the issue. New Guinea was administered separately, under the New Guinea Act, when civilian rule was restored in 1921 (Jinks, Biskup and Nelson 1973: 230).

The new Administration took over the colonial institutions of the Germans and modified them according to Australian policies. Among these institutions was the *luluai* system, which the Australians retained and continued to spread into mainland New Guinea in a hierarchical form comprising of 'paramount' *luluais* (in charge of districts), *luluais* (in charge of villages), *tultuls* (messengers and assistants) and medical *tultuls*.[8] However, they stripped the *luluais* of their magisterial function, reducing them officially to a role similar to that of the Papuan village constables. It was soon found, though, that the *luluais* were continuing to conduct courts, often with the unofficial blessing of the Administration's *kiaps*[9] who found community dispute settlement a time-consuming and often opaque business and were happy to delegate it to local 'leaders'. The *luluais*, conversely, probably regarded their dispute-settlement activities as a mandate from *kiaps* (Strathern 1975: 49–50). Similarly, in Papua village constables assumed dispute settlement to be part of their duties (Kiki 1968: 9). Chalmers (1978a: 157) points out that from the point of view of local communities, *kiaps*' ignorance of customary offences, as well as the community's lack of confidence in the *kiaps*, also contributed to the continuance of unofficial courts.

The practical advantages of *luluai* courts were observed by a territory advisor, Colonel J. Ainsworth, the administrator of Kenya, whose attitude to colonial administration combined social Darwinism with simple expedience.[10] In a report on the administration of New Guinea, Ainsworth suggested that *luluais* and *kukurais* (a term which stressed the magisterial duties of *luluais*) continue to be allowed, by ordinance, to hear minor disputes on the grounds that they had always had this right and that they were hearing cases anyway, *ultra vires* (1924: 17–18). The recommendation was not implemented, however, and the *luluai* courts remained illegal under Australian rule.

Ainsworth's suggestion prompted the sarcastic response from Murray in Papua that if New Guineans had a system of trial according to native law they must be many centuries in advance of Papuans, a 'typical lawyer's comment' according to Rowley (1965: 78). Murray's response reflected his view that law should be properly administered by specialists, though in fact rough justice in the field was common at the hands of the resident magistrates. Like MacGregor before him, Murray saw the advent of Papuan magistrates as possible only in the distant future, when the disappearance of extended kin-group loyalties and pressures and other customary influences would permit unbiased judgment. The Administration was also concerned, in a paternalistic sense, about the liability of community leaders to corruption. Some *luluais* did indeed exceed their formal duties and exploit the power given to them by *kiaps* but whether this was corruption in a real sense, or simply an extension of pre-existing strategies for gaining power and pursuing self-interest in their own societies, is equivocal (see Strathern 1975: 49–54; and cf. Berndt 1962: 319–21; Epstein 1969: 252). The Administration's attitude of mistrust may also have been affected by simplistic conceptions of indigenous regulatory procedures as crude vengeance, a view used somewhat paradoxically by the Administration in the Mandated Territory of New Guinea to justify its capital punishment of offenders as a pedagogic exercise (Nelson 1976: 28).

The Problem of 'Custom'

When New Guinea became a mandated territory, a Native Administration Ordinance was introduced consisting of a series of special regulations aimed at New Guineans, similar to the Native Regulations of Papua. With the Ordinance, Hahl's relatively liberal attitude towards 'customs' was replaced by a more interventionist policy. The Administration's official attitude was expressed in the doctrine that traditional customs were allowed to continue unless repugnant to the 'principles of humanity'—an anthropologically meaningless phrase best understood, in retrospect, by reference to conservatively imagined Australian mores of the time. The regulations were enforced through a new legal institution, Courts for Native Affairs, mostly conducted by *kiaps* on patrol in villages or at government stations. These courts were equivalent to the Courts for Native Matters already established in Papua.

The Native Regulations continued to provide the most common experience of European law for Papuans. They served as an Adminstration mechanism for separating out undesirable indigenous social behaviour from the general body of acceptable custom and classifying it as crime along with behaviour for which there were no customary precedents at all. Sorcery and the drinking of *gamada* (*Piper methysticum*),[11] for example, became offences in the same general category as failure to maintain the colonisers' roads or to attend school. Through the legal practice and discourse of Murray's Administration, like MacGregor's before it, 'custom' was conceived ahistorically to be a body of beliefs and practices of equivocal legal and moral validity requiring distinctions to be made between those which could be tolerated and those which could not. For instance, Murray was insistent that 'cannibalism and head-hunting, human sacrifice, torture, intertribal warfare and other anti-social practices must go, and go for ever, irrespective of the consequences that may ensue' (1926: 6), whereas he considered that customary land disputes could be decided 'without raising any debatable questions of law and custom', and matters of marriage and inheritance 'may be left to native custom' (7). Murray even argued in one instance that Administration intervention was supportive of custom, in attempting to deal with an alleged increase in polygamy, over-hasty marriage and a consequent discarding of wives brought about by the introduction of a cash economy. He contended that 'in endeavouring to neutralize these tendencies, whether by legislation or otherwise, an administration is really acting in support of native custom, and is preserving it against the disintegrating influences inseparable from European settlement' (8).

While the distinction between desirable and undesirable practices involved recognition of the social validity of some indigenous customs, the Australian Administration in both Papua and New Guinea before the Second World War was never prepared to acknowledge custom as substantive law (Gordon and Meggitt 1985: 192). Further, while it was known that custom was being applied in unofficial courts, its possible influence in official court findings of guilt or innocence was unacceptable, though it could be considered in mitigation at sentencing. Peter Fitzpatrick has commented that this state of affairs involved a conceptual separation of 'native custom' from traditional law, to overcome the ambiguity of colonial policies which sought to preserve the traditional mode of production (in which traditional law was functional) while refusing to recognise the legal validity of customary regulatory procedures:

> This delicate conflict was resolved by extracting something called 'native custom' from the operative dynamic of traditional dispute settlement. The perceived vices of traditional law could then be attached to dispute settlement. Provision was usually made for the recognition of 'native custom' in colonial courts, subject to broad exceptions including one that the custom concerned must not be inconsistent with colonial law. . . . Traditional dispute settlement was, on the other hand, beyond tolerance and perhaps illegal. (1980: 68)

It is hard to gauge the extent to which the exclusion of indigenous 'law' from the general body of acceptable 'custom' was a conscious strategy involving a degree of analytic understanding of indigenous regulatory practices by the Administration. It is likely that the predominant principle generating the separation referred to by Fitzpatrick was an enduring and simple ethnocentric belief in the 'rule of law', precluding serious consideration of any indigenous processes which did not appear immediately similar to Anglo-Australian legal procedure. Certainly, Murray's statement that there was 'scanty evidence' of indigenous public administration of justice (1925: 57) flew in the face of reports by government anthropologists in both Papua and New Guinea before the Second World War. Both E. W. P. Chinnery in New Guinea and F. E. Williams in Papua mentioned the existence of social regulatory procedure in indigenous societies, ranging from dispute settlement techniques to death penalties (see, for example, Chinnery 1925: 31, 123, 133–34; Williams 1976: 106–14). While Chinnery used a pre-functionalist descriptive technique and made only perfunctory mention of regulatory devices, Williams's detailed account of dispute resolution in Elema (Gulf Province) left no doubt of the existence of procedures which were public, ritualised and systematic.[12]

While the expressed policies of Murray imply an official exclusion of indigenes from all colonially sanctioned juridical practice, quasi-legal forums did exist in which villagers were given roles allowing them to judge a range of disputes and misdemeanours. These included hearings conducted by some village councils which were given powers to adjudicate and punish. Carol Mytinger, an adventurer in Papua during Murray's period, witnessed a village council at the Motu-Koita village complex popularly known by Europeans as Hanuabada at Port Moresby, in which twelve men heard what she described as 'minor cases' concerning pigs, sorcery, adultery and 'clan squabbles' (1947: 172), with power to levy sentences and fines, which she regarded as very severe. Another forum was established by the London Missionary Society in the form of deacons courts. At Hula village on the Papuan coast, for example, the deacons court, according to Nigel Oram, had 'important disciplinary functions' (n.d.: 6). As the church established increasing dominance over village sociality these courts acted as powerful sanctioning mechanisms. 'The deacons court inflicted penalties which included refusal of communion and suspension of church membership. This punishment meant exclusion from many of the social activities of the village' (11). Yet forums such as these were never developed into formal adjuncts to the introduced legal system.

The New Deal, and a Proposal for 'Native Village Courts'

The conflict with Japan in Papua and New Guinea during the Second World War made Australians more aware of their northern neighbours, and legends (propagandist and sometimes greatly exaggerated) of the loyalty shown by Papua New Guineans towards Australia during the conflict generated a sense of obligation which had not been present previously. This and a shift in Western world opinion about colonialism contributed to a post-war 'New Deal' policy from the governing Labour Party in Australia with a view to eventual political independence for the country (Waiko 1993: 123). Under the Papua and New Guinea Provisional Act of 1945 and subsequently the Papua and New Guinea Act of 1949 Papua and New Guinea became a single entity known as the Territory of Papua New Guinea for administrative purposes. A new administrator, Colonel J. K. Murray,[13] represented the new outlook of the Australian Ministry of Territories in criticising the limited development which had taken place in the pre-war period despite such apparently positive steps as the protection of the populace against land loss and excessive foreign labour recruitment and the imposition of fairly extensive labour legislation to prevent abuses by colonial employers. 'The chief impression one gains is of the largely negative and formal character of our achievement . . . safeguards and minimum standards are not enough. . . . Socially, economically and politically, the native remained backward, and there seemed to be no clear road of advancement upon which he could travel' (Murray 1949: 15). Murray worked to develop a public service and expressed special commitment towards improving education, health services and replacing the indenture system with free labour (26–38).

In the field of justice, Murray mooted the idea of 'Native Village Courts', and Section 63 of the Papua and New Guinea Act 1949 provided for the establishment of native village courts and other tribunals run by Papua New Guineans. Murray said the village constable, *luluai* and village council systems suffered from two major defects: 'Executive, rule-making and judicial power were concentrated upon the alien European officials, and there was no recognised procedure for encouraging local responsibility and initiative' (1949: 60). To give Papua New Guineans the initiative in justice matters, he proposed community-elected councils to be accorded rule-making and executive powers in local affairs, and 'native courts will also be set up with jurisdiction in minor civil and criminal matters, especially but not exclusively in those relating to native custom' (61). Impetus for these proposals came from commentaries and research by Lucy Mair, an anthropologist and writer on colonial administration, and the Pacific anthropologist Ian Hogbin, who believed the measures would not only give indigenes a degree of local government but would also offset individual powermongering by government-appointed *luluais* and other figures (Healy 1967: 25; Hogbin 1946). Murray realised his proposals would meet with resistance among Administration staff and lawyers with primitivist attitudes and he appealed to the changing nature of Papua and New Guinea society and the rise of progressive 'new leaders' whose energies should be enlisted in 'constructive modernisation' (1949: 61).

Murray's appeal was unsuccessful. The Labour Party lost power to the Liberal-Country Party in 1949, Murray was replaced and administrative control became more firmly concentrated in Canberra. The idea of native, or village, courts was fielded several times during the early 1950s (Lynch 1978: 114–16), especially by David Fenbury, a former *kiap* who was the 'Native Authorities Officer'. Fenbury, who had consulted anthropologists and others, was in favour of native village councils and village courts comprising of panels of local 'big men' (1978: 25), although he did not intend that they should follow 'custom' in their practice (Sack 1989: 384). Like Ainsworth in a previous era, Fenbury cited the existence of unofficial and illegal courts, including one conducted competently not far from the District Court in Port Moresby (1978: 108), in his attempts to convince Canberra of the viability of a community-level judiciary. In 1955 the draft of another bill for a native courts ordinance was submitted to the new Australian minister for territories, Paul Hasluck. The proposed courts would deal with both civil and criminal cases and matters arising from custom (unless the custom was 'repugnant to natural justice or morality' and in conflict with the law) and would order compensation and impose fines and prison sentences where necessary (291–300).

While native councils were introduced (in a modified form) in the 1950s as the Administration came to the view that a small degree of local government would be innocuous to overall Australian control (Healy 1967: 25–26), Hasluck was not in favour of village courts, nor was an influential conservative section of the judiciary in Papua and New Guinea. Hasluck expressed a fear that the village courts would be 'an elaborate sham', and in reality subordinate to the European system (Hasluck 1976: 187). He argued further that if they had different procedures from the European courts there would be a dual justice system, which he considered undesirable (188). Also, echoing some pre-war administrative sentiments, he considered that it might undermine the principles of justice acceptable to the Australian Government and that people would not receive justice in a village court system (188–89). Consequently the idea lapsed.

At the time the system of courts in Papua and New Guinea consisted of a Supreme Court (previously the Central Court), below which were two constellations of lesser courts, one in Papua and one in New Guinea. Papua had Wardens Courts (hearing matters of land claims and mining rights), Petty Sessions Courts, Small Debts Courts and Courts for Native Matters, the latter dealing exclusively with 'Papuans'. New Guinea had District Courts, Wardens Courts and Courts for Native Affairs, the latter dealing exclusively with 'New Guineans'. This was the height of the *kiap* era and insofar as the *kiap* was the investigator, arrester, magistrate and gaoler (Aleck 1986: 20; Chalmers 1978a: 149–51; Nelson 1990: 187), the 'native matters' and 'native affairs' courts reinforced low-level administrators' control over villagers. High conviction rates prevailed (Chalmers 1978a: 176–77) in a situation where 'the judge, prosecutor and chief prosecution witness would often be a low-level official trying someone for failure to comply with an order he gave in the first place' (Fitzpatrick 1980: 66). In addition, informal courts held by *luluais* and other Administration-appointed authority figures were rife, punishing offences with methods sometimes extremely at odds with those of the official courts whose authority they emulated (see, for example, Berndt 1962: 328–80).

Justice Reviewed, 'Custom' Revisited

While Hasluck was not in favour of a 'dual' system of law, he was dissatisfied with the existing judicial system, and in particular with the involvement of administrators in the courts. He was also opposed to the application of the law in one way for Papuans and New Guineans (through the 'native affairs' and 'native matters' courts) and in another way for Europeans. In consultation with his new chief justice, Alan Mann, he appointed Professor David Derham of Melbourne University to review the administration of justice and prepare a report, which Derham did in 1960. Derham's findings (which were not made public until 1973) confirmed the inclinations of Hasluck and Mann. Derham wanted the racially differentiating 'native affairs' and 'native matters' courts done away with (1960: 36–37) and argued for rationalisation of the legal system into a streamlined hierarchy administered by a properly trained judiciary. He criticised *kiap* justice, and questioned the conventional belief among the colonisers that even if *kiaps* did not know and follow the law exactly, they dispensed justice adequately based on their alleged knowledge of local customs and beliefs (22–25). He urged more involvement of Papuans and New Guineans in the administration of justice, as properly trained magistrates (33–34, 46). Judge P. J. Quinlivan (who toured with Derham) also mooted, in a document in 1962, the need for participation by Papuans and New Guineans (Quinlivan 1962, cited in Quinlivan n.d.: 9) and later wrote that he influenced Chief Justice Mann at the time to consider the idea of an 'intermediate court' to relieve the burden placed on higher courts by having to travel around the country (9). Derham also wanted custom to be taken into account to a greater degree, though he recognised that custom was not systematic (i.e. was not an indigenous equivalent of European law) and would be difficult to rationalise for judicial purposes (1960: 35–36). At the same time, he still wanted the European system of 'proof' to be used (36).

The Derham report, and reactions to it among officials, indicated a growing awareness by the Adminstration of the inadequacy of the conception of 'custom' which had prevailed since the beginning of colonial rule. Simplistic, dualistic and ahistorical notions of 'customs' had represented them as ethically and legally questionable indigenous beliefs and practices. These notions now began to be refined in debate over impending indigenous participation in the legal system. Opposing the concept of village courts, Derham's report made references to the lack of legal clarity about customs and to the tendency of custom to change under culture contact and become indistinct to the detriment of its applicability in court cases. In a later comment on the report, Fenbury defended his own concept of village courts and the place of custom:

> *It was never argued by advocates of a Native Courts system ... that native customary practices and institutions are either sacrosanct or immutable. It was never proposed that the native courts ... should be 'customary courts' after the style of African Chiefs courts. ...* The Derham report had apparently made some comment to the effect that the 1954 draft courts ordinance advocated native customary usages. The comment on this aspect was that while the draft courts ordinance obviously implied that a native court bench of local laymen should be more competent than a European ... to decide certain categories of civil issues ... in the light of local customary usages, this could not properly be construed as advocating the fossilising of customary usages in general. (1978: 124–25, emphasis in original)

For Fenbury, the problem, for legal purposes, of the diversity of 'custom' in Papua New Guinea would have been solved through a process amounting to juridical acculturation:

> Derham seemed to believe . . . that 'some agency of the Central Government' should be able to lay down, from time to time, just what the prevailing state of customary usage might be or should be in any particular area. On this I commented that 'The diversities in practices, no less than the wide variations in degrees of culture contact, stultify any such proposal'. *In fact, the only feasible way in which evolving customary usages can be legally veered towards Western concepts—and hence homogeneity—is by way of periodic redefinition through area council rules, enforced by local courts.* (125, emphasis in original)

Fenbury's retrospective critique demonstrates that a more complex conceptualisation of custom was developing among administrators in the 1960s. In subsequent policy general condemnation began to be replaced by attempted accommodation. Until the period of the Derham report discourse about the development of the legal system had contained a conventional wisdom—sometimes implicit, sometimes explicit—that law and custom were virtually antithetical in many respects (for instance in terms of objectivity, impartiality and systematic applicability). But more liberal administrative attitudes had developed by the mid 1960s. Together with an increasing sociological sophistication among higher-ranked officials and a realisation that Papua and New Guinea would some day be politically self-determining, these attitudes engendered a greater administrative recognition of custom as (mostly) acceptable social practice. A move was made to give more recognition to custom in the field of law, with the 'Native Customs (Recognition) Act' of 1963. The concept of custom was so loosely articulated in the Act, however, that it was hardly an improvement on the previous attitude that allowed custom to continue unless repugnant to the principles of humanity. Section Four of the Act was annotated as a definition, and stated that by 'custom' it meant 'the custom or usage of the aboriginal inhabitants of the territory . . . regardless of whether or not that custom or usage has obtained from time immemorial'. A 'Note on Native Custom' in a legal handbook in 1965 recognised the difficulty of defining customs, and said law could recognise that customs were imprecise and changeable (Quinlivan 1965: 1–22). Many questions remained unresolved, however, such as how to determine what local customs were, how long a behaviour had to be followed before it could be considered a custom, the difference between 'custom' and customary procedure, and so on.[14]

Despite the political recognition of the validity of custom expressed through the Act, the Administration continued to be resistant to the establishment of a category of legal institutions which would formally endorse custom as a major judicial component. Also, in the 1960s, the system of *luluais* and village constables was beginning to be phased out and replaced by a system of local government councils. Councillors continued the informal court system which had operated under the *luluai* system (Strathern 1972: 88–89). Nevertheless the removal of *luluais* and village constables (the bridging elements between the *kiap* and local communities) created a gap between the formal legal system and, especially, rural communities. There was a growing concern on the part of the Administration that the majority of the population was not using the formal system of justice, and unofficial courts, over which the Administration had no systematic control, were flourishing (Fitzpatrick 1980: 139–40; Strathern 1972: 2–6).

The juridical effect of the Derham Report as far as the majority of Papuans and New Guineans were concerned was the disappearance of the 'native affairs' and 'native matters' courts and their replacement by Local Courts, beginning in January 1966 (under the Local Courts Act of 1963). Local Courts could administer fines up to $100, impose gaol sentences of up to six months and could order compensation payments up to $200. The judges in these courts were magistrates. Originally they were appointed after two years in the field (i.e. they were still *kiaps*) but later they actually underwent a magistrates training course at the PNG Administration College (Chalmers 1978a: 215–16). Derham had recommended that there should be indigenous magistrates in the Local Courts and District Courts, and while the latter positions continued to be held by expatriates until 1972, when four Papua New Guineans were appointed resident magistrates, indigenous involvement in Local Court adjudication increased at a better rate. There had been only two ex-field officers in 1966 but by 1973 there were sixty magistrates and sixteen assistant magistrates (Iramu 1975: 43). Chalmers has emphasised the shortcomings of Local Courts as an important factor in the events which finally led to the introduction of the Village Court System (1978b: 57–58). These included over-formalised procedures and language difficulties, which alienated local communities particularly in rural areas, and a procedural emphasis on producing a winning litigant, in contrast to traditional Melanesian concern with the maintenance of community stability. Idiosyncratic adjudication by frequently changing *kiaps* also undermined indigenous confidence in Local Courts and contributed to a preference for the illegal alternative courts.

There was, however, a degree of community involvement in local courts, varying in different parts of the country. In the Gazelle Peninsula of East New Britain, according to Quinlivan (a stipendiary magistrate serving in the late colonial period), the Local Court in the late 1960s and early 1970s '*always* sat with important, respected, non-trained men in the villages and foreign[15] settlements' (1975: 61, emphasis in original). Quinlivan recorded surprise at finding a very different situation in Port Moresby on his arrival early in 1971: 'I was appalled: no court ever visited the villages or foreign settlements; no elder had ever been known to sit with the magistrate' (64). The local involvement to which Quinlivan referred was legislated for in the Local Courts Act of 1963, which allowed magistrates to appoint assistants from the community but not until the end of the colonial era was any significant use of the provision evident among Local Court magistrates (Chalmers 1978b: 61–62).

The Foundations for the Village Court System

Even before the practical inadequacies of the Local Courts became evident, discussion among Administration planners in the aftermath of Derham's visit began explicitly to bring together issues of legal services, indigenous participation and custom in a configuration which forcefully reintroduced proposals for a Village Court system. A 1965 paper by the legislative draftsman of the time, C. J. Lynch, saw the Native Customs (Recognition) Act of 1963 as inevitably involving a trend towards 'unification and standardisation', no matter on how gradual a basis (1965: 15). He suggested areas of 'nativisation' in Local Courts, such as mediation and assistant magistrates, regardless of their lack of professional qualifications, on the ground that professional qualification had not been a priority for colonial legal officers in the past—it was just a matter of training: 'It is continually overlooked that in providing a moderate level of training for Patrol Officers who are usually extremely young, the Administration has always worked on the basis of a relatively low-level (and indeed, up to and including the District Courts level) sub-professional academic standard for magistrates, by whatever name these may have been known—and with no alarming over-all results' (17). Lynch proposed a reform of the legal system involving 'native courts' using 'minimally trained native magistrates of the "village elder" type', and administering 'custom' or 'customary law', arguing it would provide speedy justice at a low financial cost and would be physically close to the people (27–28).

Paradoxically, then, the implementation of Derham's recommendations, aimed at negating legal pluralism and rendering the legal system more similar in form to those of Britain and Australia, created the practical difficulties which would lead to the legitimation of the 'native' or village court system which successive Administrations had resisted since the beginning of the colonial period. But the shortcomings of the Local Courts were not the only impetus towards a new justice-delivery strategy. From the 1950s there had been increasing pressure from the UN on Australia to prepare PNG for political independence, resulting in improvements in the provision of education, health services, technical training and other symbols of development and in a programme of 'localisation' of positions traditionally held by Australians. In the 1960s a growing number of Papua New Guineans were moving into positions of authority in a variety of spheres including parliament[16] and voicing arguments and opinions which could no longer be paternalistically derogated by Australian administrators. Among indigenous parliamentarians and academics in particular, a developing anti-colonial rhetoric included calls for the favouring of custom and customary law as more appropriate regulatory instruments for an emerging Melanesian nation than the imposed legal system. This body of opinion complemented the influx of Papua New Guineans into the judiciary, and added considerable weight to the resurgent notion that some form of 'native courts' might be advantageous in the light of the inadequacies of the Local Courts as far as rural communities were concerned.

Meanwhile the implementation of recommendations from the Derham Report made the late 1960s a period of intense reorganisation in the justice system, with an attendant burgeoning of reports and commentaries particularly absorbed with lower courts and village-level society. At the official level this culminated with a review of the lower court system by the Secretary for Law, L. J. Curtis, and the First Assistant Secretary of the Department of External Territories' Government and Legal Division, J. H. Greenwell (Curtis and Greenwell 1971). In the Curtis-Greenwell Report (as it was subsequently called) it was yet again noted that unofficial courts were continuing and that the problem of the delivery of justice to rural people had not been solved: the possibility of the introduction of a village court system was mooted as a solution. Curtis ordered an enquiry into the need for village courts and village constables, which was conducted by two magistrates, R. N. Desailly and F. Iramu. Their task (the terms of reference were the comments of the Curtis-Greenwell Report) was to examine the adequacy of the lower courts and police operations, particularly in rural areas, to advise on whether the policy of opposition to village justices should be changed and whether there was a need for village constables, and to set out proposals for the introduction of any system of village courts or constables recommended (1972: 2).

Acknowledging the failure of the existing legal system to provide an adequate means of dispute settlement at village level, Desailly and Iramu were unenthusiastic about customary courts 'which would perpetuate old ideas in times of change. Some old ideas are likely to fail the test of acceptability too' (1972: 3–4). At the same time they recognised that unofficial tribunals were finding solutions to disputes through debate, discussion and compromise, and commented, 'The great need is for sanctions to ensure attendance at the tribunal and conformity with the solution when reached' (4). Their recommendation was a system of village courts which, while not applying 'strict customary rules', would be 'strongly influenced by the customs of the area and by local attitudes and mores' (8). The magistrates should not be trained in the general law, and Desailly and Iramu reinforced previous conceptions of village court magistrates primarily as dispute settlers: 'If there is power to imprison or fine, administrative and supervisory arrangements become more complex and demanding' (11).

A White Paper based on the Desailly-Iramu report was tabled in the House of Assembly and debated late in 1972. By this time the majority of parliamentarians were Melanesian and custom was becoming a rhetorical component of the debate over PNG's political independence (Gordon and Meggitt 1985: 192). The Melanesian parliamentarians were mostly in favour of village courts. Some objections were raised, along the same lines as those which had been made to J. Murray's proposal of 1949, and the debate on the White Paper[17] moved through a number of issues, including tribal fighting and the continued presence of unofficial courts. Among the themes traversed in the course of discussion, Chalmers (whose 1978 LL.M thesis was the first systematic study of the delevopment of PNG's legal system from the beginning to the end of the colonial period) has stressed those of nationalism and criticism of the colonial legal system (1978a: 266–67). There was an expressed desire that 'European technicalities' be kept out of village courts (Oscar Tammur, MHA, quoted in Chalmers 1978a: 267), and that there be no interference from welfare officers and *kiaps* (Paul Langro, MHA, quoted in Chalmers 1978a: 267).

Momentum gathered: Chalmers (1978b: 69fn) reports a meeting held in 1973 attended by two parliamentarians, Barry Holloway and John Guise, along with G. Dabb (assistant secretary for law), Lynch and Fenbury, at which village courts were mooted in the context of incipient self-government as an instrument in giving a modicum of power to indigenous people. A committee set up to investigate increasing 'tribal' fighting in the highlands added fuel, by strongly recommending a system of village courts as part of the remedy (Paney et al. 1973: 6–9). In September 1973 the Village Courts Bill was introduced for parliamentary debate[18] by the minister for justice, John Kaputin, who stressed its potential efficacy in giving indigenous communities control over their own affairs. The issue of returning power to local communities was persuasive in the climate of the end of colonial rule, along with the issue of the rural shortcomings of the current legal system, and a perceived need for an emphasis on rural 'law and order' (Curtis and Greenwell 1971, Chalmers 1978b: 71–72). It overrode concerns (mostly among Europeans[19]) about the possibility of corruption in village courts (Bayne 1975b: 41; Oram 1975: 67–68; Strathern 1975), the latter portending complaints which have periodically been made during the operational history of the village court system.

With a majority of politicians, academics and educated Melanesians now favouring the idea of village courts on political, nationalist and juridical grounds legislation became ineluctable. The Village Courts Act 1973 came into force on 28 November 1974. The ideal of village courts expressed in the Act was a compendium of elements of the periodical proposals for community-based courts since Hahl's *luluai* courts in the early colonial period. Section Forty of the Act provided that no distinction was to be drawn between civil and criminal cases. Overall, mediation and the pursuit of peace and harmony in the settlement of low-level intra-community disputes were the principal aims. Magistrates were to be legally unqualified members of the local community, fines and community work were to be the predominant form of punishment for offenders, and in the last instance village courts were to decide matters 'in accordance with substantial justice' (Section Thirty). Further, Section Twenty-Nine of the Act stipulated that village courts should apply relevant custom as determined in accordance with the Native Customs (Recognition) Act. It was also clear, especially in the commentaries of legal specialists, that village courts were expected to gather existing unofficial dispute-settlement procedures into the centralised legal system (see, for example, Bayne 1975a: 33).

There is historical irony in the similarities between the eventual model of village courts and Hahl's *luluai* courts. The negation of his juridical model by the Australian Administration after the First World War can be seen as an early moment in a dialectic which led to a system seeking to exploit an ongoing 'traditional' institution—the informal courts still being convened by elders and other authority figures in local communities—both as an executive agent and as an Administration-sanctioned settler of customary disputes, as originally intended by Hahl. The early engagement between Australian law, dispensed by 'resident magistrates' and *kiaps*, and its Other ('custom'), dispensed by elders, sorcerers and other indigenous figures of authority, became dialectically complex. Indigenous leaders appropriated elements of the introduced 'court' system, interpreted in terms of their own culture, into their own dispute settlement procedures, while *kiaps* attempted to be relatively accommodating of 'custom,' a putative political-juridical alternative allowing the consideration of a subsidiary category, 'customary law'. In time, the inadequacy of *kiap* justice and other legal services in rural areas allowed the consideration of legitimising the indigenous alternatives by systematising them into a legally sanctioned service, in which 'customary law' would be articulated with a simplified application of the introduced Law.

This articulation, endearing the idea of village courts to Melanesian leaders seeking a return to 'custom' simultaneously with progress beyond colonial rule, would prove to be the most problematic aspect of the practical operations of the village courts, as we will see in chapter 3. But the systematic administration of the village courts would also be frought with problems, which is the subject of the next chapter.

Notes

1. Investing sovereignty in the Neu Guinea Kompagnie was Germany's solution to the problem of the expense of acquiring colonies during the scramble among European colonisers in the South Pacific. The Neu Guinea Kompagnie administered the territory and took financial responsibility, under royal charter, from 1885 till 1899, when the German government took control. The Kompagnie's mismanagement, highlighted by the contrasting efficiency of the recently arrived Hahl, contributed to the government's decision to take over (see Firth 1986).
2. *Luluai* is a Tolai word usually understood by anthropologists to mean war-leader, though its original sense (before being adopted by the Germans) is not altogether clear (see, for example, Epstein 1969: 251fn; Salisbury 1970: 35).
3. 'Chief' is a term which should be employed cautiously, as popular usage has rendered it very inexact. Its anthropological use connotes, usually, a hereditary position as head of a recognisable descent group, with political authority (see chapter 5).
4. MacGregor had trained as a doctor.
5. Monckton had no legal training and like most of the resident magistrates he served as a roving administrative agent. He has been described as an ambitious and aggressive character, probably the most violent of the magistrates in British New Guinea at the turn of the century (Souter 1964: 83–88).
6. He tended to assume that the social organisation of groups in the vicinity of his headquarters was typical of Melanesia in general, and his comments about the diminishing influence of sorcerers and other significant figures underestimated the resilience of indigenous political structures.
7. Motu is the language of a group of coastal people of what is now the Central Province. A lingua franca based on Motu was extended through Papua from the 1880s by the police force who accompanied colonial officers on patrol. In 1970 'Police Motu' was officially renamed 'Hiri Motu'. The lingua franca is popularly

thought to have developed through the traditional 'Hiri' voyages made by the Motu people to the Gulf District to trade pots for sago, but Dutton (1985) has persuasively argued otherwise.

8. According to Stanner (1953: 25) there were more than 11,200 of these officials in the Mandated Territory by 1939, made up of 66 paramount *luluais*, 3,705 *luluais*, 3,865 *tultuls* and 3,580 medical *tultuls*.
9. New Guinea villagers commonly used the term *kiap* to refer to any administrator in the field, up to district commissioners, while the latter used it mostly to refer to the lower ranking patrol officers.
10. He advocated, for instance, agriculture as the basis for an education system in New Guinea—an idea which met with little enthusiasm from the Administration (see Smith 1989: 297).
11. Known elsewhere in the Pacific as *kava*, this was used ceremonially in parts of what is now the Western Province. Gunnar Landtman (1927: 106ff) recorded its extensive use in the Kiwai area, referring to it as *Gamoda*.
12. The mention of 'courts' in other pre-war anthropological accounts was often frustratingly ambiguous. John W. Whiting, for example, writes of a 'court system' operating among the Kwoma (near Ambunti in what is now the East Sepik Province) during the 1930s, without clarifying whether it was a traditional institution or the result of colonial interaction (1951: 161–63).
13. No relation to the pre-war administrator.
14. Gordon and Meggitt offer a good discussion of the issues (1985: 190–209).
15. He was referring to migrants from rural areas into towns. Restrictions on the free movement of indigenes around the country were lifted at the end of the Second World War and migrant settlements quickly appeared, especially in Port Moresby and Lae.
16. The first elections for Papua New Guinea's House of Assembly (which succeeded the Legislative Council) were held in 1964. Thirty-eight of the total sixty-four members were Papua New Guinean. The standard account of the 1964 elections is provided by Bettison, Hughes and van der Veur (1965).
17. Debated September and November 1972, recorded in Hansard Vol III No. 7 and No. 10, esp. pp. 1163–68.
18. Read 28 September 1973, recorded in Hansard Vol III No. 21, p.2881.
19. During parliamentary debate one Melanesian, United Party leader Tei Abal, mentioned the possibility of bribery: recorded in Hansard Vol III No. 23, p. 3083.

2

THE ADMINISTRATION OF VILLAGE COURTS

As shown in the previous chapter, two general themes constituted the discursive context of the eventual introduction of a system of village courts. One was that the formal justice system of the late colonial period was not accessible to villagers (Curtis and Greenwell 1971; Iramu 1975; Lynch 1965: 32; Oram 1975),[1] the other was a rhetoric that the colonial legal system had been unjustly censorious of custom and customary law and that the latter should be restored and preserved (Chalmers 1978b: 266–67; PNG House of Assembly Debates 1972: 1163–68). Consequently, the Village Courts Act stipulated that the village courts' primary function was to 'ensure peace and harmony', endeavour to obtain 'amicable settlement of disputes' and apply custom 'as determined in accordance with . . . the Native Customs (Recognition) Act of 1963' (Village Courts Act 1973).[2] Further, village courts were enjoined to decide all matters 'in accordance with substantial justice' (Village Courts Act, s.27). A desire for informality was reflected in the legislation's provisions that village court magistrates would be untrained in law and selected by the local community on the criteria of their adjudicatory integrity and good knowledge of local customs (Village Court Secretariat 1975: 1).

The work of village court magistrates, clerks and 'peace officers' (executive assistants to magistrates), then, was officially viewed as a form of community service performed by people selected after deliberation among villagers. The job required no formal educational qualifications. Rather, the personnel were expected to be 'persons whom the people respect and feel confident about, that is, who know the customs of the area well, and can be relied upon to make fair decisions' (Village Court Secretariat 1975: 1). Magistrates were to receive a tiny 'remuneration' of around $2 per week, which was less than a quarter of the official rural minimum wage of the time,[3] reflecting an anticipation that their duties would be occasional and light. Indeed the stipulation that villages courts should 'adjourn from time to time and place to place' (Village Courts Act 1973) implied both informality and a low workload. The romantic expectations held for the village courts were summed up in an enthusiastic endorsement by the minister for justice, John Kaputin, who wrote: 'customary law will from now on be a real part of the national law. . . . Village Court magistrates who will be appointed because of their knowledge of customary law will be a vital source of information and, indeed, a catalyst for reform' (Kaputin 1975: 12).

Overall, the discourse of informality, wise mediation and pastoral judgment informed by the integrity of 'customary law' implied that the practical activities of village courts would be largely determined by the needs of their communities. However, the administration of the new system quickly became problematic, and the praxis[4] of village courts has, for three decades, manifested a dialectic between the ideals described above and the practical effects of legislative, financial and bureaucratic impositions. On the one hand, a lack of legal training and qualifications has sustained the legislative intention that magistrates are not preoccupied with the niceties of law. They have, for example, no law books, no need to consult recorded cases, or to have their attention drawn to precedents by lawyers. They rely largely on common sense, and a nuanced understanding of the social and historical background of the disputes they hear, as members of the local communities they serve. On the other hand, governed by legislation which places them at the bottom of a hierarchy of legal courts and thus makes them answerable to fundamental demands of law, they have become increasingly influenced by introduced ideas of how justice is achieved. They have also been dogged by the effects of equivocation over which branches of government are responsible for their maintenance. This chapter traces the tortuous history of the administration of village courts.

Initial Equivocations

Administrative control of the village courts was at first lodged with the Justice Department. It was originally planned that the Magisterial Services Commission (MSC) would be responsible, but in 1973, when the

Village Courts Act was passed, the pre-independence Constitutional Planning Committee wanted more time to examine the MSC, so the plan did not eventuate (Garo 1979: 3). There were other uncertainties over where the financial support for the courts would come from and whether it should be a central or provincial administrative responsibility (Chalmers 1978b: 76). It was hoped, according to Chalmers (1978b: 75), that the courts could become self-financing. The question of finance was still unsolved late in 1974, when in reply to a question, Chief Minister Michael Somare told the House of Assembly that cost-sharing with local communities had been considered, and the Department of Law was still working to solve the funding problem, while the government was not sure what funds were available from its budget for the year.[5]

The Village Court Secretariat (VCS), administrator of the village court system, was inaugurated unofficially in January 1974 when District Commissioner Ian Holmes, of the Dept of the Chief Minister and Development Administration, was loaned to the Dept of Law and tasked to implement the system. Holmes, serving as the Secretary, had a small group of mainly Australian staff members to assist him. These were, like himself, on loan from other departments. By the time the first village courts were established in 1975, the Secretariat staff consisted of Holmes, Trevor Bergin, a district officer, as 'Principal Village Court Officer', Tony Pryke, a District Officer, and Bob Welsh, an Assistant District Officer as 'Village Court Officers' aided by a 'clerical assistant'.[6] This appears to have been an innovation, as the positions described were not anticipated by the Act. In Welsh's recollection, 'The VC Act as I recall made no reference to VCS or Village Court Officers. According to the Act supervision was to be through DSM [District Supervising Magistrate] and other District/Local Court Magistrates'.[7] The VCS was intended to be only a temporary body, awaiting the establishment of the Magisterial Services Commission (MSC), into which it would be incorporated. The MSC was finally established in 1976, and renamed the Magisterial Service (MS), but the VCS was never incorporated into it.

Bergin and Welsh set up a trial village court at Kainantu, in the Eastern Highlands, in 1974, before the Village Court Act came into force on 28 November. This court proved successful and the VCS began organising pilot training schemes for the first magistrates. The first village courts were officially opened in early 1975 in Rigo in the Central Province and Mendi in the Southern Highlands, followed by more at mid year in Kainantu in the Eastern Highlands and Wabag in Enga Province.[8] As recalled by Tony Pryke, 'They were very well received by the public who had been calling for them for years'.[9] Other courts were inaugurated gradually around the country, and by the end of 1975 there were seventy-nine village courts in operation. Among these were a number serving urban villagers, such as the Motu-Koita, the traditional inhabitants of the land on which Port Moresby stands. Urban village courts also served migrant settlers on land which was often still owned by urban villagers like the Motu-Koita. Thus 'village' courts quickly came to serve not only rural communities, but also 'grassroots' communities in urban centres.

The administrative uncertainties surrounding the establishment of the first courts were matched by a degree of ambiguity on the ground. The first village courts were not fully prepared juridically and were still something of an experiment (see, for example, Gordon and Meggitt 1985: 220). Not all magistrates fully understood the limits of their jurisdiction, and it was a year or so before the Village Court Handbook (Village Court Secretariat 1976), containing guidelines for the conduct of courts and information about the kinds of penalties they could impose, was published.

Despite overwhelming support among Melanesian parliamentarians and progressive legal advisers for the establishment of village courts, there were fears among conservative jurists and other Europeans that village courts would be legally or otherwise corrupt and that village court officials' ignorance of the law would result in the application of anachronistic customs (Quinlivan 1975; Strathern 1975). Consequently the newly established village courts in 1975 became the focus of critical European officials. Village courts proclaimed in the Mendi district of the Southern Highlands on 20 February of that year were almost immediately visited by white officials, who challenged decisions which they saw as applying oppressive 'custom' (Martin 1975; Oram 1979, and see chapter 3 herein). The white officials were told to stop interfering with the new village courts by the Department of Justice and the Department of District Administration (Paliwala 1982: 204).

While oppressive custom may have been the concern of European critics, the need to compensate for the inaccessibility of the formal justice system to village society quickly became a more significant force in determining the juridical role of the courts. Constraints presaged in the legislation and manifest in bureaucracy shifted the operations of village courts away not only from the idealised realm of 'custom' but also from the informality which the legislative language implied. The types of cases the courts could hear were limited, and consisted more or less of a subset of the minor offences heard in local courts of the period, which included petty theft, assault, the use of insulting, threatening, or offensive language, damaging another person's trees, crops or property, spreading malicious lies, disturbing the peace, drunkenness, carrying weapons 'in a manner which frightens others', disobeying magistrates' orders, and sorcery threats and accusations. Village courts were not authorised to hear land ownership disputes, but they could hear matters involving the use of, or rights in, customary land, such as disputes over gardens, and trees. They could not hear cases of major theft, rape, murder, cases involving motor vehicle use, or divorce cases.

They were obliged to keep written records of cases, to use forms for 'summonses' and for the issue of compensation and fine orders. They could write prison orders, but these had to be countersigned by a district court magistrate. Indeed, their activities could be overseen by members of the formal judiciary, and certain types of cases were to be referred to local or district courts, which could also hear appeals by disputants against village court decisions. In a very short period of time, village court officials, selected from their community ostensibly on the basis of their 'elder' integrity and knowledge of customs, and untrained in law, found themselves structurally integrated into the country's formal legal system.

Growing Pains

The popularity of the courts added pressure for more and more to be established. This increased the burden of the VCS, whose staff had grown to nineteen by mid 1975. There were transitions in the senior positions. Holmes and Bergin left at Independence, and Pryke acted as secretary for a period, before a Papua New Guinean, Andrew Maino (a trained magistrate), was appointed to the position. After two or three years he was succeeded by Kila Garo, also a former magistrate, with Pryke as acting secretary during *inter regnum* periods.[10] The VCS continued to suffer staffing and funding problems, hampering its efforts to provide the basic pre-induction training and instruction of village court officials, and their booklets and stationery. Explanatory literature was piecemeal, and reflected the VCS's struggle to systematise village court administration in the face of misunderstanding both from within and from outside its operations. A three page document on 'Village Court Costs' attempted to explain that the government and local government councils were to share the costs of village courts, whose officials were not to be regarded as waged public servants. It listed the costs to be paid by each contributing body (Village Court Secretariat n.d.: 1–2) clearly. The Government would pay gratuities to magistrates and clerks, and the costs of training, magisterial supervision, records and handbooks, and the implementation of village court services overall. Councils would pay peace officers' gratuities and their incidental costs, and would receive all money collected in fines. Yet this straightforward vision was not shared by other elements of state, and confusion continued. In 1979 an annual report—bearing the name of the Village Court Secretary, Kila Garo, but written in fact by Welsh,[11] who was now senior village court officer—said of the administration that 'the lines of control are fragmented and inadequate' (Garo 1979: 2).

At the time, three agencies were involved in the system: the VCS, the MS and a 'Decentralisation Department' supposedly working on the decentralisation of various functions from central government to provincial governments. According to the Village Courts Act (s.6), responsibility for the supervision of village courts rested with the district supervising magistrates of each province, assisted by a provincial village courts officer, and by other magistrates directed by the MS and the Decentralisation Dept. This arrangement had not worked. There was in practice no full-time involvement at the supervisory level. Welsh comments:

> After the system got going and critical supervision shortfalls became evident . . . it became advantageous and perhaps necessary to widen and officialise VCO involvement in VC supervision and make VCO's duties consistent with relevant provisions of the VC Act. That was why it was necessary to ensure all VCOs were appointed as Deputy Local Court magistrates. As such their VC supervision was in accordance with the VC Act. Similarly, if VCO supervision of VCs was to be in accordance with the Act it would have to be under the direction of the DSM (at the time most VCOs were in fact experienced *kiaps*).[12]

In the 1979 Annual Report, Garo (i.e. Welsh) commented, 'the gradual demoralisation of the Decentralisation Dept has led to a continued decline in the capability of this dept to assist in village court supervision' (1979: 3). The Secretariat was seeking the centralisation of control of the village courts in the MS, as had been originally planned, and a greater field involvement by supervising magistrates (3–4). Co-operation was also lacking between village courts and Local Government Councils, most of which 'do not abide by their agreement with the VCS to look after their village courts' (7). Secretariat staff were also frustrated at the slow process of devolving responsibility for village courts to provincial governments (8–10), a reference to a long-term plan which would prove fateful for the village courts in the 1990s (see below). Other forms of cooperation were also lacking, such as police liaison. Welsh complained in the annual report that the police seemed reluctant to get involved with village courts (20–21), although he has commented since that

> in some areas police worked effectively with VCs. . . . For example when Inspector Paul Van Steveren (an ex kiap) was in charge of the Kagamuga Police Station in 1977–78 VC/Police cooperation was good and this resulted in an improved law and order situation throughout that area. . . . It depended a

lot on the attitude of the relevant Police Commander. When this situation became evident it was clear that the team approach to law and order problems was the most effective (ie VCs, Police and Local/District Courts working together). This, of course, came as no surprise to Secretariat Officers and others, but in at least some other quarters, VCs were regarded with suspicion and as such were not readily involved or supported.[13]

Despite its problems, the village court system had continued to grow. By the end of 1979 there were 738 village courts throughout the country, staffed by a total of 3,565 magistrates, 2,032 peace officers and 858 clerks, and 58 per cent of the population was claimed to be served by village courts (Garo 1979: app. 1, 1). The Secretariat had grown, too, and with thirty-four staff members was pursuing the system's goals aggressively. It wanted more resources for training the ever-growing body of magistrates, claiming that if it were given adequate support the village court system would handle 'law and order' in 90 per cent of the country with minimal assistance from the police (app. 5, 5). In the 1979 report Welsh suggested upgrading the secretary's position and increasing the Secretariat staff to 55 (app. 5, 5–6); he also asked for an increase in the honorarium of village court officials, arguing that the average official worked three days per week and should receive appropriate pay in recognition of this (app. 7, 1–2). He attacked what he called the 'traditional tribunals did not receive pay' argument, which he said was based on an outmoded and anachronistic concept of village courts as 'traditional' and operating on a self-help principle, when 'the purely subsistence economy has virtually disappeared' and people now needed cash (app. 7, 4).

The rates of remuneration at the time were K104 per annum for a chairing magistrate, K91 for a magistrate and K78 for a peace officer and a court clerk. The Secretariat wanted these increased to K230, K220 and K78, respectively (Garo 1979: app. 7, 5–6), and was successful, while many of its other requests remained unfulfilled. The report for the following year, also written by Welsh, began with a reiteration of the problem caused by having three agencies involved in the administration of the system (1980: 2). The Public Services Commission had approved a reorganisation proposal whereby provincial village court officers would be put under the direct control of district supervising magistrates and trained as deputy magistrates. This had improved the supervision of the village courts mainly because of an 'improvement in the coordination between this secretariat and Magisterial Services and the fact that the PVCOs are now actually doing inspections of village courts themselves' (3). Of this period, Tony Pryke recalls:

> Regular inspections were supposed to be, and in most cases were, carried out and reports were sent to the secretariat HQ. VCIs and VCOs were

empowered to and did hear appeals and reviews. Transport for inspectors was always a problem although we did get a number of small Suzuki 4x4s. We also got four small launches for the islands. I ensured that inspections were carried out on a regular basis while I was with the secretariat. . . . I laid disciplinary charges on officers who failed to heed warnings about carrying out their duty. This wasn't very popular.[14]

While the field officers of the Decentralisation Department were now under control of the provincial governments, and some of the latter had agreed to field staff involvement in village court supervision (Garo 1980: 6), there were still staffing problems and the process of setting up new village courts was virtually at a standstill—271 new courts had been introduced in 1978, 100 in 1979, but only 21 in 1980 (6).

The Travails of Expansion

At this stage, five years after the introduction of the courts, the Secretariat faced two fundamental problems. One was that while its proposals for more staff, training schemes and other needs were being approved by the National Planning Commission, funds were never forthcoming to implement them. The other was that the VCS could not persuade the Department of Justice to transfer overall responsibility for the village courts to the MS. The Secretariat saw the latter as vital for adequate supervision of the system. In a letter to the deputy secretary for justice in 1980 (Garo 1980: app. 5), it argued that a separation had developed between the organisation of the system and the overall responsibility for it. The MS, which was supposed to be responsible, assumed the VCS (the organiser) was taking care of the system, and gave little time to village courts. The village court officers for their part were confused about whether they were responsible to the VCS or the MS. The confusion was compounded by the fragmented funding arrangement. In 1980 the Village Courts Administration Act No. 10 was passed, enabling provincial governments to take over many of the responsibilities of the VCS, including the payment of village court officials' monthly allowances. Three provinces (East New Britain, Manus, Morobe) responded to this development at the time. In theory, funding arrangements were now to be divided between central, provincial and local providers. The Department of Justice paid general administrative costs, with the exception of the allowances of village court officials and their transport costs. Provincial goverments were supposed to pay the allowances, and local government councils (or provincial governments where the local councils were not operative) were supposed to pay transport costs, which were offset against the receipts for fines collected by the courts.

The fragmentation of responsibilities for the system overall required constant liaison between the bodies involved, and the VCS insisted a proper chain of command was needed to resolve the problem (Garo 1980: app. 5, 2). The longer-term plan, the transference of the duties of village court establishment and administration to provincial governments—which would take years—would not affect the basic chain of command with the MS at the top, according to the VCS, but would simply mean an increase in provincial government staff and a decrease in MS staff (app. 5, 5). Meanwhile, plans for the transfer of duties were proceeding slowly. A bill for a Provincial Village Courts Act was drafted in 1983, providing for the transfer of all administrative matters, except those concerning jurisdiction, to provincial governments. A circular was sent from the justice department to provincial government heads spelling out the proposed transfer of village court administrative functions to provincial control in three phases—limited administrative control, legislative control and 'full transfer'—and suggesting that provincial governments should begin to assume some responsibility for village courts (Keris 1988: 75–78). Three provinces, Enga, Morobe and the North Solomons, took the initiative and shortly passed their own village court acts (1985: 4).

Generally, however, there was confusion over responsibility at provincial levels. Gordon and Meggitt, writing of village courts in Enga during this period, cite reports of 'meddling' in the selection of village court magistrates by the Enga provincial government, local government councillors and village leaders (1985: 223–24). Other problems reported by Gordon and Meggitt were complaints from magistrates about a lack of support from the government, a lack of regular visits from supervisory magistrates, and limited cooperation from police (230–32). Magistrates were also complaining about the low stipend they received relative to the amount of work they did, and the delays in payment of the stipends (232). Gordon and Meggitt's descriptions of administrative attitudes to village courts provide the obverse aspect to the concerns expressed in the VSC Annual Reports. The potentially important role of the village courts in maintaining law and order in the countryside was being largely ignored by administration officials: 'The attitudes of the higher-level magistrates, the police, and the *kiaps* toward village court magistrates can fairly be described as elitist and overbearing' (234).

Nevertheless, the VCS was still successful in getting support for its expanding system, with the National Planning Office approving the recruitment of more village court inspectors, and by 1985 the allowances paid to village court officials had increased again. Chairing magistrates now received K283 per annum, deputy chairpersons received K252, magistrates K231 and clerks and peace officers K210. The VCS also appeared successful in having money allocated to expand its operations into more provinces and to buy vehicles for inspection purposes (Keris 1985: 6–7). But the new village court secretary, Peni Keris (replacing the retired Garo), was still criticising the 'three agency' problem. The Decentralisation Department had been superceded by the Department of Provincial Affairs (DPA), but the same equivocable situation of responsibility for the system remained, and nothing had come of repeated attempts to have the VCS absorbed into the MS (2–3). In the 1985 Annual Report of the VCS, Keris complained of the lack of availability of DPA staff, and a lack of co-operation from local government councils because the latter were becoming defunct and the remaining ones had a 'don't care attitude' (3–4). Responsibility for paying village court officials' allowances had been transferred from recalcitrant local government councils to the National Government.

Lack of systematic centralised control was starting to have jurisdictional effects, both from lack of support and co-operation locally, but also from occasional exploitation of village courts to provincial administrative ends. For example, Enga Province, the focus of concerns about 'law and order' in the 1970s, had been keen to acquire village courts in 1975 as a social control resource and had already been accused of 'meddling' in their administration (Gordon and Meggitt 1985: 223–24). In the 1980s there were new problems in the province, with some village courts exceeding their powers under pressure to involve themselves in a systematic attempt (known as Operation *Mekim Save* [Tokpisin: roughly, 'teach them a lesson']) to suppress 'tribal fighting'. They had been given the impression that a provision for joint jurisdiction of courts in the Village Courts Act (part 3, div. 2, s.17) allowed them to punish people involved in warfare (Keris 1985: 5). Deletions and amendments to the Act in 1986—the Village Courts (Amendment) Act 1986—were intended to clarify anomalies such as these.

Under Keris's leadership (and with Papua New Guineans replacing the departed Australians in senior positions), the village court system appeared internally healthy. Training units were expanded, and training for village court officials became a significant project toward improving the efficiency of the courts. By the end of 1988 there were 957 village courts officially in operation (Keris 1988: 26). However, funding continued to be a problem, as did a lack of co-operation from police, a lack of supervision from district court magistrates and mixed attitudes at provincial level from provincial governments to the general push to transfer control of the system to them (Keris 1988: 7–14). Keris was convinced, like his predecessors, that transference of control to provinces was the answer to the problems, and appeared to be encouraged in this by the fact that a few provinces were showing interest (7–8). At the same time, he acknowledged that some provinces were 'still dragging behind' (9), and noted a lack of initiative from provincial village court officers toward their duties (16), without appearing to see these as portents of the longer-term effects of the transfer.

Funding was becoming the major problem for the system as a whole, as its expansion had not been matched by a corresponding expansion of national budgetary allowances. Keris could not increase the number of VCS staff (fifty-four in 1988) to cover the needs of the huge number of courts needing regular inspections, supervision and training. By his calculation the VCS had seven active village court inspectors to cover 957 courts: 'Using staff from Magisterial Services Commission and Provincial Affairs has proved unsatisfactory as they concentrated on their own duties' (Keris 1988: 138). He wanted forty-five more inspectors, to meet his plan to establish a further 1,423 village courts in the next decade, and money for motor vehicles and dinghies for transport purposes (141). He also wanted an increase of fifty per cent in the allowances paid to village court officials. The popularity of the village courts had meant that the amount of work done by officials was far in excess of the expectations of the system's planners. Some magistrates were working most days of the week, mostly in mediation rather than adjudication, and the meagre increases in allowances over the past decade were regarded as inadequate by both the officials themselves and the VCS. Keris was afraid that dissatisfaction with the remuneration would make officials vulnerable to bribery and corruption (142).

His efforts to get an increase in the allowances were successful. Chairing magistrates subsequently received K32.70 per month, their deputies received K29.06, magistrates K26.64, and peace officers and clerks K24.22. This was still inadequate for the work the officials performed, and the rate remained unchanged for the next decade and a half, to the increasing dissatisfaction of village court magistrates in particular. The other support that the VCS sought was less forthcoming. Co-operation from police was ebbing, with courts reporting that the police were failing to enforce warrants issued by the village courts, or were releasing warranted offenders without consultation. Magistrates also complained that district court magistrates showed no respect for them. And while an increase in the allowances had been achieved, the delivery of the payments each month had become erratic. The training programs which Keris was attempting to expand were also beginning to falter. The VCS officers charged with training magistrates had no instruction skills themselves.

New Laws and New Discontents

The Village Courts Act of 1973 was superceded by the Village Courts Act of 1989, which contained few substantive changes apart from the replacement of colonial terminology ('territory', 'native', etc.) with terms more appropriate for an independent nation. By this time there was a noticeable difference between the idealised village courts represented in the language of the Act and the real conditions faced by many village court officials. While some courts may have been adjourning 'from time to time and place to place', for many village court workers around the country the combination of a heavy workload, community and juridical demands on them for more legal rigour and a lack of payment was intensifying a perception that they were being exploited. In 1994 I was shown a draft document of association by a small group of village court magistrates in the Port Moresby area. They were trying to develop a communicative network to form a national association or union to press for 'proper training', with the long term goal of taking over the work of the formal local courts. This initiative was partly grounded in a logic that the majority of cases heard in village courts were of the same order as those heard in local courts (local courts were abolished in 2001), and they therefore considered that village court magistrates should be treated the same way as local court magistrates. At the time the allowance of a village court magistrate was around K6 per week (paid monthly), little more than a quarter of the national minimum adult wage of K22.96 per week determined by the National Wage Board in 1992. There was clearly a rational link, in the thinking of village court magistrates, between workloads, increasing demands for legal knowledge and expertise, and rates of pay.

The payout of their entitlements was erratic at that time, but things were to get worse. In 1995 an Organic Law was passed, which among other things transferred responsibility for the administration of village courts to provincial governments, with the exception of a few matters such as jurisdiction, appointment of magistrates, provision of operational materials, and training programs. In view of the problems the VCS had already been having with the fragmented responsibilities for the courts, it had been predicted by some commentators that transferring administrative responsibility to provincial governments would not be advantageous, and that there could be serious funding problems (see, for example, Weisbrot 1988: 42). These predictions proved correct, and the deleterious effects became obvious almost immediately. The VCS attempted to make sure the financial remuneration was carried out, but found that a number of provincial governments were recalcitrant, and money received by them for village court remuneration was being used for other purposes. The payment of allowances, when it did occur, was variable in its frequency from province to province. Depending which province they were in, village court officials were often going for months without remuneration. There was also confusion over powers of appointment of village court officials, with claims of interference and nepotism at provincial level.

In the National Capital District, where financial responsibility was taken by the National Capital District Commission (NCDC), I noticed a distinct difference in morale in village court officials between my period of fieldwork in 1994 (before the Organic Law) and my subsequent fieldwork in 1999 (four years after the Law). Payment had been erratic in the earlier period, but delays had been mostly a matter of a week or two. By 1999 these delays had stretched to months and funds frequently 'went missing'. Magistrates were frustrated and angry. Their expectations were understandably that it should be a simple matter to redistribute to them a proportion of the money they collected in village courts in the form of fines and delivered to authorities like the NCDC or provincial governments. The non-payments also caused suspicions among the village court officials themselves. The chairing magistrates of each court in the NCDC area went to the commission to collect the gratuities, frequently had to report back to their fellows that there had been no payout, and were liable to be suspected of having misappropriated the money.

Meanwhile, reviews of village court officials' performance and training schemes were becoming more frequent. This was an initiative of Secretary Peni Keris, driven by the pressure of criticism of village court magistrates from various quarters, especially from legal conservatives (see chapter 3). Under changing Western ideas of informal justice and dispute resolution (such as ADR and latterly 'restorative justice') imported by development-aid agencies, the training strategies in particular have varied over time, but the findings of the reviews have remained fairly similar. Lack of adequate supervision by the various agencies charged with overseeing the courts and inadequate remuneration have been core problems, but in the absence of ways to realistically enforce these, emphasis was invariably placed on the need for better training. Until the 1990s, official commentaries on the need for training were mostly subsumed under more general reviews, such as those of the Law Reform Commission (see, for example, Law Reform Commission 1987). More specific reviews began to appear in the 1990s, one of the first being commissioned by the Attorney General's Department, and in which I was involved.[15] The review reported that the village court system was working and that 'thousands of potentially violent and abusive situations are diffused every week'. It stated that the media, academic and juristic emphasis on alleged discrimination and unjust decisions combined 'to give the erroneous impression that Village Court Officials cause more injustice than they solve'. Its suggestion for dealing with the problems of the village courts was to be echoed in all reports which followed: 'The majority of the problems and aberrations of the courts can be addressed through better and more regular training' (Eyford et al. 1992: 1).

The review team found that despite the intentions of the village court secretary, many courts had not received training. Those magistrates who had undergone some kind of formal training thought it was inadequate to their needs (Eyford et al. 1992: 8). The training strategy until that time had been simply to organise magistrates from various parts of the country into tutorial groups which were then instructed in the rules and procedures outlined in the village court handbook. Magistrates were sometimes relatively educated men in their thirties but were more often aged men with little or no education, and there were some who were non-literate. The inaugural intentions of the village court system planners, that courts should be informal, were negated as training techniques reinforced a sense that village court officials were supposed to rote-learn and rigorously apply the 'law' as written in the handbook. Many of the older men, perfectly adequate dispute settlers in their own ways, found the process confusing and frustrating. The review team commented: 'The courts work well *despite* the training provided. The training currently provided does not prepare Village Court officials for the job they are called upon to do. In fact aspects of the trainings as they are now conducted actually impair the ability of Village Court officials to do their job' (iii).

The report recommended, among other remedies, that village court trainers themselves needed training, that new training and reference materials should be developed, and that training sessions should be smaller in scale and more frequent (Eyford et al. 1992: 10, 19–20). Subsequently, new training programs were developed, but their implementation was spasmodic, depending on availability of funds and personnel. Moreover, the manuals compiled by the various advisors used by the VCS, who were usually Europeans, were hardly put to use. Some remained uncirculated, or even unfinished in production, such as the ambitiously designed 'Luksave Buk' (Tokpisin: roughly, 'guide book') for magistrates, compiled after the 1992 review. Another manual produced not long afterwards contained fashionable Western conceptions of dispute resolution techniques and the conduct of training sessions which the VCS's Papua New Guinean staff could not identify with, and was discarded (quietly and diplomatically, after the European advisors had left).

Substantively, training courses attempted to develop skills in mediation, which was regarded as a priority in the villages courts' idealised role in petty-dispute resolution. But the preoccupation of magistrates with becoming knowledgeable in techniques of adjudication (based on their observation of formal legal processes), the juridical preoccupation with *ultra vires* actions, and the need for bureaucratic accountability and the maintenance of paper work generated a bias towards training in more formal and technical aspects of court procedure. Mock courts and practical exercises in adjudication became a common feature of village court training. Training courses may or may not have been improving the skills of village court officials in various areas of their work, but to an extent they were reinforcing the dissatisfaction with inadequate and erratically paid gratuities and lack of support. Village court officials saw themselves as being trained in specialist work, and felt they should be paid accordingly. Moreover, they were told in training courses that they were part of a legal structure, overseen and reinforced by district court magistrates in particular, and supported by the police. The lack of this structural reinforcement in the real world of their operations added to their dissatisfaction.

The Legacy of the Organic Law

The transfer of administrative responsibilities for village courts to provincial governments under the Organic Law of 1995 was proving with the passing of time to have been a major mistake. Many village court officials failed to receive their modest allowance from that year onwards. The explanations given amounted to reciprocal accusations between the national and provincial administrations. The former was accused of giving so little support to provincial governments that they were forced to use the funds intended for village courts for other purposes. The provincial governments in turn were accused of corrupt diversion of funds. In 1999 questions were asked in Parliament about the non-payment of village court officials' allowances for three years, bringing assurances from the minister for justice that they would be paid within a few months. The minister blamed the non-payment on the 1996 transfer of functions: 'The expectation . . . was that the provincial government will pay them through the grants given to provincial governments. Unfortunately, these were not indicated in the Budget documents in the last three years, as well as in the provincial government budgets'.[16]

A few months later, the member for Moresby South, Dame Carol Kidu, raised questions in Parliament about cost-cutting, and the danger of the collapse of village courts in the National Capital District. She claimed that in the year 2000 the budget of K400,000 per year was cut by more than a half to K150,000, and the number of village court officials reduced from 440 to only 240 for the whole city, and further that the allowances formerly paid on a monthly basis were now quarterly. She asked rhetorically whether politicians or the NCD staff would be willing to work for two months without pay, adding that there had been no training for village court officials for the past three years, no uniforms, and no stationery for record-keeping.[17] Complaints increased from around the country that allowances had not been paid since 1996 or 1997. These occasionally prompted small payouts. For example, some magistrates in the Central Province were paid outstanding allowances (a total of more than K303,000) by the Department of the Attorney General, after publicity was given to claims they were cutting back their activities, with a resulting increase in 'law and order' problems. The justice minister, Andrew Baing, subsequently gave a general assurance that outstanding allowances would be paid. However, questions continued to be asked, and confusion ensued over which of the provincial administrations (if any) were dutifully paying the allowances and which were not.

In the Eastern Highlands Province more than a thousand village court officials vented their frustration in December 2000 by attacking one of the main provincial administration buildings and causing K300,000 worth of damage, mostly by smashing windows. Surprisingly, despite not receiving their allowances, the majority of village courts continued to operate over the next few years. Occasional piecemeal payments and ministerial announcements of imminent payments did little to assuage the general climate of discontent, however. On the contrary, rumours (often exaggerated) of massive payments of arrears in some districts or provinces served to fuel the anger of officials in other areas who had not been paid at all. Occasional assurances by individual national or provincial parliamentarians of investigation and consequent payment either proved vacuous or were negated by a change of government or minister in the volatile climate of PNG politics.

By 2003 the issue of non-payment was clouded by accusations that village court magistrates were corrupt, stealing money from the fines they imposed, or illegally charging disputants to have their cases heard. The accusations were either denied by magistrates, or countered by claims that in the absence of allowances (which were regarded as inadequate even if they were paid) court officials had no choice but to charge disputants if they were to continue their operations. Threats of strikes were becoming more frequent, and in 2004 some village courts in the Eastern Highlands Province ceased to operate on the grounds that they had not been paid for years and received no support from other agencies such as district courts and the police. Strikes proved to be an effective measure, although in restricted geographical areas, in the longer term. When they eventually came to the notice of authorities (often months after they had started) they were usually accompanied by reports of significant recent increases in local crime or 'law and order' problems, prompting quick administrative responses. In 2005 the governor of the Eastern Highlands Province arranged payment of arrears to village court officials in three districts. In return, the officials made a formal apology for the December 2000 attack on the provincial government building and arranged a collection to pay a proportion of the cost of repairs to the windows.

These were small victories, however, and for the majority of long-serving village court officials in PNG the days before the Organic Law have become mythologised as a kind of golden age, in which they received their allowances regularly, had smart uniforms to wear, and had the support of authorities and the respect of villagers. At the time of writing (2007) payment is still an issue. The current justice minister, Mark Maipakai, announced in December 2005 that the government had allocated K8.7 million for a payout on allowances owed since 1997. Time will tell whether this marks a real change in the fortunes of the village court system.

The Organic Law belatedly prepared the ground for the decentralisation which Kila Garo had been attempting to achieve in the 1970s, but provincial government in the 1990s was not as efficient as advocates had hoped it would be. Not only were there accusations of corruption, diversion of funds and provincial nepotism, but each province began to develop its own administrative structure and system. For the VCS this provided further headaches. Previously the relatively centralised administration had allowed flexibility in the way the courts operated individually and at a district level, while maintaining a fairly uniform overarching system of maintenance. Following the 1995 law, differences among the provincial administrations started to impinge on the operational flexibility and relative autonomy of the courts, and the VCS could do little about it. The Secretariat was reduced to responsibilities covering jurisdiction, the appointment of magistrates and (despite a lack of adequate funds) provision of operational materials, and training programs.

Some provincial governments thought they could legislate to give themselves power to make appointments, and to choose and remove magistrates accordingly, overriding the intention that communities should choose their own magistrates. In some places, under policies promoting 'progress' and 'change', ageing magistrates were replaced with younger ones, with mixed results, as conservative but very experienced magistrates were replaced by inexperienced ones. There had always been a legislative clause allowing the VCS to intervene in the appointment of magistrates, for example if a demonstratively inappropriate person were somehow chosen locally, but it had been rarely used. Provincial government appointments, good or bad, caused resentment, confusion and accusations of interference, nepotism and corruption both locally and nationally. In some places, particularly urban environments with a mixture of regional migrants, an administrative rationale developed that each regional group in a local community should have one representative magistrate. In the National Capital District some experienced magistrates were replaced on the ground that there had been two magistrates from the same 'region'. These variations in initiatives on appointments resulted in frustration among magistrates, who, regardless of internal frictions in their village courts, preferred continuity and stability of personnel to constant change.

Moreover, village courts as an institution fared differently depending which province they were in. Some provinces gave reasonable attention to the courts as local dispute-solving institutions and thereby valuable to the maintenance of law and order and the prevention of escalation of local disputes. Others gave them little support. Most appointed a provincial 'officer in charge' of village courts, but their placement in the administration structure varied. Sometimes they were attached to a 'law and order' section, sometimes to a community liaison office, or to a social welfare branch. Depending on the province there might be only a single village court inspector for seventy or eighty widespread courts. Inspectors were supposed to visit the individual courts on a regular basis, dealing with their local problems, and ensuring their efficiency. But many inspectors complained that their province provided no vehicles for them to visit rural courts, which were not accessible by any other means. In these and other ways, the overall village court system became fragmented into a variety of differently structured provincial systems, with differing degrees of interference or neglect. As provincial governments periodically restructured internally, responsibility for the administration of village courts became dispersed and communication gaps developed between the courts and their provincial administrators. The result was a significant decline in the efficiency of village courts nationwide.

The fragmentation of the system worked against the attempts of the VCS to keep village court officials supplied with their basic operative needs and to keep them up to date with legislative and policy changes which might affect them. The delivery of village court handbooks and stationery for court clerks' record keeping had already been a problem as the number of village courts grew and funds to produce the documents were not keeping pace. By the 1990s some magistrates were using outdated and deteriorating copies of the original handbook produced in 1976, while many others were operating without adequate written guidelines at all. Training courses were run on an *ad hoc* basis, when funding and staff numbers permitted, but were not reaching all districts. Uniforms and badges were no longer being regularly distributed or renewed, and many veteran magistrates and peace officers were still wearing the vestiges of decades-old uniforms which had become ragged and threadbare with age, while others had no uniforms or badges at all, with detrimental effects on the degree of respect given village court officials in their communities. A legacy of colonial rule is that uniforms and badges are generally recognised symbols of authority in PNG. A lack of uniforms and badges was, by the turn of the new century, a common complaint among village court officials, who argued that their authority was undermined if they were unable to display some symbol of their position. *Ultra vires* adjudication was also becoming more common, generated by a combination of magistrates' lack of clarity in the absence of handbooks, pressure from their local communities (who often preferred to have 'law' cases heard in village courts rather than district courts) and the lack of an alternative judiciary in a number of relatively isolated communities.

New Policies, and the Re-Discovery of Village Courts

By the end of the 1990s a further general decline in the village court system seemed inevitable, arguably due to the administrative fragmentation following the transfer of responsibilities to disparate provincial administrations. But other influences began to counter its potential disintegration. While the payment of allowances had become an ongoing problem under provincial administration, other aspects of village court operations began to gain attention as a result of changes in the aid and development strategies of Australia, PNG's major development 'partner'. A shift was occurring from 'top-down' development strategies to aid programs more specifically directed at community level institutions, as a result partly of the problem of corruption (funds delivered via PNG Government channels frequently failed to reach the intended recipients) and expense. The Australian Agency for International Development (AusAID) began to explore the possibility of supporting community-level institutions particularly in relation to what is popularly thought of as PNG's 'law and order' problem. A significant turn was exemplified by a PNG National Legal Convention in 1999 (with Australian input) at which it was mooted that 'traditional' dispute-resolution mechanisms be explored. At the time, 'alternative dispute resolution' (ADR) was a popular concept in legal-pluralist and dispute-resolution discourse in Australia, and village courts became a subject of interest, viewed as an accessible and cheap alternative to the expensive, complex and formal legal system which was still inaccessible for most 'grassroots' Papua New Guineans.

At about the same time a restructuring of the justice sector began. This led to a confusing body of changing abbreviations and acronyms over the next few years, including the official renaming of the VCS as the Community Courts Administration Unit (CCAU), and its positioning as a component of the Attorney General's Department (AGD/CCAU), or sometimes alternatively the Department of Justice and the Attorney General (DJ&AG/CCAU). The head of the renamed unit, Peni Keris, however, resolutely continued to refer to it in documents and verbally as the Village Court Secretariat. With renewed interest in the village courts, a project was developed in 1999, with input by AusAID, to address the reported ignorance of village court officials about their role and jurisdiction which was believed to be causing incorrect practice and abuse of their powers. A major component was the improvement of the content and delivery of training courses. With subsequent formal assessments and reports by AusAID fuelling community-based initiatives, the CCAU (or VCS) found itself supported to a degree that had been lacking for some years previously. Renewed training courses continued to put emphasis on village court procedures, and jurisdictional issues, rather than genuinely informal dispute settlement. Nevertheless, there was a degree of re-orientation resonating with the influence of ADR discourse, which was extended beyond village courts to the district and national courts. Courses in ADR for judges and magistrates at all levels of the judiciary became popular. Ironically, considering that ADR was introduced to PNG from Australia, and the courses were sometimes held in Australia, ADR was promoted as an alternative to the 'Western adversarial' legal court system, supposedly drawing on 'traditional' ways of solving disputes through negotiation.[18]

The DJ&AG issued a new village courts policy document in 2001, acknowledging that village courts were 'struggling to meet their objectives' and that provincial administration had not been entirely successful since the 'transfer of power' (5). Much of the document reiterated the original objectives of the village court system and revisited the administrative weaknesses which had developed since the 1970s. The application of 'customary law' and 'custom' continued to be advocated (9), though the progressive integration of the village courts into the formal legal system was now more or less explicit elsewhere in the document (11–13). The concept of alternative dispute resolution had by this time been superceded in documents by that of 'restorative justice' (9), a newer addition to dispute resolution discourse, emphasising healing and the restoration of social harmony in preference to punitive responses to crime (see, for example, Braithwaite 1999; Strang and Braithwaite 2001). It was a particular focus of the Restorative Justice Group in the Research School of Social Sciences at the Australian National University, and was quickly appropriated into AusAID programs for application in PNG. Its most explicit application was in attempts to bring closure to the long-running and complex dispute on Bougainville Island triggered in the 1980s by local revolt against the Panguna copper mining project. In a short time 'restorative justice' became a 'law and order' policy byword in the search for community-level institutions throughout PNG which could be drawn into the Government's justice initiatives.[19]

Training programs for village court officials conducted by the DJ&AG/CCAU quickly appropriated the philosophy of restorative justice, attempting to persuade magistrates away from punitive or win/lose court decisions. More emphasis was now put on aspects such as mediation skills, listening skills, and guiding disputants through the presentation of their case. The Attorney General's Department now had an Institutional Strengthening Project (AGDISP), essentially an annex to the CCAU, developed and staffed with AusAID assistance. By 2004 the AGDISP had completed a substantial number of training programs, not only for village court officials, but also for provincial officers responsible for overseeing village courts, in an attempt to bring some regularity to the system nationally. At the same time, however, provincial governments were beginning to enact their own Provincial Village Court Acts, under national legislative provisions, and some were announcing intentions to instigate their own training programs, portending more disparities. One of the first provincial Village Courts acts was passed by the Western Highlands Provincial Asembly in February 2004, accompanied by a press statement by the provincial governor that this would shift the power to appoint officials from the national to the provincial government, and that there was a provincial plan to reduce the manpower of the village courts system by a third.[20] This drew a concerned response from the province's village court officials, numbering some 1,900, who claimed they had not been made aware of the Act and were confused about their future and whether they would lose their powers. They duly petitioned the National Government not to approve the provincial Act.[21]

Dismayed by the trend to provincial administration, and buoyed by the new policy-oriented interest in village courts and recently commissioned reports lauding village courts as effective community-level 'law and order' agencies, Peni Keris began to lobby strongly for a re-centralisation of village court administration to his unit within the Attorney General's Department. His organisation had been reinvigorated by the input of AGDISP staff, who had produced new and updated village court handbooks (now called manuals) in English, Tokpisin and Hiri Motu. The 1976 handbooks had virtually disappeared, and tattered copies had become the prized possessions of a few veteran village court magistrates, even though they were barely relevant to current needs. The new manuals were considerably more comprehensive than the originals, and had been brought up to date, reflecting modern policies and social trends in the country. The role of mediation in dispute settlement was more clearly articulated (reflecting the 'restorative justice' policy), and 'custom' was at least acknowledged to be a vexed concept, in contrast to the simplistic references of the old handbook. Other sections reflecting changing times and the influence of Western human rights discourse (again significantly reinforced through AusAID) included one on women's rights, and a commonsense explanation of the PNG Constitution. Whether the 2004 manuals could be adequately circulated to all parts of the country in the near future was another matter, and remained equivocal at the time this book was written.

By the end of 2004, there were about 1,100 village courts in PNG, and despite the criticism they were subject to, and the paltry remuneration they received, officials were well aware of their value and importance as 'grassroots' dispute settlers. 'The government talks about a law and order problem,' a village court magistrate remarked to me during the crisis of payment in 2004, 'but if we village court magistrates stop doing our job, then you will see what a law and order problem really is!'

The historical processes reviewed in this chapter can hardly be interpreted as a tale of smooth progress towards the fulfilment of the ideal envisaged at the end of the colonial period. The growth and resilience of the village courts system over three decades was remarkable, given the administrative and financial uncertainties its magistrates and other officials experienced. Until 2004, when a few strikes occurred, magistrates continued to provide their services despite the problems discussed in this chapter. The occasional, and far from universal, training courses did little to help their real problems. These were generated by the original directives that they apply custom but follow 'the law', in which they were unschooled, and fed by reccurring criticism of their performance in both aspects of this intangible dichotomy, about which more detail is given in chapter 3.

Notes

1. But cf. Quinlivan (1975).
2. The Village Courts Act 1973 was cosmetically amended with the Village Courts (Amendment) Act 1986, and replaced by the Village Courts Act 1989, without significant substantive changes. The Native Customs (Recognition) Act 1963 was post-colonially retitled the Customs Recognition Act.
3. Rural wages were less than half those paid in urban areas in the mid 1970s.
4. In view of the current popularity and varied use of this term, I should specify that I use it in a sense grounded particularly in Marx's 1844 critique of Hegel (1974: 124–47), where the dialectic of negativity—the negation of the negation—was taken to be the 'moving and generating principle' (131) determining that no element of social reality could be investigated as complete in itself, but should be seen as an element of a social totality involved in a process of historical change.
5. PNG House Of Assembly Debates, Vol. 3 No. 36, 3 October 1974, p. 4619. The background to funding policies of the time remains unclear. One of the first staff members of the VCS, Tony Pryke, commented in a personal communication in 2006: 'The first policy decision as I remember it was whether the village court officials would be paid and it was decided they would not be'.
6. Personal communication, Tony Pryke, Bob Welsh, 2006, and see Garo (1979: app. 5, 2–3).
7. Personal communication, 2006.
8. Three courts in the Rigo district were proclaimed on 24 January 1975 (Gazette No. 007), and twelve in Mendi on 20 February. Nineteen courts in the Kainantu district and two courts in the Wabag district (Enga Province) were proclaimed on 6 June (Gazette No. 047). The inauguration of the two courts at Wabag was hastened by requests from the area in connection with a local 'law and order' issue (see Gordon and Meggitt 1985: 217–20).
9. Personal communication, 2006.
10. Personal communication, Tony Pryke, 2006.
11. Personal communication, Tony Pryke and Bob Welsh, 2006.
12. Personal communication, 2006.
13. Personal communication, 2006
14. Personal communication, 2006.
15. I took part in the first stage of this exercise, a review and investigation of the operations of the village court system. The second stage was the development of

a new training program, in which I took no part. It should not be assumed that I was entirely in agreement with all recommendations in the final report.
16. Minister for Justice Kilroy Genia in Papua New Guinea House of Assembly, 2 December 1999, noted in mimeo copy of questions in the House, Village Court Secretariat, Port Moresby.
17. Reported in *The National* (PNG daily newspaper) on 29 June 2000. Subsequent information in the following four paragraphs on the matter of village court officials' allowances and related issues is taken from twenty-nine reports in *The National* or the *PNG Post-Courier* (daily newspaper) from June 2000 to December 2005, and personal communications from village court officials.
18. See, for example, *The National*, 30 April 2001: 'Four magistrates to attend conflict resolution course', which reports a course to be held in Melbourne, Australia, and gives a description of the 'traditional', non-adversorial orientation of ADR.
19. See, for example, the Government's 'National Law and Justice Policy and Plan of Action' of 2000, subtitled 'Toward Restorative Justice'.
20. Reported in *The National*, 13 February 2004: 'WHP Assembly passes village court law'.
21. See *PNG Post-Courier*, 2 March 2004: 'New Act irks WHP magistrates', and 3 March 2004: 'WHP Govt to implement new Village Court Act'.

3

Village Courts on Trial

In this chapter I explore in more depth the legacy of the intention by planners of the village court system that village courts should apply 'custom'—an intention partially driven by a rhetoric that the colonial legal system had been unjustly censorious of custom and customary law. The planners could not have foreseen the consequences of the Village Courts Act's ostensibly reasonable stipulation that the village courts should apply custom 'as determined in accordance with . . . the Native Customs (Recognition) Act of 1963' (Village Courts Act 1973), and its provisions that village court magistrates, untrained in law, would be men of adjudicatory integrity and good knowledge of local customs (Village Court Secretariat 1975: 1). From the time when the first courts began operations with no handbooks to guide them in simultaneously applying the law (which they did not know) and custom, and no clear information about the limits of their jurisdiction, village court magistrates were vulnerable to attack by conservative jurists and other Europeans (and later, some Melanesians) on the grounds of corruption, legal ignorance and the application of anachronistic customs. These kinds of criticisms have continued to the present.

Herein I review some examples of the criticisms made of village courts. This historical catalogue not only reveals the range of criticisms—from allegations about the application of both archaic, and newly invented, 'customs' to concerns about the heavy-handed application of the law—but also indicates some recycling over time of a few early anecdotes about the courts' shortcomings. In a 1992 review of literature on the village courts Jonathan Aleck commented on the relative scarcity of literature that reflected a truly balanced appreciation of local cultural contexts or the technical administrative and legal determinants of village court practice (1992: 122). He reiterated comments by some other observers that 'the existence of demonstrably corrupt or prejudicial practices . . . is rather more a matter of cultural perspective than of objective fact' (114). Further, while there had been reports of corruption or situational bias, there was nothing in the literature to suggest that these were 'either widespread or incapable of being addressed by existing mechanisms and recommended reforms of . . . administrative practices' (114–15). Aleck was part of the review team of 1992, referred to in chapter 2, which opined that various types of publicity in combination gave 'the erroneous impression that Village Court Officials cause more injustice than they solve' (Eyford et al. 1992: 1). Arguably, this impression has continued to the present. I also discuss here the problems raised for village court officials by the ambiguous notions of 'custom' and 'customary law' with which they were burdened, and the directives that they observe the law while applying custom. It is worthwhile to begin with a catalogue of the criticisms of the courts, not only to get a sense of the range of these, but also to give a sense of the concerns behind the scrutiny by critics of village courts.

The Critical Concern with 'Injustice' and Bad 'Custom'

When village courts began to be proclaimed in 1975, critics of the system were anxious to observe their practice. The first courts proclaimed included some in the Mendi district of the Southern Highlands,[1] which were almost immediately visited by concerned European observers, who consequently made allegations of discriminatory applications of 'custom'. Nigel Oram, drawing on unpublished notes by one of the European visitors (Martin 1975), describes an incident thus:

> A village court in the Southern Highlands convicted a woman who had infringed a resurrected or invented customary ban against smoking by women. Local white officials were worried that village courts in such a conservative area might discriminate unjustly against women and strangers to the area and appealed as a test case. The district supervising magistrate granted the appeal on grounds of the village court's lack of jurisdiction, but he upheld the right of the village court to interpret local custom against the view of the reserve magistrate. The officials were also concerned lest village magistrates would use their appointments as a power base. (Oram 1979: 73)

No attempt seems to have been made to investigate, to any analytically significant degree, the cultural background or circumstances of the case or the village court's decision. Accused of *ultra vires* action, village court magistrates in these first courts in fact had no handbooks to guide them in the negotiation of legislative demands that they apply both the law and custom, and were not adequately informed about the limits of their jurisdiction (see chapter 2). The Village Court Handbook was not published until 1976, a year after this incident.

A subsequent critique of the village court system by Abdul Paliwala (1982) typified a point of view emanating from what has come to be known as dependency theory, representing Western legal systems as agents of control in non-Western societies and therefore systematically oppressive of the ruled people. According to this view—sometimes called 'legal centralism' (Galanter 1981; Griffiths 1986; Scaglion 1990)—while legislation such as PNG's Village Courts Act might appear to reinforce customary law, the courts actually impose an alien system, and depart significantly in practice from pre-existing forms of dispute settlement (Paliwala 1982: 192–201). Village courts are thus seen as agents of the state applying both custom and law oppressively to the political economic ends of a dominant class. Paliwala saw village courts as applying oppressive customs more strictly than had previously been the case, in the interests of social control over women as the most important source of rural labour power (221–22). Paliwala's article was based on research from 1975 to 1978, and contained references to the incidents at Mendi mentioned by Oram, revealing that the white officials involved were told by the Department of Justice and the Department of District Administration to stop interfering with the new village courts (204).

Legalist criticisms continued to represent the village courts as unjust and legally inadequate or incompetent. In 1980, after inspecting the Barane/Barawayi Corrective Institution in the highland town of Kundiawa, Justice Pratt commented in the National Court on the number of juvenile detainees (thirty) gaoled by the district court, local court and children's court. He was particularly concerned, however, that some were held under warrants issued out of village courts. In addition to a general concern that 'courts in this country are sending young children, some of them very young, to gaol for offences of a most trivial nature' (NCPNG 1980: 2), which he considered to be 'bordering on the inhuman and ... certainly cruel' (2), he attacked the village court system. He criticised the fact that under the Village Courts Act there was no appeal to the National Court or beyond but only to local courts or district courts, and said a review of the Act was overdue (2–3). He continued:

> With the fine provision coupled with the compensation provision which can total a period of 40 weeks imprisonment, a person coming before a village court is stripped of every safeguard which he would enjoy before any other court, including legal representation, and left with only a presumption of innocence and an assurance that 'substantial justice' must be done, whatever

that means. . . . The consequences of failing to pay an award awarded by the court in bride price or compensation for death, however, are nothing less than terrifying. (2)

Compensation, he said, was being ordered by courts against children, who could not pay, and thus 'the child is clearly being used as a lever to get the money out of the parents.' (2-3). Pratt noted that village courts had no authority to deal with children and consequently, under a section of the PNG Constitution (s.57[3]), declared village court fines and orders relating to persons aged under 16 invalid, ordering that anyone held under warrants issued on default of fines or orders, be released (4).

Subsequent criticism began to focus particularly on alleged discrimination against women in village courts, continuing to represent 'custom' directly or indirectly as an undesirable influence. In the mid 1980s Barbara Mitchell, a law lecturer at the University of PNG, brought a conventional legal perspective to bear on the courts. In a critique of the treatment of women, she pointed out the contradiction between the notion of women's equality found in the PNG Constitution and its promotion of the Melanesian family at the same time, which reinforced customary attitudes to women's role and treatment in marriage. She considered that directing village courts to apply custom was bound to result in discrimination against women, whom she believed were customarily subordinated in marriage. Mitchell conducted some comparative research in the North Solomon Islands and the Southern Highlands and attempted to achieve a balanced view of what she understood to be customary law and the way it was applied in the village courts. She noted that village court magistrates were predominantly male and regarded this as a disadvantage for women. She also described women as inexperienced and lacking skills in public speaking, to their detriment in court (1985: 88). Mitchell avoided simply categorising village courts as intentionally misogynist, blaming instead what she saw as the discriminatory customs which she believed village courts inevitably apply under the directives of the Village Courts Act, and the contradictions in the Constitution. From Mitchell's legalist perspective, which regarded custom as a conservative force impeding women's equality, education to change the views held by both men and women was essential (89).

In the late 1980s concern was expressed about an observed tendency in the Western Highlands Province for village courts to write imprisonment orders against people who did not pay fines and compensation within a prescribed time. A joint submission by the Western Highlands Rehabilitation Committee and the staff of the Baisu Corrective Institution cited figures indicating the number of imprisonments in Baisu from

January to June 1987 arising from village court orders: 164 men, 127 women and 24 juveniles (Keris 1988: 111). The submission was also concerned about harsh adjudicatory attitudes in village courts over matters such as brideprice repayments and child custody after the break up of marriages. Its recommendations focussed on a need for better instruction and training of magistrates and emphasis on the intent of the Village Courts Act that disputes be settled within villages, rather than by recourse to imprisonment. In particular, the group sought directives that people be given more time to pay fines and compensation, and (citing a report of a 5.5-year imprisonment for failure to repay a brideprice) that a limit of six months be set on the length of imprisonment a village court could order (112–13). The submission did not suggest that women in particular were discriminated against, although it commented that it should be made illegal for village courts to imprison women with small children (113), but the following year village courts in the same province were accused of sexual discrimination. Newspaper publicity was given to an incident in which a woman was freed from Baisu gaol by a National Court judge after being imprisoned for non-payment of compensation ordered by a village court. The woman was portrayed as a victim of village courts,[2] and the judge ruled that the village court had been in breach of the Constitution. No publicity was given to the subsequent finding of the Supreme Court that the Constitution had not, in fact, been breached by the village court (see Jessep 1991). In 1991 other imprisonments of a similar kind, of up to four months, received widespread publicity, when Chief Justice Sir Buri Kidu said the village courts had misused their powers and done grave injustice to the women involved.[3] Similar newspaper coverage was given to the Judges Report of 1990, a judicial assessment of the legal system in PNG, in which it was reported that 'during 1990 more than 50 complaints were made to the National Court in Mt Hagen of women being unfairly and harshly treated by village courts and sent to jail for matters which were essentially marital problems'. The National Court found errors of jurisdiction, or in the application of the Village Courts Act, or breaches of (the legal concept of) natural justice[4] in forty-four cases (Independent State of PNG 1990: 7). No comparative figures for males were given. The report claimed the errors to be evidence of conflicts between custom and the rights guaranteed under the Constitution, and the judges clearly regarded what they understood as custom to be archaic and oppressive, generalising to a polemic that: 'The human rights guaranteed under the constitution are a dead letter for the women in many areas of the Highlands and there is no attempt being made by men and specially by men in positions of power and influence and with modern education to attempt to come to terms with this' (8). The Judges Report applied the same basic perspective on the relationship between custom and human rights that Mitchell had half a decade previously, albeit with a more condemnatory attitude towards village courts and males.

A discussion by a legal scholar of some of the 1989 and 1991, while providing no cultural context to the cases involved, critiqued the village court decisions in terms of the Village Courts Act and the Constitution. It made the point that the alleged mistreatment of women in the cited cases contrasted with reports from other parts of the country, and suggested a remedy in fundamentally legal terms: better legal training and more attention to the constitutional dimension of family law at the village court level (Jessep 1991: 75–77). It is, of course, now impossible to anthropologically examine these 1991 cases satisfactorily, or to investigate the 'customary' actions which the judges considered to be in conflict with human rights. Neither can it be sensibly judged whether the women were being discriminated against 'customarily' in being ordered to pay compensation or fines in the first instance.

Nevertheless, the National Court decisions, based on an investigation of the cases, seemed a clear indication that the women had been victims of injustice in these instances, at the hands of village courts, although perhaps with a degree of complicity from district courts, for imprisonment orders written by village courts have no force or effect unless endorsed by a district court magistrate. In this respect the district court magistrate may refuse to endorse the order if he or she has reason to believe the village court has acted without jurisdiction or has exceeded its powers, and under such conditions may review a case.[5] Thus, although the district court magistrate is not required to review the evidence or conduct of individual cases if the village court appears to have acted within its jurisdiction and powers, district courts share some legal responsibility for gaolings. Theresa Doherty, a national court judge in active service at the time, commented of village court imprisonment orders being countersigned by district court magistrates: 'It was apparent many were signed automatically' (1992: 11).

While I could not examine the substance of the cases reported in the newspapers and discussed by Jessep (1991) I did talk to village court magistrates in the Enga, Western Highlands and Eastern Highlands Provinces during a visit to the highlands in 1992 as part of the review of the village court system referred to earlier.[6] I took the opportunity to investigate the writing of imprisonment orders for what appeared to be unusually long periods after the women failed to pay the compensation ordered of them. I found that the 'harsh' imprisonment of the women in 1991 resulted from the careful application by the village court magistrates of the rules in their village court handbooks, for fear of not applying 'the law' correctly. The magistrates were using the 1976 handbook, which was outdated in terms of social and judicial changes which had taken place since its publication. Prepared by a European at the end of the colonial era, it made no allowances for the fact that the rigour in the rules of law might penalise women more than men, for example in respect of orders to pay fines when women had less access than men to substantial amounts of cash. The relevant part of the handbook, in English, instructed magistrates that in the event of non-payment of a fine or compensation, a person could be gaoled for 'up to' one week for every K10 owed, with a bracketed clause mentioning that the court could order less that one week for each K10 if it chose. The highland magistrates, who were relatively unschooled and had poor literacy, used a Tokpisin version of the book, which also attempted to advise readers that the rate of one week per K10 was an optional maximum. The book had exemplary, completed order forms for magistrates to look at as a guide, which the magistrates found clearer and more helpful than the complicated textual instructions. The examples were made out for the full gaol term, thus losing the intention that it was an optional maximum. Mindful of criticism of their lack of legal rigour, magistrates were following 'the law' to the Tokpisin letter. Compared to the English term 'law' the Tokpisin equivalent '*lo*' is an ambiguous term whose glosses extend to 'rules' and received edicts—including religious teachings—which are not, strictly speaking, 'law' in the conventional English sense. It is fair to say that village court handbooks are treated as rule books by many village court officials.

Their strict application of the law indicated the paradox engendered for village court magistrates by the original plan that they should be recruited from the communities they served, and chosen by the community partly on the understanding that they were *not* technically qualified jurists but had an organic knowledge of the community's customs. In practice they found that the disputes they dealt with were actually categorised into a reduced range of the same offences that technically qualified magistrates dealt with in local courts of the time and in district courts. Most of the interventions into, or over-ruling of, village court decisions have been concerned with matters of law as interpreted by legal specialists, not matters of custom. Further, in various investigations and reviews of the workings of the village court system since its inception, when magistrates have been consulted their own assessments of their work and competency have focused overwhelmingly on their lack of expertise in law.

During the 1992 review, which covered seven different provinces (Central, East New Britain, Madang, Eastern Highlands, Western Highlands,

Enga, Milne Bay), an investigation of village court magistrates' self-perception revealed that they saw themselves as part of a legal system rather than being an essentially customary institution. The types of cases they heard were often either cases in which customary solutions had failed, or cases where customary solutions were inappropriate or could not be applied for some reason. Magistrates in the 'settlement' village courts (i.e. in communities of migrants in suburbs or on the periphery of towns like Madang, Lae and Moresby) said they faced difficulty in that disputants often came from different areas, so their customary backgrounds were different. Decisions based on custom were virtually impossible in such situations, and these magistrates wanted a better knowledge of law. They also had problems with disputants who went into town after village court cases and consulted friends in the police force or legal services, returning to challenge village court decisions armed with legal arguments. When we asked village court officials what they felt their needs were, we were invariably told that they wanted more training in the law.

Specific reports of unfair or excessive imprisonment of women by the village courts disappeared from the media after the 1991 publicity (until a single incident in 2006; see conclusion). In fact, Judge Doherty reported that a breakdown of figures for a total of forty-one women gaoled in Baisu (Western Highlands Province) in August 1992 showed thirty-five were from National Court convictions, five from district court convictions, and only one from a village court conviction (1992: 5–6). While commenting that this was a 'contrast' to the 1991 situation at Baisu (6) Doherty was nevertheless of the opinion that women, youth and the less educated members of society seemed to fare worse in the lower courts (that is, local courts—which have since been phased out—and village courts) than in the higher courts (1). She went on to give a set of conclusions—which she qualified as being personal and unresearched—about village courts which were similar to those of Mitchell, citing the Judges Report of 1990 and the imprisonment cases which had received publicity in 1989 and 1991 (4–13). Like Mitchell, and Jessep (1991), Doherty contextualised the shortcomings of village courts in a lack of proper training and knowledge of the law. She noted training workshops conducted in 1992 which revealed that the village court magistrates 'were unaware of people's rights to speak etc, they had been misled (or maybe misheard or misunderstood) that they should enforce their orders with imprisonment' (1992: 14–15), and concluded also that they did not realise they were subject to the Constitution (4).

The press carried no significant reports of village court injustice during the next few years, and there were no other immediate reports to suggest that the sensationalised cases had been part of any wider systemic injustice towards women by village courts. In fact, the findings of research by anthropologists had previously mostly presented women as confident and relatively successful users of the courts. George Westermark, for example, said of village courts in Agarabi in the Eastern Highlands: 'That women should be such frequent users of the court, when in other public contexts they tend to refrain from asserting themselves, suggests that they view the court as an effective method for responding to their conflicts' (1985: 114). Richard Scaglion and Rose Whittingham, on the basis of statistical analysis from all parts of the country, found that women used village courts more than any other forum (ranging from village moots to higher formal courts) to settle grievances. Scaglion's own research in the Abelam area of the East Sepik Province informed his criticism of Paliwala's assertions (Scaglion and Whittingham 1982: 132) that village courts were agents of women's oppression by the state: 'Paliwala (1982) argues that Village Courts attempt to control women by making divorce more difficult, and by enforcing restrictive customs more strictly. . . . These sorts of practices are certainly not characteristic of all Village Courts . . . the results reported here suggest that women in this area are winning more cases than men' (Scaglion 1990: 30).

However, the issue of women's rights in PNG was gaining attention during the 1990s partly through the longer-term effect of second-wave feminism on anthropology (see, for example, Reiter 1975; Moore 1988, 1994), but also with the dissemination of human rights discourse from the 'developed' world. The status of women in PNG was being researched not only by a new wave of anthropologists sensitised to gender issues, but also through aid and development policy–related research conducted by agencies such as the United Nations Educational, Scientific and Cultural Organisation (UNESCO) and the Australian International Aid and Development Bureau (AIDAB) and its successor AusAID. Some effects were visible in studies premised on the general inequality of women in the country. For example, in a problem-oriented and even-handed discussion in 1993 of the social control of women in PNG, Cyndi Banks mentioned the research of Scaglion, Whittingham and Westermark but relied heavily on Mitchell and Paliwala on the topic of women and village courts, and ultimately, in terms of her wider topic, favoured their negative comments on the outcomes for women over the more positive comments of the former (32–37).

By the end of the 1990s, though, catalogues of injustices to women were beginning to include references to the village courts which were explicitly judgmental. Oddly, though, they drew on old examples, rather than recent research. Martha Macintyre argued that women lacked rights 'according to customary law' and men desired to 'legitimate the subjugation of women by extending customary law into other areas' (1998: 218). She illustrated this by reference to the reported 1975 incident in Mendi (cited above). Similarly, Maev O'Collins said 'reference to custom and tradition can produce some curious results', and recalled an example witnessed by herself in 1976, when visiting Pangia in the southern highlands. Local village court magistrates, she said, had gaoled several women who had been found smoking 'store-bought' cigarettes (2000: 6). This 'example' might have been an error of memory on O'Collins's part, since no village courts were proclaimed in the Pangia region until 1978.[7] On the other hand, the cases she described were very similar to those reported in 1975 from Mendi and could have been a recycled version of the same incident (except that the women were now claimed to have been gaoled, not fined).

An influential publication in the same year as that of O'Collins was an account by a PNG campaigner for women's rights, Sarah Garap. Garap included a section about women and village courts in a general discussion of women's oppression in her own province, Simbu (2000: 162–68). The first part of her discussion echoed the conclusions of Judge Doherty (see above) with whom Garap had worked a few years earlier, though Garap's own criticisms were unqualified and more polemical. She also referred to complaints made by Simbu women to a visiting judge in 1993, and reproduced part of the Judges Report of 1990 (see above). Two of her nine brief examples of women's suffering mentioned the village courts. One described an unsuccessful attempt to obtain a divorce and the other told of a woman's unsuccessful attempt to have a village court punish her husband's polygamy (Garap 2000: 167). Village courts are not authorised to grant divorces, and polygyny is legal in PNG. Acceding to either of the requests cited by Garap would have involved the courts in *ultra vires* action.

The rhetoric that women are mistreated in village courts, while ungrounded in rigorous research and arguably selective in its sources and poorly informed about the legislative structures governing the courts, became influential in concert with general commentaries by human rights and other organisations, which cyclically publish (mostly unreferenced) summaries of crime, corruption, and law and order issues in PNG, recently including unqualified statements about village courts' discrimination against women. It is not clear how much rigorous field research, if any, has informed the latter kinds of reports. Advocates of women's rights in PNG continue to occasionally include general comments about the misogyny of village courts when speaking of discriminatory practices in PNG,[8] and Garap's account is popular, as a citation, with authors who make passing references to women and village courts (see, for example, Dinnen 2001b: 109; Lipset 2004: 66; Parker 2002).

The question of women's treatment will be taken up again in chapter 9. For the moment it is useful to note the link between the critical preoccupation with alleged misogyny in the village courts during this period, arguably lacking significant support from rigorous research, and the 1992 comment by Aleck that 'the existence of demonstrably corrupt or prejudicial practices . . . is rather more a matter of cultural perspective than of objective fact' (114). Considering that village courts have been in operation since 1975, and that there were more than 1,000 across PNG by the year 2000, the number of reliable reports of wrongdoing is slight. Occasional reports of prejudice have been given emphasis according to prevalent climates of concern among commentators. In the early days of the courts, for example, conservative colonial prejudices against generalised 'custom' guided the kinds of criticisms made of the village courts. At later stages, human rights and explicit gender issues have provided the context of concern under which village courts are scrutinised. The scrutiny itself is possibly reinforced by an understanding that village courts are parochial and therefore represent dubious 'customary' attitudes in the face of the need for modernisation and development.

More recently, as the crisis developed in the matter of the payment of allowances to village court officials, prominence was given to allegations of financial corruption and *ultra vires* practice. Unsubstantiated reports of financial corruption were common from the highlands areas during the period when village court magistrates were complaining most vociferously about non-payment and were threatening strike action (see chapter 2). Similarly, an intensification of complaints of *ultra vires* actions in highland provinces came at a time when provincial governments were preparing legislation to take greater control of village courts (see chapter 2). Legalist concerns that village courts would act beyond their jurisdiction were expressed even before the courts began to operate in 1975, and were to some extent borne out by reported cases in the system's early days. At that time *ultra vires* actions were mostly due to ignorance of the law. More recently, though, other influences have come to bear particularly on courts in areas distant from administrative centres.

Village court magistrates in rural areas with whom I discussed the matter (for example, in Enga and the Western and Eastern Highlands Provinces) admitted to conducting *ultra vires* hearings on criminal matters, including murder, but said they would avoid the practice if they could. Magistrates in these areas particularly complained about a lack of support from district courts and police, which may have contributed to their capitulation to local pressure to deal with matters well outside their jurisdiction. Their communities lacked confidence in district or national courts, and lacked access to these alternative courts. Moreover, they sometimes had an insular concern to keep their 'law and order' affairs from wider scrutiny, as police responses to reported crime in rural areas commonly involve generalised punitive action such as destruction of village gardens and livestock and razing of houses. Urban village court magistrates, in closer proximity to police stations and district courts, were less vulnerable to pressure to conduct *ultra vires* hearings. The amount of *ultra vires* practice by village courts overall, however, is unknown.

Whatever the cultural, juridical or political perspectives behind perceived corruption or injustice in village courts, we can see that the most pervasive discursive categories of allegations over time have been 'custom' (usually portrayed as undesirable, or oppressive) and 'law' (traduced, transgressed or abused in application). This returns us to the underlying dichotomy which village courts are supposed to negotiate in practice, and it is worthwhile to interrogate how these concepts have been understood and used not only by commentators but also by the village courts and the people they serve. In particular, the matter of village courts' relationship to 'custom' needs to be placed in a nuanced historical perspective, in contrast to both the nativistic view of early proponents of the courts and the condemnatory attitudes of their critics. While many of the criticisms reviewed above seem to assume that a basic problem with village courts is magistrates' ignorance of the law and adherence to (bad) custom, an examination of the attitudes particularly of rural villagers to law and custom discloses a more complex negotiation of two phenomena which are far from clear to those obliged to consider them.

The Lure of Law

Despite the anti-legal rhetoric in favour of the establishment of village courts in the early 1970s, the Village Courts Act unavoidably formalised village courts as instruments of the formal justice system, with clear directives about their makeup, jurisdiction, limits of authority, their supervision by district magistrates and the range of penalties they could impose, among other things (Village Courts Act 1973). As a legislatively created institution, then, the role of the village courts was made difficult by a substantive bias towards legalism in their operational guidelines. In effect, village court officers were instructed (on paper, at least) in some detail on relevant 'law', while being assumed to know 'custom'. If they did not know the latter, the Village Courts Act (s.29[3]) nominated Local Government Councils as a suitable body to rule what local custom was. There was, in fact, only one section out of eighty-one in the Act which addressed the application of custom, and it simply referred to the Native Customs (Recognition) Act. Custom in PNG, while being the subject of much political and legal commentary, has gained little in the way of official sanction since the colonial era (see Orr 1991: 71–89).

Not surprisingly, some of the more negative early criticisms in academic literature about the village courts as an institution emphasised their structural and operational bias towards the formal legal system. For instance, Paliwala (1982: 192–227) made a number of observations to this effect. He pointed out that village courts observed a uniform system of compensation limits and maximum fines, and theoretically they could accept customary alternatives to cash fines. In practice there was no mechanism for collecting goods rather than money, so money was always collected, regardless of the fact that the cash economy had penetrated to different extents in different societies and that some societies were rich in resources but not cash (202). Paliwala secondly noted that village court officials regarded the contents of their handbooks as 'laws', and that the books contained a wide range of offences, in the manner of a 'village criminal code' drawing the officials into a legalistic framework (203). Thirdly, he pointed out that village courts had state backing, and offenders who did not comply with their orders could be referred to other courts, or imprisoned by a village court order actioned by a higher court. This, he said, was state legal procedure, not custom (203). Fourthly, the state had ultimate control of village courts, and district magistrates made recommendations over the appointment of village magistrates and could intervene (204). Fifthly, apart from the opportunity to elect village court officials, village people had no operational role in the village court system (206, 213). Finally, some village courts had built court houses as permanent sites and ran them as a model of district courts, and did not allow the full participation of the audience (212–13). Overall, his analysis situated the development of village courts in the extension of state control into village society.

But Paliwala's interpretation is relatively narrow. While village court magistrates' perception of their legal function was affected by their role as an element of state along with criticisms of the kind described earlier in this chapter, it was not only legislative exigencies and pressure from concerned Europeans that was driving village courts away from informality and 'custom' towards formality and law. By the time village courts were introduced, most parts of PNG had experienced some application of the colonial legal system, whether it was through the formal courts of the urban areas or the transient *kiap* courts. Missionaries and the Administration had inaugurated church and civil councils particularly in coastal societies, and these dealt with minor offences, modelling their behaviour on European-style committee procedure (see, for example, Belshaw 1957: 211–26). Highland societies were also attempting to emulate Western courts in their own dispute-solving (Berndt 1962; Strathern 1972). While villagers may not have understood Western law (Iramu 1975; Standish 1975; Sam, Passingan and Kanawai 1975) they certainly recognised the trappings of the Western legal system, and the concept of 'village courts', with 'magistrates', was interpreted accordingly. Interestingly, the Desailly and Iramu report of 1972 on an inquiry into the need for village courts (see chapter 1), contained an appendix of notes from meetings with local government councillors around the country which indicated a preference for authoritarian approaches to law and order and regret at the disappearance of the *kiap* system (1972).

Community expectations were that village courts would be partially modelled on local and district courts both procedurally and architecturally. Consequently, villagers either expected sittings to be held in existing buildings in urban or peri-urban areas, or they built bush-material village courthouses and wanted regular court sitting days (see Gordon and Meggitt 1985; Paliwala 1982; Scaglion 1979; Westermark 1978). This had become common practice by the 1990s, as I found during the 1992 review referred to earlier. In the seven different provinces we toured, most of the locations we visited had a courthouse, and those which did not had a closed-off area with chairs or benches and tables. All the courthouses were built by the local community, and it was clear that it was the desire of the community, and not just of village court officials, to have a formal building or area.

In all the courts we visited, sessions started and ended with a formal announcement, with formal bowing, and sometimes a Christian prayer. Some courts had docks for the accused and witness boxes. In others, participants' roles were clear, in respect of Western courtroom models, from their spatial positions. Some courts observed strict security procedures. For instance, in courts in Enga Province disputants and witnesses tended to be frisked for weapons and were obliged to stand to attention during proceedings, due to experiences of disputants attacking each other or even magistrates. In Milne Bay Province the same problem was handled in a different style: there was no search, but participants sat on the floor and a court official sat between the disputants, thus making a surprise assault virtually impossible. Overall, in the conduct of village courts in the areas we visited, there was a distinct formality, and an attempt to maintain some of the atmosphere and procedure associated with the introduced legal system.

From the time of their introduction, then, few village courts followed the legislative directive that they would 'adjourn from time to time and place to place'. Village court users also showed ambivalence about the 'customs' which the magistrates were supposed to apply. For them, 'custom' meant 'tradition', or the ways of their ancestors. During the 1992 review, I made a point in any area that we visited of asking villagers what the customary settlement procedures were. Often I received bland and unspecific answers about 'talking things out', but more thoughtful answers demonstrated either a dissatisfaction with custom as an adequate judicial response to present-day problems, or an acknowledgement that 'custom' (that is, traditional ways of solving problems) was fast disappearing. In the village of Vunadidir, near Rabaul, an elderly villager pointed out that his area had been under various colonial influences for more than a century, and certainly beyond any living memory. Nobody really knew what the so-called true traditions were any more, he said, and problems presented themselves in different ways than they used to, and required different types of solutions. He felt that old dispute-settlement procedures were a thing of the past.

In another village, Palanataman, I was told people were not happy with the village court magistrates, whom they said were old men and biased in their decisions. They wanted younger magistrates, even if the younger people did not have the same 'customary' knowledge. At Rempi village in Madang Province people told me the village courts should be given more power, to make people respect them more. This was echoed in Kainantu (site of the first village court) in the Eastern Highlands Province when I was told, 'At first we had no respect for village courts: we thought they were insignificant'. This attitude had changed when penalties were increased (through amendments to the Village Courts Act) and when village courts started referring cases to higher courts. Again, the view was expressed that customs were disappearing, and that younger people no longer responded to customary authority, so more legalistic remedies were needed. If villagers ever had a complaint about the village court system, it was about alleged bias on the part of magistrates towards members of their own kin group. It became clear that villagers actually wanted the village courts to be as objective and unbiased in their procedure and decision-making as formal courts attempted to be.

As some of these comments imply, rural communities, who had experienced customary dispute settlement as a process beset by bias and manipulation under the exigencies of kin-ordered social organisation, regarded the general principle of disinterested adjudication represented by the colonial legal system as an attractive alternative (see, for example, Warren 1976), although in practice their social conditioning would result in their disputing tactics being more representative of the former, as we shall see in later chapters. Rather than gathering informal and customary dispute settlement into the formal legal structure, village courts were commonly regarded by disputants as a formal and public legal forum *beyond* neo-customary resources. The first extended study of a village court in operation (Warren 1976) noted all these tendencies in 'Kumara'[9] court in the Kainantu district of the Eastern Highlands Province, from its official inauguration in February 1975. It met in a courthouse next to the community meeting-house on regular days, and villagers distinguished between it and informal 'courts' presided over by councillors and *komiti* (Tokpisin: 'committee'—meaning in this case members of the councillors' ward committees of the time), and other unofficial moots (Warren 1976: 4–6). On this distinction between the official and the unofficial, Warren commented: 'The formal Village Court is a rather purely judicial institution, as it turns out in Kumara: in a narrow sense of 'legal', it represents the legal mode of social control. . . . It is concerned with the breach of rules and the perpetration of wrongs. Other procedures are much more concerned with the moral and historical complexity of disputes and much less abstracted from the social and political processes of domestic, village and Community life' (Warren 1976: 6).

However, George Westermark, after research involving five village courts in the same (Kainantu) district, presented a less dichotomised view just two years later. He criticised the analytical distinction between 'court' and 'compromise' models, which was popular with legal anthropologists in the 1960s and early 1970s. This distinction represented 'court' proceedings as involving a third party who held coercive power in the discussion of disputes, applied norms, and tried to establish past facts, towards resolution and a winner-takes-all verdict. 'Compromise' proceedings on the other hand involved only two parties with no coercive power pursuing interests instead of applying norms. The two parties were unconcerned with establishing past 'facts' because they were trying to establish their own positive position in the future, and thus seeking compromise instead of resolution (1978: 82). Westermark favoured a more flexible approach, avoiding the reification of the court/compromise dichotomy, and his research findings suggested that village courts blended 'court' and 'compromise' models to a greater extent than Warren's view allowed (83–95). Following Moore's (1973) phraseology, he argued that the village courts occupied a 'semi-autonomous social field', and emphasised the role of actors who he said were generating their own cultural systems within the confines of external forces (Westermark 1978: 89). 'Village Court officials . . . have acted as legal middlemen between their own communities and the hierarchy of officialdom, they have created a system different from what existed before and different from what was envisioned by the *Village Courts Act* 1973' (90).

Westermark's typification has come to be more commonly applied in literature on village courts than Warren's. The blend of 'court' and 'compromise' models he suggested has been observed consistently by researchers until the present (see, for example, Goddard 2000, 2003; Scaglion 1990; Westermark 1986; Zorn 1990). While Warren's representation of village court practice as being abstracted from local community sociality may not have been borne out historically, his basic point about the legalism of the village court reflects the view of most users of village courts. The Village Courts Act (s.17) intended that magistrates should attempt mediation in disputes in the first instance, moving to adjudication if mediation failed or was not possible. In fact, much of the work of village courts is mediation, commonly called *wanbel* (literally 'one belly', meaning 'in agreement') *kot* in Tokpisin, though it does not appear in court records. But villagers tend to recognise only the *ful kot* (Tokpisin: 'full court', that is, adjudicatory proceedings) as the official village court. Ironically, early criticisms of the village courts accused them of favouring adjudication over mediation, possibly because the latter was unrecorded and therefore 'hidden' from the view of transient observers. In fact, mediation is the activity that has kept village courts articulated to a degree with the informal courts from which Warren saw them as becoming separate, and through which many disputes in rural communities and urban settlements continue to be settled without reaching the village court.

The informal procedures sometimes involve still-surviving community figures used by the colonial Administration in a politico-jural capacity, such as *luluais, tultuls* and *kaunsels* (Tokpisin: councillors)— prominent males installed as village heads and problem solvers. These are the kinds of people who ran the unofficial courts to which Warren referred. Those who still exist are nowadays elderly figures, but they have maintained their status as dispute settlers by virtue of experience and reputation, and a wide range of disputes which might otherwise have gone to a village court are taken to them. In a broader context, though, Warren's informal courts (which he called 'outside courts') might be better termed neo-customary dispute-management procedures, as they have developed, and are still developing, throughout PNG from transformations in the structure of social organisation over time. For example, another forum for dispute settlement or management has been provided for many years in some south-coast societies by church organisations, wherein deacons, pastors and other church officials regularly mediate or arbitrate disputes (for an early example see Belshaw 1957). In urban environments regional groups within the community often form their own self-help associations, and disputes of certain types can be taken to these. Also, in urban settlements there are usually 'settlement committees' made up of concerned individuals and aimed at preserving stability in the settlement and attempting to improve the settlers' habitat. These committees also attempt to resolve disputes which threaten the well-being of the community. Committee members are also prominent members of the community, and sometimes a person will hold several different positions of prestige, including that of village court magistrate.

In respect of the intended strategy for village courts, that mediation is to be attempted where possible before a case comes to a full village court, this unofficial intervention in disputes has come to blur the boundaries of formal and informal dispute settlement. There are cases where an individual is at the same time an ex-*kaunsel*, a church elder and a village court magistrate. When he is approached to settle a dispute outside a formal village court hearing the formal or informal capacity in which he is acting is of no particular importance to him or the disputants. As a result of this variety of dispute-settling resources there are some communities in which the types and numbers of disputes which find their way into the *ful kot* are fairly limited, and sometimes a matter of default, in that other resources have failed to reach satisfactory results.

As well as legislative directives, and the attitudes of village court users, political concern with the country's 'law and order' problem has added a further dimension to the village court system's complex relation to law and custom. The first secretary of the VCS, Kila Garo, wrote in 1977 that 'if the procedure of a village court diverges too much from custom, the people will be unable to participate as well as they should, and the effectiveness of that court will be impaired' (59). But by the mid 1980s the PNG Government was anxious to increase the village courts' effectiveness in relation to the country's crime problem and was urging better supervision of the courts, more co-operation between village courts and the police, and an increase in 'urban village courts'. The latter, now well-established in major towns around the country, operate under the same terms of reference as 'rural' village courts, but the complex ethnic mixing in urban areas militates against attempts to involve 'local custom' in proceedings. As I observed in chapter 2, the urban milieu has increased the tendency for village courts to be perceived as a 'bottom rung' on the ladder of official courts, rather than as people's courts. In contrast to Garo's comment of 1977, his successor wrote of village court officials in 1986: 'Their legal background is very scanty and this can create complications in the executing of their duties' (Keris 1986: 74). Keris also wanted village court officials to be better educated (74), and noted 'many of our village court officials see themselves as representing the government, rather than just being lay officials, and seek external validation whenever they run into any conflict or problem with the community they serve' (71). The implied juridical role of village courts was reinforced in training sessions for magistrates which I observed during the review in 1992, where an inverted pyramid was drawn on a blackboard to represent the hierarchy of courts, with village courts at the base, and participants were repeatedly told they were the '*las kot*' (Tokpisin: 'last court', i.e. bottom in the hierarchy). By 2003 the legal role of the village courts was being fairly explicitly stated not only in the kind of policy statements referred to in chapter 2, but by members of the judiciary. A national court judge was unequivocal in declaring that since the Constitution defined the national judicial system as consisting of the Supreme Court, the National Court and other courts as established by Acts of Parliament, and since the village court system was established by an Act of Parliament, then village courts were part of the national judicial system.[10]

The Enigma of Custom

We have seen that practical exigencies have driven village courts towards formalism, against the intention of the planners of the system that their duties would be occasional and light, and that they would 'adjourn from time to time and place to place' (Village Courts Act 1973) in an informal atmosphere. But in tension with the increasing legalism has been an awareness by village court officials and village court users of the official directive that the courts are to follow 'custom'. Village court magistrates have conscientiously struggled to implement this, even in the face of the kinds of scepticism expressed by villagers to which I referred in the previous section. Despite what some commentators regard as their integrative practice, they continue to carry in their minds a dichotomous notion of law and custom. This is manifest discursively: in the village courts in Port Moresby that I have observed, phrases such as '*long kastom sait*' (Tokpisin: 'on the custom side') or '*kastom kaha dekenai*' (Hiri Motu: 'on the custom side') are common in lingua franca argument and discussion, relative to the 'law' side of a matter.

The dichotomy is also manifest in magistrates' preoccupation with establishing and stating the nature of particular 'customs' involved in cases before the court, though this has been invariably a rhetoric rather than a substantive achievement in the courts I have observed during fieldwork. In urban village courts, serving ethnically mixed populations, magistrates regard the identification and pursuit of custom as particularly vexing. In their interpretation, the directive to follow custom imposes a need for them to become knowledgeable of a diversity of customs, and burdens them with the problem of whose customs to follow in a dispute between people of differing ethnic backgrounds. While the factors generating the drive to legalism outlined in the previous section are comparatively discernable, the preoccupation with custom requires some analytic attention here.

Two distinct schools of thought are visible in the criticisms of the village courts' application of 'custom' which I noted earlier. One, represented by Paliwala (1982), emphasises a bias towards legalism in the courts. The other is the more conservative legalism presented by Mitchell (1985), which implies the superiority of Western forms of jurisprudence over others, and takes a critical view of the village courts' alleged application of what legalists understand to be 'custom' and 'customary law'. However, there is little interrogation of the notion of custom in either perspective. The particular representation of custom to which legalists subscribe is reflected in the definition taken from the colonial Native Customs (Recognition) Act (s.4) of 1963 and embedded in PNG's Constitution at Independence. Officially, 'custom' means 'the custom or usage of the aboriginal inhabitants of the country . . . regardless of whether or not that custom or usage has obtained from time immemorial.'

As we saw in chapter 1, colonial juridical ideas about custom in PNG were informed by a social evolutionist attitude to non-Western societies, and conceived custom from the beginning as a body of 'traditional' beliefs and practices of equivocal legal and moral validity. It was feared that indigenous courts, if permitted, would be liable to corruption, and bias, and that custom would influence decisions (Chalmers 1978: 70; Gordon and Meggitt 1985: 191). Before the Second World War the Administration was not prepared to acknowledge 'custom' as substantive law, and while it could be considered in mitigation in court cases, its possible influence in official court decisions was unacceptable. Law and custom were thus seen to be antithetical so far as their potential for objectivity, impartiality and systematic applicability was concerned. At the end of colonial rule, despite the greater administrative recognition of custom as (mostly) acceptable social practice, manifest in the Native Customs (Recognition) Act of 1963, the dualistic contrast between custom and law remained. Conditioned by this colonial legal tradition, even the relatively liberal view of Mitchell regarded custom as an untrustworthy guarantor of justice. Consequently, education in human rights as defined according to a Western paradigm, and expertise in Western-style jurisprudence were seen as a desirable social developmental strategy. In the light of post-colonial adoptions of Western ideas of social equality (especially gender equality) and universal (individual) human rights, custom is necessarily detrimental to justice from the perspective of legalists. Whether the discursive opposition of custom and a European system of law visible in the critiques of Mitchell and others has always existed in reality (anywhere, let alone in PNG) is of course doubtful: Jean Zorn has shown, for example, how 'custom' can stray even into the stringently legalistic proceedings of the PNG National Court (Zorn 1991).

The PNG Constitution provided for an Act of Parliament to declare the underlying law of the country, incorporating custom, common law and a judicial formulation of new law. The Law Reform Commission, set up at Independence to investigate and report on the development of the underlying law, recommended a strong role for custom in the underlying law. However, despite the state's preparation for custom to be systematically integrated into law there has been no effective progress in this direction (though there is a massive body of literature in legal journals, and conferences on customary law are virtually perennial rituals). Obvious difficulties in such a project would be the difference between 'national' custom and a huge variety of local customs, and conceptual problems concerning the fixity and historicity of customs. Also, for legislative purposes, definition of custom remains a problem. The only official definition (stipulative, lexical or otherwise) of custom in PNG now is given in the Constitution and is, as I have already observed, a reproduction of the inadequate definition in the 1963 Act. The relationship between custom and customary law has also been difficult for legislative bodies to define. The Law Reform Commission devoted an eighty-eight page publication in 1977 to 'the role of customary law in the legal system' but could offer little in the way of a clarification of what customary law was. Its definition of customary law, 'the customs and usages of indigenous inhabitants', simply collapsed customary law into the existing definition of custom embedded in the PNG Constitution. An explanatory note to the definition acknowledged this, with an added statement that 'customary law is a flexible system of law which may be different from place to place and from time to time'(17).

The anthropologist Richard Scaglion, who worked with the Law Reform Commission from 1979 to 1982 to direct a customary law–development project, reminisced some years later about the problems he encountered. As an anthropologist he regarded customary law in

PNG as 'less a system of application of formal rules to a given fact situation and more a system for insuring a just solution through compromise' (Scaglion 2005: 50, cf. Scaglion 1981: 37), and acknowledged a distinction between '*substantive law* (rules for normative behaviour, infractions of which are negatively sanctioned) and *procedural law* (mechanisms through which legal issues are actually handled)' (2005: 50, italics in orig.). Further, where lawyers were often preoccupied with statutory rules, 'anthropologists (and Melanesians) tend to be more interested in the procedures by which disputes actually get settled, and with the underlying principles of fairness implied in such settlements' (50–51). Scaglion's problem during his service with the Law Reform Commission was that he wanted to focus on procedural law, rather than 'substantive law—the "rules" that most Melanesians seemed to lack but that the lawyers seemed to think were so important. Many of the other government legal officers did not feel that this was a profitable direction for me to take' (53).

Elsewhere Scaglion argued that attempts to codify custom would freeze it and render it inflexible, and made the further point that customary law was 'personalised' inasmuch as mediators in disputes already knew a great deal about the parties to the dispute and its history. 'The facts of the matter are rarely in question. . . . The question is rather what to do about the matter' (1985: 32). Also, the relative social standing of disputants is very likely to be explicitly taken into account. A consequence of personalisation is that customary procedure towards justice is very rarely as objective and unbiased as the introduced law attempts to be. Further, disputes may not be resolved with a finality corresponding to that in formal legal proceedings and sometimes manifest themselves again repeatedly over a period of time. Zorn (a lawyer) has suggested that 'dispute settlement' may be better called 'dispute management' (1992: 29). These considerations collectively constitute a challenge to the legitimacy of such a category as customary law, or even an ostensibly sensible concept like 'traditional dispute settlement' (Young 1992: 32) relative to Western law.

Anthropologists nowadays are likely to argue that the conventional notion of customary law was generated in the course of colonialism and that the dualistic idea that in countries like PNG there is 'law' on the one hand and 'custom' on the other is a legacy. Indeed, as Melissa Demian notes, for anthropologists nowadays 'it almost goes without saying that customary law did not exist until the introduction of a sphere of political activity from which it had to be differentiated' (Demian 2003: 100). Certainly, as Zorn observes, discursively convenient phrases like 'customary law' and 'custom' are of questionable validity and have uncertain connotations and the use of 'law' in reference to the norms and dispute-management processes of stateless societies 'imposes a Western category on something that may have very different aims and effects' (1991: 27n).

Zorn's point can be exemplified from my own experience in 1985 shortly after beginning participant observation fieldwork (which was not on village courts) in the upper Kaugel Valley in the Western Highlands during my doctoral research. Observing a gathering one morning I asked what was happening and was told (employing a Tokpisin term, rather than a local language term) that it was a *kot*. I asked for details and was informed that a young woman had charged a young man with neglect of husbandly duties. The couple had originally entered into a relationship after a *tanim het* (communal 'courting session' for young people) but a brideprice had not yet been paid. He was not treating her correctly, so she returned to her own parents. The issue now was whether the couple should stay together, in which case the brideprice should be paid, or whether they were irreconcilable, in which case the young man (or, more correctly, his family) should pay compensation. If the latter was the case, the young man's group should make an initial payment as a gesture of goodwill and as *bel kol* (Tokpisin: 'cold belly') money—that is, a payment to cool the 'hot belly' (i.e. anger) of the bride's group. Seeing that the *kot* was being presided over by a respected older man who was in fact a village court magistrate, but that there were no other court officials, I interpreted what I was witnessing as an unofficial, or customary, court.

There were some initial exchanges between the young man's parents and the young woman's parents. Then an elderly man got to his feet and launched into a 'what-is-the-world-coming-to' harangue about the morals of contemporary young people, the decline in standards of behaviour during *tanim het*, and the (real or imagined) higher moral standards of his own youth. He was followed by others, who expounded on the same theme, sometimes allegorically, expanding to include commentaries on crime and moral decline in general. Rain interrupted proceedings, but at a regathering the following day speakers continued to declaim on the subject of declining social standards. Eventually, discussion turned back to the 'case' at hand, and it was decided, after some musing by the presiding elder, that the young man and woman were irreconcilable and compensation should be paid, beginning with a *bel kol* offering of K100. Everybody murmured agreement. The young man's father immediately produced K100 from his waistband and handed it over. I suddenly realised that he and everybody else had known all along what the outcome of the *kot* would be, and had also known what the appropriate *bel kol* payment should be. I was obliged to reconsider my interpretation of the event as an unofficial court, for while it had the superficial trappings of a dispute-settlement procedure, its most important social function appeared to be to provide a forum for the community's moral self appraisal and critique. One of the lessons of this example is that in opposing a category of 'customary law' to Western law we risk the reification of elements of a complex social whole at the expense of recognising their role in more substantial social processes.

Unlike the legal commentators exemplified earlier in this chapter, anthropologists are nowadays more likely to approach the putative relationship between 'law' and 'custom' from the perspective of legal pluralism, recognising the existence of multiple forms of social ordering in any society, and seeing them as fluid and interactive. Consequently they are wary of attempts to categorise and conceptually systematise these forms, although this caution itself leads to further equivocation. As Sally Merry has pointed out, 'It is clearly difficult to define and circumscribe these forms of ordering. Where do we stop speaking of law and find ourselves simply describing social life?' (1988: 878). Not surprisingly, anthropological approaches to village courts withhold judgments of the kind legalists make about their allegedly bad practices. Investigating the sociality of the local communities in which village courts operate provides an understanding of the background to the disputes they hear and of their responses and decisions. To put this another way, rather than being driven by a definable set of 'customs', each court reflects the sociality of the particular local community it serves. In this respect each court applies a complex integration of introduced law and a variety of local conventions in its dispute-management procedures (see, for example, Brison 1992; Demian 2003; Goddard 2000, 2002; Scaglion 1979, 1990; Westermark 1986; Young 1992; Zorn 1990; and see later chapters herein). Few anthropologists would nowadays be prepared to generalise about the attitudes, biases or prejudices of village courts as a whole, or their application of 'custom' or 'customary law'.

Negotiating 'Custom' and 'Law': The Snake Bone Case

While anthropologists may have reservations about the usefulness of concepts like 'custom' and 'customary law', the questions they raise have little practical effect so far as the everyday experience of village courts is concerned. The idea that there is a 'law' side and a 'custom' side to village court praxis is not only held by legal and other critics, but is also conditioned into the thinking of village court magistrates, as I said earlier. The ambiguities which can arise from this can be illustrated through an example from an urban village court in Port Moresby. The case exemplifies a number of aspects of village court praxis which have been touched on so far in this chapter, such as the blend of formality and informality, as well as the attempt to adequately consider 'customary' as well as 'legal' aspects of disputes. An allegation of sorcery began the case, which I monitored during fieldwork in 1994, and it was classified by the village court magistrates as a 'sorcery' case for the records. The term *sorcery* is used extremely loosely in PNG, and itself raises a number of issues concerning law and custom. A brief digression on the history of the term is therefore necessary before recounting the court case itself.

As we saw in chapter 1, in the early colonial period 'custom' was the range of indigenous social behaviour considered by the Administration to be significantly at variance with European norms. Of these customs, 'sorcery' was a major concern for the colonisers, and its alleged practitioners were given a six-month gaol sentence if they were found guilty. The Administration used the term 'sorcery' imprecisely, to cover a wide range of real or imagined types of personal violence not involving immediate physical attack. Words like 'witchcraft' and 'magic', used interchangeably, were subsumed under the rubric of 'sorcery' without the caution or qualification occasionally expressed in academic literature (see, for example, Evans-Pritchard 1976; Stephen 1989: 215–17, 236n). Sorcery continues to be outlawed in Independent PNG under the Sorcery Act, in which it is defined enumeratively as including 'witchcraft, magic, enchantment, *puri puri*, *mura mura dikana*, *vada*, *mea mea*, *sanguma* or *malira*, whether or not connected with or related to the supernatural' (6). While at first sight this may appear to be a reasonably extensive stipulation of acts of sorcery, it is better understood as a partial catalogue of a greater class of malevolence. In addition to the vagueness of the English terms, the lingua franca phrases cover a wide range of practices. For instance, *mura mura dikana* (Hiri Motu: *mura mura*, a strong drink or drug, and *dikana*, bad) refers to poisoning. The term *sanguma* (Tokpisin, absorbed from Sepik region) is now widely used in place of generalised 'sorcery' but originally referred to a type of attack where victims are set upon, rendered unconscious, physiologically interfered with, restored to consciousness, and sent on their way with no memory of the event, to suffer or die later. *Vada* and *mea mea* (Hiri Motu) are terms whose precise original meanings in the 'pure' Motu language (see chapter 4) have altered considerably over the past century and a quarter, and are now quite vague in their application. Both are sometimes used to refer to illness or death inflicted at a distance using personal items secretly obtained from the victim. It can be seen, then, that the transition from colonial to post-colonial representation has preserved the ambiguity of the official definition of sorcery. The modern use by Melanesians of the English term *sorcery* is an apt example of the uncritical perpetuation of imprecise colonial concepts of indigenous practices generally glossed as 'custom'.

With this critique of 'sorcery' in mind, we can now proceed to a case heard in Erima village court, Port Moresby, exemplifying village court preoccupation with the elusive phenomenon called 'custom'. Erima is the busiest of the dozen and a half village courts in the Moresby area (see chapters 4 and 8 for more detailed descriptions). The cases it hears are classified by magistrates according to a list of offences given in the 1976 Village Court Handbook which includes theft, assault, property damage, slander, insulting language, sorcery, disturbing the peace, drunkenness, carrying weapons, and failing to obey court directives (see appendix). The list is given in plain language in the handbook, with the most complex category being sorcery, which is subdivided into five offences covering 'making' sorcery or pretending to make sorcery, threatening sorcery, procuring sorcery, owning 'things that can be used to make sorcery' and paying for sorcery.

The case was represented to me in advance by the chairing magistrate, 'Chairman Andrew', specifically as a matter of 'custom'. Complainants in disputes register their case with the court by asking the court clerk, usually, to write out their complaint in plain language on a form which acts as a summons to the defendant. Consequently court officials have a rough guide to the nature of the dispute or complaint before the case is heard. Also, as the village court workers are part of the settlement community and its gossip network, they sometimes know most of the details in advance of the hearing of evidence. As the classification of offences in the court records has to fit the list given in the village court handbook, it is not uncommon for village court officials to hear disputes through almost to completion and then decide what the specific 'offence' is, for the purposes of proper documentation.

When disputants face the magistrates in Erima village court it is usual for a peace officer to stand between the two parties, both as a formality and to be ready to intervene in the event of a physical attack by one party on another. When the case under discussion here was called, by announcing the disputants' names, a man I shall call 'Sobe' and whom I estimated to be in his early 30s took his position as complainant on one side of the peace officer. A slightly younger looking woman, 'Mata', and a much older man 'Yaba', stood together on the officer's other side. The court clerk read out the complaint. Sobe accused his wife Mata and her older kinsman Yaba of 'sorcery'. Mata was alleged to have put snake bones in a cup of tea made for Sobe, with the connivance of Yaba. Sobe was from the Tari area of the Southern Highlands Province. His wife and her relative were from the Eastern Highlands Province. According to the Village Court Regulations at least three magistrates must sit on any case. Chairman Andrew (originally from Milne Bay Province) was joined on this case by the deputy chairman, Tagube, originally from the Southern Highlands Province (and from the same general area as the complainant, although unrelated) and a magistrate originally from the Eastern Highlands. The case was conducted in Tokpisin. Chairman Andrew referred to the alleged offence by the English term *sorcery*. The disputants used the Tokpisin term '*Posin pasin*'. While this term includes a transliteration of the English word *poison* (and of *fashion*), it does not always mean 'poisoning' in the strict sense, and is commonly used as a Tokpisin gloss for the indistinct range of phenomena covered by the official term *sorcery*.

Chairman Andrew asked Mata what she had to say. She admitted the charge. She said she had wanted to be rid of Sobe and to get a 'new man'. She had taken the bones from a dead snake she found, and had given them to the older man Yaba to look after while she went to the market. She had retrieved them from him when she returned, and had put them in Sobe's tea. Chairman Andrew asked her where she had learned to do this 'sorcery'. She said women in her settlement area who were from Simbu Province, and from Mt Hagen, in the Western Highlands Province, had told her about it. She said it was not a custom of her own area. Sobe, the complainant, told the court he had not drunk the tea because he suspected something was in it. He had become suspicious when he saw Yaba pass something to Mata just before she gave him the tea. When asked by the court for his account, Yaba simply denied any knowledge of the whole affair.

At this point Chairman Andrew produced his copy of the Village Court Handbook and read aloud the sections on sorcery, pretended sorcery, and procuring sorcery (I discovered part-way through fieldwork that Chairman Andrew, an extremely conscientious worker, actually knew the handbook's contents by heart: the ostentatious reading of the handbook was a strategy he used often to reinforce community comprehension of legal sanctions and to demonstrate that he was scrupulous in judgment). He said that even if sorcery was not actually done, people's fear of it could cause them to die. In response to this comment, Sobe announced, 'I have evidence' (the transliteration '*evidens*' is used both in Tokpisin and in Hiri Motu in village courts), and immediately produced a fist-sized newspaper bundle, which he placed on the magistrates' bench. Chairman Andrew cautiously teased the newspaper open with the court clerk's pen, exposing half a dozen tiny bones. He commented that he knew about this kind of sorcery. The snake was a common harmless variety that slept a lot. The victim of the sorcery would take on the snake's characteristics of harmlessness and dopiness, and become vulnerable and easy to get rid of. Chairman Andrew then asked Mata to name the women who had told her how to do the sorcery. She said she did not know their names, they were just 'settlement women' and were not in the vicinity of the court at the moment. Chairman Andrew then adjourned the case for one week. He said he wanted to establish whether Mata had acted alone or whether others had been involved. He told Mata to bring the other women to the next court sitting.

The following week, when the court clerk called Sobe, Mata and Yaba, the three arranged themselves differently before the magistrates. Mata now stood with her husband Sobe on one side of the peace officer, and Yaba on the other. Before the case was called I had seen Mata arrive with her husband, she did not appear to have brought any of the asked-for women with her. Chairman Andrew announced that this was a continuation of the previous week's case, and asked the older man Yaba what he had to say. Yaba once again denied any part in the affair. He was asked what his relationship to Mata was. He said he was a (classificatory) brother of her father. Mata was asked what she had to say. She began a narrative: her first husband had died, she had been alone and destitute. One of the magistrates, 'Deputy' Tagube, interrupted and told her to stick to the case at hand. She said only that this was the first time she had done anything of this nature. Deputy Tagube suddenly accused Yaba of putting Mata up to the sorcery. He said he had heard that when Sobe discovered the bones Mata had cried and blamed Yaba. Obviously Tagube had been doing some detective work during the past week. Yaba once more denied any involvement. Mata then said Yaba had told her that her husband was no good and would mistreat her. Yaba wanted her to get rid of him and find another husband, from the Eastern Highlands like her own kinspeople, she said.

Sobe told the court he and Mata had been together for two years: he had given her a home when she was destitute in Moresby after her first husband died. He then elaborated the story of the crime. He said Yaba had tried to persuade him to have a cup of tea when he was not thirsty. Yaba had been insistent, so Sobe had eventually said yes, and had then seen Yaba slip something to Mata. When the tea was made Sobe was suspicious. He told his affines he was not thirsty and offered the tea in turn to several of his wife's kin who were present. They all refused it. Eventually he offered it to Mata, at which point Yaba became extremely agitated. Then, he said, Mata confessed the plan, and he discovered the snake bones. After hearing this second and more elaborate version of the attempted sorcery Chairman Andrew adjourned the case for a decision. This would normally have been a one-week adjournment, but Sobe wanted to go to his village for family reasons and said he had already bought a plane ticket, so Andrew adjourned the case for four weeks. Significantly, he told Mata that in the meantime she must keep away from her own *lain* (Tokpisin: kin-group), stay with her husband, and go with him to his village if necessary.

Four weeks later the case was called again. By this time it had been written into the court record as a case of 'attempted sorcery'. Again Mata and Sobe stood together. Yaba was asked what he had to say: he denied everything. Mata confirmed Sobe's version of their marriage, telling the story which the magistrate had interrupted previously. She said her first husband had died, she had been destitute and Sobe had taken her in and looked after her. She respected him and was happy with him, but Yaba had told her that Sobe being a 'Tari' (that is, from the Tari area), he would cut her with a tomahawk. Chairman Andrew said that whoever was to blame, there was no doubt that an attempt at sorcery had been made, and the court had to do something about it. He said if it had been successful it would have led to huge trouble between Taris and Eastern Highlanders and many people would likely have died. Tagube abruptly confronted Yaba with the accusation that he (Yaba) had repeatedly asked Sobe to have a cup of tea, which was suspicious, and further that it had been Yaba who boiled the tea (none of the disputants had said this: the inference is that Tagube had done more detective work). 'Why would I do this thing?' said Yaba, 'They are like my own children.'

Then the story took another turn, as Mata disclosed to the court that there had been no snake bones in the tea at all, her feelings for her husband had made her unable to go through with the plan. So when Sobe had offered the cup around and everybody had declined it, she had drunk the tea herself because she had known it was not 'poisoned'. Sobe reiterated that he had seen Yaba pass something to Mata, had suspected the tea was poisoned and had offered it around to see what the response was. Finally Mata had confessed and given him the bones. This was the third version of the incident and by now the magistrates considered that enough had been heard for them to consider a decision. They decided to announce their finding the following week, after due consideration. Chairman Andrew said they would have to think about this carefully, because the disclosure that Mata had not actually put the bones in the tea made the matter of distinguishing between whether it was 'attempted sorcery' or 'pretended sorcery' more complex.

The following week, the magistrates gave their decision. This time Mata stood with her kinsman Yaba, as she had on her first appearance before the court, and the complainant Sobe stood alone. Chairman Andrew explained that according to the law about sorcery people could be punished for actual sorcery, pretended sorcery or attempts to procure sorcery. The maximum fine was K200 and payment of compensation up to K1000 could be ordered. He said the court had taken note that Sobe was not harmed in any way, but there had been intent to harm him, and despite Mata's feelings and her failure to actually put the bones in the tea, she had been involved. He said the magistrates had decided that Mata and Yaba were guilty of a sorcery attempt, and Sobe should be paid compensation. He then instructed the court clerk to write down that 'Yaba and his *lain*' (that is, Yaba and his group, without specifying who constituted the group) were ordered to pay compensation of K200 to Sobe within two weeks, and a court fine of K50 within one week. A week later the court fine had not been paid, and a court order was made out threatening imprisonment if the fine was not paid before the next court sitting. This order was made out specifically against Yaba, not Mata or Yaba's *lain*.

The case I have just described is procedurally typical of village courts. Some elements of legalism and formalism are evident, largely determined by the operational directives developed under the Village Courts Act. Also evident are aspects of the intended informality of the system, for instance in Tagube's detective work, exploiting his community ties to find and use information that was not actually presented in evidence (something that would not be allowed in a district court). The spatial movement of Mata from a defendant's position in front of the 'bench' to a complainant's position and back (an allegory, perhaps, of her experience of conflicting loyalties to her husband and to her hostile kin-group) as the evidence revealed the ambiguity of her role is another example. Further, there was a humane manipulation in the sentencing process, when Mata was publicly announced to be guilty (as the agent of her kin-group) but not named in official records. In this latter manoeuvre the magistrates capitulated to community views of the politics of inter-group hostility in PNG by identifying the wife with her natal group regardless of her dilemma,[11] while using the paperwork of sentencing to spare her from punishment (this aspect of the case will be revisited again in chapter 9).

Returning to this chapter's general theme, a significant aspect of the snake bone case is that Chairman Andrew categorised it to me in advance as a matter of custom. This was obviously linked in his mind to its being about sorcery. There is no doubt that according to the Sorcery

Act and the classification of offences in the Village Court Regulations this was indeed a sorcery case, regardless of the caution anthropologists might exercise in classifying it. Its customary status, however, is more difficult to ascertain. Mata denied that the use of snake bones in this way was a custom of her area, and in her initial attempt to shift blame away from her kinsman Yaba she suggested she had learned about it from women belonging to two other highland provinces (this covers a large and socially diverse area of the highlands and Mata's claim can be regarded as deliberately vague). Chairman Andrew claimed knowledge of this form of sorcery, as if it were not uncommon. I was working at the University of PNG at the time I monitored the case, and discussed it with an ethnically diverse range of Melanesian colleagues. Nobody claimed the snake bone technique as a custom of their area. But at the same time, nobody had any difficulty seeing its rationale, and neither had I during the case. It was, after all, based on a very simple analogy. My colleagues found the malevolent use of snake bones unremarkable. Fear of 'poisoning' by enemies via food or drink is common (particularly among males), and people are open to suggestion about the actual substance of the 'poison' itself. Interestingly, during the latter part of the case when Yaba's culpability was obvious, no-one asked *him* where he had learnt about snake bone sorcery, whether it was a local custom or something he had heard about from people of a different area, or whether it was his own idea.

The snake bone case falls under the general legal category of 'sorcery', which in early colonial times rendered it 'customary' in terms of the designation of sorcery as 'native custom'. Yet sorcery has always been illegal, while custom has gradually become legally acceptable practice. In the colonial period this acceptability was qualified with the stipulation it must not be repugnant to the principles of humanity, and postcolonially under the Customs Recognition Act (1976) it was stipulated that custom should not be recognised if it would result in 'injustice'. The post-colonial qualification amounts in practice to custom being recognised in courts as long as it is not against the law or the principles enshrined in the Constitution. This creates an irony in the snake bone case. We may indeed observe that while there was talk of custom in the course of the case, it was not made clear whose custom snake bone sorcery was, and beyond a casual declaration of acquaintance by one magistrate it was not established whether use of snake bones in poisoning was a custom at all. This becomes a cavil, however, since the specific customary status of the incident is legally irrelevant. Sorcery, which as we have seen is broadly defined to encompass instances of bodily harm or attempted bodily harm of varying severity up to murder without immediate physical attack, is simply against the law. When a social practice is legally regarded as an illegal custom, the question of how it should be dealt with in a village court according to custom becomes something of a paradox. In this case, as far as punishment was concerned, the magistrates followed the law, imposing a compensation payment and a fine in accordance with the penalties listed in the village court handbook, and issuing an order threatening imprisonment when the fine was not paid.

Contrary to Chairman Andrew's representation of the snake bone case to me as custom by the singular virtue of its being about sorcery, I regard the salient customary aspect of this case as a broader and less-exotic phenomenon, which is also present in many other urban village court cases. It is manifest not in the offence itself but in the inter-ethnic tension generated by the marriage in the first place (between an eastern highlander and a southern highlander in this case), which the court could not really deal with directly. Chairman Andrew identified the underlying problem obliquely in his remark that had the sorcery attempt been successful it would have led to intergroup violence. During fieldwork I saw patterns of court appearances by individuals which were implicitly recognised by magistrates and the disputants themselves as manifestations of simmering inter-group tensions perpetuated through marriage links. In the village courts, they could usually only be dealt with according to the form in which they appeared—an assault, an accusation of theft, of non-repayment of a debt, an insult, and so on. It was likely that the snake bone case would prove with the passage of time to be just one of a continuing series of cases involving disputes of one sort or another between members of Sobe's group and Yaba's group, unhappy with a marriage which frustrated corporate preferences about alliance and exchange.

The snake bone case exemplifies the contradiction between the conditioned understanding of village court officials that they are to 'apply custom' and their legally and socially determined practice. This is not to deny what we might want to call the customary issues—that is, the wider social issues—which underlie many of the cases they deal with, but which are beyond the legal and *de facto* scope of their activities. Village courts share that particular relationship to custom with every other kind of court in PNG's formal legal system, which precludes it from being considered analytically in terms of the legislative distinction between the aims of village courts and those of other courts. As I noted earlier, Zorn has suggested that the customary process of 'dispute settlement' might better be termed 'dispute management', since chronic underlying problems are held at bay (but not solved) through dealing with particular manifestations from time to time (1992: 29–30). While aspects of the snake bone case resonate with that observation it should be noted that Zorn's typification of customary processes can also be applied to an extent to the legal processes of Western courts. In the latter, individual cases, dealt with as they arise (though often in sentencing after a conviction, in the light of past convictions), are frequently known by judges or magistrates and probation officers to be linked by underlying socioeconomic factors and community tensions beyond the control of the court.

What I witnessed in the snake bone case in Erima village court was in essence what I would have witnessed if the case had been heard in a district court in PNG: an attempt to establish whether a crime had been committed, to determine the guilt or innocence of the accused and to decide on a suitable punishment. Certainly, there were procedural elements which deviated from an ideal of formal legal procedure, and there was discernable manipulation and strategy employed by the magistrates to achieve a public recognition of Yaba's culpability and to reduce the burden of guilt on Mata, the immediate victim of the affair. But this, while commonsense and maybe creative, is hardly customary in the sense intended by the village court legislation, or by the rhetoric which preceded the establishment of the village court system.

A Verdict of Sorts

Returning to the matter of criticisms of the village courts on the grounds of their application of undesirable custom or their oppressive application or misapplication of the law, the discussion in this chapter suggests that rhetoric and polemic have overwhelmed careful research in conclusions about bad practice. Particularly in recent times there has been some hasty generalisation from scant evidence, and a less than rigorous use of concepts which require considerable interrogation. While represented by some as imposing undesirable custom, the village courts in practice have not fulfilled their originally intended customary function: village justice administered by village people in accordance with local tradition, free of what a Melanesian parliamentarian called 'European technicalities' (Chalmers 1978a: 267). This is not only a result of the unavoidable legalism of an instrument of justice established under an act of parliament, but is also due to the way that people at village level tended to interpret the coming of village courts. They wanted the village courts to be part of the introduced legal system, not customary courts, and village court officials see themselves as being at the foot of the hierarchy of courts in PNG.

Moreover, customary problems in village societies are still being dealt with in customary ways, and villagers see the village court as a separate arena of justice, to be utilised when custom fails or is inapplicable. To a large degree, 'unofficial courts' of the kind described by Marilyn Strathern (1972) before the advent of the village courts flourish as they did then. Nevertheless, something which could loosely be called custom does come into play in village courts, sometimes as simple common sense, or as a nuanced perception of the wider implications of disputes, as we saw in the snake bone case. However, this is not custom or customary law in the sense implied by the critics exemplified above. Overall, I do not share the optimism of, for instance, Zorn, that integration of introduced law and (changing) customary law through magistrates' flexibility in admitting testimony and in decision-making suggests ongoing creative blending of court and compromise models in pursuit of the aims of customary law (1990: 306).

If village courts have exhibited a significant shortcoming in their practice in the longer term, it has been the impossible attempt to systematically integrate introduced law and putative local custom. They fail largely because the state encourages the use of custom in theory, but demands selectivity in practice, while being unable to codify the country's diverse customs for juridical purposes, and unable to distinguish in advance the desirable from the undesirable (beyond an appeal to unspecified principles of humanity). While rhetoricians in PNG have continued to demand the implementation of the Constitutional demand for custom to be the underlying law, the problem presented to this project by the country's extreme cultural diversity remains to be solved. It is likely, therefore, that the law and custom problem will be perpetuated by official literature and critics, while the village courts will continue to extend introduced law into village society. Further, bringing together the discussion in this chapter with that of the previous one, there is much to suggest that village court officers are economically exploited as servants of the legal system. In this respect, the notion of custom, in the context of the operation of the village court system and considering the heavy workload and low pay of its officers, is ideological rather than a genuine constituent of village court praxis. That is to say, the ideology that village court officials (especially magistrates) are organic specialists in matters of custom and customary law, selected by the community and hearing disputes 'from time to time and place to place' has served to obscure their exploitation as poorly paid agents of the legal system at the lowest jurisdictional level.

Notes

1. Twelve village courts at Mendi were proclaimed 20 February 1975. Gazette No. 010.
2. 'Judge frees village court "victims"' was in fact the headline in *PNG Post-Courier*, 17 May 1989, p. 4.
3. Typical headlines of the period included: 'Mother of four set free' and 'Village courts discriminate against the female partner—[Justice] Woods' in *The Times of PNG*, 7 March 1991, p. 2; 'Jails are not sanctions to solve family problems' in *The Times of PNG*, 4 April 1991, p. 6; 'National Court frees village court "victims"' in *PNG Post-Courier*, 10 May 1991, p. 1; 'Highlands women have been unfairly treated by village courts—PNG Judges' in *The Times of PNG*, 18 July 1991 p. 2.
4. 'Natural Justice' in legal usage requires jurists to be fair and without bias and to give all parties to a dispute the opportunity to state their case adequately. In more technical terms, it involves two principles, or rules: *audi alteram partem* (hear the other side) and *nemo judex in re sua* (no man a judge in his own cause).
5. Village Courts Act 1973, s.37(1), (3), (4); 1989 s.68(1), (3), (4).
6. The review team consisted of four academics from the University of PNG, J. Aleck, H. Eyford, N. Faraclas and myself. In the highlands we visited village courts in the areas of Wabag (Enga Province), Mt Hagen (Western Highlands), Goroka and Kainantu (Eastern Highlands) and talked to Provincial officials, village court officials and village court users.
7. Seven village courts were proclaimed in Pangia on 19 August 1978.
8. See, for example, the claim by President of the Western Highlands Council of Women Paula Mek that women are 'always made to suffer judgments against them by village courts . . . we are victims all the time' (Kumugl 2001).
9. The author's fictional name for the court.
10. Reported in *The National*, 26 June 2003, editorial titled 'Village Courts lacking guidance, direction'.
11. This is not to suggest that the community did not recognise that Yaba was the real individual culprit. Responsibility in inter-group hostility is seen as corporate so far as vengeance or compensation is concerned.

4

THREE VILLAGE COURTS AND THEIR SOCIAL ENVIRONMENTS

In the three decades since their inception village courts have spread to most parts of PNG and there are now more than 1,100 in operation. As noted in chapter 3, contemporary anthropological studies of village courts have indicated that each court reflects the sociality of the particular local community it serves, and applies a complex integration of introduced law and local convention in its dispute-management procedures. In this chapter I give some indication of the particularity of village courts in describing three in the National Capital District, and the communities in which they operate. Village courts were quickly extended into urban areas after their introduction in the 1970s, where they mostly served settlement communities and traditional villages which had found themselves increasingly within the boundaries of expanding towns. In 1994 I began a project which has been ongoing till the present (though intermittently), monitoring three of these courts for comparative purposes.

While it is a popular convention to talk about PNG in terms of a rural-urban dichotomy, the movement of people around the country and the uneven rate of 'development' creates a much more complex demography. Movement back and forth between rural homeplaces and towns is common, and a significant proportion of the people apparently living in towns can be described as in fact bi-local (see Ryan 1970). While the movement back and forth is easier for some migrants than others, particularly when the distance travelled requires the expense of a plane trip across the country, even unemployed people in town occasionally manage to visit their homeplace. Accordingly, the three village courts introduced below should not be imagined as collectively typifying an urban, migrant, multi-ethnic social setting in contrast to a rural, traditional, 'tribal', subsistence-based society. One of them serves a traditional village on the edge of Port Moresby, and it is rare for an 'outsider' to appear in court. By contrast, another serves a part of the town with an extremely diverse population, ethnically representing many regions of the country, and a third serves a community whose members mostly identify ethnically with the eastern part of the Gulf Province. In the communities served by the latter two courts, kinship networks link people strongly to rural places, even for generations who were born and bred in town, and there is a great deal of movement between town and 'village'. These three communities together reflect the hybridity of PNG societies, in contrast to the putative dichotomy of a modern urban society and a traditional rural society, or alternatively the rural-urban continuum, which is suggested in popular representations of the country.

As village courts are embedded in these diverse communities generalisations about the courts, the cases they hear, and the way in which they deal with those cases cannot be extended to the country as a whole. Each of the three courts has its own distinctive characteristics, which is true of village courts across the country. Comparing these three courts and their social environment will show how the social context is reflected in the predominant types of cases which come to the court, and in the 'style' of the courts. Despite their significant differences, however, all three occupy the same position in terms of their juridical function in the community. None of them is customary or neo-customary, none of them serves as a significant source of information about 'custom' in the sense intended by John Kaputin and others in the mid 1970s (see chapters 1 and 2). They are not, strictly speaking, exactly a mediator between customary dispute-settlement mechanisms and legal courts, because they are, *de facto* and *de jure*, legal courts, by virtue of the exigencies discussed in chapter 3.

Pari, a Motu-Koita Village

Port Moresby is situated on the traditional territory of two intermarried peoples now often collective called the Motu-Koita, or Motu-Koitabu. The Motu, or more precisely the Western Motu, traditionally built their houses at the edge of the sea in lines extending out over the water. The Koita lived slightly inland. Before European contact a number of Koita groups became allied with five Motu villages (Hanuabada, Tanobada,

Tatana, Vabukori and Pari) close to where Port Moresby would develop and the two peoples had intermarried to a significant extent when Europeans first arrived. At that time the Western Motu were settled in a number of villages along about 50kms of the coast, separated from their coastal enemies, the Lakwaharu (now called the Eastern Motu), by an inlet (Oram 1981). Both the Motu and the Koita villages were divided into residential groups with a patrilineal descent idiom. These groups were, and are, called *iduhu*, a term popularly translated as 'clan', contrary to the caution of anthropologists (see Belshaw 1957: 13; Goddard 2001; Groves 1963; Seligman 1910).

Pari is a peri-urban coastal village on the eastern edge of Port Moresby containing a mixture of Motu and Koita people, though it identifies itself principally as Motuan. The largest village complex of the Western Motu is known as Hanuabada (Motu: 'big village'), a few kilometres west of Pari. Hanuabada is actually a collection of several villages which have become so close during their growth in the colonial period and afterwards that they appear more or less continuous. The land on which the early missionaries and subsequent colonial administrators first established themselves was close to Hanuabada, and was acquired by a process of trade which Europeans considered to be purchase, but which Hanuabadans, unused to the commodification of land, probably considered to be gifting in return for permission to reside there. The Motu-Koita were unprepared for the burgeoning European settlement which followed, and missionaries, administrative officials, traders and urban service providers were well established on Hanuabada land by the 1950s. By the Second World War Australians had come to regard the town as their own, but after the war Melanesian migrants began to move into Port Moresby in steadily increasing numbers. Since Independence and the departure of many Australians the population of what has become a city has been overwhelmingly Melanesian. The development of the city has resulted in increasing loss of traditional Motu-Koita land through infrastructural installations, the construction of modern office and shopping complexes and the spread of suburban housing.

Pari has been fortunate to observe the saga of Hanuabadan land loss from the periphery of the urban area and maintains a view of itself as 'traditional'. It proudly contrasts this with what it perceives as the loss of tradition and Motu identity in Hanuabada as the latter has been swallowed by the growing city. Older villagers are well rehearsed in the history of Pari, and combining their stories with various partial accounts by historians and other interested writers, we can give a reasonable well-rounded account of the village's origins and development. Legend has it that the village was founded after Kevau Dagora, the son of a woman who was the sole survivor of a massacre at nearby Taurama, avenged his forebears in a series of skirmishes with their enemies, the Lakwaharu. After a peace was established a Lakwaharu leader helped Kevau Dagora build a new village at a coastal place called Tauata (Oram 1981: 211; cf. Bulmer 1971: 45). The village came to be called *Pari*, which villagers discursively relate to the Motu word *paripari*, meaning 'wet'. They suggest the name connotes the plenitude of fish there and the wetness of villagers' throats from fish oil.[1] The anthropologist C. G. Seligman mapped Pari in about 1904 (1910: 46), plotting approximately sixty dwellings[2] and listing eight *iduhu*.

Traditionally the women of Pari made pots for trade (Bulmer 1982: 122) and the village was one of the Western Motu villages involved in the *hiri* (Motu: a westward trading voyage). *Hiri* were voyages undertaken until the middle of the twentieth century by Motu sailors to trade pots for sago produced in the Papuan Gulf. Historically, however, the identity of Pari as a community was grounded in its specialisation in tuna fishing, chartered by the *kidukidu* (Motu: tuna) legend of the village. According to the story a woman called Uguta Vaina, pregnant to her husband Vagi Boge, secretly gave birth to five tuna on the shore of a bay near the village, and suckled them there daily. One of the fish was discovered by Vagi Boge and killed in ignorance of its parentage (an act of filicide). To save the rest, Uguta Vaina sent them out to sea, and then disclosed their provenance to Vagi Boge, who issued a set of moral principles to be followed by villagers to ensure the return of the tuna (Ikupu 1930; Kidu 1976; Pulsford 1975). This was understood to have been the genesis of a seasonal phenomenon whereby huge schools of tuna would swim into their natal bay, to be easily caught by Pari fishermen. Tuna fishing and its preparatory and attendant rituals took up a large part of the year, and social conduct in the village was held to influence its relative success or failure (Kidu 1976; Pulsford 1975).

Like a number of other villages in the region, Pari came under the influence of the London Missionary Society (LMS) before Papua was officially colonised,[3] with a resulting atrophy over several decades of much traditional dancing ritual and other activity (Oram 1976: 59, 1989: 56) although Motuans continued the *hiri* and its associated rituals for some decades against the wishes of missionaries. In recent decades the United Church (successor to the LMS) has dominated in the village. By the 1960s only older males without jobs in town attended the fishing rituals, and there was no fishing on Sundays (Pulsford 1975: 112). In 1970 an observer commented that 'most of the students who return to Pari at holiday times take no active part in the traditional dancing performed by their elders, but watch in embarrassment from the side lines' (Biddulph

1970: 23). By the mid 1970s the fishing rituals had been replaced by ritual blessing of fishing nets in church (Pulsford 1975: 109). When I began research in the village in the 1990s the rituals had disappeared, although older villagers were still enthusiastically reminiscing about them. Pari's identity as a fishing village has also been affected by the decline of the shellfish beds in the area, under pressure from an increasing population and the proximity of the town (Swadling 1982: 308–9).

During the Second World War, Pari village was evacuated, like most of the Western Motu villages (Robinson 1979: 101–10; Tarr 1973). Its population was temporarily shifted to a site near Gaire, further east of Port Moresby (Tarr 1973), and able-bodied men were taken to work for the Australian military. The period was not only socially disruptive but took a mortal toll as a lack of gardening resources and poor nutrition made evacuees vulnerable to illness. The village's population, a little less than 600 in the early 1940s, was only 477 at the end of the war (22). After the war the village (which had meanwhile been looted by Australian soldiers for timber and garden produce) was substantially rebuilt (Tarr 1973). Trade goods became more available and employment opportunities for villagers increased in the growing town of Port Moresby. Long contact with missionaries and proximity to Port Moresby and technical training opportunities contributed to increasing numbers of males becoming involved in non-traditional work, such as teaching, pastoring, carpentry and other trades, and Pari men, like those in other Motu-Koita villages, became literate and well-qualified tradesmen and followed professional careers earlier than most other Papuan peoples (Oram 1976: 52–57).

By 1970 Pari was linked to the Port Moresby water supply and there was a bus service into town (Biddulph 1970: 23). Ian and Diana Maddocks, who operated a medical clinic in the village for a period in the late 1960s and the 1970s, noted that in 1971 '85% of adult men in the clinic population work in the town of Port Moresby, mostly in artisan positions. 26% of women are employed, mainly as clerical assistants or shop assistants' (1972: 227). A map by Maddocks in 1974 shows almost 100 dwellings (1974). In 1969 a census calculated 937 residents (1972: 225). By 1990, according to census figures,[4] this had increased to just over 2000. By this time Pari was said to have seventeen *iduhu*. One of these was identified as an *iduhu* of Gulf people, an unusual occurrence in a Motu-Koita village. Gulf migrants (called 'Kerema', after a major town in the Gulf Province, by the Motu-Koita villagers) first came to the village in the 1920s as guests of one of the *iduhu*—a relationship based on pre-colonial trading partnerships between Pari and some Gulf villages. Interestingly the relationship with them was emphasised to me by modern Motu villagers more than connections with Koita (cf. Oram 1976: 57–58). Pari has remained a fairly insular community even though the village is only six kilometres by a sealed road from the industrial suburb of Badili and less than nine kilometres from downtown Port Moresby.

The results of early contact by the LMS are clearly evident. The LMS used Pacific Islanders, especially Polynesians, as local area missionaries and teachers (the first Papuan to be ordained by the LMS was Mahuru Gaudi, from Pari village, in 1884). A large church and an adjacent community hall dominate the centre of Pari, and were built with the proceeds of church donation competitions which have become institutionalised in a number of Motu villages and are known in Motu as *bou bou* (traditionally meaning 'gather'). Christopher Gregory (1982) charges the LMS and United Church with great transformational influence on Motu villages, particularly Poreporena (an alternative name for Hanuabada) village close to downtown Port Moresby, suppressing the traditional gift exchange system and usurping the power of traditional leaders. 'They have been replaced by church deacons, the "neo-big-men" of the new gift exchange system that has been established by the church in order to raise money. It was the rise of these men that saved the clan (*iduhu*) system from collapsing.' (206; cf. Groves 1954). Church collections were introduced in 1889 by the LMS, and nearly all Motu village churches were financially supporting their own pastors by 1919 (Oram 1989: 66). It is likely that the combined impact of the LMS and wage labour made necessary by the introduced cash economy was significantly affecting traditional forms of sociality, if not the basic social structure, before the Second World War (Oram 1976: 61; cf. Oram 1989: 56, 64–65). Oram points out that before the war church organisation was based on the *iduhu*, which retained its importance. 'Traditional leaders lost some of their prestige as they were no longer required to perform ritual functions at feasts and other ceremonies, but the leaders who achieved leadership in new situations gained support from kinship and other traditional bases' (1976: 61).

In the face of the growing city and its influences, Pari village as a community has attempted to preserve a sense of its own identity as a 'traditional' Motu-Koita village. It does this in a number of ways including the politicising of language, a tendency it shares with most other coastal Motu villages, including Hanuabada, in privileging its traditional language against *lingue franche*. As Port Moresby is predominantly a migrant town a majority of its people speak PNG's main *lingua franca*, Tokpisin. A large part of Papua has its own *lingua franca*, known in colonial times as Police Motu but renamed 'Hiri' Motu at the end of the colonial period. This was originally developed from a simplified version of the Motu language.[5] The mother language is commonly referred to as 'Pure' Motu. Older Motu villagers typically demonstrate a disdain for Tokpisin, which they regard as a crude language spoken by the uneducated. They regard 'Hiri' Motu as a necessary compromise in communicating with other Papuan groups but do not encourage its use among themselves. Most Motu-Koita are fluent in English, the language of missionaries and of Western education, and prefer to use it when communicating with non-Motu speakers. Their pride in Pure Motu is historically reinforced by its having been recognised by early missionaries as an acceptable vehicle for the transmission of Christianity (see Garrett 1985: 211). Due to the long history of intermarriage with their immediate inland neighbours, coastal Motu villages have a significant Koita presence, marked by a number of nominally Koita *iduhu*, and more subtly by the weight of genealogical connections. However, Motu dominates Koita linguistically as the spoken language.[6]

Pari also retains the *iduhu* system as a principle of social organisation. Mature villagers trace genealogies back to the eighteenth century, using a patrilineal idiom which admits cognatic elements. Through these means they link themselves to classical *iduhu* and *iduhu* leaders and identify with contemporary *iduhu* generated by fission, fusion and migration. *Iduhu* leaders inherit their position through agnatic primogeniture as a general rule. While many of the activities and symbols expressive of *iduhu* identity described nearly a century ago by Seligman (1910: 49–65) have long since disappeared, the corporate nature of *iduhu* in modern Pari remains the same as that implied in his explanations of descent, inheritance and marriage tendencies (66–91), and described in detail by Murray Groves half a century later (1963).

The village also takes pride in having retained its land, apart from an inland section about a kilometre and a half from the village area which it sold in the late colonial period and which is now the site of Taurama military barracks. The city has engulfed the Hanuabada area, and its suburbs have stretched several miles inland, but there is a clear stretch of land between its south-east suburbs and Pari village. In maintaining its general landholding the village has preserved in particular the geographical provenance of its moral identity, on the shores of Oyster Bay: the site known as Daugolata, where Uguta Vaina suckled her tuna children. But Pari has also strengthened its sense of being a 'traditional' Motu-Koita community through its Christianity. Christianity has become a tradition in itself since its introduction in the late nineteenth century. This is despite, for example, the persistence of sorcery as a powerful force in Motu society (as it is throughout Melanesia) and Pari villagers' suspicions that various individuals in the community are engaged in such activity, which demonstrates the resilience of non-Christian beliefs. Photographs and documents from the early days of colonialism have been preserved by some villagers with pride, including copies of a photograph of the village's original limestone church building. Church-related activities abound in modern Pari, where elected deacons head activity groups comprised of clusters of families. In former times the need for appropriate behaviour to ensure the success of tuna fishing had underpinned the village's sense of itself as a moral community. Social behaviour was believed to have a bearing on the number of fish which would return each season to be corralled and caught (Kidu 1976; Pulsford 1975: 111). In the course of the past century and a quarter the birth of Christ has replaced the death of tuna as the focus of the village's moral identity. United Church codes of morality have become a familiar discourse among villagers.

The early acceptance of Christianity, the self-conscious privileging of Pure Motu language and the retention of land, including a focal mythic site, are major factors in the retention and regeneration of Pari's perception of itself as a tradition-oriented moral community. Yet, ironically, the maintenance of this perception requires the negotiation of contradictions grounded particularly in the village's amenability to Christianity and the colonial presence. Christianity and church-oriented social activities nourished the moral identity which could have been lost with the decline of ritualised tuna fishing, but Christianity also provided educational opportunities and associated technical training which facilitated the villagers' access to more material and profane colonial resources. Pari's orientation to 'tradition' is not so rigid that the culture of commodities is rejected or the allure of urban sociality resisted altogether. Nor are the villagers collectively a model of Christian morality. Even church deacons are susceptible to Port Moresby's profane attractions.

Like most other Motu villages, alcohol and gambling are leisure activities, and older villagers express some anxiety over young people's drinking and its disruptive effect on the community at weekends. This is not a new phenomenon: alcohol became legally available to Papua New Guineans in 1962 (and had been obtainable, illegally, previously). Ian and Diana Maddocks wrote of the injuries treated at their village clinic in the late 1960s that 'severe lacerations were often *alcohol-related*, stemming from fights which arose in drinking groups. Many young men, reserved or even withdrawn when sober, become violent when drunk' (1977: 112, emphasis in original). There are no legal liquor outlets in the village, but beer is easily obtainable in the city, and a small degree of black-marketeering of beer through village tradestores is countenanced as a commonsense acknowledgement of the inevitability of village men wanting to drink alcohol. Compared to alcohol consumption and related violence in the adjacent city, Pari's problem with alcohol is relatively slight. Nevertheless, the community regards drunkenness as particularly vexing. Not only can it result in fighting among drinkers but it loosens tongues. Polite, restrained language gives way to obscenity and the expression of normally private resentments.

Pari Village Court

Pari village court held weekly meetings in the village's pile-elevated community hall when I first began attending in the early 1990s. The hall had been built some years previously and was becoming dilapidated due to a lack of finance for its upkeep. By 1999 the hearings had shifted to the area underneath the hall's raised floor. Tables and chairs were set up especially for court hearings and a national flag was hung behind the magistrates' bench. In a small community such as Pari, anonymity is impossible, and gossip networks ensure that offences are public knowledge, sometimes within minutes of their occurrence. On court days the names of disputants were called out loudly across the village by the village court clerk prior to the beginning of proceedings. For any villagers accused of wrongdoing there was thus no escape from public knowledge and scrutiny. Proceedings opened and closed with a Christian prayer. Disputants sat on a bench directly in front of the magistrates' table, and those waiting for their cases to be heard sat with other interested parties a small distance beyond. The court had a more orderly atmosphere in fact than a typical PNG district court: even the reference numbers of cases to be heard were read out from the summons forms by the court clerk. All those involved conducted themselves with emotional restraint, politeness and deference. Magisterial condemnations of the actions of those found guilty at Pari were delivered in a tone which never exceeded gentle reproach, in comparison to the occasional fulminations of officials in the other courts I attended.

As disputes between individuals or groups in Pari are essentially between more-or-less kin-related people living in close proximity, they are mostly dealt with in forums connected with the Church, whose social organisation is articulated with kin-group relations as noted above. The church forum provides a relatively informal and private way of managing problems within the village, safe from the gaze of outsiders, since formal records are not kept. Family problems and similar frictions are often dealt with through mediation by church deacons. Consequently, since there are few 'outsiders' in the village, and few outright 'crimes', Pari village court deals with a low caseload compared to other village courts in the Port Moresby area. Some of the magistrates at Pari were church deacons in fact, and some others were aspirants to positions of prestige in the Church. No *iduhu kwaradia* (*iduhu* heads: patrilineal inheritors of *iduhu* leadership) were village court magistrates, reflecting an attitude that Pari village court did not deal with the kinds of problems regarded as 'customary'. These were the realm of *iduhu kwaradia* (see chapter 5). The village court is the most formal of Pari's dispute-settling resources. Three to five magistrates sat on each case. Scrupulous in attempting to be unbiased, each magistrate would occasionally leave the bench during a day's hearing, declaring himself to be related to a disputant. A large number of the cases heard while I was monitoring the court were related to drunkenness, mostly among young men, and were often the result of complaints by mature women that they had been insulted by the behaviour and obscene language of drunkards. Drunkenness in Pari rarely involved serious fighting beyond clumsy brawls, but mostly led to rowdy behaviour, bad language and bottle smashing. The incidents were essentially disturbances of the peace, or offences against the greater community.

In the case of drunkenness, the public description of their behaviour and obscene language by the offended women in court, repeated by the magistrates with deliberate clarity, was highly embarrassing for the now sober, polite young men. Magistrates tended to make a point of repeating the alleged obscenities several times. A women's Christian fellowship group held meetings in the nearby church at the same time as the village court hearings. They sang *peroveta* ('prophet' songs), whose exquisite harmonies and beatific lyrics drifted across the main village area, providing a sonic background against which the revisited obscenities of the accused sounded all the worse. Asked for an explanation of their utterances, the offenders were commonly reduced to ashamedly mumbling that they were drunk and had not meant what they had said. The magistrates could prolong the young men's discomfort by asking for clarification of the meaning of an obscene metaphor they had used, or for an explanation of why they had addressed their remarks to the particular female complainants, bringing the ordeal to an end with a moral lecture invariably referring to self and mutual respect, and rhetorically asking what the offender had learned at school. A nominal fine (usually K5) was imposed. The final gesture of reparation was a public handshake between the complainant and the accused, after which both parties ritually shook hands with all court officials.

The strategy of the magistrates in dealing with these complaints reflected the village's self-identification as a peaceful, Christian, moral community, and was aimed at the restoration of respectful social interaction rather than at punitive attempts to stamp out drunkenness. Older male villagers, including the magistrates, conceded that they had once been young and careless themselves, that many of them enjoyed alcohol and were still susceptible to its intoxicating effects. It would be hypocritical, they said, to visit heavy penalties on youthful drunks. They were also concerned not to alienate young people by the imposition of stringent rules about alcohol consumption and severe penalties for drunkenness, for fear of driving the young people from the village into the city and undermining the solidarity of Pari as a community.

It is difficult to ascertain, from early descriptions of Motu-Koita society, whether public responses to offensive or disruptive behaviour within villages have always been restorative, rather than punitive. Seligman's early account of the Koita (which extended to the Motu) represented them as mild in disposition, while at the same time he alluded to violent physical retaliation, as well as the employment of sorcery, against offences such as theft (1910: 133). Sorcery, a secret activity, remains prevalent beneath Pari's self-conscious Christian lawfulness and is a powerful sanction, but restorative strategies have become institutionalised as the appropriate way to deal with offences against individuals or the community. While the village court is a legal institution, it can be seen that in Pari it is more than a forum for dispute settlement. The manner of its dispute settlement is a reflection of the particular Motu-Koita identity which Pari village is trying to maintain and which it expresses through a neo-traditional morality centred around the integration of Christianity into its sociality. Through the regular public ritual of explicit descriptions of drunken behaviour and obscene language precipitating shame and expiation week by week in the village court, Pari reconciles itself with its susceptibility to the profane temptations of urban modern sociality, represented by the nearby city. To summarise, the colonially created village court has not only come to reflect the juridical attitude of the formal district court, but has been appropriated into Pari's sociality as a restorative, rather than punitive, resource, reflecting a commitment to the Christian ideal of non-punitive justice. Of the three courts I monitored, Pari, and the community it served, displayed the 'harmony' which Nader has called an inherent component of social organisations and of ideologies that can evolve as a consequence of colonial political and religious policies (1990: 2). Harmony ideologies, says Nader, may be used to suppress peoples by socialising them towards conformity in colonial contexts, or they may be used to resist external control (291). Both these tendencies are visible in the history and contemporary sociality of Pari village.

The Social Environment of Konedobu Village Court

Konedobu village court is named after the suburb in which it is located, and which was the site of the colonial Administration headquarters. The court mostly serves the inhabitants of four settlements near downtown Port Moresby locally known as Ranuguri, Vainakomu (also called Ginigini), Vanama and Paga. Port Moresby's settlements are commonly misrepresented in the popular media (and in some academic literature) as the squatter habitats of maladjusted unemployed migrants who live in poverty and who are mostly responsible for the country's urban 'law and order' problem. The findings of properly conducted research in settlements over a number of decades show that this categorisation is quite misleading (see, for example, Barber 2003; Goddard 2005; Jackson 1976: 49; 1977: 32; Umezaki and Ohtsuka 2003). Contrary to popular portrayals of settlement-dwellers as transient 'squatters', workers living in formal housing estates are often more transient than people in some of the long-established settlements (which could be better described, perhaps, as informal housing areas). The settlements contain people in all manner of employment, both formal and informal, including politicians, public servants, shopkeepers, secretaries and clerks. It is useful at this point to give some history of the settlements that Konedobu village court serves, as they are among Port Moresby's oldest.

The biggest settlement in the Konedobu area is Ranuguri, which provides a handy model for an overview of the development of urban settlements in the immediate post-war period.[7] For that reason it is described historically here in more detail than the other three settlements in the area. *Ranuguri* is a Motu word meaning a spring or water well. The settlement came into existence in 1946 at the inland end of Spring Garden Road, which was constructed shortly after Port Moresby was first established, in 1885, as the capital town of the British Protectorate of Papua (Oram 1976: 20–26; Stuart 1970: 41–44). The area was the site of a traditional spring, at which a settlement of Koita people had existed in the nineteenth century (Belshaw 1957: 11; Norwood 1984: 54). The spring, at the foot of a local landmark known by Europeans as Burns Peak, still served as a local water supply for modern settlers during the wet season in the early 1990s.

The ground which Ranuguri settlement occupies is partly government-owned land purchased during negotiations between the British administrators and Motu-Koita landowners in 1885 and 1886 (Oram 1976: 23–24), and partly customary land (UPNG 1973: 5; Norwood 1984: 54). The settlement was established when migrant workers from the Gulf district were invited to move into buildings abandoned by the

Australian army at the end of the Second World War. According to Dawn Ryan (1970: 19) the arrangement was intended as a temporary measure by the Administration while it built proper housing for employees, but the settlement quickly grew with passing time. While this suggests that the Administration itself told the settlers to move into the buildings, there is equivocation among the settlers over who issued the invitation. I was told by a long-term settler that the customary (Motu-Koita) landholders invited his people to take over the buildings. His interpretation was predicated on the old trading relationships between Motu and Gulf people, and on an established pattern of Motuans inviting individuals from their trading partner groups to settle on their land (this is the case with Vainakomu and Vanama settlements, see below). As the buildings were constructed by colonisers on 'government land', the settler's interpretation also evokes the question of whether customary landholders recognised land deals with the early colonial administrations as outright sales, or interpreted them as matters of permitting land use for an unspecified period.

While some settlements in Port Moresby have developed a wide mix of ethnic groups from different parts of the country, Ranuguri has remained until very recently (see below) overwhelmingly a community of Gulf people, originating almost exclusively from the Malalaua district, in the east of the Gulf Province. They often refer to themselves collectively as 'East Kerema', following a common tendency in Port Moresby to identify people in relation to the larger towns (in this case Kerema) of their province of origin. The Ranuguri community is subdivided into smaller groups, identifying themselves respectively as Toaripi, Moveave, Miaru, Karama and Lese. Toaripi is a tribal grouping, and nowadays a council district, situated around the mouth of the Lakekamu River on the Gulf coast, and Moveave people live in the hinterland. Lese and Miaru are names used to refer to village clusters in the Moripi council district south-east of Toaripi. Karama is, likewise, a village name used metonymically to refer to a cluster of villages on the coast west of Toaripi.[8] Central District people sometimes refer to the Malalauans collectively as 'Toaripi' (as well as 'Kerema'). According to Dawn Ryan there is a tradition of hostility between Toaripi and Moveave people relating to early land struggles (1965: 5), but I found no evidence of significant hostility in Ranuguri settlement. The Moripi people traditionally enjoyed a reasonable relationship with the neighbouring Toaripi, with occasional enmity and apprehension of sorcery between them (5). It is not clear which subgroup were the original settlers of Ranuguri. Elderly men from both the Moveave and Toaripi contingents told me their kin were the 'first' people to move in.

In addition to being traditional trading partners of the Motu people, the Malalauans, and particularly the Toaripi, developed trading relationships with colonial Port Moresby before the Second World War. This followed a complex history of contact with missionaries, miners and British and Australian Administration agents which resulted in a significant break with traditional ritual life, especially under missionary influence (the missionary James Chalmers arrived in the area in 1881, and the LMS predominated). Ryan, in the 1960s, noted that the Toaripi showed 'a reluctance to dwell on details of the old way of life' (1965: 9). During the war many men from the Toaripi area served as carriers and labourers for the Australian army, and learned skills such as plumbing, building and painting. At the end of the war they began to drift into Port Moresby looking for work and negotiating with Motu-Koita landowners for places to build homes. Often working as independent subcontractors in the public works field, they employed their own kin and affines, resulting in growing clusters of related people around the city (1970: 20). They quickly became the largest settler group within the Port Moresby area. Oram (1964: 41) estimated that in 1964 three-quarters of the town's settlement dwellers were migrants from the Gulf District. In 1963 and 1964 Ryan counted 1,310 Toaripi scattered through Port Moresby. Nineteen per cent of these lived in public service housing, twenty-two per cent in housing provided by private employers and fifty-nine per cent in settlements (Ryan 1970: 18).

According to some Ranuguri informants the originally invited settlers had been living in buildings on the site already, employed by the Australian army during the war.[9] The settlers tore down the army buildings, and replaced them with dwellings more to their liking. The settlement followed a common pattern of growth; original settlers invited kin to stay, and gradually more houses sprang up. Other migrants from the same general area, but different local groups, arrived and set up neighbouring blocks of houses. Over time the different groups arranged themselves territorially within the settlement area, roughly reproducing the geographical relationships of their natal groups in Malalaua, with roads and walkways marking boundaries between them. In 1973 a University of PNG research group counted ninety-five dwellings in Ranuguri and gave its population as 770 (UPNG 1973: 3). In 1982 Norwood mooted a population of 740, in 125 houses (1984: 54). By 1994 there were more than 150 houses. Periodic population counts can give only a rough impression of community size as settlement members tend to be mobile, moving back and forth between their 'home' area and the settlement, and also between settlements, visiting and staying with kin. The increase in the number of households did, however, indicate that Ranuguri had become a well-established community.

Towards the end of the colonial period the Administration came to accept that migrant settlements were an unavoidable part of urban growth, and efforts were made to improve conditions in some of the established settlements. The sections of Ranuguri on government land were upgraded in the mid 1970s in a program which included the improvement of the inland end of Spring Garden Rd to provide vehicular access, the provision of concrete footpaths and street lighting and advice to settlers on improving their houses (Norwood 1984: 54, 99, 101). In subsequent years, as Administration personnel vacated office buildings adjacent to the settlement and shifted to a new complex in the suburb of Waigani, Ranuguri residents moved quickly to strip the buildings of useful materials for their own houses. In the mid 1990s the entrance to Ranuguri was an odd landscape of iron skeletons of office buildings while the settlement itself was a marvel of architectural bricolage.

Ranuguri exemplifies the complex economic profile of most settlement communities in Port Moresby, with a wide range of occupations, both formal and informal, represented in the population. Some residents have long-term skilled and semi-skilled labouring positions on the waterfront and in stores and business premises in the downtown area, and support extended families. Bilocality is common among Ranuguri's inhabitants, and integrates elements of urban and rural economic activities. Settlers occasionally trade, for instance, in vegetables from their home areas. Norwood's assessment in 1982 that 75 per cent of the men of working age were employed (1984: 54) remained accurate in 1994, given the analytically confusing synthesis of 'formal' and 'informal' economic activity which typifies settlement communities like Ranuguri. Small-scale gardening is widespread, though often frustrated by problems with the water supply during Port Moresby's dry season. In 1994 the water supply problem (taps are provided in the settlement) was particularly acute, as it was with other downtown settlements (see the account of Vanama settlement, below).

There is a strong United Church presence, and the centrally-sited community church, a largish building preserved from the Second World War, is a focal point. Community members take some pride in claiming (not entirely accurately) that they are extremely law-abiding,[10] and point to a relative absence of alcohol consumption as a major contribution to the peaceful atmosphere of Ranuguri. Over a period of time there has been intermarriage among the different groups (mostly with virilocal post-marital residence) and some intermarriage of settlement dwellers with local Motu-Koita. All these factors contributed to Ranuguri settlement being a close-knit community enjoying a reasonable relationship with the large Motu-Koita village complex of Hanuabada nearby and having, relative to a number of other settlements around Port Moresby, a reputation for being fairly free of 'law and order' problems, in the early 1990s.

In recent years the character of Ranuguri has begun to change. Towards the end of 1994 the inhabitants of Ranuguri settlement learned that a highway was to be built connecting Port Moresby International Airport to downtown Port Moresby. Ranuguri settlement was said to be directly in its path. After surviving for half a century, and being dependent on their proximity to the downtown area and its formal and informal employment opportunities for their urban livelihood, the settlers faced the possibility of eviction, or at best relocation out of town, at the stroke of a town planner's pen. At the end of 1996 the earthworks for what was to be known as the Poreporena Highway obliterated a number of buildings surviving from the old Administration complex at Konedobu, but missed the edge of the settlement by a matter of metres.

Whatever relief Ranuguri settlers may have felt was quickly displaced when proposals for feeder roads were made public. The fate of Ranuguri continued to be equivocal, as the provision and placement of feeder roads was debated against financial considerations and local (Motu-Koita) landowner concerns. The final position of the feeder roads spared the settlement dwellers in one respect, as they were not required to move. But the exercise created vacant areas of land where there had previously been bush or old buildings, and the settlement was now fully visible from the new highway. New arrivals began to take advantage of the vacant land, and the insular, long-established residents found themselves flanked by strangers from other regions, particularly the highlands. Ranuguri settlement was undergoing a transformation in its social organisation. Sadly, the provision of the highway also destroyed the spring from which the settlement took its name, and which for more than fifty years had been providing the settlers with fresh water supplementing unreliable town water supplies.

Less than a kilometre from Ranuguri is the younger Vanama settlement, hidden from view by the offices and printing plant of PNG's oldest daily newspaper, the Post-Courier, and some small industrial premises. Vanama is on customary Motu-Koita land and began its life in the early 1960s. Its name is a shortened form of *vanamage*, a Koita word meaning a pleasant breeze. Lohia Doriga, a Koita man, is locally acknowledged to have been the owner of the land, and moved onto it from nearby Hanuabada village to consolidate his control in about 1950. In recognition of old family trading relationships he gave an east Kerema family permission to settle on the land, and the settlement grew with the arrival of more migrants from the Gulf area.[11] In this respect the development of Vanama, with subgroups of people from different village clusters in the Gulf Province, has been similar to that of Ranuguri and of most settlements dominated by Gulf district migrants. A wider geographical selection of Gulf Province societies is represented in Vanama than in Ranuguri, with people from Kikori (western Gulf), Orokolo, Karama and Sepoe (eastern Gulf), arranged territorially within the settlement. A small rent was paid to the Motu-Koita landholders in the settlement's early years but gradually lapsed.

Vanama has not grown to the size of Ranuguri. In 1982 Norwood recorded seventy houses (1984: 43) and by the mid 1990s there were still less than one hundred households. As the settlement is not on government land it has not been subject to any official upgrading programmes and does not have noticeable internal boundary markers like the sealed roads and footpaths of Ranuguri. Over a period of time a few people from the highlands, Goilala, Samurai and the Morobe Province were allowed by Lohia Doriga to join the settlement, but it has remained relatively free of interethnic tension or any other behavioural problems. This has been largely due to the authority of the resident landlord, who could deal with troublesome people simply by evicting them, as all the settlement dwellers are dependent on the landlord's goodwill in the absence of rent arrangements. Friction with the landlord, for instance, resulted in the departure of the Morobe group in the late 1980s. Lohia Doriga, who had been the chairing magistrate of the Konedobu village court in the latter part of his life, died in 1990, and his son Dirona Lohia (also a village court magistrate) took over residential control of the settlement. Dirona Lohia maintained the same relationship with settlers that his father had, though he told me he was thinking about putting part of the land to commercial use, perhaps developing its real estate potential (which would involve evicting settlers), and had curtailed the influx of new settlers.

The community has a number of water taps but due to the unreliable state of Port Moresby's water-supply system water is a problem. For the latter half of 1994 none came through the pipes and Vanama people were forced to obtain water from sources outside the settlement. The most visible activity during my visits at that time was a constant trickle of people along the access road with buckets and plastic containers, and the occasional arrival of utility trucks with large drums of water. The water problems make crop production an unreliable source of income, although Vanama had, in 1994, more extensive gardens than Ranuguri. A reasonable number of the male inhabitants were employed in the downtown Port Moresby area, but in relatively unskilled positions which did not guarantee long-term security. As Vanama is a younger settlement than Ranuguri its residents have not enjoyed the same long-established integration into the downtown workforce, and there is more formal unemployment among them, but among the residents from the Gulf Province (who are in the majority) there is a significant degree of bilocality, and betelnut is brought back from the home province and sold as a source of income. With the landlord in residence, Vanama is a quiet community which, like Ranuguri, receives very little publicity regarding 'law and order' issues or welfare issues, compared to a number of other settlements around the city.[12]

Vainakomu is a small area of land a few hundred metres west of Ranuguri traditionally owned by a Motu-Koita family in Hanuabada. A small group of Motu-Koita describing themselves as descendants of the original owners now live at the foot of a ridge of Burns Peak, just off Spring Garden Road, at a place whose name on formal documents and maps is given as Kinikini. Local people pronounce the name *Ginigini*, which is a Motu word meaning a thorn, and they commonly refer to nearby Vainakomu settlement also as Ginigini, by extension. The settlement is accessible by a track from Ginigini and in the early 1990s was hidden from general view in a small valley behind the old Konedobu administration complex. The name Vainakomu is interpreted by local people as a compound of two Motu words; *vaina*, a small string bag, and *komu*, to conceal oneself. I was told a legend about a woman gardening on the land in former times who temporarily left the garden but neglected to take her string bag with her because it was hidden among plants. While she was away, someone set a fire which destroyed both the garden and her bag.

Like Ranuguri and Vanama, Vainakomu's development began with an invitation to a family from the Gulf district to settle on the land. Norwood (who records the settlement's name, incorrectly, as Mailakoum) gives the date of settlement as 1967, when a Mr Nohore was invited by a woman called Kiowa Koke to build a house on the land, in recognition of previous hospitality to her late husband (1984: 56). These details were disputed by Ginigini residents with whom I spoke who represented themselves as descendants of the original land owners. They said the first settler was a man called Haro (Nohore, they said, was second), at the invitation of a woman called Geua Vani.[13] The settlement remained very small by the 1990s, and consisted of two groups of people from the western part of the Gulf Province. The first group (as one approached from Ginigini) originated from Kiuru and comprised a dozen households. A little further on were six households originating from Vailala.

The early settlers gave tributary items to the landlord (Vainakomu people have extensive gardens), but the system has now lapsed. As the settlement is tiny and on customary land it has received little attention from urban authorities and has never been upgraded (i.e. provided with basic infrastructure or advice on self-development). Like the Ranuguri settlers, Vainakomu residents scavenged materials from disused Administration buildings nearby to maintain and improve their houses. The profile of Vainakomu given in Norwood's survey of Port Moresby settlements (1984: 56) remained substantially the same in the mid 1990s. It was a small, stable community of which the majority of adult males were employed in labouring or semi-skilled jobs in the downtown area. As the settlers were from 'west Kerema' rather than 'east Kerema' they remained a little insulated from the neighbouring settlement of east Kerema people, and had come under the influence of the Seventh Day Adventist Church in contrast with Ranuguri and Vanama whose residents, like most Papuan communities originally Christianised by the LMS, are dominated by its successor the United Church. The construction of the Poreporena Highway and its feeder roads in the 1990s was of great concern to the Vainakomu settlers. Previously their settlement could only be reached by a foot track extending from the rear of a group of houses including that of their customary landlord. They were thus well hidden from public view and untroubled by unwelcome outsiders. However, one of the highway's feeder roads ran close to Vainakomu, making them easily accessible and vulnerable to encroachment by outsiders, although the proximity of the customary landowner continued to act as a deterrant to squatters.

The fourth settlement served by Konedobu village court is Paga. Paga Hill, at the tip of the finger of land which is now downtown Port Moresby, was one of a few pieces of land in the area acquired without payment by the colonial Administration at the beginning of the twentieth century. Regarded by Papuans at the time as a useless place of 'rocks and stones', the land was taken by the Administration as 'waste and vacant' in 1901 (Oram 1976: 24). Its higher slopes on the inland side gradually became an elite housing area overlooking the downtown area. On another side some industrial development took place and the top of the hill became a popular tourist lookout in the late colonial period while the town's waste was dumped into the sea on the furthest side from town. That side was known as Paga Point, and was too steep on its lower slopes for colonial residential or industrial purposes. *Paga* is a Motu word meaning shoulder, and a popular humorous story tells that the hill acquired its name at the beginning of the colonial period when a European wanting to identify the area grabbed a local man by the shoulder and asked, 'What is this called?'. The traditional name for Paga Point is *Elakurukuru*, also a Motu term (*kurukuru* is commonly used to refer to a point of land, the bow of a canoe, or a nose) but has been superceded by the 'official' colonial term.

Norwood (1984: 44) names a Mr Mairi Nakaia, a 'night soil collector', as the first settler in the 1960s, building a shelter on the lower slopes of Paga Point so he could look after his employer's equipment there. Settlement residents told me however that the original settler was Papua Amogoa, the driver for a sewage disposal contractor.[14] To enable him to guard the contractor's equipment he was permitted by the city authorities to live temporarily in a concrete gun emplacement which had been built during the Second World War above the sewage disposal pipe at Paga Point, with the assurance that he would be found proper accommodation. The alternative accommodation was not forthcoming, however, so in 1969 Amogoa built his own shelter nearby with the aid of kin. During the next few years he was joined by kin and by other downtown workers, predominantly members of the waterside workers union, and Paga Point developed into a settlement. Although Papua Amogoa was from Kikori in the western Gulf Province he did not live at Paga by arrangement with a customary landowner, and the settlement did not develop in its early life as an exclusive community of Gulf people like Ranuguri, Vanama and Vainakomu. People from the Southern Highlands and the Central Province joined the settlement on the basis of their acquaintance with Amogoa and their working proximity. In more recent years contingents from Simbu and Goroka Provinces, in the highlands, have expanded the community.

Lohia Doriga, the landowner at Vanama, became a patron of the Paga settlement as it grew. Norwood described the settlers as being 'under the (erroneous) impression that he [Lohia Doriga] has land rights' (1984: 44). The late Doriga's son, Dirona Lohia, however insisted to me in 1994 that Doriga really was the landowner.[15] Older settlers told me that Lohia Doriga claimed the land at the base of Paga Point on the seaward side after the war, arguing that the Administration had occupied it without consultation or permission when they built the cluster of gun emplacements during the war (the emplacements were still there in 1994, and a settler family was living in one of them). His claim was rejected, but he refused to accept the official decision. He championed the settlers when colonial residents high on the hill complained about the growing community of 'squatters' down below, and campaigned successfully for them to get a water supply and road access. No rent was paid by the settlers. Older residents remember Lohia Doriga with great respect. As the settlement grew the predominance of waterside workers lessened and the community became a mixture of both formally employed and unemployed people.

Norwood (1984: 44) recorded twenty-five houses at Paga in 1982, with one trade store (of kiosk size, as is common in settlements, selling rice, tinned fish and other basic supplies). By 1994 the number of houses had increased to sixty-four, and the settlement had four trade stores. This expansion began in earnest with the arrival of a Simbu man, David Kemi, who had previously been living in another part of town. His story is an interesting tale of ambition and enterprise. Kemi, employed in semi-skilled work in downtown Port Moresby, became friendly with workmates from the Paga settlement and met Lohia Doriga. He arranged a huge feast for the Paga community as an act of goodwill. Lohia then invited him to live at Paga. He moved there during the 1980s, and subsequently brought other people from Simbu and Goroka (eastern highlands) into the community. He had building skills and contributed to the development of the settlement by building better houses for residents (they provided the materials by scavenging at their workplaces and building sites in the area). His prominence in the settlement community well established by these gestures of largesse, Kemi began to consolidate his standing authoritatively through settlement committee membership (most well-established settlements in Port Moresby have some system of community 'elders') and the village court system. He became a peace officer in 1993, pursued his duties vigorously, and by the end of 1994 had become a village court magistrate. The ethnic mixture of Paga settlement and the fact that it is not dominated by Gulf people makes it different from the other three settlements served by Konedobu village court, and potentially more volatile, yet it is a relatively quiet settlement, and insulated by its position, hidden at the back of Paga Hill.

Konedodu Village Court

Konedobu village court was established in 1977 when the village court system was beginning to be extended into urban areas following its perceived success in some rural locations. It was officially gazetted in 1979. At the time of my research Konedobu court had five magistrates, a court clerk and fifteen peace officers (the latter are executive assistants to magistrates, responsible for tasks such as delivering summonses, making sure disputants present themselves at court sittings, and so on). It was one of the few village courts in the country with a female magistrate, and the only one to my knowledge in which the female magistrate was the chairperson.

When I began attending the court in 1994, it had only recently moved its location. There had previously been friction with the Motu-Koita Council (a body representing the interests of Motu-Koita generally in the National Capital District) over attempts to conduct the court in an annex of the council's rooms near Konedobu. It was now being held under the stilt-raised house of one of the magistrates once a week. This area contained a table with a wooden bench on each side, one for the magistrates and the other for the disputants. On the morning of court days a cloth was put on the table, two vases of flowers were added, and the PNG flag was hung behind the magistrates' bench. The 'courtroom' was bounded by chicken wire and only court officers, disputants and witnesses to each case were allowed inside, although court proceedings were visible and audible to anyone standing beyond the chicken wire. Three magistrates sat for each case, the minimum number specified in the legislation (there can be more magistrates but it has to be an odd number). When all evidence in a case had been heard the disputants went outside while magistrates came to a decision, and were then called back in to hear it. When a decision was made, a magistrate would carefully read out the nature of the offence and the penalty from the village court handbook, to make absolutely clear to disputants what the law was in regard to the case. The court was conducted in Hiri Motu, the lingua franca of south-coast PNG. Sometimes—usually when emotions ran high—people would drift into Toaripi, a language from the eastern area of the Gulf Province which was intelligible to most of the settlement population.

Many disputes in the settlements never reach Konedobu village court, as they are taken instead to alternative dispute-managing institutions of the kinds mentioned in chapter 3 such as settlement committees, church elders and other community leaders. Indeed, in the downtown settlements some people simultaneously hold a number of positions which could be glossed by the term 'community leader'. As a result of this variety of dispute-managing institutions and of the regional unity of most of the settlement dwellers (which prevents inter-ethnic conflicts of the kind experienced elsewhere in Port Moresby), the types of disputes which find their way into the village court are fairly limited, and sometimes a matter of default, in that other forums had failed to reach satisfactory results.

I found in Konedobu village court that cases which came to court were rarely offences or disputes concerning property or material resources, or physical violence. The majority involved alleged threats of sorcery, insults, or perceived insults, and malicious gossip. The extent to which people in non-Western communities are sensitive to the semantic density of language has frequently been noted particularly in linguistically oriented anthropology. As William Foley has observed, 'The meaning of a word is not exhausted by what it refers to in some objectively known, pre-given world, but also includes the world of cultural and social understandings it brings into being when used' (1997: 186). He was citing an observation by Alan Rumsey, based on research on Australian Aboriginal language, about a lack of distinction between direct and indirect discourse. His statement and Rumsey's observation certainly resonate with Melanesian approaches to language. In everyday discourse the metaphorical possibilities, in particular, of utterances are recognised to be substantial. It is not uncommon for people to hear a slight or insult in a mundane statement and to confront the speaker with an accusation of slander or a counter-insult (see chapter 7).

The complaint that one has been publicly insulted, defamed or is the subject of malicious gossip is not of a kind that holds the possibility of mollification through private mediation or relatively confined arbitration. A public vilification requires a public withdrawal, in the common view, and the village court served in these cases as a very public recourse, with complainants demanding compensation of K100 or more at the outset. But clearing the air or gaining a public admission of wrongdoing, or a public apology, mattered more to complainants than substantial compensation. Initial demands for a high fine or compensation payment served to express anger or distress on a complainant's part, and magistrates would routinely lecture the guilty party on the evils of malicious gossip or incautious remarks and the potential disruption to community peace and order of such behaviour. At the end of a hearing a nominal compensation (commonly K10) was usually accepted by the aggrieved party, and a public handshake between disputants was not uncommon.

Most of the disputes brought to the court were among residents of Ranuguri, the largest of the four settlements, and were mild in nature, compared to those heard in many other village courts. Residents of the small settlement of Vainakomu rarely brought any kind of dispute to the court, neither did those of the more ethnically mixed settlement of Paga. The population of Vanama settlement, relatively small and with its Motu-Koita landowner in residence, was rarely involved in village court disputes. The nearby Motu-Koita village complex of Hanuabada (closer, in fact, than Vanama and Paga) had its own village court, and while Konedobu village court had a Motu-Koita man among its magistrates, Motu-Koita in the general area took their disputes elsewhere. Overall, the caseload of Konedobu village court was very low, compared to other village courts around Port Moresby. Nevertheless, court hearings were lengthy, and individual cases, sometimes centred on an accusation of insult drawn from the interpretation of a single word, would last for hours.

During the last two or three weeks of my fieldwork in 1994 Konedobu village court hearings were perfunctory affairs, if they happened at all. Plans for the new Poreporena Highway had been publicised, and the disputants and court officers alike were preoccupied with fraught discussions about their future and with trying to get definite information about the highway. By 1999 the highway had been built, and the most threatened settlements, Ranuguri and Vainakomu, had survived the potential damage of the earthworks. But as noted above the highway construction had created vacant areas of land at the edges of the settlements and new people were moving in. They were not 'Kerema', being mostly from the highlands. Coastal peoples and highlanders have never enjoyed particularly cordial relationships, and the potential for the influx of strangers to generate conflict quickly became visible in the village court. Where previously the caseload had consisted mainly of accusations of insults and threatening behaviour, there was now a significant proportion involving minor assaults and more serious complaints about threats of violence. The complainants were overwhelmingly the 'Keremas' and the respondents were from the newer parts of the settlement. A new set of problems and preoccupations had clearly developed. It remains to be seen, at time of writing, whether they will displace older ones.

Like Pari village court, the court at Konedobu had adopted the trappings of a formal court, and also terminology such as 'complainant', 'defendant', 'witness', 'evidence', 'adjourned' and so on. The magistrates spent considerable time in mediation work, but in the formal court hearings proceedings were oriented towards findings of 'guilt' or 'innocence', or a declaration of 'case dismissed' (all juridical terms were pidginised). In this respect the critical observation that village courts have served to extend the colonially introduced legal system into local communities (see chapter 3) is true of Konedobu, as of nearly all village courts that I have observed around PNG. But at the same time Konedobu court, again like Pari, was concerned to keep the community's internal problems from coming to wider attention, and also explicitly contextualised individual disputes in the encompassing issues of the settlements. In this respect its decisions on guilt or innocence, and its consideration of appropriate penalties manifested a sensitivity to communal dynamics, rather than the severity of the offence, or the 'previous record' of an offender.

The Social Environment of Erima Village Court

The third village court I monitored was Erima village court. It is the busiest village court in Port Moresby and serves an area of more than eighteen square kilometres, including four densely populated suburbs which have burgeoned in the northern part of the city since the late 1950s. The area contains not only several large low-covenant and high-covenant housing estates (such as Hohola, Tokarara, Waigani, Gordons Estate), but also a number of habitats which should perhaps be called settlement complexes, rather than 'settlements', as the latter term implies that they are more discrete and formally bounded than is really the case. Unlike the downtown settlements or Pari village, these habitats are multi-ethnic, and have grown quickly and fairly haphazardly. Within these complexes is a variety of housing of different types, from squatters' makeshift shelters to more substantial dwellings built of corrugated iron, wood, and fibro on rented blocks. Inhabitants commonly upgrade their houses over time if they are able, and the city's expansion has created suburban estates ever further afield from its downtown 'centre'. Consequently, the distinction between squatter settlements, legitimate settlements and planned low-cost housing estates has become increasingly unclear in the outer suburbs of post-colonial Port Moresby, not only conceptually (although the popular media perpetuates a simple distinction between 'squatter settlements' and legitimate housing) but demographically. Enclaves of squatters who established themselves unnoticed on peripheral unused land in the 1960s became swallowed up in the spread of suburbia by the late 1980s. Conversely, the untidy development of suburbs with basic infrastructure provided the opportunity for individuals or families to establish illicit dwellings in the interstices of communities of mixed ethnicity where few questions of legitimacy are asked unless serious trouble arises.

A survey conducted in 1988 (none that I know of has been systematically conducted since) referred to more than forty habitats in Port Moresby as 'settlements', of which twenty-seven were classified as unplanned (Iopa 1988).[16] Five of the settlements described in the survey are situated within the territory covered by Erima village court, and are listed as June Valley, Hohola Rifle Range, Gordons Ridge, Fourmile/Garden Hills and Erima. By the early 1990s none of these communities were, strictly speaking, the discrete entities implied by the survey. However, a brief recapitulation of their history may help the reader to understand the significant difference between the overall community served by Erima village court and those served by Konedobu and Pari village courts.

June Valley settlement was one of the first self-help housing areas to be developed under new housing policies in the late 1960s which allowed for the provision of serviced blocks on which people could build their own houses (Oram 1976: 195–96). It began with one-hundred 'no-covenant' blocks and developed into a mixture of several hundred people from several parts of the country including the Eastern Highlands, the Gulf District, Milne Bay and coastal areas of the Central Province. Gordons Ridge settlement, in contrast, was unplanned. It began in the early 1960s when highland migrants squatted on government land which was officially zoned as open space. In the late colonial period the suburb of Gordons was an exclusive European housing area, and the appearance of makeshift dwellings on the ridge above it met with local and official disapproval. Somehow the settlers survived (although some moved to other suburbs) and the little enclave grew beyond one-hundred houses. By the early 1980s the settlers had upgraded their habitat to the extent that it was recognised as a permanent fixture. Two communal water taps were supplied by local authorities and a proper access road provided in 1981 (Norwood 1984: 34). The inhabitants are mostly from Simbu Province, with some Koiari people (highland fringe dwellers whose homeland is located within the boundary of the Central Province), and the majority support themselves through informal economic activities.

Hohola Rifle Range settlement began in 1983 beside a rifle range used by a gun club in the late colonial era and is partly on government land and partly on customary land. In general, those settlers living on customary land pay a rental to the landholders, but many of those on government land are squatters. By the early 1990s the settlement had become annexed to the burgeoning suburb of Hohola. The population is extremely mixed, containing several hundred people drawn from the Eastern Highlands, Simbu, Morobe, Eastern Gulf and the Sepik region. As well as pursuing a range of informal sector activities, settlers find employment in the industrial sectors in the eastern part of the suburb of Gordons and 'Four Mile', both of which are less than half an hour's walking distance away.

The Fourmile/Garden Hills settlement is very small, containing a little more than one-hundred people. It began during the 1980s on Government land in a suburban area close to a major intersection and shopping centre. Its immediate environment is constantly being developed for both housing and industrial purposes and thus the enclave has little chance of expanding. Its inhabitants, from Simbu, Eastern Highlands and Milne Bay Provinces, are non-rent-paying squatters and it does not have the benefit of officially provided basic services. In contrast, Erima settlement, on the north-eastern edge of town, is one of the fastest growing of Port Moresby's settlements. It began in 1987 as a legitimate self-help settlement area on government land with plots rented at K18 per annum. A massive leap in the cost of rental plots to K50 per annum over the next year did nothing to deter migrants from making their homes there, often acquiring their building materials one way and another from the nearby Erima sawmill. Informal subdivision and sub-leasing of rented sites is not uncommon, resulting in great architectural diversity and a crowded atmosphere in some sections of the settlement, and a large and fluctuating population. The settlement dwellers represent a wide range of societies from all areas of the highlands, the Gulf Province and the north coast.

As can been seen from the brief descriptions, the inhabitants of these communities originate not only from the early points of post-war migration like the Gulf district and the Papuan highlands north of Port Moresby (the latter migrants popularly referred to as 'Goilala') but from many other areas of PNG, reflecting the increasing influx of migrants towards the end of the colonial era and since. The settlements themselves are volatile, since they contain mixed populations competing for housing and jobs and forced to share restricted space. Within these communities, regional groups form cheek-by-jowl enclaves, and try to get along with their neighbours as best they can. Violent confrontations are common, especially when alcohol consumption exacerbates chronic friction among diverse and mutually suspicious ethnic groups. Consequently police intervention is frequent, and a high proportion of trouble cases are immediately taken beyond the ambit of the village court.

Erima Village Court

When I began attending Erima village court it was held in a small building in the centrally placed Gordons market, the biggest produce market in Port Moresby. There was an ongoing disagreement between the village court officials and the market's managers over whether the village court should pay rent, which led eventually to the court shifting to Erima settlement, within which it was continuously relocated and its siting was constantly renegotiated with residents (see chapter 8). Finally, it settled into regular hearings under a lean-to beside the house of one of the magistrates. The court had twelve magistrates, twenty peace officers, and one court clerk, the large number of officials being an indication of the size of the population it served. Between five and seven magistrates would occupy the bench on any case. Even during the period when the court was shifting from site to site, an effort was made to provide a 'bench' for the magistrates, and a table, however makeshift. Sessions always opened with a prayer, a statement that the court was 'in session', and bowing by all officials, mimicking district court procedure.

Disputants stood, rather than sitting as they did at Konedobu and Pari, and a peace officer stood between them.

While the settlements served by Erima village court have settlement committees and a (multi-denominational) church presence, the ethnic diversity of their constituents means the structure of these institutions is not woven into extended kinship networks as it is in the downtown Kerema-dominated settlements or Pari village. In the absence of those relatively intimate links between individuals and communal institutions, there is less possibility of small disputes between individuals being dealt with in neo-customary forums, and thus the village court has a very large caseload which ostensibly covers a wide range of disputes and complaints, including personal and property violence, insults and malicious gossip, debts and financial defaults, sorcery, adultery and petty theft. On closer examination of the evidential content of the cases, however, I found that a common thread in the majority of them was marital problems or marital breakdown.

Migrants in the mixed settlements are cut off from the bulk of their extended kin groups and the social structures into which marriages in PNG are traditionally linked (and which are grounded in clan-ordered landholding) are not present locally. Lacking the customary resources and sanctions on which marriage partners would draw in a habitat typified by extensive kin networks, the marriages of urban migrants can be comparatively fragile. Also, single adult migrants are likely to enter into relationships and hastily arranged marriages with people from ethnic groups other than their own. Women are especially vulnerable to these liaisons for economic reasons. In such cases, as the bride's father and immediate family are absent, more distantly related kin substitute for them to receive small promissary payments which commonly take the place of properly negotiated brideprices.

In this situation of relative estrangement from the customary context of marriage alliance, discord can develop quickly, and manifests itself in accusations such as neglect, adultery and personal violence between the marriage partners, and confrontations and accusations between affines or quasi-affines as the latter's putative alliance is transformed into a state of hostile estrangement. When a new marriage breaks down gifts which were given and accepted as part of the development of ongoing ties of obligation and reciprocation between the kin of marriage partners become the subject of accusations of debts unpaid. Cash which served as nominal brideprice is demanded back, material things taken under the aegis of affinal rights become the focus of accusations of theft. Even if the married couple are content in themselves with the union, inter-ethnic marriages can be unpopular with those related to the marriage partners. Discontent with a marriage which has frustrated the logic of clan-based production and exchange alliances becomes manifest in confrontations of various kinds between individuals from the two micro-ethnic groups involved. These were the types of cases chronically heard by Erima village court, and when analysing my ongoing records of what appeared initially to be unrelated cases I commonly found sets of individuals whose diverse disputes were actually linked by marital issues.

The volatility of life in these settlements was reflected in the village court hearings, where violent confrontations between disputants were not uncommon, necessitating physical intervention by court officers and sometimes temporary adjournments to allow tempers to cool. Experience of people producing and brandishing weapons, including knives and bottles, during disputes had led to a rule that disputants could not carry bags into the area in front of the magistrates. This was applied particularly to women, who carried *bilums* (net bags) on their backs, and were adept at extracting weapons (usually glass soft-drink bottles) from these in the same moment as they swung them to the ground while taking their position before the magistrates. There was also a greater tendency by disputants to challenge the decisions of the court, which involved magistrates in frequent appeal hearings at the district court. Disputants who were found guilty also had a greater tendency to default on fines and compensation payments ordered by the court, which resulted in frequent threatened and actual referrals of cases to district courts for penalties more severe than village courts are permitted by law to impose. The incidence of non-cooperation by disputants with Erima village court decisions compared with Pari and Konedobu reflected, I think, the relative estrangement of disputants from each other and the lack of an underlying sense of kinship with its accompanying need for the integrity of social relationships to be maintained in the long term.

The three village courts described here, then, reproduce to some extent the formality and physical trappings of the colonially introduced legal system, and all rely heavily on the prescriptions of the village court handbook in classifying cases and offences, and in determining the penalties. They do not apply 'custom' in the sense used by some critics of the village court system. That is to say, there is no range of stipulated customs that they draw upon, even in the 'tradition'-oriented village of Pari. However, their 'style', so to speak, reflects the sociality of the communities they serve, and their decisions are implicitly, and sometimes explicitly, concerned to address the better interests of those communities rather than being concerned solely with delivering justice to the individual disputants, as we shall see in chapters 6, 7 and 8. Peter Lawrence's apt comment on the maxim *fiat justitia, ruat coelum*, that Melanesians are more concerned with keeping the sky up (1970: 46), is certainly demonstrated in village courts.

Notes

1. An alternative explanation of the name was given me by one villager, who said that it was changed from *Tauata* in the distant past in honour of a man named Pari, from the Gulf Region, who saved the village from orchestrated sorcery attacks.
2. There are more than sixty buildings shown on the map, but it is not clear how many are actually dwellings. Maddocks and Maddocks (1972: 225), presumably referring to the same map, say there were fifty-eight houses. Seligman's plan is actually 'upside-down'—a compass indicating 'north' and pointing to the top of the page is pointing to what is actually the south, in relation to the lines of houses.
3. London Missionary Society operatives were active on the Papuan coast in 1872. The Reverend W. G. Lawes arrived in Port Moresby in November 1874 and immediately began posting missionaries to local villages (see Garrett 1985: 206–8). A Papuan interpretation of the arrival of the Rarotongan missionary Rua Toka in 1872 is given in the memoirs of Kori Taboro (Goava 1979: 74–76).
4. National Population Census, Final Figures, Census Unit Populations, National Capital District, p. 6. National Statistical Office, 1993.
5. In Pari village it is still mostly called 'Police Motu'.
6. A measure of this dominance is that the Motu word for the Koita, *Koitabu*, is commonly used in Papua New Guinea in preference to *Koita*, with the acquiescence of the Koita themselves. On one occasion, when I asked a Koita resident of Pari which term was 'correct', he confessed to not knowing, but advised me, 'Don't say *Koita*'.
7. The 40-year-old study of Rabia camp by Hitchcock and Oram (1967) remains the best account of the establishment, growth and lifestyle of an urban settlement in Port Moresby.
8. F. E. Williams, the Government anthropologist in Papua before the Second World War, employed a similar method of using names of 'main villages' in the Gulf area to refer to 'a number of local and dialectical units which we may call tribes, but for which it is quite impossible to give any generally and consistently recognized names' (1976: 76).
9. The Motu-Koita living in the nearby village of Hanuabada (Motu: 'big village') moved away in wartime, during which the village was destroyed by fire. A war veteran, Sari Ume, who had been stationed at Konedobu, told me that apart from army personnel and recruited labourers the area immediately around Konedobu was uninhabited during the war. The Motu-Koita moved back after the war, and the Administration rebuilt Hanuabada with timber and iron.
10. There is a tendency for any given settlement community in Port Moresby to claim that most other settlements are iniquitous compared to itself. This partly reflects the impact of an expedient state rhetoric that 'squatter settlements' are a major source of 'law and order' problems.
11. Oram (1976: 97) appears to have mistaken Ranuguri for Vanama in a reference to Moveave and Miaru people being invited in 1949 and 1950 to occupy huts left by the army 'at Vanama settlement near Konedobu'.

12. Norwood (1983) listed Vanama as 'Newtown' after the suburb in which it is situated, but I have never heard it referred to as such locally. He gave 'Vanama 1' and 'Vanama 2' as alternative designations, but in 1994 the '1' and '2' distinctions were not being used. The history of Vanama settlement given here was collected from Dirona Lohia, who largely agreed with Norwood's account (1982: 43) when I subsequently showed it to him.
13. Personal communication, Joe Maniti and family, 1994. Joe Maniti is Motu-Koita, his wife Josephine (at one time chairperson of the village court magistrates at Konedobu) is of Lese, Gulf Province, descent. I was shown genealogical documents by the Maniti family listing their *iduhu*, *Kwaradubuna Idibana*, descended from Motu Morea and including Geua Vani, and a map of the area. They regarded the two documents in concert as constituting conclusive proof of ownership. The Maniti family's disagreement with Norwood's account (which I showed them) reflects the ongoing tensions both among and—as in this case—*within* local groups about land ownership, exacerbated by urban growth and the progressive commodification of land.
14. Papua Amogoa died some years before my fieldwork. His son, in middle age and a village court peace officer in the 1990s, had preserved his employment identification card and driver's licence, which was shown to me as confirmation of the story of the settlement's genesis. My main informant was Dauri Kisu, one of the early settlers at Paga, a relative of Papua Amogoa and the chairman of the local ward committee in 1994. The name Mairi Nakaia did not seem familiar to settlers I consulted.
15. Doriga is incorrectly referred to in Norwood's account as Daniga (1984: 44). Dirona Lohia expressed his disagreement with Norwood's comment in terms which appealed to equivocation over land 'deals' between the colonial Administration and local groups. As the higher land on Paga Point was acquired as 'waste land' and the area the settlement now occupies was ignored by the Administration until the Second World War, when gun turrets were erected, the issue of ownership is especially moot. The general area from the edge of the Hanuabada village complex through Konedobu and the downtown business section of Port Moresby has been the subject of ongoing claims over land ownership ultimately grounded in differing perceptions of early colonial land deals.
16. This commissioned document contains brief descriptions of the 'settlements', and a substantial amount appears to be cribbed from a 1984 publication by Norwood who described nineteen 'squatter areas' and seven urban villages. Norwood used the term 'squatter' unwillingly, capitulating to popular usage (1984: 82).

5

Village Court Politics

This chapter discusses the politics of being a village court official, using examples from the three courts introduced in chapter 4. As magistrates and other officials are chosen from the particular communities they serve, they are inescapably enmeshed in community politics. Not only do the 'style' and decision-making of village courts reflect the sociality of their community, but social dynamics and attitudes can play a large part in determining who becomes a village court official. The legislative intention had been that village court magistrates would be selected by the local community on the criteria of their adjudicatory integrity and good knowledge of local customs (Village Court Secretariat 1975: 1). This implied a communal trust in wise elders to soothe a community's occasional moments of friction, as if villagers lived in a social climate where Durkheimian consensus succeeded most of the time in maintaining equilibrium. Melanesian societies, however, are no less politically dynamic than any others, and village courts are avenues for the pursuit of status, prestige and power which attract people whose ambitions are not exclusively directed to the dispensing of wise judgement on disputes.

As village courts in Port Moresby hold their meetings on weekdays, while employed people are at work (although when formally employed people are summonsed by the courts they are obliged to take time off work to attend), village court officials are rarely people employed in the 'formal sector'. Magistrates, peace officers and court clerks are nearly all formally unemployed, though some are in part-time work. Commonly they are people engaged in informal income-earning occupations. In settlements such as those described in the previous chapter, informal money-earning activities are visible everywhere. Smallgoods, softdrinks and blackmarket beer are sold from tiny tradestores and 'tucker boxes', betelnut and baked or fried snacks are sold from small stalls near their traders' houses. Card games, bingo games and dart-throwing competitions, all played for money, are endemic. Small-scale usury is a common practice. These and other activities re-distribute money through the community but some are also opportunities for their organisers to gain some measure of local social prestige. Other opportunities for prestige in the settlement community are offered by church-related activities and membership in the various committees set up to protect and improve the living conditions of settlement dwellers. Males in particular vie for membership and positions of authority in these committees to enhance their own prestige and gain a degree of control over their immediate social environment, and village court work offers similar prospects, though without great monetary rewards.

Magistrates are periodically elected or re-elected by the community, and then choose from among themselves a chairperson and deputy chairperson. The court also requires a court clerk and a number of peace officers. All the officials are supposed to be issued with a uniform of blue shirt and trousers or skirt and fabric badges of office. In practice, the uniforms are issued rarely and haphazardly. Magistrates and peace officers covet these symbols of authority and wear them with pride, even when they have become ragged and threadbare with age. The various positions in the village court, then, provide an opportunity both for the symbolic and the practical expression of authority and are often sought by men with little education or vocational or professional training, some of whom hope the court will serve as a vehicle to higher goals such as careers in politics or public service administration.

The Gender of Village Courts

Most village court officials are male, which has been a point of concern to some critics since the system's inception. Mitchell, for example, regarded the predominance of male magistrates as a disadvantage for women, whom she described as inexperienced and lacking skills in public speaking, to their detriment in court (1985: 88; see also chapter 3). In recent years, concerns over women's social and political inequality in PNG have influenced strategies to ensure that there are more women magistrates. These have included relatively aggressive schemes such as intervention in community selection of magistrates to make sure each court has at least one woman, and less intrusive suggestions that women simply be strongly encouraged to stand for selection in their community. These strategies invariably fail, in the face of community attitudes which are more complex and diverse than some discourses of women's rights imply.

It is conventionally held that in most parts of PNG men and women alike 'traditionally' regard public judgement as a male domain. This broad statement, however, needs qualification in consideration of varying gender attitudes and politics in the different societies throughout the country. In highland societies, where it is generally true that women of child-bearing age are not regarded as authoritative in political or judicial discourse, elderly women can be publicly judgemental with real effect. Conversely, authoritative males can lose their public effectiveness as they become old. On the other hand, in some coastal societies in which group leadership is hereditary and mostly male, deference is given to such leaders even in their old age. However, these elderly 'chiefs' have a qualified understanding of their areas of authority, including the type of dispute in which they see fit to intervene. Melanesian dispute settlement and public judgement has not traditionally been the exclusive domain of male 'elders' or 'chiefs'.

In recent times, when the number of women moving into positions of political, bureaucratic, economic and social prominence and authority has increased, women in search of status or prestige make astute choices based on a balance of personal goals and community values and attitudes. Few choose village courts as a vehicle for their social advancement. Village court magistrates are targets for violent retribution by disgruntled disputants or their kin, they are frequently accused of bias and corruption, they are poorly remunerated, if at all, and their work is extremely time-consuming. While positions in the village courts are potential avenues to prestige and power, then, they are not without their disadvantages, for men and women alike. Preoccupied with gardening, care of animals and child-rearing in the traditional sexual division of labour, women are less likely to be attracted to working in village courts than men. Womens' business groups and church fellowship groups are much more popular avenues for women seeking social advancement.

While broad statements are sometimes made that there are no women village court magistrates in any given region,[1] women do in fact serve as magistrates. The number of women village court magistrates in PNG is actually unknown, since no centralised long-term data on sitting magistrates has been efficiently maintained. It is popularly claimed that, in particular, there are no women magistrates in the area that is generally used as the basis of claims of misogynist practices, the 'highlands' (an imprecise category roughly encapsulating part or all of the Southern Highlands, Enga, Western Highlands, Simbu, and Eastern Highlands provinces as well as the higher-altitude fringes of several coastal provinces). Yet no-one has pursued exhaustive empirical surveys of the gender of magistrates in any of the constituent provinces. Nevertheless, it is probably true that there are very few women magistrates, especially in highland village courts.

Women working in village courts frequently serve as court clerks, where secretarial skills are valued. The majority of court clerks in the East New Britain and Milne Bay provinces, for example, are women.[2] Two of the three village courts I have monitored in the NCD have had women court clerks most of the time since 1992. The other practical office in the village courts is that of peace officer. Each village court has several, acting as messengers for the magistrates, serving summonses and delivering court orders, ensuring that disputants attend court, standing or sitting between disputants to prevent physical assaults by one party on another, and acting as peace wardens in the community. Women frequently serve in this capacity, though overall males dominate numerically as peace officers around the country.

The magistrates in Erima village court are mostly male, but have included women. Two whom I have known, both from the Western Highlands Province, could roughly be described as women's rights advocates, and have been involved in women's groups and projects around Port Moresby. They have not been exclusively devoted to village court work, seeing it as only part of their sphere of activities. They attempt to temper their work as magistrates to avoid the politicking of their male colleagues, many of whom are preoccupied with gaining prestige through becoming the chairperson or deputy chairperson of the court. This preoccupation was explicitly addressed by one of the women referred to above, Mege Baru, when she was nominated by a male colleague as a candidate in 1999, while the magistrates were electing a new chairperson from among themselves. She declined the nomination with a short speech in Tokpisin, which gained admiring comments and applause from her male colleagues and a watching (male and female) crowd, and which I will give in translation here:

> Thank you for nominating me, but no. If I become chairman, some of you men [magistrates] will behave like small boys. You will want to be chairman, and you will try to destabilize me. This will be bad for the village court. I have no patience for this kind of behaviour. I prefer to remain just a magistrate. If you men want to fight [i.e. try to take over the chair], fight among yourselves. That's all, thank you.

In comparison, the chairing magistrate's position in Konedobu village court has been occupied by women most of the time since 1991. Before I began to monitor it, the location of the court had shifted several times, culminating in an unsuccessful attempt to establish it in an annex to the Motu-Koita Council Office near the Hubert Murray sports stadium. The combination of the micro-ethnic territorial groupings of the residents of the local settlements (who are predominantly of Eastern Gulf origins), territorial claims by local Motu-Koita and a degree of intermarriage between Gulf and Motu-Koita people has made the location of the court politically redolent. The chairing of the court, while ostensibly a matter of periodic election after voting among officials, is actually a matter of negotiation in which the siting of the court is a significant factor. The Motu-Koita landholder in residence at Vanama settlement had, for example, been the 'elected' chairman at one point when formal meetings were held there.

After the displacement of the court from the Hubert Murray stadium, it was re-established under the house of Josephine Maniti, a magistrate married to a Motu-Koita man living on his own land between Ranuguri and Vainakomu settlements. Josephine had secretarial training and organisational skills and was well qualified in those respects to deal with some of the administrative aspects of the village court which are nominally the province of a court clerk but often overseen by a chairing magistrate. However, the fact that she and her husband had agreed to the court being held under their house, with the weekly nuisance of dozens of people in attendance, had much to do with Josephine's election to the chairing position. While all court officials publicly agreed to Josephine's elevation, it did not please all her fellow magistrates. It was known that the most elderly of them, Tati Marai, a previous chairman who lived in Ranuguri settlement, felt that his seniority in age and his long service as a church elder made him a more appropriate chairperson than Josephine, though he did not publicly dispute her election, and accepted a position as deputy chairperson.

Josephine suffered from some medical problems, mostly abdominal, which became severe enough for her to have to give up chairing the court on a couple of occasions. As is common in PNG when (in particular) chronic and severe abdominal pain is experienced, Josephine attributed her illness to 'sorcery', suspecting this was generated by jealousy or perhaps resentment at some of her magisterial decisions (a common fear among village court magistrates). On these occasions Tati Marai took over as chair, only to have to relinquish the position when Josephine recovered. Tati himself was becoming frail as the years went by, however, and there was speculation about how long he could continue with village court responsibilities. By the late 1990s the constant non-payment of court officials' allowances by the NCDC had created a climate of distrust among magistrates in the NCD's village courts, including Konedobu court. As it was usually the chairperson's duty to collect the allowances or, more likely, to return with the news that they had not been paid out, chairing magistrates were particularly the subject of scrutiny and rumours of misappropriation by their fellow magistrates. The stresses of administration, combined with her poor health, eventually led Josephine to decide she no longer wanted the responsibility of being a chairing, or even deputy chairing, magistrate.

Josephine's resignation led to a great deal of friction among the magistrates as several coveted the unstable 'chairman' position which had been shifting diplomatically between Josephine and the increasingly frail Tati. The court clerk during part of Josephine's chairship was Molly Vani, a woman who lived in a nearby house, but was from the Hula area, some 100 kilometres south-east of Port Moresby. Molly was involved in local church fellowship work and had a reputation for honesty and integrity. She was soon asked to be a magistrate. She had expressed no ambition to be the chairperson, but in the climate of distrust and bickering among the magistrates following Josephine's resignation attention focused on Molly's unblemished reputation. She was urged to become the chairperson to settle the prevailing friction, and accepted.

The Hula share some cultural characteristics with the Motu of the Port Moresby area and the peoples of the Eastern Gulf area who dominate the population served by Konedobu village court. One of these is an understanding that women do not publicly give advice on, or express judgements on, juridical matters. Molly reconciled her adjudicatory office with this customary understanding with ease. She was a skilled mediator, and devoted most of her time to non-adjudicatory work. In formal sittings, where adjudication was necessary, Molly participated in the questioning of disputants and witnesses and the discussions among the magistrates who sat on each case. But she always formally invited one of her male co-magistrates to announce the court's judgement, thus negating the apparent contradiction between her adjudicatory work and community attitudes towards women and judgement.

In contrast, there have never been any female magistrates in Pari village court. It is unusual, traditionally, for Motu-Koita women to take public positions of political or judicial authority, although divination was a prestigious activity among women in former times. A noteworthy exception occurred when Dame Carol Kidu, an Australian-born woman who had been married to the former chief justice of PNG, Sir Buri Kidu, and lived in Pari village, successfully ran for parliamentary election after

Sir Buri's death. She later commented on her decision to enter politics: 'In Motu society politics is seen entirely as a male domain and for a widow to enter into politics is almost unthinkable. I actually felt guilty for placing the family in such a difficult situation' (2002: 149). Asking for support for her venture from her local community, she sensed reluctance from the younger married women, and was surprised at support from older widowed women whom she thought would be 'steeped in tradition and might vigorously oppose me as had happened when Dobi [Kidu's daughter] asked her grandmother to go against custom and expected behaviour in breaking her betrothal' (152–53). Overwhelmingly, women in Pari involve themselves deeply in church fellowship activities, an extension of the role they played traditionally in ensuring the wellbeing of the village as a community of linked family groups. It would be extremely unusual for a woman to want to become a village court magistrate in Pari.

Village Court Magistrates and 'Wise Elders'

The broad statement that village court magistrates are elected by their communities elides a number of subtleties concerning which individuals present themselves as candidates for election. As we have seen, policy-oriented calls for more women magistrates take little account of how women might perceive their role and worth in any given society. Aside from gender issues, a number of other factors can determine whether individuals want to be magistrates. These can include a desire for prestige and power, or a genuine desire to maintain peace and good order and to dispense justice with integrity. But other political and social considerations can take precedence over these personal intentions. Pari village offers a good example of this, insofar as significant traditional principles of social organisation have survived a century and a quarter of Christianity and other influences associated with colonialism. In particular, the sociality of Pari demonstrates the equivocality of assumptions that in a society which recognises and venerates elders for their cumulative wisdom, 'wise elders' are the most likely people to become village court magistrates.

Very elderly people, referred to as *iahu* in Motu society, have usually passed on whatever specific skills or authority they may have had to their children, and are relatively inactive. They serve the community largely as important repositories of oral history. Leaders and authority figures in Motu society are more likely to come from a less elderly stratum who could be generally referred to as *eregabe* (mature and responsible), or if they are becoming aged but are still relatively active, as *iahu eregabe*. Within this range, for example, are found the active leaders of *iduhu* (quasi-patrilineal groups—see chapter 4), who inherit their position through a principle of agnatic primogeniture when their father dies or voluntarily relinquishes leadership on becoming *iahu*. The role of *iduhu* leaders, or *kwaradia* (pl. of *kwarana*, from *kwara*: head), was not clearly understood by early researchers, who tried to portray them as 'chiefs', and were unable to discern what practical authority they had. William Y. Turner, for example, wrote in 1878: 'The chieftainship descends from father to son. The distinction between these chiefs, and who they are chiefs of, we cannot yet determine. These chiefs as a rule possess little or no authority and have little power in quelling a disturbance. They are however consulted in any matter affecting the interests of the village' (53).

In fact, the degree of political authority which Turner sought in 'chiefs' was rare among traditional Melanesian societies, where elements of social control were embedded in kinship and exchange relations, sorcery and the sanctions of tutelary spirits, rather than centralised in individual political leaders. Motu notions of leadership and authority are more complex than Turner and others (see, for example, Seligman 1910) thought. The Motu term *lohia* is most commonly translated as 'chief' even by Motuans themselves nowadays, under the influence of long-term application of the latter word by Westerners. But *lohia* is best interpreted for analytic purposes to mean a venerable man or man of renown, rather than a chief or headman. It is used of *iduhu kwaradia* as a matter of respect, but also of other men who have achieved renown by notable behaviour. In traditional times a man could become a *lohia* through successfully leading a *hiri*—the seasonal long-distance trade expedition by sea to the Gulf district, discontinued by the mid twentieth century—or organising a festive dance. The latter were normally instigated by an *iduhu kwarana*, but other senior males could achieve renown through organising a spectacularly successful dance ceremony representing an *iduhu*'s resourcefulness (Groves 1954: 80, 82).

The *iduhu kwarana* is not a political figure of the type early ethnologists sought in 'chiefly' men, but is a personification of the idiom through which the *iduhu*, as a political corporation, expresses its identity. As his position is inherited through agnatic primogeniture, he is an incarnation of the particular genealogy linking a contemporary *iduhu* to its apical ancestor. The authority of the *kwarana* lies in his symbolic polyvocality: he represents the living *iduhu* to other groups and to the ancestors (this used to be manifest in his facilitation of feasting and dancing, for example), and importantly, he represents the ancestors to the living *iduhu*.[3]

For this reason the types of 'dispute' in which an *iduhu kwarana* would involve himself are very limited, and his displays of authority traditionally were directed towards the activities of the group as a whole, rather than the control of individuals within the group. Hence to observers such as Turner these 'chiefs' appeared to have 'little power in quelling a disturbance' (1878: 53). In modern times, *iduhu kwaradia* rarely make public demonstrations of their authority as most of the traditional activities through which their particular type of leadership was evident have disappeared. The kind of authority manifest in village court magistrates is not perceived by them as relevant to their own status, and none serve in that capacity.

In the modern world of the Motu-Koita, business success, high rank in public-service employment, and success in provincial and national politics can also bring men recognition and deference in village society. These men are in fact referred to as *lohia* (I have never heard the term applied to a woman) particularly if their power is seen to be used for the benefit of their own people, that is to say, if their position in the integration of the village with wider society and its administrative bureaucracy has been advantageous to their group and not just to themselves. Within villages, church deacons have become authority figures. They organise church activities, and lead groups made up of clusters of families in competitive charity and fund-raising activities such as *bou bou*, the church donation competitions held yearly in Motu-Koita villages. They are often businessmen, or employed in fairly prestigious jobs in town. Some, however, stay more or less permanently in the village, financially supported by their employed offspring and others. These deacons, mostly in their late forties or fifties, are likely to serve also as village court magistrates. They are ascribed integrity based on their positions in the church, and are available for mediations and formal court hearings by virtue of not being employed in town. Other permanently village-based men of the same age group, who either aspire to be deacons, or have a similar concern towards community welfare, make up the complement of the magistrates.

Little Big Men

We have seen thus far that cultural and gender issues, and participation in formal weekday employment, are significant determinants in the number and type of potential candidates for village court work. Other influences are also present, sometimes to the detriment of the efficiency of a village court. An example is provided by the village court serving the Port Moresby suburb of Morata (containing formal housing and a settlement area, and not far from Erima), which was burdened in the early 1990s with an aged and feeble chairman. He had, in colonial times, served as a *luluai* in his home area and had also been a councillor before moving to Port Moresby. He retained his old cap and other regalia from colonial service and had offered himself as a magistrate when the Morata village court was first proclaimed in 1983. At the time, deference was given to his age and experience by the community, which was composed mostly of migrants from the highlands, and he was elected chairman. Micro-ethnic politics kept him in that position for several years, through the machinations of a group of migrants from his own area (a phenomenon known locally as *wantokism*, from the Tokpisin term *wantok*, meaning, roughly, someone from the same language group with whom a relationship of reciprocal obligation is maintained). However, his age and his inability to grasp the basic principles provided by the village court handbook caused diplomatic problems for his fellow magistrates, who tried to compensate for his inadequacies while maintaining deference to his senior position.

The old man's lack of understanding of his job was painfully visible during a 'training' workshop he attended in Port Moresby in the early 1990s, but the VCS was reluctant to diverge from its policy of non-interference in the community election of magistrates, and as the old man had not committed a crime or offence which would disqualify him from service, he was allowed to continue. He insisted on chairing the bench in every dispute the court heard, and his irrationality created difficulty for the other magistrates, affecting the efficiency with which they dealt with disputes. Disputants from Morata began taking their disputes to other village courts, either trying to represent themselves as belonging to those courts' constituencies, or openly pleading that Morata village court was incompetent. The other courts, however, refused to hear the cases, since they operated according to strict rules about the areas they served,[4] and in any case, not knowing the background of the disputes (as they usually did in the case of disputants from their own areas) were not willing to commit themselves to decisions. The population of Morata, especially in its settlement area, was steadily growing, and the caseload pressure on the court was making the old man's incompetence unbearable. Finally, in 1994 the VCS intervened, and the ex-*luluai*, still wearing his colonial regalia to court in preference to a magistrate's uniform, was removed.

Erima village court, like Morata, serves a mixed population, and in the absence of a dominant regional culture like that encountered at Konedobu village court, or of the village politics of Pari, personal motivations are more significant in determining who becomes a magistrate. Compared to the relatively stable personnel at Konedobu and Pari courts, magistrates come and go fairly frequently at Erima, depending on people's reasons for becoming a magistrate, or their fortunes in the politics of re-election. One of the dominant figures in the court from 1986 till the time of writing was a man who appeared to have the ideal qualities of a village court magistrate. He was dedicated to the welfare of the community at large, wise, fair, and hardworking, and appeared to have no personal aspirations which might compromise his integrity. The story of the rise and fall of the man known as 'chairman Andrew', though, is revealing of the politics of a village court in the volatile environment of multi-ethnic urban settlements.

Andrew Kadeullo was from Milne Bay, and had worked in clerical positions in Port Moresby for a decade until illness and hospitalisation cost him his job. He recovered his health, though he was less robust than before. He obtained a block of land in Erima settlement soon after it was established in the 1980s, and built a small house. He was unable to find employment of the kind he had previously enjoyed, but immersed himself in community work, joining the settlement's self-help committee. His clerical background and skill with paperwork made him a valuable member, as negotiations between settlement dwellers and city authorities over land blocks, amenities and services were a chronic part of the life of this fast-growing community.

He joined Erima village court as a court clerk, but, by his own account, was taken under the wing of the chairman of the court, an elderly man who noted that Andrew had a knack for solving problems. Andrew recounted this period to me as if it had been a personal apprenticeship, with the old man engineering his election as a magistrate, grooming him in the skills of dispute settlement, and finally, in failing health, ensuring Andrew's election as the next chairman before dying (as if passing on his mantle). Andrew attributed whatever skills he had as a magistrate to this personal schooling, and saw his work as a mission. He was continually re-elected as chairman into the 1990s, and was commonly known as 'chairman Andrew' throughout the nearby settlements.

Andrew was not physically imposing, was extremely mild in disposition and made no gestures of self importance or patronage. But I found, as I became familiar with Erima settlement, that he was regarded with great respect, as a man of integrity with the best interests of the community at heart. He was an excellent mediator and resolver of disputes, bringing a remarkable memory and understanding of wider social contexts to the disputes he heard. He was also adept at bringing his co-magistrates around to his point of view when they retired to consider 'verdicts' on cases, without perceivably forcing them to concur. Although he was formally unemployed, and his only official income was his magistrate's allowance, Andrew subsisted partly on gifts of betelnut, beer and food items from disputants rewarding him for his efforts as a mediator. In this regard he worked beyond the normal call of duty of village court magistrates. Normally, if a mediation fails and disputants move to the 'win-lose' process of a formal village court hearing, the case proceeds to a final decision by magistrates on someone's 'guilt', frequently after one or more week-to-week adjournments. Andrew, though, would often manage to effect a mediation during the adjournments, even after particularly acrimonious accusations and apparently irreparable estrangements in the formal court.

He had learnt the old (1976) village court handbook by heart, and kept his carefully preserved copy up to date with changing policies and rules by way of marginal notes and corrections. While decisions on cases in the court were often informed by, and directed at, community interests beyond those of the particular disputants before the court, Andrew was able to persuade disputants most of the time that the judgements were fair to them. He had a knack of publicly referring to the handbook, which he kept on the magistrates' desk, and reading from it, to indicate that decisions were scrupulous in their reflection of the 'law'. Nevertheless, while Andrew's decisions may have been both fair and in the best interests of the community at large, they did not always suit the individuals immediately involved in the disputes. Disputants would sometimes appeal against the court's decisions under a legal provision enabling them to take the matter to the district court. Weekly trips to the district court were part of Andrew's routine. The appeals were rarely successful, for Andrew was as persuasive of his legal superiors as he was of his fellow village court officials. There seemed no malice in the appeals. Indeed, Andrew appeared to regard them good naturedly as a kind of battle of wits, and announced his rare losses publicly in the village court when a case returned to be re-heard, or when a fine was reduced by an order of the district court.

He kept an account of all cases, whether they were dealt with by mediation, or in the court, or in the informal, post-court meetings at his house, and the Erima village court records were faultless. This was despite the shortcomings of some of the court clerks who came and went over the years and who displayed varying levels of commitment, integrity and competence. Through a variety of diplomatic strategies, both during and between court hearings, Andrew would make sure their mistakes were corrected, their lapses breached, and if necessary their incompetence masked. In a very benign fashion he controlled the village court, one way and another. The weekly hearings began at 9:00 AM and continued through to the evening. This was an arduous day, and Andrew would occasionally declare himself in need of a rest, retiring to the rear of the court area to chew betelnut while the deputy chairman and fellow magistrates managed a case or two without him. But even on these occasions he watched and listened, drifting in during the magistrates' deliberations to guide the discussion to a decision which his fellows regarded as their own.

It was easy to regard Andrew as an ideal village court magistrate. He was wise, fair, combining formal and informal notions of justice with ease, he was respected by everybody, and his fellow magistrates acknowledged his skills and good judgement. They were a diverse group. One aspired to be a politician, and saw the village court as a stepping stone to gaining public support. The women magistrates included village court duties in wider activities in women's and community groups. Some of the other village court officials had been encouraged by Andrew to become magistrates or peace officers by virtue of what he regarded as their integrity, their authority in one of the ethnic groups in the area, or some particular relevant skill. A few of the magistrates and several peace officers were nakedly ambitious for prestige. As all of them were elected by the community, Andrew could do little about those which (he told me privately) he regarded as incompetent or lax, and he worked with them as best he could, mostly able to compensate one way or another for their shortcomings.

Suddenly, in 1998, having always appeared to have the full support and respect of his fellow magistrates, Andrew lost his position as chairman, to a man who he himself had encouraged to become a magistrate. The man, whom I will call Reto, was an ageing rogue, a hard-drinking gambler incessantly in search of cash by dubious means, and formally unemployed. He had begun his involvement with the village court as a peace officer, but in Andrew's opinion he was suited to be a magistrate in the volatile context of Erima court, since he was tough and courageous, and frightened of no-one despite his age and short stature. He could not be intimidated, and for this he had the respect of many settlement people, despite their being exasperated by his roguish behaviour. He was non-literate and lacked a sophisticated grasp of the areas of law within which the village court was obliged to function, but had proved to be a good interrogative magistrate. Reto enjoyed being a magistrate, for it offered an opportunity to gain prestige for a person such as himself, who was too old and did not have the resources to achieve big-man status through the manipulation of exchange relationships as he might have in his natal (highland) place. In an election held among the magistrates in

1993 Reto had become deputy chairman, and this had appeared to be the limit of his success, for in the intra-magisterial elections in late 1994, he had lost the deputy position (possibly due to his fellow magistrates' misgivings about the amount of trouble he got into in his everyday life). He had been disappointed but continued to serve as a magistrate.

Then, four years later, he suddenly and publicly accused Andrew of misappropriating his fellow village court officers' financial entitlements, paid out by the NCDC. Andrew was shocked at his colleague's allegation, but as his integrity was being questioned he immediately stood himself down from the chairing position, forcing an election among the magistrates. He had expected support from his fellows, but they elected the self-nominated Reto as the new chairman. Reto achieved this result by simple gifting (common at all levels of politics in PNG). Moments before the vote, Reto had pressed a small amount of money into the hand of each magistrate. The imperatives of the gift permeate all areas of Melanesian society: Reto's aggressive, carefully timed gifting would have been almost impossible to refuse, and obligated his fellows, in the moment, to give him their vote. Andrew had never used such a direct method to achieve his own ends, and was taken by surprise.

Once in the chair Reto became publicly autocratic, imposing his own will irascibly on court decisions and alienating his colleagues. His judgements proved to be hasty, erratic and harsh, and lacked the systematic rationality of the judgements made under Andrew's leadership. The magistrates quickly realised that Andrew had been falsely accused of misappropriation, and regretted their capitulation to Reto's machinations. They asked Andrew to return to the chairmanship, under the impression that with their support he could simply declare Reto to be an imposter and reclaim leadership. Andrew reminded them that legally Reto would be harder to dislodge, and for him to return to the chair would require a formal election process. He refused to be part of such a process anyway, as he was still hurt by their lack of loyalty. Nevertheless, he remained committed to the work of the village court and was willing to continue to handle the bookwork, appeals cases and behind-the-scenes mediation and negotiation with court disputants to prevent what he saw as the social damage which Reto's erratic judgements threatened to bring about.

After clinging to the chairing position for a year, Reto was caught out in 1999 in exactly the misappropriation which he had accused Andrew of committing. An internal shake-up in the NCDC had resulted in a well-publicised large payout of overdue allowances to village court chairmen for distribution. There was clear evidence that Reto had collected the money for Erima village court officers, but it had never been distributed. It was never found, and Reto pleaded ignorance of what had happened to it. Legally lacking enough evidence to prosecute Reto for misappropriation or theft, the NCDC and the VCS nevertheless refused to countenance his continuance as chairman, as did his outraged fellow magistrates. Andrew refused invitations to reapply for the chairmanship, and, under the careful scrutiny of an NCDC officer, the magistrate who had political aspirations was elected. He gave an acceptance speech in which he acknowledged Andrew's long service in the chair and reaffirmed the court's trust in him, making it clear that his wisdom and clerical skills would be relied upon in the future. Reto continued to serve for a while as a magistrate, but was duly dispensed with altogether. Andrew continued his avuncular relationship with the court, working hard, but refusing to officially declare himself a magistrate, even though he capitulated weekly to requests that he sit with the other magistrates and hear cases. In 2004 the politically aspiring chairman was himself accused of misappropriation and lost his position. Andrew again refused to reapply for the chair, despite the encouragement of senior staff at the VCS, yet continued his voluntary service as a magistrate, and default court clerk, while yet another magistrate took over the chair.

The story of the changing chairmanship of Erima court indicates the degree to which village courts are articulated with the political life of the communities they serve. My own assessment of Andrew after a few months of fieldwork had been that he was indispensable as the chairman of Erima village court. This was based on my observation of his remarkable skill at solving disputes, managing community tensions and discord, and keeping the court's juridical affairs in order. Certainly nobody denied Andrew's wisdom and skill, and I doubt that anyone in the community would have questioned his appropriateness as chairing magistrate according to the criteria I had used. But his long-proven trouble-managing ability was not enough to preserve him when Reto seized his chance. The village court chair was a coveted position, and crude as Reto's accusation may seem, it was a clever exploitation of the chronic issue of non-payment, and his aggressive gifting during the election process elicited a cultural response which superceded any considerations related to village court administration such as Andrew's character, past record and chairing skills, or concern for the efficient running of the court. Interestingly, Andrew continued his role as a dispute manager to the community at large, albeit beset by the complications wrought by Reto. Importantly, Andrew's dispute managing took place largely beyond the formal precincts of the village court, away from the public gaze. While he was hurt by Reto's accusation and the immediate lack of support shown by his fellow magistrates, Andrew remained secure in the value that the community at large placed on his wisdom. Indeed, he continued to be called 'chairman Andrew' regardless of the chairmanship of Reto or his successor.

Respect

The rugged public politicking of Erima village court was absent at Konedobu. The factors determining who became a magistrate, or a chairing magistrate, at this court have been partially discussed already in this chapter. Each settlement served by Konedobu court was represented by at least one magistrate, and in the absence of explicit personal ambition, there was little change in the personnel over several years, compared to Erima. Magistrates would relinquish their position usually in the event of increasing age, or a decision to return, or make a long-term visit, to a homeplace in 'Kerema'. As noted earlier, while magistrates putatively attained the chairing position through a formal election among themselves, the matter was largely negotiated in relation to where the court was held. But beneath the relatively orderly and tranquil conduct of the court were tensions which were, much of the time, suppressed in the interests of co-operation among the magistrates and peaceful co-existence in the downtown settlements. The settlements were commonly referred to by their inhabitants as *hanua* (Motu: village), a reflection of the parochial nature of these communities, which were older and smaller overall than the settlements served by Erima court. Ranuguri, Vanama and Vainakomu in particular were linked by complex affinal relationships, generating a dialectic of reciprocal obligations and petty resentments.

Many of the disputes in Konedobu court arose from this dialectic, and magistrates themselves were equally caught in its dynamics. Earlier in this chapter I referred to a degree of jealousy between two of the magistrates, Josephine Maniti and Tati Marai, and to Josephine's apprehension of 'sorcery' from disgruntled disputants. There was more to the friction between magistrates than jealousy, however. The issue of non-payment of allowances to village court officials cast a cloud over their operations in general. It was the job of Josephine, when she was chairperson, to go to the NCDC office in another suburb to collect the allowances, which were often not available. As we saw earlier in the chapter in the case of chairman Andrew at Erima, the non-payment of allowances caused suspicion among magistrates that their own chairperson was misappropriating the money. Josephine expressed anxiety to me about the possibility of accusations of this nature against herself. Tati, as her deputy, was also authorised to collect the payments, but Josephine tended to deputise another magistrate for the task if she was unable for some reason to travel to the NCDC office herself. The reason for this was disclosed by that other magistrate, who told me that some years previously Tati had been acting as the village court clerk and was rumoured to be spending the court's collected fine money. On the eve of a visit by a village court inspector Tati had burnt all the village court records. He had consequently been dropped from service in the village court, but settlement dwellers later voted him back as a magistrate. As a result of his earlier actions, suspicion automatically fell on him when allowances did not arrive, and efforts were made to ensure that Tati was kept away from anything to do with village court money.

Attempting to dispense 'substantial justice' in such a parochial climate was a tortuous business. The inherent tension was reflected in Josephine's habit, when she was chairperson, of giving pep-talks to her fellow magistrates and, in particular, to the village court peace officers at the beginning of court days, before officially 'opening' the court to disputants. She would reinforce principles of conduct, the need to wear uniforms properly to ensure respect, and the responsibility village court officials had to the community. Parochial concerns were raised in these pep-talks, such as untidiness and littering in the settlements, or noise from radios and tape recorders being played at high volume. Josephine urged peace officers to control these annoying aspects of settlement life: 'Do not be afraid to use your authority. Make sure you are wearing your uniform, and the police headquarters is nearby if you need reinforcement'.

Like village court magistrates in many parts of PNG where the community is a complex web of near and distant kin relationships, Josephine and her co-magistrates were caught between two roles. On the one hand they were involved themselves in the discontents of extended kinship relations in the community, and on the other hand they were cast in roles of authority as dispute settlers and magistrates. The latter duty required acquiescence from people who could bring cultural values to the interaction which challenged the assumption of respect which was putatively the village court magistrate's right. This problem is exemplified in the dialogue below, which occurred during a dispute brought to a formal court hearing by one of the magistrates. I reproduce the incident here also because it handily encapsulates other aspects of the politics of being a village court magistrate which I have discussed in this chapter.

Josephine, who was the chairing magistrate at the time, had tried to mediate in a family dispute. Two of the disputants, an elderly man and his daughter, became disgruntled and walked out on her mediation attempt. Josephine was affronted by this and decided to register the matter as a dispute, bringing her own complaint against the pair to a formal village court hearing. As will be evident from her comments, she had taken the rejection of her mediation personally, perceiving it as a further sign of a lack of respect that she had already felt was present in the community. Tati Marai, the magistrate who deputised as chairman to hear her complaint, also used the occasion not only to emphasise the need for magistrates to be respected, but to assert his own status. Josephine and Tati maintained a mutually respectful relationship publicly, though as noted earlier each saw the other as a rival for the coveted chairing position. Josephine thought Tati was too old for the job, and Tati though Josephine was too inexperienced. Two other magistrates, Ben Aravape and Andrew Moiri, were on the bench with Tati during Josephine's dispute. There was a significant degree of reiteration in various statements by Josephine and Tati, but I have not attenuated the dialogue in the transcript below, as their preoccupations are nicely evidenced in the repetition.

I used a combination of tape recordings and written notes during all court hearings I attended, obtaining complete transcripts of the cases with breaks of only a few moments when a tape ended and was replaced. The dialogue in Josephine's case is presented here in free translation, but phraseological stumbles and breaks in speech have been left in. The language used in Konedobu court was mostly Hiri Motu, rendered here using standard typeface. Sometimes English was used, mostly by magistrates in their discussions with each other (the magistrates were fluent in English, as were many disputants). Shifts between languages were unpredictable, and sometimes occurred in mid-sentence. When English is used in the dialogue below, I have rendered it in italics. The other language used was Toaripi (an eastern Gulf language shared by many of the court's attendees), especially when people became angry. The shifts into Toaripi, and subsequent returns to Hiri Motu, are indicated below by a note in brackets. Interpolations and minor clarifications by myself to aid reading are also in brackets. The section of dialogue given here begins after the formal introduction of the case, when magistrates and disputants had already taken their positions on the benches provided:

> Magistrate Tati: [addressing the disputants] The law is not only written in books. We are the representatives of the law appointed by the people of this settlement. Whatever I say in this community represents what the law says. No-one should disobey that. Because we are Kerema people [i.e. historically from locations near Kerema, in the Gulf District], you see us and you say we are peace officers and magistrates, but you do not respect that. It's against the law. The law says no-one should walk away from a mediation. That is why

you are appearing here. During the mediation, when you walked away you thought you were above the village court. You thought you had power to walk away, and that Konedobu village court had no power to stop you. You, this old man and this young lady, you thought you had power. That is why you said, 'This Konedobu village court is below us—if we walk away they will not do anything.' That is why you walked away. [to Josephine] What do you want to say about this?

Josephine: I will say this—the reason why I am angry is that they walked away. One of the reasons is that the lady originally called on me for help and I answered. But during the mediation they had no respect. Second, I will say, they always face problems in the settlement. They ought to move out from the settlement, *that's what they want, that's what they are wishing for*. The lady and her husband should build a house somewhere, and they should take the old man in, *so that the mother can be alone. That will make sense*. Because their problem is that—they know that one of their mother's sister's children is working with me [i.e. as a peace officer for the court]. *She asked me if they are facing problems down there and I said 'Yes, I have given them advice but they will not listen. I was giving them advice during the mediation but they would not listen and walked away. They are walking away from the court so I am taking them to court on Monday.'* The lady [the peace officer] *agreed with my decision. So that's my decision*. When the lady [disputant] came to my house that's what she was yelling, accusing me of being one-side on [i.e. biased towards] her mother. But it's not one-side. Mediation calls upon the family. I try to give good advice how to live in one house. During the mediation she was more powerful [i.e. aggressive and uncooperative]. *No respect for court area, no respect for magistrate, I want you people to charge her a court fine. That's my request*.

Magistrate Tati: [to man and woman] You two have heard what she said. . . .

Josephine: [interrupting] Because in Konedobu area I have heard many people. . . . This is my third time. . . . I heard it from two of them. . . . First—now the District Office [i.e. the NCDC office which paid out allowances], *this is what they told me, I am always one-side on people*. In this court I have always struggled to get cases all the way to welfare court so that people can be compensated. [Josephine is getting angry now and stumbling over her words. She is referring to thankless attempts to help families deal with the welfare system bureaucracy.] And they did not take it back to me. *I really struggle, myself*. Whenever I take them to court they walk off and accuse me of being biased. *I don't want to hear any more 'one-side' business*.

Magistrate Tati: *Okay, we have heard what Josephine has said. I will not be biased towards Josephine, or support her unconditionally. The law says we will not call each other sisters and brothers because we are in the village court* [i.e. fellow magistrates will not show bias towards each other in court cases]. *But today I am sitting here, it is just, only law. I am Law*. I am . . . these people are young. I have been nineteen years in Konedobu village court. I have seen all that is written about these matters. That is why—you know that in my life I have been an important man in the church. That is why—from the point of view of the church, too, people break the law. I know a lot about the law.

Now that you, the old man and the young lady, have walked away from the mediation you have broken the law. That is why *I am going to charge you, to prove it*. And secondly, I said we are the law. Our words are law. If anybody disobeys us, we will charge that person. If anybody does something like this lady, accusing Josephine of being biased—everybody says that to us. When they say that, they are going against the law. The law says we can send them to prison for one month. Or otherwise I will fine them. We, the magistrates, we do not charge people for nothing. If, *if you say I am one-side—my decision . . . you said I am one-side—I've got a certificate to arrest that fellow.* [adopting an angry tone and flourishing his village court magistrate's certificate] *My decision, I give—I give to that fellow—is, you know, because I got a certificate to give it. You got a certificate? And you say that my decision is no good. You are nothing, you haven't got a certificate. You can't arrest a person, you can't charge a person, if you haven't got like this* [waving the certificate]. If anybody later on, here in this village [i.e. settlement], says anything, I have already told you that I used to be an important man in the church, that is why I treat people with respect. But I know the law. If I left the church, I would send everybody to prison... *If you've got money to* [pay a] *fine*. You have heard what Josephine said before, She did not make any decision, she was just explaining the case. And you go away saying she is biased. *That means you are against the magistrate, huh? Are you a lawyer? No, huh? You are an ordinary person.*

Elderly disputant: Excuse me—it is true that we walked away from the mediation. The reason why we walked away was that during the mediation . . . the matter was already public knowledge. While we were talking she interrupted. She said she had heard about the problem already. The first time she interrupted, I excused her. The second time, we walked away.

Magistrate Tati: Now I will make a ruling on that. Mediation is not a court. If different parties have disputes, and come together during a mediation, it is only for mediation, otherwise jealousy would arise, or something bad might happen within the family. When we say 'mediation' it means listening or sorting out differences, otherwise family life will be spoiled. That is why people must come together and discuss among themselves what the problem is, and magistrates or peace officers would advise people, to remove the problem. To prevent harm to the family, you would all come together, make a little feast and then forget your differences. Mediation is not a court.

Elderly disputant: You have heard what Josephine said. What I want is that you listen to what we say before you decide what is right. We—in our family, this young lady [his daughter] is causing problems for us, what I want is that you look into this.

Magistrate Tati: *Okay*. One thing, when you walked away from the mediation. You should have realised 'I have not listened to the mediator and I have walked away'. You should have gone back, but first you walked out. And then later you said '*wantok system*'. The magistrate is following the '*wantok system*' [i.e. favouring her own kin or friends]. The magistrate looks at the case and decides whether somebody has broken the law or not. Sometimes a defendant will fight or run away from trouble but the complainant tells the truth. And the defendant, because he is trying to get away from trouble, will try a lot of tricks. Magistrates have to look at this, and the law—whether the complainant or the defendant is telling the truth. They will have to look at this, the magistrate will not just do whatever they want. That would be wrong.

Josephine: *Okay.* [momentarily addressing one of the other magistrates] Andrew, you listen, you were not here during that mediation we had on Monday. And all three of us were together. When we heard the complaint, it was like two daughters fighting against the mother. It was their mother. I was only trying to advise them on their disagreement, but during my advice they would not listen because they had had some problems during the weekend. And you see, for example, [now addressing the elderly disputant] your elder daughter, if she marries, and if her marriage goes wrong, you will look after her children until she remarries. *You had a feeling about it.* If the small one was sick, you would have to take it to hospital day after day. If the mother advises the children on how to live, will you help the mother in advising the children, or would you take the child and go against the woman. Which one is right? [The final seconds of Josephine's comments and the opening phrases of Magistrate Tati's response were lost as I changed the recording tape.]

Magistrate Tati: . . . I know all about these kinds of people. I would like to give you some advice but *I am feeling sick of* these kinds of people. Every time I say these kinds of things, you twist what I say, and you accuse me of being biased. That is why *I got fed up with it.* I don't want it. I know all about these kinds of people. I don't want to sort out their problems. Last time you heard what they said about Tati Marai [i.e. himself], they said 'Tati Marai, he would not do it,' because I know these people, I know the way of life in this village [i.e. the settlement]. Not only you people in this community, I have also dealt with other people. If they bring their complaints to me I will say *'Go. Find any old magistrate to make your way, not me.'* [becoming visibly angry] *How many times am I going to make it?* We are human beings, yes? If this kind of problem arises we should all sit down and listen. Have respect! [switching to Toaripi language] You must really have respect! Sit down! Listen! Think to yourself! [switching back to Hiri Motu] Don't accuse one another. You will have to think about the future, and say to yourself, if I lead people in that manner [i.e. wisely] there will be no problems. [speaking directly to the old man] You should realise you are a father-figure. The family is like that tree there, you are the trunk of that family. If you sway, the children will also sway. [switching to Toaripi] If the mother gets angry with the children, you should realise it is because they are doing something wrong. You should think about helping the mother to advise them that what they are doing is wrong. You should think to yourself, 'If I don't do that they will get worse.' [switching to Hiri Motu] You don't do that, that is why you face a lot of problems. The mother speaks on her own, that is why I don't want to deal with your problem [i.e. it is not his job to advise their children]. . . .

Magistrate Ben: [interrupting] *Okay,* I will ask you all—whether these two women show respect for their parents or not. It is the parents' job to ensure that their children respect them. . . .

Magistrate Tati: [interrupting] That is something aside from this matter. What we are talking about is that these two walked away from the mediation. We have heard all that. We are now trying to give a decision. . . .

Magistrate Andrew: [interrupting] *Okay*, let's finish now, [to disputants] you go outside and we will make a decision.

The foregoing dialogue illustrates many of the issues which have been discussed not only in this chapter but in previous chapters. The potential conflict between the culturally determined community perception of village court magistrates and the self perception of the latter as dispute settlers and adjudicators is fairly clear, particularly in its gender aspects. Josephine's attempted mediation had foundered partly on a disjunction between her attempt to give advice and the elderly disputant's perception of her as a female and younger than himself. This is a difficult position for a female magistrate to be in, as conservative elder men in 'Kerema' society believe it is inappropriate for younger women, in particular, to make judgements on them or give them advice. Josephine, an educated woman with public service training, regarded him as refusing to co-operate, and as being the most recent of a number of people who had shown inadequate respect for her authority. Josephine's frustrations, as a woman magistrate, are very evident here, and imply that the complexities of gender politics in village courts would not necessarily be lessened simply by appointing more women magistrates. As noted earlier, Molly Vani—Josephine's eventual successor as the chairperson at Konedobu—negotiated the gender politics of her job very well. She rarely encountered the kind of problem which Josephine complained about in the case above. The two women were of different temperaments: Josephine had a tendency to adopt the demeanour of a workplace supervisor when in the village court, whereas Molly was consistently Socratic, using dialogic skills which invited disputants to reflect and make judgements on themselves.

The embeddedness of magistrates in the sociality of their community is made clear by Tati, who represents himself not only as a magistrate and church elder but as a community elder as well (in his latter comments). Significantly, though, Tati presents himself as representing 'the law', and implies (wrongly) that the law does not permit people to leave a mediation. His assertions reflect the influences that have led village court magistrates to see themselves as agents of the formal legal system rather than as 'customary' dispute settlers. At the same time, Josephine's anger at the behaviour of the people between whom she was attempting to mediate is expressed partially through an appeal to her supportive role as an advice giver and helpmate, rather than as a magistrate. Her complaint about the lack of appreciation for her efforts to help settlement dwellers deal with the bureaucracy emphasises the non-adjudicatory activities of village court magistrates. Accusations that magistrates are biased are common among village court disputants, especially when a case is 'lost' in formal court sittings. Both Josephine and Tati indicate a sensitivity to such charges, though their public responses (Tati brandishing his magistrate's certificate and asserting his legal authority, Josephine appealing to her dedication to helping people) are very different. But while Tati demands respect on the grounds of his authority and 'church' background, he also shows a more avuncular concern with his fellow Keremas' behaviour, applying the imagery of a tree to the family and lapsing into Toaripi to admonish them for their attitude to one another.

The motives for becoming a village court magistrate, the kinds of people who become magistrates, and the politics of being a magistrate, are shown here to be very different among Konedobu, Pari and Erima courts. Clearly village court magistrates are not people elected purely on the grounds of their adjudicatory integrity and good knowledge of local customs. Further, we can make few generalisations about their motives in becoming magistrates. Some appear to be genuinely committed to the welfare of their community, while for others the village court is a vehicle for the achievement of status or power. In the latter case, however, we should note the implication of some examples given here, that magistrates are not necessarily powerful figures and may be vulnerable to the malevolence of others by virtue of their work.

Notes

1. This is the substance of occasional claims by political advocates for women's rights (see, for example, Kumugl 2001; cf. Garap 2000: 163, Mitchell 1985: 88, and chapters 3 and 9 herein).
2. Noted in visits 1992 and 2004, and personal communication (1992) J. Takuna, Village Court Secretariat Regional Liaison Officer, New Guinea Islands Region; (2004) N. Mark, Principal Advisor, Milne Bay Provincial Liaison Office; K.Piniau, Acting East New Britain Provincial Village Court Officer.
3. For further elaboration of these aspects of leadership, see Goddard (2001), and cf. Groves (1954, 1963), Oram (1989).
4. Village courts can hold 'joint sittings' involving magistrates from other areas, if the dispute is between someone from their own area and a person or persons from another area. Joint sittings are more common in town than in rural places.

6

Pari Village Court in Action

In this and the two following chapters I present examples of cases heard in Pari, Konedobu and Erima village courts, developing the observation made in chapter 4 that each village court has its own style. Not only does each court reflect the sociality of the community it serves, but the range and type of cases heard differ from court to court. This chapter presents Pari village court in action, dealing with offences and disputes in a Motu-Koita village which is trying to preserve its identity in the face of the modern sociality represented by the growing city nearby. Christian sobriety is an important characteristic of this identity, for as we have seen, over a period of more than a century the village has incorporated the congregational Christianity of the LMS and the subsequent United Church into its sociality, and its attempts to maintain its communal integrity are publicly oriented to the moral tenets of Christianity. Of the three courts examined in this book, Pari particularly displays the effects of what Nader has called 'harmony ideology', which she typifies as evolving as a consequence of colonial political and religious policies (1990: 2).

The range of case-types in Pari village court is narrow. The majority of cases are concerned with drunken behaviour, usually consisting of loud obscene language and the smashing of emptied beer bottles. Occasionally a degree of brawling is involved which could lead to charges of assault, but as the brawling occurs mostly among drunken males and therefore does not involve assault on anyone but themselves it is rarely raised as a complaint in court. While they are presented in the first instance as complaints about drunkenness and associated behaviour, these kinds of cases reveal conflicts which are normally suppressed in everyday life in Pari. The villagers make a concerted effort to maintain an atmosphere of peace and calm, orienting village life largely to church activities. Normal interaction is polite to the point of appearing bereft of emotion to an unfamiliar observer. Inebriation risks the revelation of tensions which are suppressed in sobriety, such as jealousy, simmering anger over land issues, family disputes, impatience over unpaid debts or unfulfilled obligations. In court the drunkenness is treated as the relevent issue so far as identifying cases for official records is concerned, and the 'settlement' of the dispute is presented as a decision by the magistrates on the culpability of the drunkard.

The underlying issues revealed in drunken confrontations often remain unresolved, as they are either beyond the jurisdiction of the court (as in the case of land disputes), or matters of a nature which disputants regard as unsuitable for explication in the village court (as in the case of intra-family disputes). In this regard the village court rarely resolves a dispute of significance. Rather, it attempts to restore the normal relationships which are important to the villagers. Thus reconciliation, and reintegration of weekend drunkards and other offenders into a communal sociality, are the real aims of the court. Indeed, magistrates display a degree of distress when they cannot achieve this. This was particularly visible when I was regularly attending court hearings in 1999. An outbreak of 'steam' consumption had occurred among young males. 'Steam' was a local name for a fruit-based, alcoholic concoction claimed by enthusiasts to be 90 per cent alcohol, produced with the use of an improvised still. The steam brewing was, in one respect, a signal that a significant group of young males in the village was rebelling against the 'traditional' identity which the village was trying to maintain (see Goddard 2005: 179–205; and chapter 4 herein). A number of the youths did not respond to court summonses, and those who did attend appeared to be unaffected by court proceedings. The village court magistrates had the power to issue prison orders against people who did not comply with village court directives, but were unwilling to do so, and found themselves impotent in the face of the youths' lack of co-operation. Their concern was that the socially disruptive behaviour of a growing number of young men under the influence of the very potent homebrew would cause increasing friction in the village, and probably bring the attention of the police to Pari. Nobody wanted a police raid (these are relatively rough affairs in PNG). Nor did they want the consequent gaoling of a significant number of the village's young men. The recalcitrance of the young men was not only a challenge to the authority of the village court, but more importantly it frustrated the social imperative of the village court—reconciliation and reintegration. The latter was more important to the court than the 'punishment' of offenders.

In addition to cases of drunkenness, the court heard cases involving, for example, minor theft (better described as pilfering) and arguments over gardens. The latter might be taken by a non-villager observing the court, at first encounter, to be accusations of a different order, such as theft of garden produce. However, claims that somebody had taken produce from a garden were likely to be contextualised in underlying and often publicly unspoken-of disputes over garden boundaries, as the first of the cases described below indicates. Some kinds of disputes, such as those within families, were taken to church deacons if they could not be resolved, and thus were only rarely aired in the village court. Certain other activities which could be glossed as 'crimes' or legal offences remained unacknowledged by disputants and the court. Sorcery, for example, is an offence listed in the village court handbook, and is often blamed for misfortune in Pari, but sorcery accusations are not brought to the village court. This is partly because accusations are hard to sustain and the fear of retribution prevents people from openly accusing other villagers, even though there are some who have fairly public reputations as practitioners. But it is also because the overtly Christian village is reluctant to publicly acknowledge the existence of practices which, its Church teaches, are obsolete and doctrinally untenable.

Pari court cases, though few in number compared to several other village courts around Port Moresby, were mostly lengthy, and the hearing of even a simple case of drunkenness could stretch for some hours. This was a marked contrast with Erima village court, where a large number of cases were dealt with in short order. The length of the hearings in Pari reflected not only the general demeanour of the village (leisurely, contemplative) but also the deeper issues in which nominal disputes were grounded, as observed above. While Pari village court magistrates could not explicitly deal with, for instance, a land dispute whose dynamics were implied in an instance of drunken abuse, there was usually an acknowledgement of its existence. The partial disclosure of these deeper issues imbued the proceedings with a gravity which precluded expeditious decision making.

Table 6.1 indicates the way Pari village court classified offences and disputes according to the category headings given in the village court handbook. The handbook lists eighteen 'offences' which are punishable, and a further category called 'disputes', which do not carry punishment, but in respect of which the court can make certain orders regarding compensation, etc. The 'dispute' category is used as a default by village courts for issues which they do not wish to classify as offences but which are nevertheless within what they believe to be their jurisdiction. Adultery, desertion, unpaid brideprices, unpaid compensation, outstanding debts, are all classified as 'dispute'. A full list of the offence categories in the village court handbook is given in the appendix.

Table 6.1. Offences and disputes as officially designated in Pari village court during two periods of eighteen weekly hearings (monitored to their completion by the author in 1994 and 1999)

Official identification of offence	Number in 1994 period	Number in 1999 period	Comments
Disturbing the peace	19	9	Most alcohol-related behaviour was subsumed under this heading, including insults, obscene language, minor fighting, property damage.
Theft	1	1	Theft from a garden, and theft of wood from a house verandah.
Insult	1	0	A woman publicly insulted a man. N.B. If this had been a drunken insult by a male, it probably would have been classified as 'disturbing the peace'.
Damage to property	2	0	One case involved youths writing graffiti on the walls of the village pre-school, the other was about damage to garden plants.
Failure to obey village court order	7	1	Mostly failure to pay fines and compensation ordered by the court.
Dispute	6	3	Mostly intra-family disputes and including, e.g. arguments over use of family property, distribution of brideprice, neglect or desertion, all brought to village court after attempts at settlement through church deacons, etc, had failed.
Total	36	14	

The classification of cases in table 6.1 into only five types of offences should not be taken to mean that other types of offences do not occur. Accusations connected with sorcery are not aired in the village court, as already noted, and further, the classification 'disturbing the peace' is used to encompass a number of other offences which could be classified differently. Drunkenness, insults, offensive language, and slander are all listed separately as offences in the village court handbook. Most of the cases classified by Pari village court as 'disturbing the peace' could have been classified at least as drunkenness, and by extension offensive language and slander (in the handbook this is described as being 'if somebody says something bad and untrue about someone else'). The preference of the court for classifying them as 'disturbing the peace' reflects the magistrates' preoccupation with the overall atmosphere the village attempts to preserve. But the consequent absence of statistics for 'drunkenness' in the official record of cases heard by the court (the records are forwarded to, and kept by, the VCS) also hints at the dilemma faced by a village which has adopted Christian sobriety as a tenet of its integrity yet enjoys commodities such as beer and has to negotiate the negative consequences. Official statistics of cases heard by any village court rarely reflect the types of cases actually heard (see Goddard 2005: 51–76).

I witnessed the cases referred to in table 6.1 in 1994 and 1999. I monitored Pari village court cases over a period of eighteen weeks in each year. The total number of cases given in the table, however, does not reflect the total number of cases which were actually brought to court. As with other village courts, numbers of cases are withdrawn by disputants after the court has commenced to hear them, or are referrred to other courts, or adjourned but then 'settled' informally before they are due to be heard again. To ensure a reasonable degree of rigour, I have listed only those cases which I was able to hear from beginning to end and so could have no equivocation about the court's findings and declared course of action. The disparity between the total number of cases witnessed in the 1994 period (thirty-six) and the total in the 1999 period (fourteen) should not be taken to mean that there were significantly less problems in the village in the latter period. For example, of the nine cases of disturbing the peace in the later period, one was the 'steam' case referred to above. This involved a dozen youths the first time it was heard and adjourned, but gradually the number of youths identified as offenders grew in successive hearings until up to twenty were involved, and represented a major problem for the village as a whole. All the court proceedings I attended in both periods were tape recorded with the magistrates' permission, and I also took handwritten notes. The language used in all cases was 'pure' Motu. The length of hearings was a factor in choosing the examples given here. Many cases continued through several court days and in written form are simply too long to present in the space of this chapter. The transcripts below are annotated where necessary to aid the reader's understanding.

Three Cases From Pari Village Court

Cassava theft

The first case described here exemplifies the point made above that disputes which appear to be simple are frequently grounded in deeper issues. There were, for instance, some disputes which, on looking at the court's list before a day's hearing started, I had assumed would be trivial and of potentially short duration in court, but which would stretch to hours of discussion. They often required a nuanced understanding of village history, which I struggled to acquire through extensive questioning of the magistrates and other older villagers after the day's hearings had ended. The case described here was less complicated than many, and (in contrast to some marathon hearings) short enough for its transcript to be included here. Initially it involved a claim that some youths had stolen cassava (*M. esculenta*) from a family garden. As the hearing progressed, however, indications of an underlying dispute over garden boundaries began to emerge.

Five magistrates, led by the chairman, Gaba Gaudi, sat on the bench. Pseudonyms are used here for the complainants, the accused and others referred to in testimony. The case began with the complaint being put to the youths:

> Magistrate Gaba: On Tuesday the 27th day of September, the following people, Ahuia, Badu, Sibona, Dika and Etai, went and stole cassava from the garden of Finau, Gavera, Hitolo and Irua. Is this true?
>
> Defendant group: [together] Yes, true.
>
> Magistrate: [asking each defendant in turn and receiving a nod of assent] Ahuia, is it true? Badu, is it true? Sibona, is it true? Dika, is it true? Etai, is it true? All say it is true. Sibona, Dika and Ahuia, what did you do on that day?
>
> Sibona: I went to town for pleasure.
>
> Magistrate: From there, where did you go?
>
> Sibona: I went to the school place.

> Magistrate: You went to the school place and met the others, and where did you go?
>
> Sibona: From there we went to the garden.
>
> Magistrate: Dika, where did you go?
>
> Dika: I was in the house and Etai's mother asked me to go with the boys to the garden to plough it. When I went to the garden they were already eating cassava.
>
> Magistrate: Etai, on that day where were you?
>
> Etai: I was there, too.
>
> Magistrate: When Badu and Ahuia did this, did you know about it?
>
> Etai: Yes I did know about it.
>
> Magistrate: Did you know about it?!
>
> Etai: When they did it, I was the one who took the cassava.
>
> Magistrate: You took the cassava plants, and you smoked them all?
>
> Etai: Yes, we smoked them all.
>
> Magistrate: Ahuia, where did you eat these cassava plants?
>
> Ahuia: We ate them in the garden.
>
> Magistrate: Is it true, Badu? Where did you get the cassava plants?
>
> Badu: I went later. When I got there they were smoking the plants already. I joined them and ate with them.
>
> Magistrate: Gavera, please tell the court the circumstances of this matter.

Gavera was the main complainant and spoke on behalf of the owners of the garden from which Etai and his friends took the cassava.

> Gavera: I was in the house when some people sent their children to tell us that some boys were stealing cassava plants from our garden. When I heard this I took my small axe because I thought it was Kerema boys stealing from our garden again.

The 'Kerema' boys referred to by Gavera lived in a settlement a few hundred metres from the village, on land belonging to the village. The settlement had been established some decades previously, by arrangement with the villagers, who had a traditional trading relationship with people in a group of villages in the Gulf Province, from where the settlers originated. Over time the settlement had grown to the point where Pari villagers were becoming anxious about the number of 'foreigners' on their land. Some Kerema people were also married into the village, and lived in the village itself. Pari villagers were quick to blame 'Kerema', often unfairly, for trouble in the village.

Gavera: When I arrived Ahuia, Badu, Dika, and Etai were in Etai's mother's garden smoking the cassava plants. They were not in our garden. As I arrived I met Dauma [another village man] and I knew he would help me. Ahuia and the others saw me and were talking fast. When I got there Uncle Kidu told me that they were there on Tuesday too, but I just left them in the garden because they said they were getting cassava from their own garden. Later I met Ahuia and asked him where they got the cassava from, and he replied that they got them from our garden. Then I asked him how many cassava plants they dug up. He said they only dug up one plant. When I went to the garden to check, they had dug up four. I didn't believe what they had first told me [i.e. that they had obtained the cassava from their own garden] because their cassava plants are still young. I asked him who had ploughed the garden and he said it was Etai who ploughed it.

The magistrate turned his attention to Etai, and while his questions superficially seem aimed at clarifying where the youth had ploughed, they hint that he was aware that there was more to this case than a simple theft:

Magistrate: Etai, which garden did your mother ask you to plough?

Etai: She asked us to plough our garden at X———.

Magistrate: At X———. Which part of X———? Above Y——— or below Y———?

Etai: Below Y———.

Magistrate: The road leads to the gardens past Lohia's house, Kidu's house and Morea's house. At the end of the road are the gardens [sketching a quick diagram on a notepad and holding it up]. This garden belongs to widower Irua, where you will see a red cloth. Which garden did you plough, this side or the other side?

Etai: We thought we ploughed on our land, but we found that our garden block was not big enough.

Etai's reply at first sight appears to be a statement of a simple error: as if he had thought he was on his family garden land, and had not realised the small size of his family's block, compared to the neighbouring block belonging to Gavera's group. But the magistrate knew this was an oblique reference to the real issue behind the theft, a land dispute. The reference to the small size of Etai's family block was in fact sarcasm. The magistrate knew the import of Etai's remark, and attempted to prevent the explication of Etai's real reason for 'stealing' the cassava, by giving a short history of the putative ownership of the garden block:

Magistrate: The court knows that this garden block belonged to Irua's wife because this was the place where she made her garden while she was alive. That is why you will see that their garden block is very big—and you thought part of it was your block because your block wasn't a big one. Because of that you also thought that the cassava plants were yours and you dug them up, and ploughed the land too. That means the cassava plants you dug were not yours, they were in Widower Irua's garden. Did you hear that, boys? He is not happy because you went right over to his block. That is why he brought you to court. I, personally, don't know the family relationship in regard to this land. The right people to talk to would be grandmother Oloa and Piri. They are the ones who understand the issues about this area of land. We have to be careful about this, Gavera [addressing a complainant] because this land might belong to old man Kevau, Piri or some other relatives, including your mother. We have to be clear or we are in trouble.

Village courts, while permitted to hear disputes involving gardens and their produce, are not permitted to hear land disputes. This is a distinction Pari village court magistrates welcomed, as land disputes usually had very long histories, were extremely complex and regenerated fierce contentions when publicly discussed. Traditionally intra-community land disputes were addressed, if possible, by negotiation between the parties involved, with guidance from elderly people who recalled previous arrangements and apportionments of the land in question. This is the import of the magistrate's reference to 'grandmother Oloa and Piri'. Settlements achieved by this method lasted for a period of some years, before a later generation began to argue over the land, negotiating a new settlement. The outcome of this negotiation might be different from that of the previous one, guided by now-elderly witnesses of, or participants in, the previous debate, who offered their memories of what the previous issues had been, and what had since transpired. And so the process continued, with passing generations. Sometimes, if land disputes could not be settled in this way, they were referred to an elder, perhaps a *hanua kwarana* (village leader) or other person recognised as a *tano biaguna* (overseer of the village's land).

In modern times, the development of land courts has meant that decisions about land ownership which were once flexible (in that they were able to be re-negotiated at a later time) become rigid, under the legal system. This is a state of affairs which sometimes appeals to younger, litigious villagers, but causes unease among elders. To the latter the old system of negotiation and re-negotiation was a way of minimising the tension in the village caused by long-simmering resentments over land. The magistrates in the cassava case were keen to keep the dispute from developing into an explicit land issue, and preferred not to acknowledge the real cause of the cassava incident. In the beginning the simple theft of cassava could be glossed at least as an error, and easily dealt with through a compensation payment.

> Magistrate: The case brought before the court is about cassava, not a land dispute. [addressing the complainant Gavera] Etai thought the cassava plants were theirs, because when he saw that their block was small he moved on to

your block and got them and ploughed the land too. Do you have anything else to say?

Gavera: When we made this garden, we built a fence around it to separate it from the others. They made these two paths across the garden because, I know for sure, they wanted to dig up those cassava plants.

Magistrate: As we said in the first place. . . .

Gavera: The main thing is, why did they make the two paths right through the garden? And they also dug up cassava and moved right over to our block.

The real issue was continuing to show itself. Gavera was moving beyond the actual theft and beginning to directly address the issue of the boundary between the two adjacent blocks. The magistrate tried to guide the argument back to the cassava theft, by asking one of the youths to clarify where they had taken the cassava from, as if to determine whether it was from one garden or the other, and whether the youths had been confused over whose garden they were in:

Magistrate: Ahuia, where did you get the cassava, and where is their garden?

Ahuia: Their garden is at X——.

Magistrate: Which one, the place which they ploughed or the new garden?

Ahuia: The new garden.

Magistrate: The new garden which Etai ploughed. Etai thought it was their garden. That's why he dug those cassava plants. Who did you go with? Etai?

Ahuia: I went with Sibona and Dika.

Magistrate: This is becoming clearer because we now know that this garden belongs to Irua and his children, and not Etai's mother. The upper garden is a new garden and the lower gardens are the old ones. Ahuia, you, Sibona and Dika have to pay a fine.

Ahuia: I don't have any money.

Magistrate: Ahuia, who told you to dig the cassava?

Ahuia: Etai told us to dig the cassava.

Magistrate: Whose cassava did you dig, Etai's or Gavera's?

Ahuia: Etai told us to dig cassava in his mother's garden.

Magistrate: Etai, is your garden a new garden or an old garden?

Etai: It is a new garden.

The magistrate now tried further questions aimed at clarifying whether the cassava had come from Etai's family's new garden (in which case they would be small and not ready to eat), or from the older garden of Gavera's family (in which case they would be more mature and edible). But this led to an important declaration from Etai which implied more strongly his underlying reason for the 'theft'.

> Magistrate: In your new garden, do you think you have cassava which are ready for eating?
>
> Etai: The cassava plants we dug are very young ones which are not for eating.
>
> Magistrate: You dug the young ones.
>
> Etai: Yes, the young ones. They are still very young for cooking.
>
> Magistrate: You dug some cassava in your garden and some in Gavera's garden?
>
> Etai: No, I am only talking about the ones we dug in our garden, where the gardens are separated.
>
> Magistrate: Gavera said the line of cassava you dug up belongs to them. The path you made through the garden—that block is also theirs.
>
> Etai: The rain tree that stands there is ours.

Etai's simple declaration was potent with contention. It invited questions which could have expanded the cassava-stealing case into a complex land dispute. For example, if the rain tree belonged to Etai's family, a question arose as to whether it had originally been planted on what was thought to be Gavera's land with the permission of his family, or whether it had been planted on what was thought to be the land of Etai's family at the time. The magistrate was quick to prevent the discussion developing in that direction:

> Magistrate: That is something I do not know. This court case is about stealing cassava. It is not a land court.
>
> Etai: I am talking about it because it is in our garden block.
>
> Magistrate: Please address this problem properly. This has arisen because you have moved right over to Gavera's block. To solve this, pull out all the cassava and redo the separation of the gardens into their proper blocks. Remember, digging up cassava for no reason is nothing to laugh about. At this time there is a drought and if there were no European food stores we would be suffering and maybe dying of hunger. Badu [addressing another of the youths], you said you didn't dig cassava in the garden.

The magistrate had now made it clear that the court would not countenance an explicit land dispute, and suggested a resolution to any equivocation over the cassava, as if a recent confusion over boundaries had occurred. With his final questions to Badu he resumed an earlier theme, clarifying who had actually been involved in the digging of the cassava.

> Badu: As I said earlier, when I arrived they were smoking them.

Magistrate: When you arrived, did they finish smoking them?

Badu: When I arrived they had finished smoking them and we sat and started eating them. I didn't know whose garden they dug them up from.

Magistrate: Gavera told us. Etai, if there is a dispute about your family's garden block and Gavera's block, you must talk about it between your families, or go to a land court. We will not discuss it here. Give us [magistrates] some time, now.

The disputants moved away to sit at the back of the court, while the magistrates discussed the matter among themselves. Eventually they were called back to the magistrate's table.

Magistrate: Ahuia, Badu, Sibona, Dika and Etai. It is clear that some of you took cassava belonging to Irua [the elderly widower, father of complainant Gavera] and all of you ate it. This was Irua's cassava, and you were wrong to take it and eat it. Each of you must pay K2 compensation to Irua. You have two weeks to pay this to the court. If there is a dispute over gardens, then we cannot hear it in this court. This case was about taking the cassava. If there is a dispute over gardens, settle that dispute. Then maybe there will be no more complaints about stealing cassava. This is finished.

All the youths then shook hands with Gavera and those of his family who had brought the complaint to court, following which all the disputants shook hands with the magistrates and other court officials. Forming a moving line, they then shook hands with everyone in the court area. The handshaking was an important ritual in Pari village court, signifying reconciliation and the restoration of the unity of the village. However, it was clear that the issue of the boundary between the garden blocks of the families of Etai and Gavera would remain contentious.

Obscenities

The second example represents a very common complaint in Pari village court, of obscene language used by drunken young men in the vicinity of mature, married women. Like the case of cassava theft, there was also an underlying issue, although it was less potent than a land dispute. The immediate reason for the case being brought to court was an accusation that two young men ('George' and 'Vagi') had used obscene language to a woman and her husband. The incident occurred in the aftermath of a local council election. Voting in elections at all levels in PNG, from those involving national parliamentary candidates to those involving aspirants to parochial councils, is overwhelmingly determined by kin-group allegiances. Tensions which might normally be suppressed between groups in a community are commonly exacerbated during election campaigns.

Two candidates had substantial support in Pari village, and friction had occurred between factions of supporters. However, it had been largely repressed in the atmosphere of calm and dignity deliberately maintained by the overtly Christian village. Under the influence of alcohol, however, self-control diminished. In this instance the drunken young men, who were brothers, had used obscene language towards a man and women who had voted for the opposing candidate, 'Ageva' (who had lost to the candidate supported by the two brothers).

The obscenities had been uttered both in Motu and English, and also in Tokpisin. The use of the latter language deserves a comment, for mature Motuans in particular regard Tokpisin as almost an obscenity in itself. Their preferred lingua franca apart from English is Hiri (or 'Police') Motu, which has been in existence for more than a century, formerly used by people of the different language groups along PNG's south coast for communication among themselves. Tokpisin is the preferred lingua franca of people with ethnic roots in other parts of the country, and thus is identified by mature Motuans as the language of foreign usurpers of their territory, who they regard as less educated and less 'civilised' than themselves. Younger Motuans, however, are less discerning. They have grown up within the influence of a spreading city, with imported popular music and its attendant commodities and a significant degree of interethnic communication. In common with other young people in town they have appropriated Tokpisin into a discursive register which combines it with both Hiri Motu and English, and also creates slang innovations drawing on fashionable phraseology from music videos and advertisements. Young, street-wise Port Moresby urbanites, like young people or cliques elsewhere in the world, have thus created a relatively exclusive argot for themselves. This town-oriented argot is normally not used publicly in Pari, where young people feel the influence of the values of their elders, who particularly frown on Tokpisin.

Sexual terminology is not taboo in itself in Motu-Koita society, but when used deliberately to insult, sexual metaphors are regarded as obscenities. Drunken obscenities are not tolerated by married women in particular, who are quick to take offenders to court. Thus, in this case the woman's complaint was about three phrases: '*Ageva ena au badana oi ania*' (Motu: you eat Ageva's 'big tree'), 'fucking bastard', and '*kaikai kan*' (Tokpisin: eat cunt). The latter two phrases were directed at her husband. In court, the two now-sober young men were obliged to sit beside their accuser and her husband, with potential witnesses waiting to the side, and five magistrates facing them across a table. Many other villagers, young and old, sat within hearing distance—village court hearings were a weekly spectacle. In this austere atmosphere, the young men's obscene utterances were read out loudly and pedantically by the court clerk.

> Court Clerk: The complaint is this. George and Vagi—on Saturday night you two said insulting words to 'Mary' and 'William'. This is what you said: 'You eat Ageva's big tree', [switching to English] 'fucking bastard', [switching to Tokpisin] 'eat cunt'. [returning to Motu] Mary says George was the real cause of the complaint.

The leading questioner was the deputy chairing magistrate, Sisia Baeau, who began by asking the young men if they had used the words as alleged.

> Magistrate: George and Vagi, we heard that on Saturday night, you were drunk. Is that true? You said some insulting words to the complainant and her husband.
>
> George: [head lowered] We were joking. We did not mean what we were saying.

Magistrate Sisia moved quickly into a shaming tactic frequently used by magistrates in cases of this kind, constantly reiterating the obscene language, and asking for its meaning. Quoting the phrases with slow deliberation, he asked which of the brothers had actually said them.

> Magistrate: So what happened? Who said 'You eat Ageva's big tree', [switching to English] 'fucking bastard', [switching to Tokpisin] 'eat cunt'? [returning to Motu] These words were spoken in front of everybody. People say George said to this lady 'you eat Ageva's big tree'. Ageva was standing in the election. 'You eat Ageva's big tree.' Did you say that?
>
> George: I did not intend that. We were all joking. We were all at the side of the road when the lady walked by. We did not say it directly to them. I did not mean to swear at them.

Feigning ignorance of the metaphorical content of one of the phrases, magistrate Sisia now intensified the shaming tactics, playing on an anomaly which arises if the phrase '*au badana oi ania*' is interpreted literally. *Au* is Motu for 'tree', *bada* is 'big', and *na* is a possessive suffix, turning *bada* into *badana*, and *au bada* into *au badana*, giving the meaning 'big tree of' or 'big tree belonging to'. *Oi ania* is 'you eat [it]'. The phrase *Ageva ena au badana oi ania* is grammatically correct Motu, and is categorically correct if its metaphorical (phallic) meaning is taken. Sisia, however, deliberately used a literal interpretation and pretended to be confused.

> Magistrate: But the court wants to know: 'big tree of'. What is the meaning of this? 'Big tree' can be a Mango tree, Okari tree or any kind of tree. In the Motu dictionary, I cannot find the meaning of this. So what is 'you ate [his/her/its] big tree' [*ena au badana oi ania*]? Can you find the meaning of these words [i.e. this phrase] for me in the dictionary? I have been looking for

this meaning in the dictionary. So, I don't know what you meant by this. What is it?

George: [head down] It is not true, I did not say this.

Magistrate: Vagi, what is the meaning of this 'big tree of'?

Vagi: [head down] I don't know.

Magistrate: So why did you say [uttering slowly and precisely] 'big tree of'? I have been looking in all the books, including the Motu dictionary, and I can't find the meaning of these words. Did you say [using the English words untranslated] *fucking bastard* too? Did you say that? And [using the Tokpisin words untranslated] '*kaikai kan*'. I don't know this, and in my books this '*kaikai kan*' is not written, so what is '*kaikai kan*'? Vagi, what is '*kaikai kan*'? Tell me, because I could not find this in any book or dictionary. So which of you said this? George, 'big tree of', *fucking bastard* and '*kaikai kan*'—can you tell me the meaning of these?

The two young men remained silent, with their heads lowered. After creating acute embarrassment for the brothers with the repeated requests for the meaning of the phallic metaphor and the non-Motu phrases, the court moved to witnesses' testimony confirming what had been said, and the drunken comportment of the brothers. During this testimony the issue behind the immediate dispute, compounding the reasons for the woman's complaint, began to emerge. One of the brothers had claimed during the incident that the candidate, 'Ageva', had bribed the couple with K100 to vote for him.

Mary: [complainant] We didn't hear them say '*kaikai kan*' but it is true they said 'you eat Ageva's big tree'. '*Kaikai kan*', I didn't hear that. Only 'big tree of' and *fucking bastard* were said. George said to me that Ageva's K100 fooled me, therefore I was following Ageva.

Magistrate: Anything more?

Mary: He said, 'Only this K100 made you vote for Ageva'. I was shamed in public by this. Because in a public place what he said was not good for someone to hear. I was walking in front, they were walking noisily behind me. They walked until they were close to me. George was the noisiest of them. I want to know, in this court, why? George knows I am not a small girl. I am a mature woman. If he had approached me with the right words I would have answered. He did not physically attack me, but what he did was not good. The person who stopped him was Ageva's own son. So George did this until he grabbed hold of his arm. So I turned round and told him what he was doing to me was not right and he should have some respect for me. On my side, I did nothing, but if George was a good man he should have approached me in the right manner, and I would have replied appropriately. But he was very drunk and abusive.

Magistrate: George, a peace officer has informed us about this. You did this. We know. So give us some time and the court will make a decision on this.

All the disputants moved to the rear of the court area while the magistrates conferred, and were subsequently summoned to their former positions in front of the magistrates' table to answer more questions.

> Magistrate: George, you attempted to start a fight with the older woman, so why were you so angry towards her?
>
> George: I was not trying to start a fight. It was a joke among ourselves, and she took us seriously. We did not mean to give offence to her. At that time we walked up the cemetery road to the community school and regarded the matter as just a joke.
>
> Magistrate: So were you on the road or, where were you?
>
> George: She was walking down while we were walking up.
>
> Magistrate: Complainant [i.e. Mary], where did this happen?
>
> Mary: It was on the main road next to George's house.
>
> Magistrate: Peace officer, did you see anything happening?
>
> Peace Officer: Yes, I will tell the court. This is what happened. Yes, I did see George and the others. That night I saw George and his friends in the middle of the road. They were drunk. I heard what they said. The other thing they said was 'who are you, you *kaikai kan*'. This was said when I was watching from my house. So, [turning and addressing George] George and the others, you said 'Who are you, you *kaikai kan*'. I can assure you I am telling the truth. I heard you say this to the woman and her husband. I had found it hard to sleep, so I was sitting on my verandah. During that that time one of you called out 'who are you' and the other called out '*kaikai kan*'.
>
> Magistrate: Let us bring this back to the complainant. [to Mary] What are your thoughts?
>
> Mary: This is not very bad, but I felt upset by what they said, that is why I brought this to the court. I am a mature woman and this is why I should be respected.
>
> Magistrate: Vagi, what do you have to say?
>
> Vagi: Nothing.
>
> Magistrate: Then we will have to make you do some community work, maybe around the church, because you have nothing to say. Does either of you have anything to say?

There was no response from the two brothers, and the magistrate terminated the questioning and the shaming of the youths at this point, moving to a more direct criticism of their behaviour.

> Magistrate: The court knows that at that time [the time of the election result] people were very happy, and George, you should be happy because your side won. I cannot understand why you said this. Insulting words are not good. You

two have no excuse. The court found that the two of you, because you were drunk, did as the complainant has reported. The problem we have here in the community is that breaking bottles, and public insults, are always caused by drunkenness. So we found two things in court here. One is your lack of respect for your elders, and two is your lack of respect for yourselves. That is why the court wants you to bear it in mind that if anything happens in future you will be punished. You could pay a court fine or go to jail. So whatever happens in future, you think when you drink and respect others. Ok, give us a little time.

Once again the disputants moved to the back of the court and the magistrates conferred. The disputants were summoned back, to hear the court's findings. The magistrates decided to not to punish the young men. This was a common outcome in the court, emphasis being placed instead on the need for good relationships, and the bad effects of beer on people's behaviour.

Magistrate: Mary, George, Vagi, all listen. All these things arose from the election. We had an election campaign for quite a while. All we did was support the two candidates, and in the end one lost and one won. When a person wins, we are happy, because he got the most support and we should be happy. The other got less support and lost, and we lost with him. After the election, we did all sorts of things. For example, the losers accused the winners, and the winner's supporters created problems. The only advice I can give is that if you had not been drunk you would not have said these things and you would not be in this court today. Only beer made you do what you did, and you are in court today. We also found that because there were losers and winners, this dispute arose from the election. So the court's decision is that from today's date we should forget our differences, because the election is over. So, all of you take notice. The case is closed, and when you leave here you will not say these things again, and we advise that both sides forget what happened. So don't do it again. All those bad words which were mentioned today, don't say them again. Because I could not find them in the books, so you should not say them. And you young people should respect your elders and learn from them, so when you become an elder yourself you will set a good example. If a child acts in a bad manner, then another child will follow in its footsteps. That is why we must set a good example. If you are drinking, be sensible. So the court is ordering that matters relating to the election, and brought to court, should be forgotten from this time and never mentioned again. So, if the complainant and defendants meet again it should be as if nothing happened. This matter is now closed.

The disputants, in the customary gesture of reconciliation, shook hands among themselves, then with each magistrate in turn and then with everybody else who had attended the hearing.

Black market

This third case indicates again the village's concern over drunkenness, but from a different perspective than that of the above case. In accordance with its Christian identity, Pari village has for several decades tried to control its alcohol consumption. On some occasions church leaders and elders have attempted to enforce rules banning the consumption of alcohol altogether in the village (perhaps recalling the colonial era ban—until the early 1960s—on the consumption of alcohol by Papua New Guineans), but without success. Many people in the village like to drink, and alcohol is readily available from the town. Village court magistrates, some of whom drink alcohol, recognise that complete village abstinence is not feasible, and concern themselves with attempting to discourage drunkenness. Beer drinking in the village mostly occurs at weekends, and imbibers are encouraged to drink in their houses, rather than in public. Liquor traders in PNG require a licence, but illegal trading is common, from tradestores in villages and urban settlements. Adapting a slang phrase from English, an illegal beer trading enterprise is referred to as a 'black market' (a much narrower application of the term than that of Westerners). While black markets are a taken-for-granted part of informal trading throughout Port Moresby, they are formally discouraged in Pari, as a way of controlling alcohol consumption. At the same time, many villagers use the one or two black markets which operate quietly, and intermittently, in the village. In this case, three people, a woman ('Geua') and two men ('Tau' and 'Dobu'), were charged with operating black markets. The leading questioner was the chairing magistrate, Gaba Gaudi.

> Clerk: Geua, Tau and Dobu: The reason for this Pari village court summons is that, in our village, you are operating a 'black market'.
>
> Magistrate Gaba: The three of you were called because, as the clerk read out, you are accused of operating a black market. Tell the court, do you operate a black market?
>
> Geua: I do operate a black market but it is on behalf of someone else, I have been asked to do this to raise school fees and other expenses.

The deeper issue quickly emerged. The real concern of the court was drunken behaviour, which had been increasing in the village recently, and was exacerbated by 'steam' drinking. Steam is referred to below by an alternative slang term used mostly among Motuans—*paina*. A new councillor representing Pari village on the local Motu-Koita Council[1] had been discussing the general problem with village elders, church leaders and village court magistrates, and they were looking for strategies to bring it under control.

> Magistrate: Drinking beer in Pari village is not approved of by our own council. The court brought you here because you are selling beer illegally, without a licence. If you are caught you are charged with operating without a licence. If this case were in a higher court you would be punished heavily. That is why, last week, the village councillor was invited to attend, and the matter

was discussed between him and us [the magistrates] before you were brought to court. We agreed you were operating without a licence, and you have been brought to court because trading needs a licence, and you have no licence to trade. The village councillor also commented that if any one of us intends to sell goods, there are application forms to fill in, including for a licence to trade beer. The court is not only concerned about the black marketing of beer, but also talk in the village of marijuana and *paina* [the distilled homebrew]. These things are also causing trouble. That is why the court is trying to find a way to get rid of all these things, now. If these things are stopped, the community will be better.

Geua: I am selling to one person only. He told me to bring it in and he would buy it from me.

Magistrate: I understand, but you have no licence. You are aware that this year we have asked the peace officers to move around and advise us of anyone making illegal sales, like you have made. We intend to stop it. Sometimes the peace officers have seen you people but not reported it. The new councillor is very strongly opposed to this black marketing, so we must act against it.

Tau: Since last year I have stopped selling beer. But this year I have faced some problems like school fees. So I brought in five cartons and sold them. I am no longer selling them.

Magistrate: That is good. But it has given a signal to others. So now Dobu is involved, too.

The village court magistrates were unhypocritical about beer drinking. Individual magistrates commonly conceded, when hearing cases of drunkenness, that they themselves used to drink to excess when they were young men. Many people in the village drank beer, and bought beer from the black markets, including magistrates and peace officers. There was a degree of duality in the efforts of village court officials to police activities in which they themselves were often complicit. What emerges in the magistrate's comments below is that this was a problem for the village as a whole, not simply a prosecution of black marketeers.

Magistrate: Some of you are saying that peace officers are drinking too. But they have not been reported so I can't comment. I like beer too, and sometimes I buy black market beer. So, this court case is not because we are drinking, it is because people have no licence to trade beer. So if you want to serve the community, do it properly by getting yourself a licence to trade.

Geua: It is true. We apologise in court for selling it. We should try to find a better way of proceeding.

Magistrate: There was a person operating last year, he was brought to court because he had no licence to trade. If you start doing it again this year you could find yourself in higher court. Some peace officers complain that they pretend to come and buy from you [to catch the sellers], but as you recognise their faces you tell them there is no beer, but you sell it to other people.

Everybody should be treated the same. If you want to trade, apply for a licence. The reason we are here is because we don't have a licence to trade in the village. Drinking beer is not the issue. Everybody can drink, but drinkers often do not behave. The NCDC can issue licences, a six-month, or a twelve-month licence. So when you have a licence you can trade beer. Some of us in the village like to drink, but because you do not have a licence, we are all at fault, and we can all be blamed. Dobu, where do you keep your beer and where do you sell it, from the house or the store?

Dobu: From the store.

Magistrate: And your father, what did he say to you previously? You are selling without your father's permission. Whatever your father says, you should follow. Your father does not drink beer. First, you should listen to your father. Second, you are selling beer without a licence. We must be clear about this—if only you had licences nobody would have a right to complain. The two of you, Tau and Dobu, you know your own background, and you go to church, but then you go selling beer. So people in church are talking about you and laughing about you behind your backs. So sometimes at church you will hear people talking about selling beer. They cannot point at you, but they are talking about you. So if you were careful, the beer selling would not be talked about in church. So, you two have a reputation and a record of selling beer. I am not mentioning this to spoil your name, but because I have heard talk about you inside and outside the church. That is why I am asking you to stop selling beer. Geua, you mentioned that because of your child you were selling beer for school fees. I remember one afternoon when I was at your shop when people asked you for beer. You told them there was no beer, because I was there. But the problem is not that you are selling beer. There would be nothing wrong with that, except you have no licence. Some boys went away without beer. While I stayed you did not sell. After I left you started selling again. I do not want to be a part of dishonesty. I will not say things against you, except in court. You are not here because of what I saw. You are here because peace officers brought the matter to court, because you have no licence. So think carefully. If you still want to trade we can think about it together and organise to apply for a licence. For example, last year, in December, it was arranged that the police would come into the village, and charge people and take them to court [see below]. So we are saying that from now on, you must do things properly and get a licence. Because the government's law is that there should be no black market.

Magistrate Sisia [deputy chairman]: The relevant offence number is number seven, 'disturbing the peace and harmony of the village' [he is referring to the list of types of offence, in the village court handbook—see appendix]. There is always trouble with beer. For example you, Geua. You sell the beer and some people take it to their house, but others sit where they are and drink it and play radios and make a noise and disturb the peace. They continue till very late, and this disturbs the neighbours. So we all have to look at it carefully. The basic problem is that you have no licence. You only have tradestore licences and you cannot sell beer on tradestore licences. So we can only stop you from selling beer [i.e. the court is not concerned to stop Geua trading other items under her tradestore licence]. Last year we brought some people to court and they ceased operating, except for you and a few others.

Gaba Gaudi had made a reference (see above) to a potential police raid on the village some months previously which would have resulted in people being arrested and charged. Pari was an insular community and did not welcome the attention of external authorities. Gossip about the existence of black markets could have brought more attention. Another magistrate now elaborated on this, citing his complicity in the potential police raid referred to by Magistrate Gaba, which was to have been carried out in response to requests for help with rising alcohol problems:

> Magistrate Puka [a third magistrate]: Last year, on the 22nd day of December, I arranged that a raid should take place, but the former councillor thought innocent people would be caught, so the letter I wrote was not delivered. It was a letter on behalf of Pari village court to the Badili [a suburb nearby] police commander. But the councillor stopped it because the raid would have taken place on Christmas Eve, which would not have been good. So out of respect to the people we did not send the letter. Defendants, you knew that this beer is brewed by Chinese[2] and anybody here in PNG. Sometime back in 1975 there was a certain person who had been selling beer in this village. The police took him to court. The court fined him K1000. This man is in the village, but I cannot mention his name. Another person in church told the congregation that they wanted a licence to trade beer in Pari, and those people in church refused. They refused because they knew that if beer was sold here it would spoil the village. So if you people sell beer without a licence there will be problems. Geua, you know that where you and I live the neighbours complain about the beer drinking. They [beer drinkers] sit on the cement and make a lot of noise. You should tell them to take the beer home. There was a paper that this court drafted, about 1993. In this paper it said 'no beer drinking, and no selling beer in the village'. This paper was distributed to every house in Pari. In the paper it said anyone caught selling beer would be punished. After two years it was forgotten about and the whole thing started again. It is not the seller that causes the problem. It is the buyers, because they buy and drink the beer and disturb the village. So these papers would enable you people and the whole community to control the beer drinking. So, as the chairman said, you see that these things must be dealt with carefully.

> Magistrate Gaba: Dobu, do you have anything to say?

> Dobu: Yes. I do sell beer, but all my beer is warm, so no-one bought it. It is still there. There is no disturbance in my area. People go to the other store, because their beer is cold.

> Magistrate: Geua?

> Geua: Yes. I do trade beer, but it is not correct to say that people sit and drink around my area. I always advise my customers to take the beer away. It was only one occasion—that man from Hanuabada [i.e. a visitor from another village], who was drunk, came to get more beer from me. Since those men were already drunk I had difficulty controlling them. So we had some hard words, but afterwards they went away, so it was all right. So it is not me who tells them to sit there and drink. Because they are already drunk, they find it

easier to sit there and drink, so it is hard to make them go away. Thank you for the court's advice, and we should all try to get the proper papers so we can sell the beer legally.

Magistrate: Tau?

Tau made a short comment, in a low voice inaudible to myself and to my tape recorder. The magistrates brought the case to a close, with no punishment to the offenders, who had been summonsed under public pressure. Again, the underlying problem was alluded to:

> Mag: We'll leave the matter there. Because of the public complaints, we have to bring this to court. Or the people would think we are doing nothing. Because we know you, we have brought you here. But there are others who are operating black markets too. Beer and other things disturb the community, that is why we have to deal with this in court. Because we know that those people who do not drink will complain, and those who do drink will enjoy it, so it divides the village. The court cannot make any decisions, or issue preventive orders to prevent people from drinking. But after what you have heard from us, think about it, go back to your homes. Get a licence before you trade again. So if you want a licence, you can go to the NCDC and apply for documents. This is the only way we can keep the people from complaining, and keep everybody safe inside the law. This is finished. All of you can go now.

The case closed with the customary handshakes between all attendees and court officials.

The Ritual Role of Pari Village Court

The three cases described here demonstrate that punishing offenders was not a primary aim of the Pari village court. Compensation to the aggrieved was frequently ordered, but this was a gesture of reconciliation, and was often a nominal amount, as we saw in the case of the cassava theft. More commonly, offenders were warned of the consequences of their behaviour for relationships within the community, and the ritual of handshaking reintegrated them into the conventional sociality of Pari village. There was no evidence that people felt particularly guilty about having committed a 'crime', even if the terminology of guilt was used in court. People rarely 'denied' the offence they were accused of—as can be noted in the cases described here—and repeated offending was common, for instance, in the case of drunkenness. The village treated the latter as a regrettable component of weekend socialising which could never be eradicated. Its unpleasant effects on village harmony—the traducing of respectful behaviour to others—could, however, be repaired through the regular ritual of reconciliation in the village court.

Literature on traditional Motu-Koita society suggests that the subordination of the individual to a sense of communal responsibility contributed to a lack of guilt feelings over the kind of behaviour Westerners commonly regard as criminal. When the missionary W. G. Lawes attempted to retrieve a stolen item from a Motuan in 1873, 'the thief coolly demanded payment before he would give up the stolen property' (King 1909: 69). The missionary ethnologist Turner (1878: 492) commented judgmentally: 'Deceit and lying seem to be part of their very existence. . . . They steal as readily from each other as from strangers, nor is it looked upon as a crime unless a thief is taken in the act, when he is severely handled'. Seligman (1910: 131) wrote that 'homicide and theft are not considered reprehensible in themselves, but only become so when directed against members of the community or tribe', and declared that 'individual morality scarcely exists'.

Groves, writing half a century later of the Motu village of Manumanu (west of Port Moresby), couched a brief discussion of Motuan morality in terms of 'sin' and 'expiation'—words which perhaps should have been used with caution, given their Christian implication. Notwithstanding his choice of terminology, his observations were similar to those of the anthropological majority in Melanesia: 'It is sinful to disrespect lineage elders, to withhold a gift or favour due to some other member of the lineage, wilfully to subvert an important lineage enterprise, to bring public scorn upon the lineage, etc. All acts endangering the harmony, strength, continuity and repute of the lineage are considered to be sins in Manumanu. They are offences not only against other men, but also against the gods; for in symbol and in sacrament the lineage, its members and its gods are indivisible'. Also typical of anthropological observation in Melanesia in general was Groves's emphasis on what he termed the 'secular moral principle' of reciprocity: 'The Motu owe no duty to mankind at large other than a duty to repay debts with interest' (1955: 11). Traditional sanctions on offenders within a group tended to involve sorcery and manifestations of ancestral displeasure (see, for example, Kopi 1979). In either case the result was that the offender suffered misfortune which would be alleviated through compensation to, and reconciliation with, the aggrieved party. Sorcery is still greatly feared in Motu-Koita society, and misfortune is often attributed to sorcery connected with either jealousy or retribution. Compensation and reconciliation retain their importance in Motu society in the interests of maintaining group integrity. To a degree, Pari village court can be understood as working alongside traditional sanctions, including sorcery, in the interests of group integrity in modern times.

Shaming was part of the ritual of reintegration, particularly in the case of drunkards. The technique of shaming is common in Melanesia. Whether shame and guilt feelings are the same thing has been a subject of some debate. Early modern anthropologists such as Mead (1937) and Benedict (1946) suggested that the emotion of 'guilt' was likely to be found in societies which used education and the internalisation of notions of sin, whereas 'shame' was more common in societies which used external sanctions and force to control behaviour. Thus, 'primitive' societies were typified as 'shame' societies, while Western societies were 'guilt' societies. While social dichotomisations such as these have become less fashionable in more recent times, the external/internal distinction between shame and guilt has remained a distinguishing characteristic in some models. Gabriele Taylor (1985), for example, makes a significant distinction, that shame requires an audience while guilt can be felt by a person in isolation. Taylor's argument acknowledges that a person's feelings of guilt or shame involve a consideration of what other people think of them, but in the case of guilt the 'other people' are an abstract consideration, rather than a real and present audience. Arguments of this kind resonate with those that in some societies wrongdoers do not experience 'guilt' (see above, citing Turner and Seligman) but might experience 'shame' if they are found out (implying that if they are not found out they are not ashamed). Later distinctions have emerged in the literature on shame, such as that between legal guilt and guilt as a felt emotion. According to this distinction a person can be found guilty of wrongdoing according to law, yet feel no guilt, or on the other hand can feel guilty about something which is not legally perceived as wrong. Bracketing the notion of legal guilt, and attending to the psychology of felt guilt, the relationship of 'guilt', 'shame' and 'embarrassment' have been explored as possible variants of the same underlying affectual state (see, for example, McDonald and Moore 2001: 134–35; Harris 2001: 106–28).

In the court case described above, and others like it which I witnessed at Pari, there was no evidence that guilt (the 'internalised' feeling according to some of the theories referred to above) was either the intended or resulting response to the tactics of the Pari magistrates. Neither did the young men exhibit any behaviour suggesting that they felt the deep shame of those people who are chronically unable to fulfil socio-economic obligations. Indeed, when a large group of youthful offenders were charged with making and consuming 'steam' (see above, and Goddard 2003)—under whose influence their behaviour was considerably more obnoxious than that of the youths in the 'obscenity' case transcribed here—a major concern of villagers and the court was their withdrawal from customary everyday activities. Yet those youths who bothered to respond to the summons displayed unconcern about the condemnatory gaze of the gathered villagers, and boredom with the court proceedings. In issues like the 'obscenity' case above, it was tacitly understood that drunken offences of this kind could not realistically be prevented, but incidental social damage to social relations could be mended. Feelings of guilt could not be expected in the youths, but intense *embarrassment*—a demeanour directly responding to public scrutiny—was deliberately generated as a precurser to the reiteration of the need for respectful relations and the eventual gesture of reconciliation.

Reconciliation, and the reintegration of offenders into the community (symbolised by the ritual communal handshaking) was the fundamental aim of Pari village court in respect of most of the disputes I witnessed. It was grounded in a perception of the village as a corporate entity whose integrity was dependent on the maintenance of its communality. This is evident in the 'black market' case, where the aim of the hearing was not to punish the beer sellers (who readily admitted their 'guilt'). Rather the court was attempting to address the more disruptive problem of drunkenness and drug use—'the community will be better'. As observed in chapter 4, the maintenance of Pari's perception of itself as a tradition-oriented moral community requires the negotiation of inevitable contradictions generated by the villagers' involvement with the sociality of the nearby city. The village could not be a model of Christian morality, and as the magistrates acknowledged, many villagers including themselves enjoyed alcohol and were susceptible to its intoxicating effects. Neither did they want to alienate younger villagers in particular with heavy penalties, for fear that their young men might decide to move to more permissive communities such as the city's settlements (older Pari villagers viewed the latter as uniformly degenerate).

The three cases described here reinforce the point made in chapter 4 that while Pari village court is a legal institution, it is more than a forum for minor dispute settlement. It is a social ritual, part of the attempt by the village to maintain its identity, as a 'Christian' Motu-Koita village, practicing a neo-traditional morality and chronically wrestling with the effects of the 'profane' sociality of Port Moresby. The lapses the court deals with represent the susceptibilities of the village as a whole, as much as those of individuals within it. It is not only individual youths who are embarrassed by public reiteration of their drunken obscenities, it is the village as a community.

Similarly the theft of cassava, superficially addressed by magistrates as a boyish misdemeanour, exposes to the participants the potential of deeper ruptures which threaten the community itself. The youths were not fined, and the amount of compensation they were ordered to pay was slight, since the magistrates recognised in fact what they attempted to avoid explicating in court—that the theft was not a random stealing, but a manifestation of a recurrent land issue. The case showed something of the legal limitations to the court's putative ability to 'apply custom'. Village courts are not allowed to deal with land disputes, which means the Pari magistrates could not become involved in an attempt to renegotiate the boundary dispute in a customary way. It could only suggest that the disputants negotiate among themselves, or go to a land court. The latter course would be likely to produce a rigid settlement, favouring one or other of the current disputant parties, and negating the future negotiations which would be more conducive to harmony among the villagers involved.

Despite the formality of the court, and despite its adherence to a 'courtroom' model based on perceptions of district court procedure, and the limitations placed upon its 'customary' orientation by the Village Court Regulations, we can see that it has been appropriated into Pari's sociality as a restorative, rather than punitive, resource.

Notes

1. In December 1981 a commission of enquiry was conducted into suitable forms of government for the National Capital District, which includes a proportion of Motu-Koita territory. The commission proposed that the NCD should from 1982 be governed by a body which became known as the National Capital District Commission, with an elected Motu-Koita Assembly having special powers over the Motu and Koita villages in the NCD. The Assembly's powers were not made clear, and an unsettled period followed. In 1992, under the NCD Act, a body called the Motu-Koita Council was established under a similar rhetoric as its forerunner, the Motu-Koita Assembly. Its exact political role remained unclear, so far as its relationship to the NCD was concerned. It did, however attempt to represent the interests of the Motu-Koita to Government and the media.
2. A mildly derogatory reference. While there had been a significant Chinese community in towns in the Mandated Territory of New Guinea for much of the colonial period, they were excluded from Port Moresby until a legal change to their status in the 1950s. Subsequently, Chinese people established themselves in the town mostly through business ventures. By the end of the colonial period, 'Chinese tradestores', as Australians called them, were ubiquitous. The relative insularity of the Chinese (in the face of a degree of discrimination both by Australians and by Melanesians) and their success in business contributed to a popular assumption that their business dealings were in part illicit. Magistrate Puka, who had been a young man during the consolidation of Chinese presence in Port Moresby, had been conditioned by the local suspicion of that period that Chinese were 'shady' and a bad influence. A handy historical overview of the Chinese presence in PNG until the end of the colonial period (1970s) is provided by Inglis (1972).

7

Konedobu Village Court in Action

While the four settlements served by Konedobu village court are not villages, they are nevertheless fairly close-knit communities. Their proximity to each other, as well as longstanding relationships with Motu-Koita landholders living in the nearby Hanuabada village complex, has bound them over time into a community that sees itself as something akin to a cluster of traditional villages. The Motu term *hanua*, meaning 'village', is commonly used by inhabitants to refer to their own settlement. While they are very close to downtown Port Moresby (an area which some urbanites now refer to as the 'CBD') and many of them walk to work, they maintain a degree of insularity from the town around them, though this is not as marked as that of Pari village. They are relatively peaceful, compared to a number of other settlements (including most of those served by Erima village court), and consciously try not to attract the attention of police and city authorities to themselves.

Konedobu village court had a lower official caseload than Pari village, although this observation needs to be qualified with reference to the large amount of mediation conducted by the magistrates. Mediation took up a great deal of their time, and was not recorded officially. I could not observe mediation procedures as they involved informal meetings, often at people's houses, and thus much of the court's activity could not be quantifiably recorded. As with Pari village court, the Konedobu magistrates were less concerned to punish wrongdoers than to restore good relations. Fines and orders for compensation payments rarely exceeded K10. The latter were mostly accepted by plaintiffs, whose occasional original demands for 'K100' in compensation were expressions of anger or outrage at the person who had given them offence. Mollification came with the public exposure of the wrong, the lecture to the guilty by magistrates, and the final handshake of reconciliation.

Table 7.1 lists the types of cases heard by Konedobu village court during two eighteen-week periods, one in 1994 and one in 1999, and monitored by myself from beginning to end. I have not included cases which, for example, had already been partly heard before the monitoring period, or which were settled 'out of court' after a first hearing and adjournment. I have classified the offences here according to their designation by the magistrates, and as with those heard in Pari village court, the designations reflect something of the sociality of the settlements involved. A number of the offences and disputes could have been classified differently. For example, sorcery is a common offence in village courts throughout PNG, and I heard cases involving sorcery in Konedobu village court, which principally serves a micro-ethnic community representing a part of the country where sorcery is well recorded as being a prevalent tradition (see, for example, Williams 1969: 103–9 and passim; Inglis 1982: 7–15; Morauta 1984: 14; Ryan 1965). Sorcery is threaded into the consciousness of the downtown settlements and its power is pervasive. However, no cases of sorcery were ever recorded as such by the court. The avoidance of any mention of sorcery in the court was part of an exercise in self protection, a tacit concern to keep from officialdom any mention of a practice that the inconspicuous communities served by the court feared would bring them to the attention of police or other intrusive authorities.

Sorcery accusations were consequently classified as 'insult', 'slander' or 'dispute', and sorcery threats classified as 'disputes'. These classifications were justified (when I queried them) reasonably well by the magistrates. A threat of sorcery, for example, was explained away as an 'emotional outburst, not really intended', and accusations of sorcery could also be explained as unwise outbursts of anger intended as insults rather than statements of fact. Elsewhere (Goddard 2005: 51–76) I have described a particular sorcery accusation in Konedobu court, demonstrating how the collusion in keeping mention of sorcery out of official records extended to clever circumlocution in giving evidence in court, so that the words 'sorcery' or 'sorcerer' were never uttered. In everyday life and discussion, in contrast, it was common to hear these words used. Nevertheless, people avoided using them in the presence of 'outsiders'.

Table 7.1. Offences and disputes as officially designated in Konedobu village court during two periods of eighteen weekly hearings (monitored by the author in 1994 and 1999)

Official identification of offence	Number in 1994 period	Number in 1999 period	Comments
Disturbing the peace	1	0	Drunken behaviour.
Slander	5	1	Includes sorcery accusations.
Insult	5	1	Includes sorcery accusations.
Assault	2	3	Connected with family problems, desertion, adultery.
Damage to property	2	0	Involved drunkenness, and arising from suppressed friction.
Drunk in village court area	1	0	A young drunkard broke bottles and interrupted a mediation hearing.
Failure to obey village court order	0	1	Failure to pay compensation as ordered by village court.
Dispute	9	5	Includes accusations of adultery, desertion, brideprice issues, intra-family disputes, sorcery threats and accusations, unpaid debts or compensation.
Total	25	11	

As can be seen in the table, insults and slander were the most prevalent complaints brought to the court, both as 'offences' and as the substance of cases classified as 'disputes'. Two of the three cases described below were of this kind.

Three Cases From Konedobu Village Court

'Kalakala'

The first case discussed here is typical of the majority heard in Konedobu village court, and displays the characteristics described in chapter 4.

The disputants were from Ranuguri settlement which has a long history of intermarriage among its inhabitants, micro-ethnic groups originating from the eastern Gulf region, as well as intermarriage of settlement dwellers with local Motu-Koita. Ranuguri settlement is a close-knit community and major disruptions to the flow of its social life are few. I have already indicated that the majority of cases brought to Konedobu village court during my periods of fieldwork involved alleged threats of sorcery, insults or perceived insults, and malicious gossip. Everyday discourse is metaphorically dense, and people are conditioned to consider meanings beyond the literal interpretation of any utterance. In such a climate, accusations of insults or malicious gossip are frequent, and aggrieved people use the village court as a public theatre for their outrage. Initial demands for a high fine or compensation payment serve to express anger or distress on a complainant's part, and magistrates commonly lecture disputants on the dangers of malicious gossip or incautious remarks.

The case reproduced below concerned an insult, or imagined insult, which was simultaneously seen as a slander. As I have already noted, complainants in these kinds of cases commonly demanded large compensation payments at the outset, but accepted a small payment such as K10 at the close. In this case no particular amount was demanded, but as with other cases of its kind the village court was used as a place to clear the air and to attempt to dispel the mutual hostility between the disputants, rather than to administer severe punishment. At the end the 'defendant' was charged a K10 fine and ordered to pay K10 to the 'complainant'.

The incident which gave rise to the complaint occurred in Port Moresby's downtown area, where many of the women of the settlements shop or informally sell items such as betelnut or vegetables which are either grown in gardens near their settlements or brought to town by village-based relatives. They also gather at habitual roadside spots to relax and talk. The dispute arose from a response to an overheard remark at one of these spots. Both of the two disputants, Lena and Betty (not their real names), had formerly been in relationships with Australian men. The incident leading to the complaint in court had occurred when Lena, whose children included some from a relationship with a white man, had been admonishing a younger cousin for her dalliances with white men, warning her of the possible consequences (eventual abandonment and single parenthood). Betty, at a distance, had heard part of Lena's admonition, and had inferred a disparaging reference to herself. She had responded angrily. Lena claimed in court that Betty's outburst had included the term 'kalakala', a Tokpisin slang term which was highly charged in the particular context in which it was uttered.

'Kalakala' can simply mean 'several colours', but Lena heard it as a disparaging reference to her own children, and to the potential offspring from her cousin's dalliance with white men.

Lohia Dirona (who acted as leading questioner), Andrew Moime and Ben Aravape were the magistrates hearing the dispute. Disputants waiting for cases to be heard sat outside the court area, and Lena and Betty approached when their names were called and sat side by side facing the magistrates. The dialogue reproduced in the transcript was mostly in Hiri Motu and Tokpisin. Occasional use of English is indicated by italics. Interpolations to aid reading are in brackets. References to 'sister', 'aunt' and 'brother' by disputants sometimes express conventional biological or classificatory kin relationships but can also be polite terms of address, which classify people as fictive kin according to their gender and age in relation to the speaker. This is common in the downtown settlement communities (an indication of their close-knit nature), and can be confusing for an outsider. Lena and Betty, for example, were unrelated, but used the term 'aunt' in referring to their interaction. Lena's 'sister' (see below) was what Europeans would term a cousin.

> Magistrate: [in Hiri Motu] Lena, you talk.
>
> Lena: It is this. Tuesday I was relaxing in front of the DCI office along the road. I didn't know that she [Betty] and her husband came in with the vehicle. She came past. I saw my little sister, in front of Big Rooster.

Lena's 'sister' worked at the 'Big Rooster' fast-food shop, and had an Australian boyfriend. She had invited Lena and another woman to go out with her and her boyfriend.

> Lena: She said, 'I'll come and pick you up and we'll go'. She [indicating another woman present at the court] didn't want to go, she was scared. She has a husband and it would not be right. In this world you don't go fooling men for nothing. So I scolded my younger sister, 'When you become involved with these men you are fooling yourself. What has the white man done? These white men take people and fool around with them and then abandon them.' This lady went by and she overheard these words and she thought we were talking about her. A white man had been involved with her and abandoned her. And she accused us. She should have said, 'Aunt [colloq.], are you talking about me?' As I was scolding my little sister, she should have said, 'Are you talking about me, or who are you talking about?' She didn't say anything, she kept on walking. She was walking away and she swore at me. She said, 'Their children are "kalakala" [Tokpisin slang: 'several colours'], they have different fathers'. My cousin [colloq.] heard her, and asked my sister, 'Who is sitting in the road? They are only girls.' I had come to Big Rooster and they were gathering round me. I got up and scolded my sister, then this woman got up and swore at me and said, 'The children have different fathers, they are black and white.' That refers to me. I have two white children and two black children, one died and only three are left.

Magistrate: Who were you with?

Lena: I was with my little sister. There were plenty of us, my witnesses are here, I have plenty of witnesses. I got up and tried to straighten things out. I went and said, 'Betty, who came and told you this, that you swore at me for nothing? I want to hear that word first.' The whole crowd got up and started arguing. I'm the person who married a white man. So I told them, 'Calm down, I have no fight with you.' They got up and started fighting with us. She started talking about the passport. [addressing Betty] Am I like you? [to magistrates] Talk to her about the passport. I also have one, it is with me, but I do not want to show it [these oblique comments about a passport were not pursued, and their meaning is unclear].

Magistrate: Have any of your witnesses come?

Lena: They are here.

Magistrate: Betty, you talk.

Betty: These words—I never said 'kalakala'. Whether she heard it herself, or whoever heard it, I never mentioned 'kalakala'. I never said anything like that.

Magistrate: Were you dropped off by a vehicle?

Betty: Yes, but that was earlier.

Magistrate: When they were talking what were they saying?

Betty: When they went for dinner, this 'Big Rooster' woman, she has a white boyfriend. She said, 'We are going for dinner', [becomes emotional] I replied to my aunt [colloq.], that was the end. They didn't mention my name, but—that was the end. Who mentioned 'kalakala'? I didn't say anything.

Having heard Lena's accusation and Betty's denial, the magistrate asked Lena's witnesses to testify. Lena left her place on the disputants' bench to make way for these. The first, an eye witness who had been walking along the road, confirmed Lena's accusation, although reporting slightly different phrasing. She spoke in Tokpisin, beginning with a digression into what she had been doing before the incident. The magistrate interrupted, telling her to give only relevant testimony. She continued:

Witness: [in Tokpisin] We had been playing cards at Simona's house, and we were coming along the road. She called out, 'The children are "kalakala."'

Magistrate: [indicating the accused, speaking in Hiri Motu] This woman? Called out?

Witness: [replying in Tokpisin] Yes. 'The children are "kalakala", black and white. The father could be any kind of man.'

Magistrate: [in Tokpisin now] And you heard this?

Witness: Yes. And sister [colloq.] heard this and got angry. Then an argument started.

Magistrate: Before this, did you hear this woman [indicating the complainant] say anything insulting about this woman, or not? Did Lena say something insulting about Betty, or not?

Witness: I don't know what went before. We heard this and we became angry.

Magistrate: Is that all you want to say, or is there some more? [pause] That is all, Huh? [pause] *Okay*, you go, and we will hear Lena's second witness.

The second witness reported Betty's alleged words, but had not heard them directly, having arrived at the scene after the initial exchange.

Magistrate: [in Hiri Motu] This is also Lena's witness? Will you speak Motu or Tokpisin?

Witness: Tokpisin.

Magistrate: Tokpisin. [in Tokpisin] *Okay.* Continue.

Witness: A woman told me this woman said that Lena was going out with a white man. That is what she told me. She said this woman [indicating Betty] said that later they would have a black and white baby, that is what she said.

Magistrate: Oh, you did not hear this with your own ears, another woman came and told you about it?

Witness: Yes.

Magistrate: Ok, that's enough. Which woman actually heard this with her own ears? Tell her to come.

Witness: Mona heard it, with her sister.

Magistrate: She actually heard it?

Witness: Yes, she is her big sister.

Magistrate: Is she here?

Witness: No, she did not come.

Magistrate: Oh. *Okay.* Lena!

Lena returned to sit in front of the magistrates with Betty, and the magistrates attempted further clarification about what witnesses had heard.

Magistrate: [in Tokpisin] I will question Betty first. How far away were you standing from these people when you called out?

Betty: This woman who came in as a witness—she was not there, her big sister went and told her about it. . . .

Magistrate: [interrupting] I know, I know. They told me, I have heard it already. Now I want to ask you, when you went to the road, where were they?

Betty: They were in front of me.

Magistrate: Close to you, huh? And their conversation, you could hear it?

Betty: Yes. They were talking to some women selling betelnut. They told them this story while I was walking nearby, I heard it.

Magistrate: They did not say your name?

Betty: They didn't say my name. But they made this accusation. And I did not talk about 'kalakala'. Who heard it and went and told this woman?

It was not clear to the magistrates whether Betty had in fact used the offensive term, and Lohia Dirona took the opportunity to warn the disputants (as was common in these kinds of cases) of the dangers of 'loose talk'.

Magistrate: *Okay*. Lena, [in Motu] do you understand Tokpisin? [she nods, and he continues in Tokpisin] You understand it, *okay*. You had said something which affected her. Her feelings have been hurt, because something you said was insulting. Whether you said her name or not, when she came by, this is what you were talking about. She thought these words were about her. I do not know whether she said 'kalakala' or not, but I want to say this. All this kind of talk, it is troublesome, it starts fights. Whether you said it to her, or someone else, before the court you are not able to make clear, it's hard—but I want to say this. All this kind of talk, loose talk, it is bad. . . .

Lena: [interrupting] I took this case to the police station first, but they told me to bring it here, so I have brought it here.

Magistrate: Yes, Yes, I know. I know your side of it, but I am talking about, in the first place—all this kind of talk brings fighting and trouble. Whether you said this to her, or someone else, she heard it and she was upset, she thought you were talking about her. And then, maybe she said something unkind, too, I don't know. Whether she said 'kalakala' or not—because in the first place you had said something bad. Is that true?

Lena: This talk, we didn't address it to her. We didn't know about her.

Magistrate: I know, I know.

Lena: We were talking to someone else and she heard a bit of it and she swore at me. And who was she angry with? We didn't know. And why did she swear at me? If she was offended, she could have asked, 'Hey, aunt, are you talking about me or someone else?' And I could have said, 'No. I wasn't talking about you.' But she got angry at me for nothing. I didn't have any bad feelings towards her and I went and spoke to her properly. I said, 'Hey, I want to know, you are angry with me, huh? Who has offended you, I want to know.' And she said, 'You were talking to me, said I married a white man.'

Magistrate: *Okay*, that's enough. Betty, you could have asked them what they were saying, but you did not do anything, did you say anything?

Betty: They said these things, I was ashamed.

As neither Lena nor Betty seemed prepared to accept any blame, the magistrates called back Lena's first witness to recapitulate her testimony. She gave the same version.

> Magistrate: Now you must talk in front of the court, and we magistrates and peace officers, and everybody, will hear what you say. Anything you say which is false, you might be charged for, so everything you say must be true. *Okay*, you talk. Whatever these women said, you tell us.
>
> Witness: She walked by and she said, 'This child, the father could be any kind of man. Black and white.' That is what she said.
>
> Magistrate: Betty said this?
>
> Witness: Yes. I and a sister heard her.
>
> Magistrate: *Okay*. Betty. Which woman went with you two to the police station? Her [pointing to the witness], or someone else?
>
> Betty: Someone else.
>
> Magistrate: What was her name?
>
> Betty: Selena.
>
> Magistrate: *Okay*. Betty and Lena, the court is adjourning this case to next week because Selena is not here. The defendant has more defence [i.e. testimony from a witness] for her case, so we have to hear it next Monday. *Okay*. So come back next Monday.

At the resumption of the case the following week, Andrew Moime took over the questioning from Dirona Lohia. After a brief recapitulation of the substance of the accusations the witness, Selena, was called. Her testimony however was not a 'defence' of Betty, but a reinforcement of the contention that Betty had used the term 'kalakala'.

> Magistrate: [in Hiri Motu] You heard Betty. What did you hear?
>
> Selena: I will speak in Tokpisin. [in Tokpisin] She said—she walked down, down to the corner. She said, 'This Lena, her children are kalakala, the fathers are different.' That is what she said.
>
> Magistrate: From the mouth of Betty?
>
> Selena: Betty, yes. That's what she said. Her and my brother and my little sister who spoke last time [i.e. gave evidence in court] sat down, and she said this. *Okay*, so I went and asked my brother, 'Who is sitting over there? It's the family sitting there.' He said, 'No, she said her children are kalakala, the fathers are different.'
>
> Magistrate: *Okay*, Thank you. Go now. Betty! Lena! [Betty and Lena return to sit in front of the magistrates] Now all the statements from you two from last week have been taken into account by the court. And the court will ask you questions, and you will answer. Betty, is it true you did not say these things: 'The children are kalakala, the fathers are different'?

Betty: I didn't say that. I didn't say 'kalakala', or 'the fathers are different'. Who truly says I said that?

Magistrate: Lena. Did you hear it from her mouth or did a witness tell you?

Lena: [stumbling over her words] This sister of mine—I didn't know, I was sitting down below. She said—the woman went up and my brother went up. The woman went down to the road. She heard—she said, 'kalakala, different fathers'. That refers to me, only. My sister heard—my brother went—my sister got up, my cousin got up, she asked my brother. My brother said, 'This woman down below doesn't have a man. This woman and her children are being blamed.' What I am saying is, she was talking about me. 'Kalakala children' refers to me, and 'different men' refers to me only. And my sister heard it and came and told me. And who was angry with her [Betty]? I didn't say anything against her. I was not angry at her.

Magistrate: *Okay*. Both of you listen. We have heard all your testimony. Your testimony and the testimony of your witnesses, we heard them last week. Now we are going to think about what we have heard. So you give us a little time, you go and wait outside for a little while.

The disputants went outside while the magistrates conferred among themselves. These conferences were lengthy, and the magistrates usually 'wrote the case up' at this point. One of them would either dictate the details to a court clerk or write the account himself or herself into the official record of the case. Disputants and interested onlookers would commonly wander away from the court area to gossip and chew betelnut during this long break in proceedings. When the magistrates had finished their deliberations and called the disputants back, there was often further delay while they were located and made their way back to the 'courtroom'.

Magistrate: Betty and Lena. The court has found that: first, Betty—at the time that Lena and her companions were talking—whatever they were talking about, you didn't know. You didn't hear, and you assumed that they were talking about you. You thought about this, and you went up and spoke to some people. When you spoke, some people heard you and they have testified in court. They say you said, 'The children are kalakala and they have different fathers.' The court has found that this testimony is true. First, you did not go and find out whether this group was talking about you or someone else, or what they were talking about. . . .

Betty [Interrupting]: I heard them.

Magistrate: Yes, yes. You thought they were talking about you, so you started talking insultingly too. And as to whether you said it or not, witnesses have testified already. And it was wrong. All this kind of talk is wrong. I said this before [i.e. the previous week]. It is better that you *investigate these matters rather than you jumping on* [sic] *a conclusion* and talk insultingly about people, because then a problem arises. So the Court is charging you under *Village Court Act chapter five, section five*, [reading from the Village Court Handbook] which says, '*If somebody says something bad and untrue about someone else . . .*' and in this case you said something bad about her, and it affected her, and upset her too, and made her ashamed. So the Court is charging you K10 court fine, and K10 compensation, *just because of those words*.

Commonly disputants accepted decisions of this kind, which involved relatively small payments. However Betty remained resolute that she had not said 'kalakala', and declared that she would take an appeal against the decision to the district court.

Betty: I am going to appeal. I will go to the district court.

Magistrate: That is allowable. That is the decision of the village court, and if you don't want to accept it, you have the right to appeal. Enough. It is finished.

Betty: [leaving] They are telling lies, I didn't say that. I'm going to the district court.

Magistrate: Enough, both of you, go now.

It was normal for disputants to shake hands after the magistrates' decision had been made (although they did not then shake hands with the magistrates and other attendees, as in Pari village court). Betty, however, left without shaking hands with Lena. She was still declaring her intention of appealing to the district court, but no appeal was subsequently made and Betty eventually paid her fine and compensation within the customary two week period allowed for small payments.

Rumours

As with the 'kalakala' case, the dangers of 'loose talk' are a theme of this second example. Mischievous gossip appeared to be at the bottom of this case, in which three men brought their concerns to the court. Their specific complaint was that 'John' had been spreading false stories, of a wife's adultery. These stories had caused a great deal of friction, as the husband had consequently been interrogating his wife at length over her implied indiscretions, and other relatives were being drawn into the prevailing atmosphere of distrust. The distressed husband 'Jacob', a male relative, 'Paul', and a village court peace officer, 'Sam', brought a complaint against John to the court, with Paul, the senior male of the three, acting mostly as their spokesman. They wanted John to either properly substantiate his stories, or desist.

The magistrates hearing the case were Andrew Moime, Ben Aravape and David Kemi, with Andrew acting as the leading questioner. As some of the dialogue implies, something of the case was already known to the magistrates, as the complainant, 'Jacob', had earlier told one of them about his concerns.

> Magistrate: [in Hiri Motu] John, you are in court because people have complained that you have spread false stories. Is this complaint true?
>
> John: Who is complaining?
>
> Magistrate: Paul, Jacob and Sam.
>
> John: They are complaining because I went to Murray Barracks.

'Murray Barracks' is the name of a military barracks in another suburb of Port Moresby. In local use the term is extended to refer to a group of shops at a major road intersection near the barracks. John was using the term in the latter sense.

> Magistrate: The court is now asking you, are the things in the summons true?
>
> John: No. It is not true, it is a lie.
>
> Magistrate: Uh huh. Paul, you speak.
>
> Paul: John has been spreading false rumours. He went to the office of another man's wife, and this kind of behaviour, for example, this spoils the relationship between our families. This is why we have summonsed him to court. We want you to tell him now to stop taking stories back and forth. It would be best if he stops. We do not know whether he is telling the truth or not. We want to find out from you what John has said—whether he is telling lies. We said to ourselves, we can wait until Monday [the day on which the village court sits]. When John is here we can straighten out the discussion. But whether he is telling the truth, or telling lies . . . the decision is with the court. Because while this is not solved, the problem continues. I am leaving everything in your hands.
>
> Magistrate: John, you heard that. Do you understand?
>
> John: Yes.
>
> Magistrates: Do you have anything to add?
>
> John: No. Yesterday I went to the market, and he [Jacob] was coming by. So we went together to the bus stop, and he asked me some things at the market. That's all.
>
> Paul: [in English] *Excuse me.* [in Hiri Motu] What he said—after he left, Jacob was upset. When he [Jacob] went, he didn't do the right thing. He got his wife and he kept on asking and asking. He was forcing the woman to talk about wherever she has been. Whenever John is around, he gives us a lot of problems. We want you [the court] to get back to her and find out what is going on, so that we don't have to pass stories back and forth, because this is damaging our families.
>
> Magistrate: Stories are going to the woman, or the man?

> Paul: The man [i.e. Jacob]. The woman used to work at one place, but because of the stories, she left and got a job somewhere else. Somebody must have said something again, so the man went to the woman and was trying to force information out of her. The whole family got involved in the problem. It went on till midnight. So the reason why we summonsed him [John] is so you can speak to him, so he can look after his mouth.
>
> Jacob: *Excuse me.* When I asked him I said, 'If I gave you the Bible, what would you say?' He said, 'It is not true.'

Jacob's statement needs a little elucidation here. The implication is that John's response was ambiguous, reflecting his mischievous manner of spreading gossip. That is, if pressed for the truth of the gossip, he would imply that he was only passing on what someone else had told him. Therefore, if forced to swear on a Bible, he could opine that the gossip he was passing on was untrue. This becomes clearer with the next statement, which indicates that John claimed he was merely passing on to Jacob something someone had told him.

> Jacob: The story he passed on, I had already heard, he said was from a boy. 'You go to Murray Barracks and you'll see your wife behind the store. Your wife is inside one of the houses. She is sleeping with a man.' So I went to fetch my wife, but when I got there, there was no one there. Luckily, there was no one there.
>
> Paul: For people living in the settlement, this kind of thing causes a lot of problems, just like what this person has done, passing false messages. The husband can go and cause a lot of problems for the wife. That is why we want you to advise this man. He should not do this sort of thing again.
>
> Magistrate: John, did you hear what Paul has said? It has been repeated twice. Have you got the right message?
>
> John: Yes.
>
> Magistrate: Do you think it is good? It is not good.
>
> John: It was them who asked me, 'Where did you see my wife?' So I went and caught the bus right away.
>
> Magistrate: First you said you went to the market, then you said you went to Murray Barracks. Now you are changing the story.
>
> John: No, I didn't go to Murray Barracks, I was standing at the Gordon's market bus-stop. He came and asked me where his wife was working. I said, 'You go to Murray Barracks.' That's all.
>
> Magistrate: Is there anything else?
>
> John: No, no more.

The offhand demeanour displayed by John at the beginning of the hearing had now gone, and he was shifting his legs nervously and had lowered his head.

Magistrate: You are a mature man. This sort of behaviour is not good. Do you think what you have done is good? You did not see anything, but when the problem arises, you are very scared. You seem to be happy with whatever comes out of your mouth, you enjoy making mischief. But when you come back and see the problem you have caused you are scared. You wouldn't have the courage to approach the person yourself.

Paul: *Excuse me*. He sent him [John sent Jacob], he was very upset, so when he went and caused a problem, who is he going to come to next? You ask him.

Magistrate: [to John] As I was saying, after the fun you have had with your big mouth, who are you going to next, if the whole thing backfires? You enjoy spreading rumours to your friends and relatives. Who is going to take the burden next? [changing to Tokpisin] You look me in the eye, and answer what I am saying to you. Don't look at the ground. The ground is not talking to you. I am talking to you. [John is silent.] You enjoy spreading talk among friends and relatives, but you have nothing to say here. Don't go spreading rumours, making cruel jokes, you are spoiling people's lives. When people find out the truth, you will be in trouble. Now I am talking to you, and you have nothing to say. Do you think you have done a good thing? Bits of gossip go there, bits of gossip come here—Is that good? You answer! 'Yes' or 'No'?

John: No.

Magistrate: 'No.' Talk goes and comes. Why do you do this?

Paul: *Excuse me*, he said these things and he (Jacob) went and asked his wife.

Magistrate: Yes. [to John] Have you anything else to say? No. *Okay*, all of you wait outside. We [magistrates] will make a decision on this.

The disputants went outside, and the magistrates conferred at great length, and wrote up the case, before calling them back in.

Magistrate: This is what the court has decided. As it is your first time in court, we are giving you a warning. Next time, you should not spread lies. Do not do it again. If you, John, do this again, you will pay a fine to the court. Do you understand? Spreading lies from one person to another has caused a lot of problems. Who carries the burden of this? It all comes back to you. Enough. This is finished.

John shook hands with his three accusers.

Recompense

The third case shows the enduring links between the people in the downtown settlements and their places of origin. The disputants were from Paga settlement. While Paga (unlike the other three settlements served by Konedobu court) was not actually a community of 'Gulf' people, these particular disputants were originally from Kikori, in the Gulf

Province. The background to the case involved a workplace death in Port Moresby. A man had died in an accident in a timberyard. His body had been taken back to Kikori, his homeplace. The woman complainant, a classificatory sister of the dead man's mother, had provided food for the mortuary rituals, but had never been recompensed for her service. She was now claiming compensation from the dead man's father through the village court.

Among other things, the case exemplifies the confusion which can arise from the informal way in which testimony is given in village courts. In the early part of the transcript it appears that the mortuary ritual had taken place a little more than a year previously. Later it transpired that it had occurred twelve years previously. A number of things were unspoken during the testimony, and I was confused, when attending this case, by the equivocation over the length of time the woman had been waiting for her money. The chairing magistrate was also momentarily confused, but by the end of the case he had realised what had actually occurred. This was not made explicit in the hearing, and was explained to me afterwards by the magistrates.

The deputy chairperson of Konedobu court at the time, Dirona Lohia, who was from Vanama settlement and therefore not directly connected with either disputant, chaired the court and led the questioning of the disputants. With him on the bench were David Kemi, a magistrate from Paga settlement, and Ben Aravape, a magistrate from Ranuguri settlement. The case was conducted in Hiri Motu.

> Magistrate: The complainant says she wants to get her rights from the defendant here in Konedobu village court. [to the woman] Tell us your problem.
>
> Woman: This is about the bigman's son. ['Bigman' was a deliberately polite term, the man was not of high status.] At the workplace. He died, and I did this work, to help. When he died I was at the village. I got a message through the local school that when they brought the body to the village, if I helped out with mortuary preparations I would get a little money. So I came, I made some food. I am still waiting for the money. It is one year three months now.
>
> Magistrate: [to the man] Your son died? [to the woman] After the accident you wanted to help?
>
> Woman: Yes.
>
> Magistrate: So when you helped them, you went to the village?
>
> Woman: Yes. It was my own desire to help. But the boy's father said that because of my help they would give me some money.
>
> Magistrate: [to the man] Do you have something to say about this?
>
> Man: He was looking after the timber and he died when the timber fell on him. We did not get the compensation [accident compensation payout].

Magistrate: Why is the woman asking for money?

Man: Because of the things she did, preparing food. She didn't get the money so she got angry.

Magistrate: So you made this agreement between yourselves?

Man: Yes.

Magistrate: Is this woman related to you?

Man: Yes, on my wife's side.

Magistrate: [to the woman] How long have you been waiting?

Woman: One year three months.

This statement led to confusion as the hearing progressed. The woman's answer elided the fact that she had been waiting *at the settlement* for more than a year, having come there from the village. Previously she had been at the village most of the time since the mortuary rituals twelve years previously. I was informed of this after the hearing by magistrate David Kemi, who knew the background to the case, and clarified the matter for the chairing magistrate (Dirona) in asides later during the hearing.

Magistrate: So where are you living now?

Woman: At Paga.

Magistrate: I don't really understand the dispute about your help. Isn't it a matter of custom to help?

Man: This is not a matter of custom, just assistance given to the family. For two days there was no food, so this woman helped. So this is the reason why compensation is being asked for.

Magistrate: This was your son?

Man: Yes.

At this point Magistrate Dirona turned to Magistrate David (from Paga settlement) and there was a murmured exchange between the two which my tape recorder did not pick up. Evidently Dirona was seeking one or two points of background from David. He resumed publicly with a statement which summed up what he understood to be the problem.

Magistrate: The woman is complaining that she did not get compensation for her work, but the agreement which was originally made is still standing. He is not arguing with that. When the accident happened, he didn't get the son's money. But he knows, when he gets the money he'll sort out the agreement. It would have been better not to come to the court in the first instance. It would be better to attempt a mediation with a magistrate. Things like this take time. The man is trying to pay her back for what she did. So I think that if he gets the son's compensation he will sort things out. This should not be brought to court, it's not very serious. So maybe we should dismiss the case. Until the man gets his payment, however long it takes, six months, or eight months, or one year. [to the woman] Is there anything else you want to say about the help you gave?

Woman: No.

Magistrate: [to the man] Are you working? Since the woman is upset about this, perhaps you could give her something in a few weeks' time or a few months' time.

Man: I am working, but there's not a lot of money to spare as I am the only one in my family working. Life is hard.

Magistrate: *It's okay.* And [to the woman] you understand, let's give him a chance, since he is working and he has to buy food from day to day. I know he'll pay, we'll give him time. If he doesn't pay you, then the magistrates and peace officers are there at Paga settlement, they'll know. You can always come back to us, it's not a big problem. If we get cross for nothing we might create other problems. [to the woman] Is that acceptable, what do you think?

Woman: It might be alright, but I'm going back to the village again.

Magistrate: You are going to live in the village. How long have you been in town?

Woman: I've been here since last year, June 21st.

Magistrate: If you go back to the village, he'll know. He'll pay you. *That's a big thing in PNG custom.* He'll give you the money, or he'll pass a message. We won't take sides in this. In the village, life is easier, city life is very hard. You understand. When did the young man die?

Man: 1982.

Magistrate: Where did this woman help?

Man: At the village.

Magistrate: In the same year, 1982?

Man: Yes.

Magistrate: So you have been owing her since 1982? I thought this problem happened last year!

Man: It has been one year six months.

At this point Magistrate David Kemi interrupted to talk to Dirona in a whisper, and the three magistrates huddled on the bench murmuring among themselves, with the disputants remaining in their place. My tape recorder did not pick up the magistrates' conversation, and I could not hear it from my position at the side of the table. Later I learned that David was clarifying the issue about the time lapse. The woman had been waiting twelve years for payment, and had eventually come to Paga settlement to shame the man into paying her. This period in the settlement was the 'one year six months' referred to by the man, and represented as 'one year three months' by the woman earlier. The man had still not paid her (he did not have money to pay a substantial amount), so she had eventually brought the matter to the village court in desperation, as she had to return to her village. An implication is that there was more behind this compensation request than was being disclosed by the disputants in court, but the magistrates chose not to investigate that possibility, taking the dispute at face value.

> Magistrate: I thought it happened last year, but it was 1982? So the poor woman has been waiting since 1982. It has been a very long time. Almost twelve years since you people made the agreement. She has waited for a long time. I was thinking this was a 'last year' problem. [to the man] From 1982 till now, have you done anything?
>
> Man: The money was supposed to be K92,000 [i.e. the original accident compensation for the timberyard death] but we received only K21,000.
>
> Magistrate: You've got 21,000 already?
>
> Man: No, I didn't get anything. [He made a further statement, but it was inaudible to myself and on the recording tape.]
>
> Magistrate: It would be better to settle this out of court. It's not a big problem. We'll hold this paper [summons] at the village court. I'll give you time. Go back to your family. Get together and they will contribute. And make a little feast for the woman. You don't have to do it alone, the whole family will help. The people who help must be listed, and when you get the boy's payment you can return the money to them. But I want you to help the woman first, because it has been so long.

While it is not explicit in his words, the magistrate was suggesting in the last sentence that the man should make some kind of promissary payment as a sign of good faith. This is a common gesture in Melanesia, and usually can be quite small.

> Magistrate: I thought it was last year but it was 1982. Anybody would agree that is a long time. I won't specify a time for payment, but make it quick. You were the person who promised to pay her. Please get your family together and do something for her. This is not the village, so just prepare some food to make her happy. So when you do the ceremony make it official, and village court officials can witness it. So it's up to you now, because if you don't do it this lady will continue to worry about it. You don't have to do it yourself, the family can contribute, ten toea [PNG currency equivalent to cents], K5, or something. We'll keep this paper, so something is recorded with the court. [to the man] What do you think? I'll give you a little time so you can organise it with your relatives.

> Man: This will take time. We have some problems with money, and we are still waiting for the compensation [for the accident].
>
> Magistrate: We'll leave it for a while and see what happens. We'll give him a little time, and if the son's compensation comes through—If it takes a long time you can come back to the magistrate. I am going to close this case. . . .

Magistrate Dirona paused here and waited. He was creating an opportunity for the man to publicly show his goodwill to the woman. After some moments, the man produced a K50 note and put it on the magistrates' table.

> Magistrate: He is putting K50, so if you accept it. . . .

Another pause from magistrate Dirona, and after some hesitation the woman picked up the money.

> Magistrate: . . . we'll close the case. This is finished.

The man and woman shook hands, but it was unclear whether the woman was fully satisfied with the outcome. Implicitly the man had committed himself, with the K50 payment, to paying a larger amount at some time in the future but there was no guarantee that this would be soon. The confusion over the passage of time since the woman's contribution to the mortuary feast suggested also that there was something more to this dispute than was made explicit in court, but this possibility was not investigated by the magistrates.

Reconciliation Versus Punishment

To a degree, Konedobu village court showed the same bias towards reconciliation, rather than punishment, as Pari village court. Magistrates were reluctant to fine disputants, and compensation ordered for offences such as slander and insults was slight. Village courts are permitted to fine people up to K200, and order individuals to pay compensation of up to K1,000 (and in the case of *groups* found to be at fault in matters of brideprice, death or custody there is no limit on the compensation the village court can order), or order offenders to perform manual labour for eight hours a day, six days a week, up to twelve weeks. Konedobu village court fines and compensation orders were uniformly low, however. The largest compensation order I observed was for K20, and concerned a sorcery threat (though this was glossed as a 'dispute' for the records sent to the VCS). Village court magistrates are supposed to attempt mediation before a case is taken to full court, and Konedobu magistrates certainly pursued this end resolutely. But they were sometimes alerted by peace officers to a reported offence appearing serious enough at the outset that a heavy fine or other significant punishment would eventually be imposed on a guilty party. In such instances they attempted to avoid dealing with the case, advising complainants to report it to the police, even if it was well within their jurisdiction. The police might refer it back to the village court, but on the other hand it might find its way to the district court. The combination of serious mediation attempts and referral to the police served to reduce the number of cases brought to full court, and also lowered the risk of magistrates having to impose high fines or compensation orders on local people.

The magistrates' reluctance to 'punish' people was made explicit when I discussed cases and decisions with them. It was explained partly by reference to the lack of wealth among the settlement-dwellers. One magistrate, Ben Aravape, summed the situation up in terms of a vicious cycle: 'People can't afford to pay big fines, so if we give them big fines or compensation orders we are causing more problems for them, and that means trouble later, and so we see them in court again.' But magistrates also argued that people were quick to anger and that symbolic and physical violence were regrettable manifestations of the unavoidable jealousies and suspicions of community life. As the magistrates were intimately connected to the same community, I wondered also how much their mild treatment of offences reflected their own apprehension of reprisals. The rationale presented by the magistrates is implicit in the three cases described above, where small fines, or no fines at all, were imposed, and rather than order a fixed amount of payment in the 'recompense' case, the magistrate merely suggested that some kind of promissary payment would be appropriate, and left the man to produce an amount which the woman would find acceptable. As we shall see in the following chapter, this contrasts with the willingness of Erima village court magistrates to stipulate relatively punitive compensation amounts.

The pace of the Konedobu court hearings was slow, and testimony could be extremely repetitious. Repetition was not simply a discursive tendency of the disputants themselves, but was often instigated by magistrates revisiting testimony, or hearing many peripheral witnesses to the same dispute. This is not particularly evident in the cases presented above, whose relative brevity allowed full transcripts to be reproduced here. Another case, for example, continued over three weeks, and was about an altercation among members of an extended family during which a knife had been brandished. Repeated testimony from those involved served to confuse, rather than clarify, the facts of the incident. The disputants and various eyewitnesses contradicted not only each other, but themselves, as they revisited their own testimony at the request of the magistrates. By the third week two different people had been identified as the brandisher of the knife, and the identity of the person at whom it had been brandished had changed, as had that of the person who had snatched the knife from the brandisher. But while an observer preoccupied with establishing the 'facts' towards a finding of guilt on someone's part might have been frustrated by these changes, the magistrates were unperturbed. The dramatic brandishing of the knife was, after all, symbolic of the shared anger, and no-one had actually been hurt. The real issue was a disagreement (arising from a marital problem) which had simmered to the point of physical confrontation. The lengthy talking out of the incident served as a catharsis, and the magistrates, in their 'findings' emphasised the need for peaceful co-existence, fining the two main disputants K10 each. Finally, the disputants shook hands complacently.

There are some resonances in this—and in the three cases presented above—with the notion of 'restorative justice' which has been advocated recently as an appropriate alternative to punitive systems of justice in Western society (see, for example, Braithwaite 1999) and in Pacific Island societies (see, for example, Dinnen 2003). John Braithwaite and Heather Strang point to two conceptions of restorative justice. The first is a 'process' conception, according to which all stakeholders affected by some harm that has been done meet and come to an agreement on what should be done to right the wrong (2001: 1). The second is a 'values' conception, whereby 'the value of healing is the key because the crucial dynamic to foster is healing that begets healing. The dynamic to avert is hurt that begets hurt' (1–2). In an ideal situation, according to Braithwaite and Strang, the two concepts are interrelated: 'Ultimately we . . . think that to be fully restorative justice, both restorative process and restorative values tests should be passed. Equally it is clear that these joint requirements can define a continuum of how restorative any given practice is' (12).

However, in the case of Konedobu village court—and given the extensive kinship networks and persons who can potentially be affected by a 'wrong'—it is doubtful whether all 'stakeholders' are ever involved in mediations or court hearings. Further, the romantic ideal of 'healing that begets healing' is not really applicable in the settlement environment. The magistrates were attempting to contain an atmosphere of jealousy, and suspicion (in which they themselves had to live) as best they could. Lawrence's observation that Melanesians are mostly concerned to keep the sky from falling (1970: 46; and see chapter 4), seems more appropriate to the strategies of Konedobu court than does the concept of restorative justice. The 'recompense' case, with its hints of some deeper problem which the court left unexplored, suggests that the court was wary of publicly exposing or acknowledging more discontents in the community than were neccessary to bring a nominal dispute to an end. A more realistic goal in the social climate of the downtown settlements is simple reconciliation. The magistrates attempted both to reconcile disputants with each other and to reconcile them with the social exigencies of settlement life, requiring caution and reflection in everyday behaviour. Reintegration, an aim made visible in Pari village court in shaming and communal handshaking at the end of cases, was not an evident intention of Konedobu court. While the downtown settlements were closeknit and relatively insular, they lacked Pari village's conscious sense of being a corporate group whose integrity depended on communal commitment to a focal historical identity.

8

Erima Village Court in Action

In contrast with the sedate atmosphere of Pari and Konedobu village courts, Erima court hearings were volatile, sometimes to the point of physical violence between disputants. The ethnically mixed nature of the suburbs served by the court, and the competition among unrelated migrants for urban resources ensured friction, suspicion and distrust between groups. While the populations of these outer suburban settlements present a common front to authorities and other outsiders, the ethnic groups which inhabit them recognise only limited social commonality among themselves. Violence is common, exacerbated by alcohol consumption on paydays and weekends. The caseload of Erima court was heavy, and daylong court hearings were conducted in a crowded atmosphere. Dozens of people waited for disputes to be heard, and clustered around whatever area the magistrates demarcated for the court. Hearings were punctuated by demands from magistrates that onlookers step back and give them space. Onlookers, relatives or friends of disputants, commonly interrupted with shouted opinions, accusations that disputants were lying, remonstrations, or supportive rhetoric. Occasionally magistrates would fine these interlopers K5 on the spot, as a warning to others, but like the grudging retreat of the pressing crowds, the lapse into silence was mostly short-lived.

Disputants stood, rather than sat, in front of magistrates, with a peace officer between them. Physical assaults, or attempted assaults, among them were not uncommon. In some cases, the court hearing was the first encounter for some time that a complainant had achieved with a 'defendant' who had been avoiding him or her. Taking advantage of the rare meeting, complainants sometimes immediately launched themselves, or swung a makeshift weapon at, the object of their wrath before the peace officer could intervene. The majority of these attacks were by women, who carried *bilum* (net bags) in which weapons could be concealed (men were usually empty-handed). It was common for women disputants to be told to leave their *bilum* outside the court area, for this reason. The volatile atmosphere of the court hearings echoed in the constant site-shifting of the court itself.

Erima court has shifted its location several times over the decade and a half that I have been acquainted with it. With such a large population to serve, and with its very large caseload, the 'place-to-place, time-to-time' ideal of village court sittings contained in the original legislation has always been an impossibility. When I first began monitoring the court the chairman had gained permission to use a small concrete building in Gordons market, a large produce market fairly centrally placed in the overall area served by the court. This arrangement became unstable when the market's managers demanded rent from the magistrates. The magistrates argued that as they were financially governed by the NCDC, to which the market's managers were also responsible, they should not have to pay rent. The court officials had been consolidating their occupancy by installing makeshift benches and a table for the magistrates and the chairing magistrate, Andrew Kadeullo, asked the VCS to weigh in on the court's behalf to settle the debate over rent payment. Before anything came of the request, the market managers took matters into their own hands, and the court officials and dozens of disputants arrived one morning to find the smashed courtroom furniture strewn outside the building, whose door was locked.

Andrew Kadeullo announced on the spot that the court was adjourned and would be held the following week at Erima settlement, and set about negotiating a location in the settlement to conduct day-long sessions. This was difficult, due to the mixed ethnicity of the settlement and the apprehension people felt at the prospect of having a large crowd of strangers near their house. Andrew eventually persuaded one of his fellow magistrates to allow the court to be held near his house, in a lean-to with a cleared space around it big enough to accommodate a milling crowd. After two or three weeks the magistrate wanted to use the lean-to for other purposes, and agreed to let the court use instead an area under his stilt-raised house nearby. The wife of the obliging magistrate was less than happy to have a noisy crowd underneath and around their house. At one sitting, involving a disputant related to the magistrate's wife, the latter shouted—from inside the house—her displeasure at some testimony in the dispute which she could hear below. The magistrates scolded her for interrupting the court, but she continued to voice her anger at one of the disputants till the case was over, and threatened to evict the court from her domain. The hearing continued for the rest of the day, but she later berated her husband and demanded that he charge a large rent from his colleagues if the court were to continue to be held under their house. The following week the court moved its location again.

Two other moves followed, with equally unsatisfactory results, and eventually chairman Andrew decided to hold the court at his own house. This was extremely inconvenient for him and his family, as the constant crowd took a toll on the small garden his wife attempted to maintain in their yard, but he tolerated it until the incident described in chapter 5, the accusation of misappropriation brought against him by a fellow magistrate which resulted in him losing the chairing position. Andrew's tolerance of the disruptions caused by weekly court hearings dissipated, and before long the court moved yet again. And so it continued. At the time of my most recent visit the magistrates were using a partly-built 'clubhouse', whose completion, by the side of an open space designated for development as a 'sportsfield', had been curtailed by the lack of promised funding from a local politician.

Table 8.1 lists the types of offences in Erima village court as classified by court officials during the two eighteen-week periods in which I monitored this and the other two courts in 1994 and 1999, and like tables 6.1 and 7.1 it contains only cases which I was able to witness from beginning to end. Not only were many cases dealt with by mediation, and thus not available for systematic monitoring by myself, but the intervention of chairman Andrew after initial hearings of cases resulted in a significant number of them disappearing after being 'adjourned' for a week. As noted in chapter 5, Andrew Kadeullo was skilled at effecting reconciliations, or mollifications, through informal meetings with hostile disputants after appearances in court. My fieldnotes and tapes from Erima court were littered with half-heard cases which I anticipated hearing to completion in subsequent weeks but which simply vanished. They never appeared in official records, as the paperwork for cases heard formally was completed when the court made its final finding. I pursued some of the vanishing cases by asking Andrew what had transpired, but most of them eluded my investigations.

As with the tables of cases heard in Pari and Konedobu courts, many of the cases in table 8.1 could have been classified differently, and the magistrates' classifications given here reflect the social nature and preoccupations of the overall community which Erima court serves. Assaults were very common in the fractious atmosphere of the nearby settlements, yet this is not reflected in the official record, in which most cases involving assaults were catalogued under other headings. These headings were based on the magistrates' assessment of the contextualising dispute or problem during which the assault occurred. In fact, assaults (and gross insults) occurring after a number of interactions between disputants which had failed to solve

Table 8.1. Offences and disputes as officially designated in Erima village court during two periods of eighteen weekly hearings (monitored by the author in 1994 and 1999)

Official identification of offence	Number in 1994 period	Number in 1999 period	Comments
Disturbing the peace	0	1	An encounter between a peace officer and a drunk escalated into a prolonged noisy episode involving property damage.
Slander	2	1	Malicious gossip suggesting someone was a sorcerer, or sexually profligate.
Insult	5	2	Usually loud public outbursts including derogatory sexual comments.
Sorcery	1	1	An alleged sorcery attempt, and a threat of sorcery.
Assault	7	13	Assaults were very common in disputes, and the classification 'dispute' (below) subsumed most. Usually, only physical assaults occurring in isolation from a more complex dispute, and resulting in injury, were recorded as such
Damage to property	2	0	Damage to trees, damage to a market stall.
Theft	6	2	Mostly property theft, rather than money.
Failure to obey village court order	8	6	Failure to pay compensation or fines as ordered by the village court, failure to comply with 'prevention orders'.
Dispute	58	62	Includes accusations of adultery, desertion, brideprice issues, unpaid debts or compensation. Incidents involving assault, slander, sorcery threats and accusations, insults, damage to property were often involved in confrontations leading to the case, but were subsumed under the 'dispute' categorization.
Total	89	88	

a problem, were often simply the 'final straw' which led to the underlying dispute being brought to court. While complainants might describe an assault when the court clerk asked them for their 'complaint' in order to write the summons to the 'defendant', they were likely to show less concern about it in court than about other matters which had led to the violence.

It can be seen in the table that there were few recorded offences explicitly involving public nuisance—such as drunkenness and disturbing the peace—of the kind dealt with in Pari village court. Drunkenness and noisy behaviour were part of life in these settlements, especially on Fridays and Saturdays, and such behaviour in itself caused little concern to the community unless it was connected with some other issue. We can also see that the most commonly used category was 'dispute'. Cases entered under this category covered a wide range of problems and incidents, including sorcery threats and accusations, slander, insults, assaults, unpaid debts and property damage (and sometimes several of these together). The underlying issue in a great many of these cases was marital problems, or marital breakdowns.

As we saw in chapter 4, single adult migrants in town are likely to enter into relationships and hastily arranged marriages with people from ethnic groups other than their own, for economic reasons. These liaisons, lacking the customary resources and sanctions on which marriage partners would draw in 'traditional' circumstances governed by the dynamics of kin-ordered production and exchange, can be comparatively fragile. As discord develops, so do accusations of neglect, adultery and the like between the marriage partners. But also, the relations of exchange which the marriage generated between affines or quasi-affines turn to hostile estrangement. Gifting relationships between people who had classified themselves as affines become issues of debt, or accusations of theft. Nominal brideprice payments to kin of the bride are demanded back. If the married couple were not from the same ethnic group, tensions and confrontations develop between other individuals from their respective groups. Quite correctly, then, the court identifies many cases involving assault, insult, slander, threats and property damage as being really about the complex disputation arising from failing or failed marriage alliances. Thus, chairman Andrew and his fellow magistrates frequently came to decisions about 'guilt' or 'innocence' which appeared not to rationally accord with the ostensible nature of a complaint by one individual against another as described on the summons sheet. They were concerned with the more complex and often far-reaching issues which transcended incidents of insult or violence between two people.

Disputes which arose from failed marriages presented the court with a fundamental problem, especially where it might seem that annulling the union and making 'prevention orders' to keep the parties away from each other would provide a practical solution. Under the Village Court Regulations, village courts are not permitted to grant divorces, and thus are hindered, for example, in extricating women, in particular, from marriages which are clearly dysfunctional. The regulation about divorce hearings begs technical questions, though, about what constitutes a proper 'marriage'. In the case of couples who have met and 'married' in town, the complex preliminary and ongoing reciprocations which would occur between members of the two linked kin-groups in a customary marriage are, mostly, simply not possible. Consequently, the status of the union becomes equivocal. In this respect, the question of whether a brideprice has been paid becomes central in defining what constitutes a marriage, in the view of village court magistrates. While brideprice is a common term, it is actually a difficult thing to define in itself, as Colin Filer (1985) showed in reference to a debate in the 'letters' columns in a PNG newspaper. Nevertheless, it has become the defining transaction of marriage for many people in modern PNG, regardless of whether marriages are established in 'customary' ways, or through Christian church services. While popular sentiment tends to bemoan the escalation of cash brideprices in recent decades (Filer 1985; Lohia 1982; Marksbury 1993), brideprices in the settlements served by Erima court can be quite small in cash terms. I have recorded brideprices of less than K200 in this environment, in contrast to the thousands of kina commonly paid among families who are members of the country's political and professional élite.

Erima village court's ability to end dysfunctional unions, by its own rationale, depended on whether a brideprice had been paid. If an amount generally agreed to be a full brideprice (regardless of its size) had been paid, the magistrates regarded themselves as legally unable to annul a marriage, even if a woman asked for a divorce. In the latter case, they would advise her to go to the family court or district court. On the other hand, if the brideprice had not been paid they would sometimes declare a marriage 'finished' if at least one partner wanted it and had what the court regarded as reasonable grounds. Also, former cohabitants whose 'marriage' had clearly been terminated for some time, but who were engaged in ongoing recriminations, often used the village court as a public forum in which to formalise the end of the relationship and therefore the recriminations. The court would make a terminal ruling on compensation payment amounts, constituting closure of the relationship and its associated disputes.

While marital issues are an underlying factor in many cases heard by Erima village court there are, of course, many cases which have no such complications, as the examples given below will indicate. Many cases were dealt with quickly (in contrast to the pace of proceedings at Pari and Konedobu), and chairman Andrew organised the summonses on his table into piles, of which the first consisted of cases which required only summary attention, allowing those disputants to go home early. These were often cases adjourned from previous weeks, or cases in which Andrew had already given advice to disputants about what they could hope to achieve in the court. When the latter were called they mostly proceeded in the manner of this example:

> Magistrate Andrew: David, you were complaining that John has owed you K300 for a year and has not paid. John has got a job now and he will get paid next fortnight, so he will be able to start paying you. Is that right, John?
>
> John: Yes, I will give him K50 next fortnight, and I will make payments every fortnight after that.
>
> David: This is alright, but I have waited a long time already. He told me previously that he would pay me in a few fortnights, but he did not pay.
>
> Magistrate: That is true, but he has said before the court he will start paying you next fortnight. So if he does not, you can tell us and we can bring him to court again, or even issue a prison order [a document which would need to be countersigned by a district court magistrate] if he does not do what the court has ordered. He understands that. You understand, don't you John?
>
> John: Yes, I understand. I will pay the money.
>
> Magistrate: Okay. So John is fined K10 for the trouble this has caused. He has a fortnight to pay that. And he is to pay K50 to the complainant in one fortnight. And he is to pay the rest of the money in payments every fortnight after that. If this does not happen, David, you can bring this to court again. Thank you. Next case.

Proceedings in the court were conducted in Tokpisin. As the population within the court's jurisdiction included migrants from many parts of the country, there were occasionally disputants who spoke no Tokpisin. In such cases a person was found from their own region to act as a translator. At least five magistrates (there are twelve in all in Erima village court) occupied the bench for each case. The complexities behind many of the cases, involving, for example, underlying conflicts between groups in relation to marriages or settlement resources, together with the out-of-court interventions of chairman Andrew, have limited the range of examples I can present here in transcript form. My transcripts of court cases at Erima frequently made little sense in relation to the outcomes without lengthy annotations about the cases' backgrounds, explanations made to me by magistrates afterwards, and other information from my own investigations in the settlements. Transcripts of such cases, if presented here, would need even lengthier annotation for the reader unfamiliar with the community, severely limiting my ability to present a representative collection within the confines of this chapter. The cases presented below, then, are those which are reasonably easy to understand from transcripts with minor annotations (as with the examples from Pari and Konebodu).

Cases From Erima Village Court

A physical injury

We have seen that disputants in Pari and Konedobu court were largely honest about their actions when giving testimony, though they may have felt some embarrassment about discussing them, or been recalcitrant about motives. In Erima court, by contrast, disputants frequently gave conflicting accounts of events, as 'defendants' denied wrongdoings or even attempted to turn the tables on their accusers by presenting themselves as the victims. Magistrates were sometimes faced with equivocation as to which disputant was telling the 'truth'. The question arises in the case cited here, when a woman, 'Nansi', was accused of attacking and injuring another woman, 'Josi', who was a 'tenant' on her settlement land block. However it was only a contingent issue and, as we shall see, the magistrates dealt with it quite easily. The complaint of physical injury was a manifestation of an underlying issue involving a tenancy arrangement. While the popular media implies that settlement dwellers in Port Moresby are 'squatters', many settlements are in fact collections of leased blocks, on which lessees are permitted to build houses at their own expense. It is not uncommon for people to subdivide their blocks, or to allow other people to build a lean-to dwelling on them, for a small rent. This was the case with Nansi's block.

As tenancy arrangements of this kind are not official and there are no signed 'agreements' involved, the potential for conflict between the parties is high. Tenants can be accused of breaching the terms of the arrangement (which are invariably implicit rather than explicit), and the landlord or landlady can be accused of making unreasonable demands of the tenants, or of treating them harshly. Such was the case with Nansi and her tenants. Friction had developed over what kind of access the tenants should have to toilet facilities and water. Water supplies are meagre in the settlements, and it is considered a luxury to have a pipe and tap on one's block. Neighbours without their own tap negotiate permission to fill buckets or pots from those who have one, and it is not unknown for the latter to charge a small fee for the service.

This was the issue underlying Josi's complaint of physical injury at Nansi's hands. Nansi had refused Josi and her husband 'David' access to a toilet and water supply on her block. Eventually the tenants tried to get water by attaching a length of hose to a water pipe. An altercation ensued resulting in Josi requiring hospital treatment. Josi wanted compensation for the monetary costs arising from getting hospital treatment. However, Nansi was quick to argue that Josi and her husband were the aggressors. Five magistrates were on the bench for this case, led by chairman Andrew.

> Magistrate Andrew: *Okay*. Josi, your complaint says Nansi attacked you and you are asking for K500. And you have brought a medical certificate.

Assault victims who had received hospital treatment usually brought medical certificates, and sometimes x-rays, to the court to consolidate their claims of injury. Josi handed a medical certificate to Andrew.

> Josi: She hit me with a piece of wood. You read this.
>
> Magistrate: *Okay*. What does it say here? [reading out relevant phrases in English] *'Severe bruising left chest . . . bruising upper left abdomen . . . . difficult breathing . . . injuries consistent with heavy blunt instrument.'* [in Tokpisin] Thank you. Now, what has happened here?
>
> Nansi: [speaking before Josi has a chance to respond] This woman and her man have caused trouble for me before. They hit me. I want them to leave my block.
>
> Magistrate Tagube: Where do you live? 'Five-mile'?
>
> Nansi: Yes. They tried to kill me!
>
> Magistrate Tagube: But Josi complains that you hit her. She went to hospital.
>
> Nansi: They tried to kill me! The man held my hair, and the woman was behind me. She wrapped a hose round my neck [gesturing the strangling motion]. They pulled me down on the floor. One of my hands was loose, and I went like this [extending her arm sideways and back in a desparate flailing motion]. Luckily I found a 'two-by-two' [a length of two-inch by two-inch timber]. I swung it like this [demonstrating]. It hit the woman, and they let go. . . .
>
> Magistrate Tagube: [interrupting] Wait, Wait! Josi and her man are living on your block? They are paying rent?
>
> Nansi: Yes. They attacked me. . . .
>
> Magistrate Andrew: [interrupting] Okay, Josi is the complainant. Nansi, you have told your story. Now let Josi speak. Josi, what is your story?
>
> Josi: She hit me with a two-by-two. We were trying to get water.
>
> Magistrate Tagube: What water?

Josi: Water in the pipe. We are paying rent, but she would not let us have water, and she would not let us go into her toilet. We asked plenty of times. This time, we tried to connect a hose to the water pipe. She attacked me with the wood. I went to the hospital in a taxi. I had to pay for that. I had to pay for the x-ray. I had to pay the hospital. She has to pay the cost for these things.

Nansi: They attacked me. I have a witness.

Magistrate Andrew: Oh. Is your witness here? We'll hear the witness.

Nansi gestured to a man in the crowd, who stepped forward and stood alongside her.

Magistrate Andrew: What did you see?

Witness: This woman [indicating Nansi] called out. I went there from my house [he is a neighbour of Nansi]. They were shouting. I told them not to fight.

Magistrate Andrew: Did you see Josi hit Nansi, or did you see Nansi hit Josi?

Witness: I did not see that. I went when the woman called. I told them not to fight. I went back to my house.

Magistrate Andrew: *Okay.* You did not see. That doesn't help us. Thank you, witness [the witness returns to the crowd]. Josi and Nansi, we have two stories here. We magistrates are going to think about this, so we will call you again when we are ready. Thank you.

The disputants moved away, and the magistrates conferred. The large crowd became noisy in the interim, as was common at Erima court hearings. When the magistrates were ready, peace officers began shouting at the crowd to quieten down, while the court clerk yelled out the names of the disputants, who returned to stand before the magistrates. The magistrates' decision dealt neatly with the muddy account of the altercation, which the magistrates knew could never be clarified, and was a contingency of the ambiguous conditions of Nansi's subletting scheme. This was the ground of problems which were likely to continue for as long as Josi and David stayed on the block. The best the magistrates could do in the latter respect was attempt to keep future friction to a minimum by issuing a prevention order under which all parties would be charged if they fought again:

Magistrate Andrew: The court finds. . . .

Magistrate Tagube: [to the noisy crowd] Shut up! If you interrupt the court, you pay K5 each. . . . [in English] *'Contempt of Court!'* [laughter from the crowd, which then becomes quieter].

Magistrate Andrew: Josi and Nansi, you told two stories. These stories did not fit together. But, Josi has evidence of injuries, Nansi does not have evidence of injuries. The court finds that the story of the fight is not clear. But one side [i.e. party] has injuries to be compensated. So, the court orders Nansi to pay compensation. The compensation is K500. Nansi, you have one month to pay this. And all three people, Nansi, Josi and her man—'David' I think? Yes, David—all three will pay a K10 fine to the court for fighting. A 'preventive order' [a document signed by the magistrate and specifying prohibited behaviour: breaches of the order are punished] will be given to you to stop more fighting. The court clerk will give you the preventive order. You understand? *Okay*, case finished.

Sanguma

'Sorcery'[1] is endemic in PNG, and takes many forms. *Sanguma* is a term which was absorbed into Tokpisin from a language of the Sepik district. Originally it referred to a specific form of sorcery but it has become a generalised term for any of the activities which people might imagine 'sorcery' to include, and is also used of any kind of practitioner of 'sorcery'. Accusations and threats of sorcery are taken extremely seriously. People unjustly accused of being a *sanguma* are quick to take offence, even in the case of accusations which Europeans might interpret as humorous or momentary petty insults. The case whose transcript is given here arose from a card game in which the loser attributed her loss to *sanguma*. The complainant, 'Janet', accused the card loser, 'Karua', of referring to her (Janet) publicly as the *sanguma*, thus she wanted compensation. In the first instance Janet had gone to Erima settlement's self-help committee, which was sometimes used as a dispute-settling resource. The outcome had not been satisfactory, and she had subsequently brought the matter to the village court.

> Magistrate Andrew: The complainant is Janet. She complains that Karua told people she [Janet] was a sanguma woman, and she wants K40 compensation for being 'shamed'. Janet, give us your story.
>
> Janet: I told the settlement committee, and a member told her [Karua] to pay me compensation, but she refused. So I am complaining to this court.
>
> Magistrate: Why did she tell people you were a sanguma woman?
>
> Janet: We played cards. She lost her money, K10. Then she told people I was a sanguma. I was shamed.
>
> Karua: [interrupting] I tried to give her K20 because the member [i.e. settlement-committee member] told me to, but she refused to take it.

A conflict can be seen here between the two women's testimony, as to whether Karua had refused to pay the compensation suggested by the settlement-committee member, or whether Janet had refused to accept it. The court did not investigate this. There is a possibility that Janet had not considered K20 adequate compensation, or that Karua had been told to give Janet K40 and had only offered half that sum. But people accused of sorcery commonly seek a very public retraction of the accusation, to clear their name, which may have been why Janet pursued the matter in the village court, which was always attended by a large crowd of onlookers.

> Magistrate: Did you tell people she was a sanguma?
>
> Karua: No. I did not say her name. I did not say she was a sanguma. I said, 'I have lost all my money playing cards, there must be a sanguma nearby.'
>
> Magistrate: *Okay*, this is not a difficult case. We magistrates will talk about it and give a decision. Thank you.

The disputants retired, and the magistrates conferred, subsequently calling the disputants back over the growing noise of the chattering crowd.

> Magistrate Tagube: [to the crowd] Shut up! [in English] *'Court in Session!'* [In Tokpisin, to disputants] Stand up and listen.
>
> Magistrate Andrew: The court finds—Karua, even if you did not say Janet's name, it is still clear that you were talking about her, because you lost at cards to her. When you said 'sanguma' people would think about Janet. So Janet was shamed. The problem here is [playing] cards. We know in the settlements that cards lead to trouble. People lose their money, and there is trouble. We have talked about this plenty of times. So you are both fined K5 for playing cards for money. And Karua, you will pay Janet K40 compensation for her shame.
>
> Karua: I will pay the fine, but I will not pay the compensation!
>
> Magistrate Tagube: Listen to the court! K40 compensation! Don't be a big-head!
>
> Karua: I tried to give her K20 but she would not take it! [walking away and grumbling over her shoulder] You did not ask her why she did not take that money.
>
> Magistrate Andrew: You can appeal against the court's decision [i.e. to the district court]. You know. Case finished. Thank you.

The re-married wife

This case demonstrates the links between town and migrants' homeplaces, and the problems faced by people who do not or cannot maintain social obligations from a distance. Ostensibly the case centred on a complaint by a man, 'Simon', that his wife, whom he had sent from

Port Moresby to their rural homeplace near Gumine in the Simbu Province, had been given away to another man in marriage. He was therefore charging two of the woman's male kin with arranging the second marriage. They argued in response that events at Gumine had given them little option, in Simon's absence, other than to marry off the woman into another group with whom they had sought refuge after a war. Underlying the issue, however, was a question of neglect. The marriage seemed to have been troubled in Port Moresby, and after sending his wife back to Gumine Simon apparently made no effort to maintain his ties, or fulfil his customary obligations to her and her kin-group. He was demanding compensation of the brideprice, said to have been K800. Customarily a brideprice has to be repaid one way or another if a marriage ends, but implicit in this case is the suggestion that Simon might not deserve the full customary compensation. Tagube Epi acted as chairing magistrate in this hearing.

> Court Clerk: [reading from summons] The complaint is, 'Alois and Ranji, you gave the wife of Simon to another man.'
>
> Magistrate Tagube: Simon, you are complaining that your tambus [affines] married your wife to another man. You talk.
>
> Simon: I sent my wife and my daughter home [to Gumine]. My tambus here gave my wife to another man, and she is now pregnant. They have also arranged for my daughter to marry.
>
> Magistrate: [to Alois and Ranji] You two talk.

Commonly in the highlands, from where the disputants originated, it is taboo to utter the names of close affines, that is, the close relatives of one's spouse. In Tokpisin, people commonly refer to these affines, or address them, instead as *tambu* (Tokpisin: taboo).

> Alois: Our tambu here left his job at PTC [Post and Telegraph Commission, in Port Moresby]. Then there were money problems, and marriage problems. The woman came back to our place [Gumine] in 1989. We received no letters from our tambu. No messages came. No money came. We did not know what happened to him. Then there was a war [at Gumine]. We had to leave our land and go to stay with another group. After a time some women were married into this group. This woman [Simon's wife] was also married into this group.

Alois was referring to an obligation sometimes generated by situations where routed groups were given refuge by other groups. Being driven off one's land in war is a humiliating experience. Refugee groups bear the stigma of weakness and resource poverty. When given refuge by other groups they have little to bargain with, and it is not uncommon that women are married into the host group. In this case, in the absence of any communication from Simon for five or six years, his wife was treated as a single and available woman and given to the host group in marriage. An inference is that Simon was neglectful and had not fulfilled his duties as a husband.

> Magistrate: [to Simon] Did you pay a brideprice for this woman?
>
> Simon: Yes. I paid K800. I want compensation.
>
> Magistrate: Okay. This is a problem between tambus, and you two [indicating Alois and Ranji] have come to Moresby to straighten this out. We will adjourn this case to next week. We are not going to make a decision now. While you are waiting for the next court hearing, maybe you will straighten things out between you, and then this court will not have to make a decision. Go. Next case!

The following week the disputants were back. Again Magistrate Tagube acted as leading questioner, and had already ascertained that the problem had not been settled out of court. He had also meanwhile clarified one or two things for himself about the case, and reiterated the content.

> Magistrate Tagube: You have not straightened this out in the past week. This case is about Simon's woman. The woman went back to her homeplace. Her group married her to someone else, who also adopted the daughter. Her group says Simon never went to them, never wrote to them, never sent anything to them, never talked to them, after the woman went back. There was a war, the group moved, and lived with another group in another place. She was married to a man in the group they lived with. Simon had given K800 for her. He wants this money back.

There was an interjection at this point from the back of the crowd:

> Interjector: Give him nothing! He is fucking rubbish!
>
> Magistrate: You! Come here! [The interjector comes forward and stands in front of the magistrates' table.] K5 fine! [in English] *'Disturbing Court!'*
>
> Interjector: I don't have K5.
>
> Magistrate: K5! Pay now, or two week's prison. We'll make a prison order.

Such an order would have to be signed by a district court magistrate, who would most likely refuse to consign a person to prison for such a petty matter as interjecting. Magistrate Tagube was bluffing. His aggressive response was deliberately aimed at dissuading any other potential interjectors. Controlling the rowdy crowd was a chronic problem for the magistrates, and Tagube frequently used a tactic such as this. The situation was resolved by one of the disputants, who paid on behalf of the interjector.

> Ranji: Sorry. He is our relative [hands Tagube K5, which Tagube passes to the court clerk].

Magistrate: *Okay.* [to interjector] Go!

Alois: There is a little problem with the brideprice. Our tambu [i.e. Simon] gave K800. We gave K200 to a relative. He is dead now. He used the money before he died.

Magistrate: *Okay.* Enough. Go and wait.

The disputants retired into the crowd. The matter of the K200 allegedly given to a relative who used it and died could have been contentious, if the claim for compensation had been heard under different circumstances and without the complicating factor of Simon's long period of non-communication with his wife and her kin-group. He might have argued that the recovery of the K200 was his affines' problem, and that he was entitled to the full amount. An inference here is that the affines were not willing to pay the full amount because of Simon's neglect of his obligations (this was the import of the interjection by a 'relative' of the wife's kin), and Simon was hardly in a position to insist on this in Erima village court under the circumstances. The magistrates conferred and subsequently recalled the disputants.

Magistrate Tagube: We have talked about this. Our brother [indicating one of the four other magistrates on the bench] is Simbu [i.e. from the same general area as the disputants] and he knows the ways of your people. The marriage between Simon and the woman is already finished. We are not talking about that here. And we are not talking about the daughter. These are not things for this court to decide [i.e. they are matters beyond the village court's jurisdiction]. Simon paid a brideprice and he is asking for compensation. We have decided on that. We are cutting the K200 which the relative used. He is dead, so that is lost. Alois and Ranji, your group must pay K600 compensation. You must pay within two months. Any other problems between you people must be taken to a court at Gumine. They [i.e. other potential repercussions of the demise of Simon's marriage] are matters of your homeplace, and we cannot hear them in Erima village court. Case finished.

Jacob's house posts

Erima court, more than Konedobu and Pari courts, borrowed legal terms and concepts from district court procedure. The discourse of the magistrates, while largely in Tokpisin, appropriated English words such as 'proof', 'adjourn', ' (case) dismissed', 'evidence', and 'contempt (of court)' among other terminology which was readily understood by most disputants.[2] Magistrates also invoked the burden of proof in cases involving offences such as theft and property damage. Complainants who could not provide adequate evidence against the accused were likely to have their case 'dismissed'. But the trappings of formal legalism were being appropriated into a community-based institution, where local knowledge, infused with the biases and prejudices of parochial sociality, also had a significant influence on people's fortune in court.

In the example below, 'Jacob' had accused 'Moses' of stealing some house posts, damaging the walls of Jacob's jerry-built house and verbally insulting him. Moses had acquired some house posts while Jacob was away visiting his homeplace in Simbu Province, and Jacob believed these were his own missing posts. Jacob's case was undermined not only by the difficulty of proving his accusation, but also by his own bad reputation in the settlement. Moses on the other hand had a good reputation, and Jacob had already shown himself to be antagonistic and troublesome to neighbours. Indeed, one of the magistrates remarks, in the transcript below, that Jacob had difficulty fitting into the settlement community and should perhaps return to his rural homeplace. A degree of community prejudice against Jacob is evident in this case, and is acknowledged and acceded to by the court. A finding against Moses may have generated resentment in the community, resulting in retaliation against Jacob, and an escalation of the nascent problems caused by his presence. Nevertheless, the court attempted to deal fairly with the underlying, and unexplained, antagonisim between Jacob and Moses.

> Magistrate Andrew: [reading through the summons] Moses, Jacob's complaint says, first thing, you stole five iron posts, house posts I think, costing K20 each. Second thing, you damaged some walls of his house when you two had an argument. Third thing, you called Jacob a 'rubbish man' and a 'sanguma' [roughly, 'sorcerer', implying that Jacob brought misfortune on others]. Is this true?
>
> Moses: No, it is not true. I built my house. I bought things to build the house. The posts, I got them from a man.
>
> Magistrate Tagube: What man?
>
> Moses: His name is James.
>
> Magistrate Tagube: Where did he get the posts from?
>
> Moses: I don't know. I got them from him, that's all. I did not break anything at Jacob's house. I don't know about that.
>
> Magistrate Andrew: Did you call Jacob a 'rubbish man' and a 'sanguma'?
>
> Moses: No. I did not say those things. Ask people who live around me—I am a peaceful man. This man, Jacob, he has come to my house before, when he is drunk. He has made trouble for me, but I have never taken him to court about this.
>
> Magistrate: Jacob, what is your story?

Jacob: I went to Simbu [Jacob's home region]. When I came back to the settlement, my posts [house posts] were not there. Later, I saw them at Moses's house.

Moses: They are not his posts. I have a witness.

Magistrate: OK, we'll hear him. Witness! Come.

A man came forward from the crowd and stood beside Moses.

Magistrate Andrew: What do you know about this?

Witness: What Moses says is true. He is a quiet man. These things this man [nodding towards Jacob] said, this did not happen. Moses did not steal the posts.

Magistrate: *Okay*. Thank you witness. [the witness retires into the crowd] We know about things that have happened between you two before. I am thinking about making a preventive order. Do you know what a preventive order is? It means you two are not allowed to argue or fight, or the court will charge you. I have heard stories about you two before. I have heard about Jacob coming to your [Moses's] house when he is drunk, and causing trouble. Things are not good between you.

Jacob: I have a witness.

Magistrate: Oh. *Okay*, we'll hear him.

Jacob: He is not here. I will bring him.

Magistrate: *Okay*, we will [using the English term] *adjourn* this case for one week. Jacob, you can bring your witness then. We will send peace officers to look at the house and the posts, and they will report next week. [In English] *Case adjourned!*

The following week, when the case was called, Magistrate Andrew resumed with the report of the peace officers.

Magistrate Andrew: The peace officers have seen the house and the posts. They cannot see what damage was done to the walls. That is not clear. This is not a 'covenant' house [the inference is that damage is hard to discern in a house built with improvised material]. The peace officers have looked at the posts, too. Moses said he got these from a man called James. The peace officers cannot say if these posts were stolen from Jacob. There is no proof. Jacob, is your witness here?

Jacob: No. He has not come.

Magistrate Tagube: Yes! He has not come! Listen, there have been plenty of problems with Jacob for a long time. We know this. I think Jacob is not able to behave properly in this settlement in Moresby. It would be better for him to go back to his homeplace.

Magistrate John: [a third magistrate] It is true, Jacob has not behaved well in the settlement. He has gone to Moses's house when he is drunk, and caused trouble plenty of times, and Moses has never taken him to village court. [addressing crowd] True? Or not?

A section of the crowd, presumably from the same settlement area as Jacob and Moses, called out 'True!' and individuals began calling out that Jacob was a 'trouble man' and a drunkard.

> Magistrate John: *Okay, okay*. Jacob has no witness. But Moses has plenty of witnesses. We can hear them.

> Magistrate Andrew: *Okay*. Jacob, there is no proof that Moses stole your posts. There is no proof that Moses damaged your house. There is no proof that he called you a rubbish man or sanguma. That was your complaint, and there is no proof. So, [in English] *'case dismissed.'* [in Tokpisin] There has been trouble before with you and Moses, so I am going to make a preventive order. You two cannot argue or fight or you will be charged by this court. Did you hear this? Jacob, did you hear? *Okay*. See the court clerk afterwards and get the preventive order. Thank you.

Megi and Karo

This case involved a man and a woman from the highlands who had entered into a *de facto* marital arrangement in town, though no brideprice had yet been paid. The woman, Megi, was claiming compensation for deception and abandonment.

> Magistrate Andrew: [looking at summons] *Okay*. Karo, Megi says you lied to her. You sent her to your homeplace for three months. Then you got another wife, and when she came back from your place you threw her out. Is this true?

> Karo: It is true. She is not a good woman. We were in a big house. It was always full with her wantoks [relatives and acquaintances]. There were many other women in the house. I did not feel like I was her husband. She played cards a lot. She was out and about a lot. She didn't cook. This house, the rooms had no doors, and too many people. We two could not be together as a man and wife. I do not want her to come back.

> Magistrate: Megi, what is your story?

> Megi: He sent me to our place [i.e. homeplace, which was near Mt Hagen]. He did not send money, he did not send any talk. I made gardens and worked at our place. Then I came back to Moresby. He was not at the house, they told me he had gone to another house. I went to that house. There was a woman. He [Karo] was away. I pretended to be a wantok [in this context 'wantok' implies distant relative] waiting for somebody. I stayed around. Then he came home. The woman then knew I was his wife. She ran away.

> Karo: I sent her to our place for nine months. She came back in three months. I did not like the way she behaved, and I told her to find another man.

> Magistrate: Karo, do you want Megi to come back to you?

Karo: No. I am not happy with the way she behaved.

Magistrate: Karo, your behaviour was not good. You did not act like a married man. You should have stood up. You were the boss of that house. If you were unhappy with your wife you should have told her. It was wrong to send her away and then get another woman behind her back. That is not the right way for a husband to behave. Megi, what do you want to do? Do you want to go back to Karo?

Megi: If he wanted me to go back to him, I would go back to him. But he wants to get rid of me. That's alright, I will go back to Mt Hagen.

Magistrate: How long have you been married? [they were not married, in fact, by any legal measure; Magistrate Andrew is referring to the length of time they had been together under a *de facto* agreement].

Megi: Two years.

Karo: Nine months. Starting November last year.

Assessments of time periods beyond a few months were commonly vague in settlement communities, and contradictions like this one between Megi and Karo were not unusual. For the majority of settlement dwellers living day-to-day, the longest practical measure of the passage of time is a *fotnait* (Tokpisin: literally 'fortnight', but also 'payday', reflecting the two-week pay period in formal employment). Economic activities are planned in relation to *fotnait*, and references to time periods longer than a few *fotnait* are generally imprecise.

Magistrate: Hmmm. *Okay*, go and wait. The court will think about this.

The magistrates discussed the case among themselves for several minutes, then the disputants were called back.

Magistrate Andrew: *Okay*, my brothers and sister [i.e. fellow magistrates] have talked, and this is what we have decided. Karo, if you were unhappy with your wife, you should have told her. You should have behaved like a husband. It was wrong to send her away and get another wife without telling her. You must pay compensation to Megi. You must pay K400. You have one month to pay. And you must pay for a plane ticket so Megi can go back to Hagen. And you will pay a court fine of K50. You have one week to pay the court fine. Do you understand? *Okay*, case finished.

The case was not, however, finished. Four weeks later, Megi and Karo were back in court. Karo had been to chairman Andrew's house, complaining that Megi had come to his workplace and harrassed him about the compensation payment. But the one-month period allowed for the compensation payment had now ended, so Karo's complaint eventuated in a return to court, where he was warned about non-compliance with the court's orders. While Karo had been ordered formally to pay K400 compensation within a month, the court was usually lenient in cases where a significant sum was involved. Had Karo paid at least a portion of the compensation within the required time he would have been allowed to pay the rest at a comfortable rate. However, he had paid nothing, so the court was relatively severe.

> Magistrate Andrew: Karo and Megi. Karo has complained that Megi came to his workplace and made trouble, asking for compensation money. Karo, the court ordered you to pay K400 compensation, and ordered you to pay it in less than one month. Now one month has passed and you have not paid. You have not paid any money, or given Megi a small part of the compensation. *Okay*. Karo, the court orders you to bring some money and give it to Megi in front of me on Friday. If you do not do this, the court will make an imprisonment order. That means you will go to prison because you have not done what the court ordered. [in English, gesturing towards his open copy of the village court handbook] *'Failure to comply with a village court order.'* [in Tokpisin] Do you understand?
>
> Karo: I have some problems. It is hard for me to pay this money. And she is not behaving well. It was wrong for her to come to my workplace. . . .
>
> Magistrate Tagube: [interrupting] Listen! Don't humbug! [adopting a whining tone] 'I am not able—She does such-and-such. . . .' [in his normal voice] Hah! Give her some money or you will go to prison!
>
> Karo: I am not happy. The court has not done the right thing.
>
> Magistrate Andrew: That's alright. You can appeal to the district court. Case finished. Thank you. Court Clerk, next case.

Jimmy's Dog

Issues of proof and 'evidence' are again important in this case, in which two men are claimed to have stolen, killed and eaten the dog of a third man. While groups in some areas in the highlands are popularly thought to eat dogs, dog-eating is not common in Port Moresby. Meat is relatively expensive in town, however, and more-or-less stray dogs wandering the streets are occasionally killed and eaten. Dogs killed by passing cars quickly putrefy in the heat and dirt, and their corpses are unlikely to be taken for human consumption. Nevertheless, the two accused dog stealers claimed in court that they found the dog dead on the road.

> Magistrate Andrew: Gama and Ben, Jimmy's complaint says you two stole his dog, and you killed this dog and ate this dog. He asks for K100 compensation. Is it true that you stole this dog and ate it?
>
> Gama: We did not steal the dog. We found it on the road. It was dead. We did not know it belonged to Jimmy, we thought it was a wandering [i.e. stray] dog. It was already dead, so we cooked it and ate it.
>
> Jimmy: It was not a wandering dog, it was my dog. It did not go on the road. They stole it.

Magistrate: *Okay.* Jimmy, did you see Gama and Ben steal your dog?

Jimmy: No. They killed it.

Magistrate: Do you have a witness who saw them steal it? They have said it was on the road.

Jimmy: I don't have a witness. But, they killed the dog.

Magistrate Tagube: But, do you have a witness? Did someone see this?

Jimmy: They killed it!

Magistrate Tagube: That is not what we asked. Listen, did anyone actually see these two men kill this dog?

Jimmy: No, but. . . .

Magistrate Tagube: [interrupting] That's enough! That is all we wanted to know.

Magistrate Andrew: This is not an easy case. In bush places [i.e. rural or village societies] dogs can roam around far from home, and it would be wrong for anyone to kill the dog, or eat the dog. Dogs go about with freedom, and everyone would know the dog belonged to someone. They would probably know who the dog belonged to. But in town people are supposed to look after dogs and keep them near their house. There are roads and cars in town. In town, people cannot allow their dogs to roam around in the same way as they allow them to in the bush. We often see dead dogs on the road, and in town we know there are dogs who don't belong to anyone, who are just around. So if there are no witnesses, we just have two stories here.

Gama: Excuse me, this dog was dead. We found it on the road.

Jimmy: You stole the dog!

Magistrate Andrew: Hmmm. I am going to [using the English term] *adjourn* this case for one week. Maybe we can find a witness. Our peace officers will ask questions around. [in English] *Adjourned one week.*

The following week the case resumed. Peace officers had reported back to chairman Andrew that somone had seen the dog at the house of Gama and Ben, already dead.

Magistrate Andrew: We have a report that the dog was at the house of Gama and Ben, but it is not clear whether Gama and Ben stole the dog, or whether they found it dead on the road. There is no proof that Gama and Ben stole the dog. So Jimmy, the court will not order K100 compensation.

Magistrate Tagube: There is no proof that you two stole the dog, but you two ate the dog. It is not permitted to eat dogs in the 'NCD' [National Capital District]. This is not a bush place!

Magistrate Andrew: Yes, my 'brother' [Tagube] is correct. And it was Jimmy's dog. So he will get some compensation. We order K50 compensation for Jimmy. Gama, you will give K25 compensation to Jimmy, and Ben, you will give K25. And Gama and Ben you will pay court fines of K10 each, because it is wrong to eat dogs in town.

Ben: I am not happy. It is not good to fine us for eating the dog. Meat is expensive.

Magistrate Tagube: Listen! It is the law!

Magistrate Andrew: Yes. That is the court's decision. You have one week to pay. Case finished.

Law and Justice

A contrast with both Pari and Konedobu village courts is evident in these cases, in respect of issues of proof and reliable witnesses. Where witnesses' testimony was considered, for example, in some cases at Konedobu recorded in the previous chapter (in respect of gossip and insult), inferences were drawn from it by magistrates about the kind of aggrievement felt by the complainant and the social effects of the incidents. But preoccupation with proof, reasonable doubt, or equivocation over the veracity of evidence did not affect magistrates' considerations to the degree where cases were dismissed. In cases in Erima court, however, the burden of proof, the veracity of testimony and the reliability of witnesses were explicitly taken into account. The court's quasi-technical considerations suggest a preoccupation with the precise administration of law (and therefore, in principle, justice) to the individuals before the court, as is the case in Western courts of law. Yet this was not entirely evident in Erima court, even though the magistrates' decisions were more punitive, and less reconciliatory, than those of their Konedobu colleagues, and lacked the reintegrative imperative of the Pari magistrates.

In the ethnically mixed settlements served by Erima court, the obligations and imperatives of kinship-ordered sociality were not as strong as in the 'Kerema'-dominated settlements served by Konedobu court, or in Pari village. Most disputants were not related to each other by kinship, even distantly. Those who had a connection through a marriage were frequently not from the same 'tribal' area, and their affinal relationship was likely to be acknowledged only grudgingly and lacked the reinforcement of other kinds of ties which might have integrated the marriage partners' groups in a rural homeplace. The relative estrangement of disputing individuals was reflected in their divergent accounts of incidents and their contradictions of each other's testimony (as in the cases of Nansi and her tenants, the sanguma accusation and Jacob's house posts). They had few qualms about accusing each other of lying or contesting 'facts' if they thought it was to their advantage. Yet the court remained sensitive to the social and political exigencies of life in the settlements which have been described in previous chapters. Regardless of their differences, the settlement dwellers had to cohabit as best they could. Consequently the technical application of the law to disputants as individuals was tempered by consideration of social issues as the case examples above indicate. Erima court's magistrates could not be socially disinterested jurists, despite their recourse to formal juridical principles.

The Erima magistrates' adoption of techniques from formal courts indicates the effects of the pressures and criticisms discussed in chapters 2 and 3 which have generated a preoccupation among village courts in general to apply 'the law' correctly. Chairman Andrew, in particular, attended every available 'training' course he was able to, and in addition to knowing the village court handbook by heart had gone to some lengths to educate himself in the law as he had seen and heard it applied in the district court. The application of tenets such as the burden of proof and the interrogation of veracity stopped short of the requirement that people giving testimony should swear to tell the truth. Disputants and supporters in court, cognisant of the 'swearing in' that took place in the district court, occasionally produced and flourished Bibles to support their version of events. Magistrates discouraged this, telling disputants that Erima was not a district court and people were not required to take an oath of veracity.

The adoption of legal principles of proof and veracity has the potential to dispose the court further towards individualised justice (*fiat justitia, ruat coleum...*) but this is countered by the preoccupation with communal equilibrium which is evident in some of the court decisions above (Nansi and her tenants, and Jacob's house posts). The magistrates' failure to capitulate further to the technicalities of socially disinterested, individualised jurisprudence should not, however, be completely reduced to their reflective concern with the need for the ethnically diverse settlement community to maintain its social coherence. For while the population served by Erima court is not a village (like Pari), or a sub-regional enclave (like the settlements near Konedobu), the magistrates and disputants share with Melanesians in general a more fundamental disposition towards communality than a superficial consideration of the disputes and the decisions might suggest. This disposition, and its relationship to the putatively individualised cases dealt with by village courts, is addressed in more depth in chapter 9.

Notes

1. Any attempt to define precisely what is meant by 'sorcery' here would be a waste of time (see chapter 3).
2. Tokpisin, the most widespread lingua franca of PNG, is subject to significant variation around the country, and foreigners can find this confusing, in the same way that regional dialects and phraseological idiosyncracies in Britain are confusing for (even English-speaking) foreigners. In Port Moresby, more than in other areas, many resident Tokpisin speakers sprinkle their conversation liberally and confidently with contemporary English terms, both slang and technical, even when they are not fluent English speakers.

9

BETWEEN GROUPS AND INDIVIDUALS

A theme running through the previous four chapters is that the 'style' of a village court is significantly shaped by the particular community it serves. A corollary of this is the degree to which local sociality is taken into account in hearings and in the decisions of magistrates. In Pari, for instance, the integrity of the village was a major consideration, and a preoccupation with the reintegration of offenders and the maintenance of good interpersonal and inter-*iduhu* relations, rather than the punishment of individuals, was implicit in the practice of the court. In Konedobu court, individual disputes were contextualised in larger issues of settlement life, and communal dynamics were clearly part of the considerations of magistrates when dealing with offences which in Western legal discourse would be reduced to the actions and responsibilities of the individuals involved. Even in Erima court, serving ethnically mixed settlements with an accompanying degree of estrangement among disputants, magistrates were sensitive to the dynamics of the local community. In this chapter I address the tension between the village courts' embeddedness in their community and the fact that, as I have also noted in earlier chapters, they are legal institutions governed by rules which ostensibly oblige them to treat disputants as legally responsible *individuals*.

Relationalism and the Legal Individual

Since the earliest ethnographic accounts (for example, Landtman 1927; Malinowski 1961 [1922]) anthropologists have, one way or another, conventionally portrayed Melanesians as traditionally lacking the individualism of Westerners, and subjugating individual 'rights' to those of the group. Individual aspirations were seen to be constricted by the relationships in which a person was inextricably enmeshed. According to this understanding of the dynamics of Melanesian societies even the stereotypical, aggressively entrepreneurial, highland 'big-man'[1] would be misrepresented by the label 'individualist'. The traditional 'big-man' may have been a successful entrepreneur and thus individually distinctive by reputation, but he attained this only by astute manipulation of inescapable relationships with kinsmen, and his individual prominence waned as he aged and others skilfully usurped the web of obligation and reciprocation he had nurtured. The degree to which the traditional Melanesian is sustained by relationships used to be reflected in anthropological literature in dichotomous terms contrasting the 'individualism' of Westerners with the 'communalism' of Melanesians. More recently, and especially after Marilyn Strathern's influential critique of gender relations (1988), the term 'relationalism' has gained currency. Joel Robbins typifies a significant body of recent writing: 'Melanesian cultures value the creation of relationships over that of other cultural forms (e.g., individuals, wholes) and . . . reckon the value of relationships rather than of the individuals who make them up or the larger structures of which they may empirically be a part' (2004: 292).

A potential challenge to Melanesian relationalism was presented by Western individualism, which has been linked historically with the rise of Christianity and subsequent transformations of the early conceptualisation of the Christian as an individual-in-relation-to-God (Dumont 1986). Individualism was introduced to Melanesians not only through Christianity, but also through capitalism, and through the imposition of Western law, which emphasises the legal accountability of the individual. The degree to which Melanesians have embraced individualism has been a matter of debate. While missionaries might be encouraged by the relative enthusiasm with which many Papua New Guineans have adopted the rhetoric of individual salvation, anthropologists have sometimes questioned the degree to which Melanesians have actually internalised Christian individualism (see, for example, Robbins 2004) or secular individualism (see, for example, Gewertz and Errington 1991). Similar doubts have been raised in respect of capitalist individualism. An influential publication by Christopher Gregory indicated that the introduction of commodity exchange, whereby 'alienable' objects are transacted by 'aliens', had not undermined traditional gift exchange, whereby 'inalienable' objects are transacted by 'non-aliens' (1982: 43). Gift exchange in Melanesia is a process explicitly maintaining interpersonal relationships, linked to the sustenance of group identity and, importantly, to group ownership of land (116, 163–65).

The effect of Western law on relationalism is equally moot. Ethnographers have noted the way in which aspects of Western legalism, as experienced through the administration of justice by *kiaps* (patrol officers) as well as in formal courts, were appropriated by Melanesians in the colonial era (for example, Berndt 1962; Strathern 1972). Yet there have been suggestions that localised 'unofficial courts' (sometimes encouraged by *kiaps*) derived their influence and acceptability not so much from the jurisprudence represented by colonial *kiap* and formal courts as from their perceived power (see, for example, Gordon and Meggitt 1985: 49–54, 167–69). The prominent Papua New Guinean politician and lawyer Bernard Narokobi (1977) went so far as to claim that Papua New Guineans did not understand Western law. A critique of Narokobi's rhetoric by Gordon and Meggitt pointed out that many Westerners do not understand Western law either and that Engans of the PNG highlands, for example, had a shrewd understanding of what Western law entailed, but that neither Engans nor ordinary Westerners understood 'the abstract mystification of legal concepts' (1985: 209fn).

Moreover, the unofficial *kots* (courts) of the late colonial period had some characteristics which distinguished them from the courts they partly mimicked: 'The fact that a wide range of evidence and discussion was allowed often gave the appearance that cases in these kots were disposed of in a manner contrary to established administration norms; this was another feature that could serve to mollify the litigants. Sittings of kots were generally well attended . . . it was important for [people] to see what was happening and to be able to support their clans' positions' (Gordon and Meggitt 1985: 167). The final statement in the quotation could perhaps be taken to imply that behind putatively individual litigants are clan dynamics which may have a bearing on local understandings of responsibility and accountability. Gordon and Meggitt, however, did not pursue this avenue, arguing instead that 'the recognition of individual responsibility is very much a factor that initiates and steers action'. Further, they saw the traditional sanction of expelling an individual from a group as an indication that 'although responsibility might seem to be collective to the outside observer, for the insider it is indeed individual' (201). This last observation, however, does not enable us to confidently assume a degree of individualism in traditional Melanesian societies. In fact, from a relationist perspective, the expulsion case may be more complex than Gordon and Meggitt recognised, for insofar as identity was dependant on membership in a group, the ability of an 'individual' to exist outside a group is questionable. Possibly, expulsion amounted not to the isolation of an individual, but to the negation of 'personhood'. Maurice Leenhardt, writing of New Caledonia in the 1920s, suggested that expulsion from a group consigned a man to 'perdition', and that deprived of his participation in a group he had, in effect, no existence (1998: 251). Leenhardt's point was contextualised in an argument that traditionally New Caledonian Melanesians were *personae*[2] and necessarily sustained by relationships, lacking a sense of themselves as individuals in the Western sense (248–51).

Less concerned with existential themes, but perhaps more useful for contemporary understandings of the reception of legal individualism by Melanesians, was an observation by Marilyn Strathern in a discussion of informal courts in the highlands shortly before the introduction of village courts. She argued that Hageners (of the western highlands) 'do have a concept of individual responsibility' but added the important qualification that Hageners made a contrast 'between responsibility for an act and liability to make amends for it' (1972: 142). Further, she noted that '"settlement" may seem to be more important than the rights of individuals' (143). Strathern's reference to Hageners' contrast between responsibility and liability is important, for it marks a disjunction with Western legalism's emphasis on the connection between responsibility and liability. The disjunction is problematic for village courts, for unlike the informal courts which they were intended to obviate when they were introduced, their regulations and institutional terms of reference explicitly represent Western jurisprudence. The individualism on which this jurisprudence is predicated is particularly visible in cases where mediation is inappropriate or unsuccessful, upon which individuals are summonsed by name, and if thought 'guilty' they can be individually fined or sentenced to community work. If they do not co-operate with court rulings, individuals can be recommended for imprisonment. Prevention orders can be issued restraining individuals from particular behaviour. These and other expressions of individual liability in village court practice have sometimes been interpreted as leading to an adoption of principles of legal individualism by the local community itself.

The advent of legal individualism in village society is argued, for example, in Donald Tuzin's discussion of changing times and attitudes among the Ilahita Arapesh, of East Sepik Province. Tuzin noted that the introduction of the village court had increased people's appetite for litigation: 'For matters great and small, villagers are now committed to the idea of having their day in court. Moreover, they participate in the legal process as individuals' (1997: 44). He places particular importance on the individuality of disputants:

> The effect of the village court system—descended, as it is, from Western principles of jurisprudence—has been to locate legal identity and accountability in the person, thereby undercutting group ties. Traditionally . . . an individual who had been wronged would frequently adopt a morose passivity, expecting kinsmen or ritual allies to act on his behalf. Nowadays, if asked, the simple advice to one's brother is, 'Take him to court!' The grievance is now the victim's own, and the institution that created this new situation stands ready to service it. The lesson, namely that the individual is legally self-sufficient and responsible, is repeated several times every fortnight before a large and attentive audience, in the village courthouse. It marks a change of great sociological moment, for it liberates the individual from legal dependency on the group. (44–45)

Yet while it is true that disputants face a village court mostly as individuals, Tuzin's argument requires a great deal of qualification if it is to be applied more generally to village courts and the communities they serve. We have seen in the case of Pari village court, for example, that great emphasis is placed on offenders' membership in a village sharing a particular identity, and the court attempts more or less explicitly to reintegrate errant villagers. Complaints about 'individuals' are considered at least implicitly in the light of local group dynamics and history. Examples given in chapter 6 indicate something of this, but I will give an account here of another case in Pari village court which demonstrates more explicitly that while legal identity and accountability may be putatively located in the person under the rubrics of village courts, group membership can be an implicit, and vital, consideration in the village court's view of a dispute.

A Simple Case of Property Damage and Assault?

Superficially, and as represented on the summonses, the case involved mutual claims of property damage between two neighbouring households, and a man of one household was also accused of assaulting two women of the other household. It is possible to represent the case in a simple form, based on the court testimony. At the centre of this dispute were three Pari-born women related by birth—'Janet', 'Mary' and 'Anna'—who were married to non-Pari men. Mary was married to 'Tom', a man from another part of the country (hereafter called 'Gabuamo'), and had lived at other locations around Port Moresby as Tom moved from job to job. Anna was married to 'Sam', also from another area. About ten years previous to the court case, Mary and Anna and their husbands had decided they wanted to settle in Pari, after having moved from location to location for some time. Having no land themselves in the village, they negotiated permission to live on land controlled by a senior village man. The *tanobiaguna* (land controller) gave his approval for them to bring other people to live with them on the condition that all parties lived peacefully and looked after the land. Mary and Anna consequently invited Janet to establish a house next to theirs. Janet's husband, 'Jack', was also from Gabuamo, and was the son of Tom's sister. Jack, like his mother's brother Tom, had previously been living at various locations around Port Moresby.

At first the neighbourly arrangement worked satisfactorily but gradually friction developed between the two households, and eventually Mary and Anna decided that Janet and her husband had to go. The ultimatum came at a time when Janet and Jack were establishing a permanent house, after living in a temporary dwelling for some time. Things came to a head when, without consulting the *tanobiaguna*, they gave Janet and Jack one week to leave and informed them a bulldozer would subsequently arrive to level the area they were occupying. Janet and Jack worked frantically to dismantle their stilt-supported house, but when the bulldozer arrived the houseposts were still in place, and these and some plants and gardens were casualties of the subsequent levelling of the area. In distress Jack got drunk, damaged water tanks, plants and other property of the household of Mary and Anna, and punched the two women. Hence the two parties came to the village court accusing each other of damage and claiming compensation.

A complication arose from the relationship btween the two men from Gabuamo. In hitting Mary, Jack had assaulted the wife of his (Gabuamo) mother's brother Tom. Jack was the son of a hereditary clan leader, and the assault on his affine had been conduct very unbecoming. In an affidavit to the court, Tom, who was sitting at some distance from Jack, said he was currently unable to talk to his sister's son, and this state of affairs would continue unless and until Jack delivered a pig to Tom's family house in Gabuamo as compensation. The estranged relationship between the two Gabuamo men would damage the chance of reconciliation between the two neighbouring households in Pari. The court asked Jack for a response to Tom's statement, and Jack replied that he was shortly going to Gabuamo to deliver the compensatory pig. Having obtained this assurance, the court dealt with the case in what would seem to a casual observer to be a relatively straightforward manner. It announced it would adjourn the case for a week for the parties to consider whether they thought themselves reconcilable and able to cohabit peacefully in the future, or whether they should move to locations more distant from each other (the adjournment would also allow for some cooling off). The court would then itemise and estimate the cost of the damage for compensation purposes. However, the dispute had far more dimensions than were explicitly addressed in court, and my efforts to understand it adequately involved me in a great deal of genealogical and archival research in addition to lengthy conversations with magistrates and senior village men over some months.

A clue to the complications behind the case, and to its embeddedness in group relations and historical issues, emerged when the disputants returned the following week to report on their prospects for reconciliation. Janet, speaking for herself and her husband, told the court they had moved to another location in Pari territory, and would not consider trying to return to the area where Mary and Anna lived. During this statement to the magistrates Janet commented, in an audible aside to Mary and Anna, 'If I leave, then you will leave.' I did not realise the potency of her comment at the time. The court then decided on the compensation to be paid. The property damage claims were found to be roughly equal in financial measure. While the amounts cancelled each other out mathematically, it would not have been unusual for the court to direct the disputants to pay each other the cost of the damage, to ensure that a ritual of compensation took place. However, the magistrates declared the damage on both sides to be equivalent and left it at that. The remaining decision was the compensation for the assaults on Mary and Anna. Jack was ordered to pay each of them K100, and the case was closed.

Immediately after the hearing, the last for the day, there was some discussion among the magistrates and the *tanobiaguna* which contextualised the dispute in wider social issues. The magistrates were lamenting the disruption to landholding arrangements and rights when foreigners moved into the village, became partially absorbed into local social and political structures, and then departed, leaving descendants with equivocal rights. I learned that two of the three women were adoptees, and all three of them were descendants of a foreigner. The magistrates were concerned about the future prospects of Mary and Anna, neither of whom (the magistrates said) belonged to an *iduhu* even though they were brought up in the village. Some genealogical elaboration is necessary at this point, to better understand the social and historical context of Janet's dispute with Mary and Anna.

Mary, Anna and Janet were descendants of 'Paul Simpson' (see figure 9.1), who was himself one of more than a dozen children of a foreigner who arrived in Port Moresby late in the nineteenth century. Paul Simpson's father had married a Pari woman, of Idibana *iduhu*, who was working as a domestic servant in a European household. They had lived some distance from Pari, and the marriage had not introduced the man into Pari society. At the turn of the twentieth century and for much of the colonial period, the children of such marriages were labelled 'mixed race' (the term is still used in modern PNG) or 'half-caste' and were commonly marginalised in colonial European society and often unwilling or unable to immerse themselves in indigenous society.[3] Paul Simpson himself married a woman described to me by older Pari people as a 'South Sea Islander' (a term they often apply to Polynesians) and had eight children, of whom Mary was the last born. In the 1960s—as Port Moresby was growing rapidly and the cash economy was well established in nearby villages like Pari—the Simpson family, including the ageing Paul and two adult sons, opened a trade store in Pari village. They were given permission to reside and operate their store on land belonging to Idibana *iduhu*.

Several of Paul Simpson's daughters were married to Australians and Anna was the child of one of them. When her Australian father left the country Anna was adopted by Paul Simpson himself (her biological grandfather) and became, in social effect, Mary's younger sister. An older brother of Mary married a woman from Hanuabada whose brother was in turn married to a Pari woman. The marriage was short-lived, but shortly after its demise the woman gave birth to a child, Janet. Janet was adopted by the mother's brother, who had moved from Hanuabada and lived in Pari with his wife, who was a member of Idibana Taulamiri *iduhu*. Idibana Taulamiri was one of three *iduhu* resulting from the segmentation over time of Idibana[4] and is acknowledged to be the senior *iduhu* of the village since its core lineage

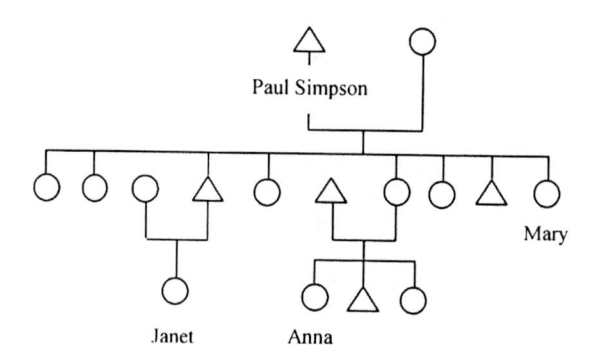

Figure 9.1. Natal relationship between Mary, Janet and Anna (marriages and children of Mary's other siblings are not shown here).

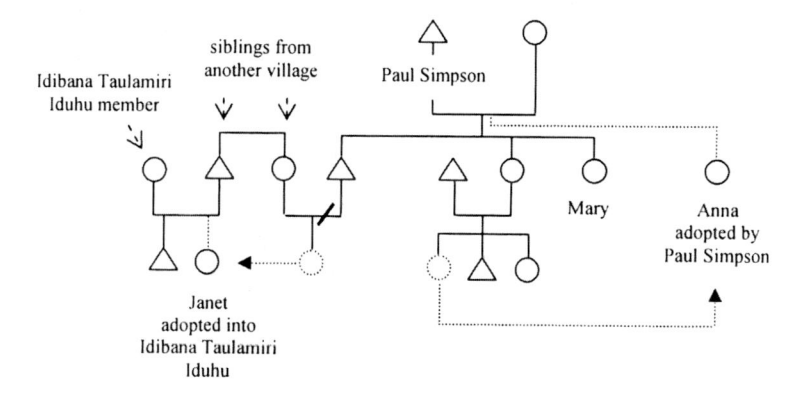

Figure 9.2. Adoption of Janet and Anna. Janet was now a member of the senior village iduhu, Idibana Taulamiri, while Mary and Anna remained in the Simpson family.

descends agnatically from Kevau Dagora, the founder of Pari. In discourses of descent the Motu-Koita use an idiom of patrilineality, but in practice cognatic elements are not uncommon. In Janet's case, since her adoptive father was an immigrant to the village and not part of a local lineage, she was classified into her adoptive mother's *iduhu*, Idibana Taulamiri (see figure 9.2). Her *iduhu* membership would prove to be a fateful distinction between herself and her biological father's sister (Mary) and father's sister's daughter (Anna). All three women married outside Pari village.

With the passage of time the males and some females in the Simpson family either died or moved to Australia. Left without male parents or brothers and married to outsiders, Mary and Anna had no claims to *iduhu* membership and no rights to land (see figure 9.3). Having given them a place to live at Taurama beach, the *tanobiaguna* was pleased when Mary invited Janet and her husband, Jack (Mary's husband's sister's son), to live with them as Janet was a member of the *tanobiaguna*'s own *iduhu* and consolidated, by occupation, ongoing *iduhu* control of that particular piece of land against other potential claimants. The subsequent falling out between Janet and the other women was disturbing in this regard since it was Janet, who had recognisable rights, who left. In fact, longstanding jealousy between Mary (landless, and lacking *iduhu* membership) and her fortunate niece-by-birth Janet (landholding and a member of the senior village *iduhu* by adoption) was the major contributor to their falling out.

The *tanobiaguna* was thus faced with the diplomatic problem of what to do about Mary and Anna. Their own marriages, to outsiders, annulled any possibility that they could become attached to an *iduhu* and develop initial affinal connections to land. They had no rights in relation to the land they occupied with his permission, and had broken his stipulation that they should live in peace. He commented in discussions after the court case that he would probably have to ask them to leave. This eventuality had been the import of Janet's aside—'If I leave, then you will leave'—during the dispute hearing. In this regard there was an encouraging aftermath to the case. Despite Janet having told the court she would not return to reside with Mary and Anna, the women effected a reconciliation a few weeks after the case. They ritually slaughtered and consumed a pig, and appeared—for the time being at least—to have settled their differences, opening the way for Janet to return to the piece of land if she wished. For Mary and Anna, repairing their relationship with Janet was vital for their survival in the community.

Behind the village court case, then, was a complex history bearing on the friction which eventually led to the property damage and assaults, all of which was known to the court, but never explicated. In discussions among the magistrates about the case and with myself, Mary's and Anna's lack of land was seen as the underlying problem and explained by their lack of *iduhu* membership.[5] This, in turn, was blamed on the systemic disruption brought about by impermanent foreigners.

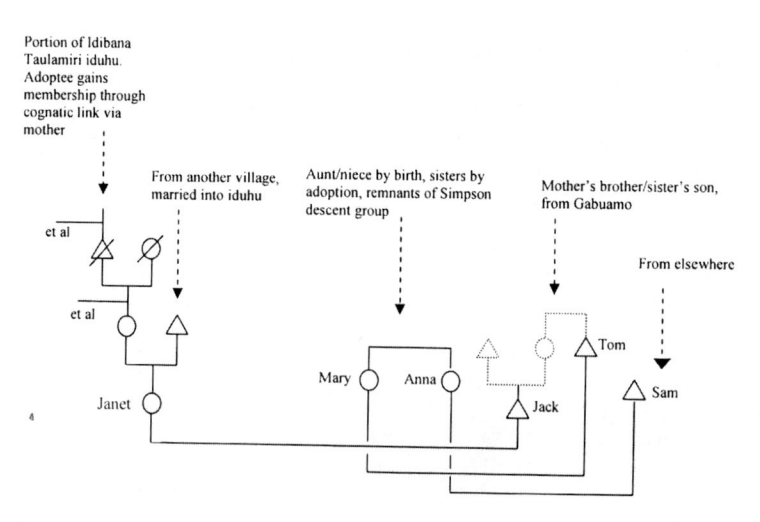

Figure 9.3 Marriages of Janet, Mary and Anna to men who are not Pari-born (all have children, not shown here). Janet is the only one who has *iduhu* membership.

Returning to Tuzin's comments on individual disputants, we can see in the example above that while the disputants faced the court as individuals, and the court's decision appeared superficially to have treated them as such, issues of kinship, descent and group affiliation played an important part in the magistrates' understanding of the affair, and in their concern about the future of the two women who had no *iduhu* membership. Legal identity and accountability may have been putatively located in the individuals concerned, but this did not undercut group ties (or the lack of them) or liberate the individuals from legal dependency on a group in the sense which Tuzin implies. Indeed, had Mary and Anna been members of an *iduhu* the case would have developed differently in court.

Relationalism and Individual Justice

To speak of the influence of 'relationalism' in village court practice in the face of the Western jurisprudential individualism to which the courts are putatively bound is to reaffirm, in currently fashionable parlance, Peter Lawrence's (1970) observation about Melanesian preoccupations with keeping the sky up. Importantly, this is a characteristic of the communities the village courts serve, inasmuch as the courts' decisions mostly accord with community attitudes about right and wrong, responsibility and liability. Consequently, attempts to judge whether village courts discriminate against individuals, or classes of individuals, take us into difficult territory. Village courts are, of course, no less capable than any other kind of court—formal or informal, 'higher' or 'lower'—of making bad or unjust decisions by any criteria, whether foreign or local. The period during which Reto was the chairing magistrate of Erima village court, described in chapter 5, is an example. Reto's autocratic decisions dismayed his fellow magistrates and most disputants alike, as well as the onlookers.

Claims of bias or prejudice in village courts are common among losing disputants though conversationally they express disgruntlement about the fine or compensation they are ordered to pay, rather than about being found 'guilty' (Strathern's observation about responsibility and liability is particularly relevant here). Given the local social context in which any village court operates, the possibility of apparent injustice to individuals is always present. But as we have already seen, the fate of individuals in a village court is sometimes determined more by the need for harmony and good order in the community at large than by principles of either Western or so-called 'customary' law. Further, the subjugation of individual 'rights' to wider community issues is intrinsic to local perceptions, governed by the 'relationalism' which I have discussed above. Under the circumstances, decisions which appear to a Western observer to be unfair to an individual disputant may be regarded as perfectly just by the local community. By way of example, I will briefly review the 'snake bone case' which I discussed in chapter 3, in which a woman, Mata, a member of a group from the Eastern Highlands Province, was accused with her group of attempting to sorcerise her husband Sobe from Tari in the Southern Highlands Province.

Mata was, in fact, personally innocent, according to Western jurisprudential principles. She had been coerced by her kinsmen, particularly by her 'uncle', Yaba, into the attempt and had in the last instance not gone through with the act of placing the sorcerised snake bones into her husband's tea. Chairman Andrew pointed out during the case that had the sorcery plot been successful it would have led to conflict between groups from the two districts probably resulting in a number of deaths. The court found Mata's group guilty. As Mata was recognised to be a member of the responsible kin group, she was included in the 'guilty' verdict. The exclusion of Mata from the judgment of guilt would have been extremely controversial, amounting to an implication that she was being publicly separated from her natal kin group. It would certainly have been regarded by the community as unjust, while it was recognised that the real 'culprit' was Yaba. However, when the verdict was dictated to the court clerk by chairman Andrew, the guilty parties were described as 'Yaba and his *lain*' (group), without specifying who constituted the *lain*. In the public view, this was also perfectly correct, as it loosely identified the kin-group as a whole as being responsible. When the ordered court fine had not been paid in the designated period of one week, an order was issued threatening imprisonment. This was made out against an individual, Yaba. Mata was excluded from any punishment by this paperwork. It is useful to recall, once again, Strathern's distinction between responsibility and liability here. Mata, included in the category of those responsible, was ultimately not held to liability in the court's ruling.

The finding of 'guilt' against Mata might offend Western legal sensibilities (indeed she could be perceived as a victim in the affair), but it was not unjust to her in any practical way. Her husband Sobe bore her no personal ill will, and she continued to cohabit with him during and after the case, against the wishes of Yaba and other kinsmen. In our discussion after the case chairman Andrew expressed concerns to me about the continued cohabitation of Mata and Sobe in the settlement. He feared that this would cause continued discontent from Yaba and his kinsmen, and he expected more disputes related to the marriage would be brought to court.

In contrast to this case, in which an 'innocent' woman was found 'guilty', another case from Erima court exemplifies a contrary situation, in which a man's accusations against his wife were dismissed. The man brought his young wife to court claiming that she had committed adultery. He said he was certain she was seeing a man, 'George', in another suburb. The wife denied this. After some questioning which provided no enlightenment, the village court decided it needed more evidence. It adjourned the case for a week for George to be found and brought to court as a witness. By the following week George had not been found. After a further adjournment, with no sign of George, continued denial by the wife, and no other evidence or witnesses to the alleged adultery, the village court dismissed the case. This might appear at first sight to be a favourable decision for the wife. However, the case was more complicated than might be inferred from a superficial observation.

The village court magistrates, needless to say, knew more about the background to the dispute than had been disclosed in court. Chairman Andrew told me that the 'marriage' in this case had been secured by only a nominal brideprice. By 'customary' criteria the ritual of exchanges between groups (including a significant brideprice payment) which consolidated a marriage had not taken place. It was the kind of urban marriage described in chapter 8, regarded as legitimate by grassroots townspeople, despite its equivocal legal (or 'customary') status, and of which payment of a nominal 'brideprice' was the informal criterion used by the village court in deciding whether or not it was a 'real' marriage. If a sum agreed upon by both parties as a 'brideprice', however small, had been paid, then the union could not be annulled, according to the village court's criterion, even if it had become an unsatisfactory union in other respects according to one or other of the disputants.

The *de facto* marriage of the disputants before the court was known to be unstable and the husband was known to be a violent man. The wife had never complained about his violence[6] or about the marriage, and unless she or her kin brought a complaint against him the court could not take action. But Andrew had hoped, nevertheless, to use the adultery accusation to extract the woman from the marriage. The union was of the kind which the village court normally refused to annul, using its rule-of-thumb method of defining marriages in town. However, disputants in marriage-related cases often gave conflicting accounts of the amount of money which was agreed on as the brideprice, and of the amount of time a man had been given to pay the amount (brideprices were frequently paid in instalments by low-income earners in town).

There were also debates over the categorisation of occasional cash payments by a man to his 'wife' or her kin. Such payments were sometimes argued by the man to be a brideprice instalment, and by the woman to be in a different category such as a gift, compensatory payment, or some other kind of contribution (therefore not acceptable as a brideprice contribution). These equivocations created a 'grey area' whereby the village court sometimes prevaricated over the classification of the union. The court might declare a troubled relationship 'finished' (i.e. not really a marriage, and therefore within their jurisdiction to publically annul), or alternatively 'unable to be finished' (i.e. a definite marriage, which was beyond their legal power to annul).

In the case at hand, Andrew had been hopeful that with some manoeuvring he and his fellow magistrates could raise doubt about the legitimacy of the marriage. He was hoping that either the wife or George would admit to the liaison, for George really existed, and the magistrates knew who he was. Desperate attempts had been made to locate him and persuade him to come to court, without success. Neither were the magistrates (or Andrew at least, who was skilled at these kinds of manoeuvrings) able to approach the woman separately from her husband to discuss their strategy with her, as the jealous husband was not letting her out of his sight. After two adjournments, the court could no longer prevaricate and had to let the case slip away. Had the adultery been admitted, the magistrates' plan was to exploit any inconsistency in accounts of the marriage's status to declare the 'marriage' finished. They could then order the wife to repay the small 'brideprice' (in reality her kin, rather than she, would probably make the repayment), and issue a preventive order against the ex-husband to keep away from the ex-wife, passing a copy of this to the village court serving the area where George was known to live, to ensure the wife would be safe. She could then have married George, reportedly a better prospect than the current husband. Instead, the dismissal of the case, superficially a finding in favour of the woman, consigned her to staying with her undesirable husband.

These two cases demonstrate attempts by a village court to achieve justice, negotiating community attitudes on the one hand and legal strictures on the other. The tensions between individual responsibility and liability, implied by Western jurisprudence, and the contingent responsibilities and liabilities of relationalism are visible in the snake bone case in particular. In the adultery case we see the constrictions placed upon the court's sense of a just outcome by legal requirements manifest in the burden of proof on the husband, the wife's right to deny the charge and the need for the 'other man' to be identified and made accountable as a witness or co-defendant. The complexities evident in the two cases, as well as the case above from Pari village court, reinforce the point made several times in previous chapters that an understanding of social context is vital to an appreciation of the workings and decisions of any village court. Certainly, knowledge of the social context is more useful in understanding their treatment of disputes than conventional notions of 'custom' or 'customary law' (cf. Zorn 1991). Further, assessments of the degree to which individual rights might be traduced by village courts, or to what extent the courts discriminate against, or are oppressive of, certain types or classes of individuals, also need to be informed by an understanding of the social context.

Relationalism and Discrimination

The most common accusations of discriminatory practice in village courts in recent times have been about their treatment of women, as we saw in chapter 3. If we acknowledge relationalism to be a paradigm governing the way rights, responsibility and liability are understood by the majority of Melanesians, we face difficulty in accurately testing whether women, when they individually go to court, are discriminated against. It is commonly argued that women as a whole are subordinated to men in Melanesian societies, from which it would be easy to take the inference that village courts, whose officials are overwhelmingly males, can simply be added to a catalogue of institutions used by males to oppress women. In chapter 3 I gave a number of examples of legalist criticisms of village court treatment of women made from the 1970s to the early 1990s. I also noted that after abating for a while the issue of discrimination has re-emerged in recent years, partly under the impetus of human rights and gender-equality concerns pursued through policy-related research connected with international aid and development agencies. As I have already pointed out, some of the evidence or examples offered of village courts' discrimination are recycled stories from the 1970s (for example, Macintyre 1998; O'Collins 2000) which are not supported by up-to-date research and appear to serve a purpose more polemical than analytic.

The particularly influential criticism by Sarah Garap (2000, and cited, for example, in Dinnen 2001b: 109; 2006: 413; Jolly 2003: 272; Lipset 2004: 66: Parker 2002) was accorded legitimacy partly by virtue of the fact that she was herself from Simbu Province, in the highlands, where women are said to be particularly oppressed. However, the examples she gave (2000: 167) were of cases in which women disputants had unsuccessfully sought *ultra vires* decisions in the village courts (see chapter 3). Garap's paper serves better as an example of local misunderstandings of village courts' intended role and jurisdiction than as evidence of their misogyny. In contrast to Garap's criticisms, which suggested that highland courts were more prone to misogyny that courts in other areas, a series of short reports provided by Papua New Guineans in 1986 with occasional references to village courts in highland provinces and (very brief) examples implied evenhanded decisions towards male and female disputants (Warus 1986: 61; Tua 1986: 67–68; Asea 1986: 80; Kakaboi 1986: 89).

Contrasting with legalist and polemicist criticisms, anthropologists and others whose fieldwork has involved a degree of observation of village courts in action have commented positively on the treatment of women. As village courts became established around the country and teething problems were overcome in the late 1970s, it seemed that women found them more amenable to dealing with their discontents than previous dispute-settling arenas (see, for example, Westermark 1985: 114; Scaglion and Whittingham 1985: 132). In a 1990 publication based on a ten-year retrospective analysis of Balupwine village court in the East Sepik Province, using statistics gathered by himself, Richard Scaglion wrote:

> Clearly, Abelam women are now making good use of the Village Court in pursuing their grievances. In 1977, they were the plaintiffs in only about 22 per cent of disputes resulting in Court Orders. It was clear from the context of many of these disputes that males were bringing cases on behalf of their female relatives. By 1987, however, it appears that women have taken matters into their own hands: they were the complainants in 53 per cent of all Orders. It thus seems that Abelam women are now able to remove their grievances from the male-dominated forum of village politics and still have them heard by a body that recognizes local custom. (1990: 29)

More recently, in respect of the Ilahita Arapesh, Donald Tuzin noted 'the women's newfound legal assertiveness' (1997: 50) manifest in their use of village courts, and 'the extent to which the village court functioned to articulate and protect the interests of the traditionally disenfranchised: women and young men' (45).

The axiom that women are traditionally subordinate to men, on which both the negative and positive views of village courts above are based, has been challenged recently by arguments that male-female relations in Melanesia have been problematised reductively by Western points of reference. Annette Weiner (1992) and Marilyn Strathern (1988), for example, address the issue in relationalist terms, arguing that theories of exchange in particular need to be reconfigured to shift analytic attention from a preoccupation with the economics of exchange to what is being expressed in the relationships which gifts manifest. Strathern takes the issue up particularly with reference to the conception of the exchange of women in marriage, conventionally seen as an oppressive objectification of females by males, particularly in the PNG highlands. At one juncture Strathern engages explicitly with the issue of men's physical dominance of women, their demand for obedience, and their overriding of women's concerns, reinforced by physical violence: 'Frequently this is quite explicit as to gender: it is by virtue of men being men that women must listen to them' (1988: 325). She continues: 'Yet . . . domination cannot rest on the familiar (to Western eyes) structures of hierarchy, control, the organisation of relations, or on the idea that at stake is the creation of society or the exploitation of a natural realm, and that in the process certain persons lose their right to self-expression. More accurately, men's acts of domination cannot symbolise such a structure, for it is not an object of Melanesian attention' (1988: 325–26).[7]

Whether or not we accept the particular relationalist model Strathern proposes in the work from which this quote is taken, her point is well taken. The difficulty of representing the Melanesian phenomenology she seeks to apprehend is evident in the same book, where she acknowledges the problems of pursuing her project within the constrictions of Western thought and language (1988: 328–29). Entering the debate on whether women are discriminated against or not in village courts, then, is a capitulation to the terms of reference under which the legalist and anthropological critiques above were pursued. I can do little more in that particular sphere of discourse than offer quantitative evidence from the three village courts I have monitored, and measure the relative success or failure of male and female disputants numerically. This begs the question, of course, whether the categorical structures applied here are valid, according to the relationalist viewpoint raised earlier in this chapter. For the purposes of the comparative exercise, I have adopted the conservative method used in tables in previous chapters, enumerating only the cases that I witnessed from beginning to end, and of which I am thus sure of the courts' final decision.

Success and Failure of Disputants by Gender in Three Village Courts

The three tables below refer to the same catalogues of cases listed in tables 6.1, 7.1 and 8.1 in the preceding three chapters for the two periods during which I monitored Erima, Konedobu and Pari village courts in 1994 and 1999. The sex of plaintiffs and defendants is distinguished, and I have also made simple distinctions between those cases involving two disputants only and those involving several disputants. In the latter cases I have indicated whether parties on each 'side' of the dispute are male, or female, or both male and female. Decisions are classified according to whether they favour the plaintiff or defendant, or favour neither. I think this gives a reliable picture of the correlations of the sex of disputants with their success or failure in court.

In respect of the simple question 'Does the village court discriminate against female disputants in favour of male disputants?' I would argue that my method here is valid and can provide an adequate finding, according to what we might call the 'legal individuation' perspective which frames the negative and positive claims above about women and village courts. The abstraction of 'women' as a class of individuals who can be collectively favoured or disfavoured by courts analytically discounts other factors influencing courts' decisions, and thus I regard my method here as extremely reductive, in the light of much of what I have written in foregoing chapters.

Erima

The table below shows that the number of complaints brought to the full Erima court by women overall exceeded the number brought by men, and that the women received far more decisions in their favour than men. This at least indicates that women are relatively successful users of the village court, compared to men. Few decisions were made in favour of respondants. The table further shows that the majority of the cases brought by women singly were against a male respondant, and that in such cases recorded there was never a decision in favour of the male respondant (forty-three—more than two thirds—in favour of women, seventeen other outcomes). This compares positively with cases brought by males singly against a woman. In the twenty-four cases in this category, eleven decisions were in favour of the male plaintiff (less than half), two were in favour of the woman respondant, and there were eleven other outcomes.

Of the sixty cases brought by women singly against men my fieldnotes showed that thirty-three were marital problems. Of these thirty-three, eight included complaints that no brideprice had been paid. In these cases the court asked the woman if she wanted to stay with the man, and some women said they would so long as he paid the brideprice. All cases included charges of neglect, manifest sometimes

Between Groups and Individuals 259

Table 9.1. Dispute outcomes by sex of plaintiffs and respondents in 185 cases monitored at Erima Village Court, 1994 and 1999

Disputant Number/sex Pl'tiff	Resp'nt	Number of disputes	Decision in favour of Pl'tiff	Decision in favour of Resp't	Other outcome#
1 M*	1 M	36	17	2	17
1 M	1 F	24	11	2	11
1 M	2< F/M	19	11	0	8
1 F	1 M	60	43	0	17
1 F	1 F	17	10	0	7
1 F	2< F/M	19	16	0	3
2< M	2< F/M	1	0	0	1
2< F	1 M	2	2	0	0
2< F	1 F	1	0	0	1
2< F&M	1 M	4	4	0	0
2< F&M	1 F	2	1	0	1
Total		185	115	4	66

* M = Male, F = Female, F/M = Female or Male, F&M = Female and Male, 2< = Two or more.

'Other outcomes' can include transfer of dispute to another court, settlement which favours neither disputant, mediation or other factor resulting in withdrawal of complaint, etc.

in non-provision of living expenses, sometimes in lengthy absences, sometimes in adulterous behaviour, sometimes all three. If physical violence by the husband was mentioned by the woman, it was introduced into her evidence additionally and after the other complaints. None of the marital cases was instigated specifically on the ground of physical violence, although some of the non-marital cases brought by women involved complaints of assault by men other than their husbands, and by other women, as well as complaints of insults, malicious gossip, debts, theft and damage to property.

Of the thirty-three marital disputes, in twenty-four cases the court ordered the man to pay compensation (up to K1000) to the woman, as well as a court fine (up to K50). In ten cases they declared a *de facto* marriage 'finished' (which they would not have been able to do in the case of properly constituted customary marriages). They usually ordered the return of all or a large part of the nominal brideprice to the man if he had paid one, but sometimes ordered compensation to be paid by the man to the woman. Overall the data suggests that women are not disadvantaged in Erima village court, compared to men.

Konedobu

The sample in table 9.2 is small, so not a great deal can be made from the superficial observation that more women bring complaints to full court at Konedobu than men (nineteen compared to thirteen). It can be noted again that complaints brought by women singly against a male were the most frequent type, and further that no decisions were made in favour of defendants.

Of the nine complaints brought by women against a man, five could be classified as marital. Three of these were accusations of neglect, resulting in admonitions and preventive orders issued to two husbands, and an order to the third to pay compensation. The fourth marital complaint was about a failure to pay brideprice, which the court ordered the husband to pay forthwith. The fifth was a claim of serious insult, which the man was warned not to repeat, on penalty of a fine. Of the three complaints by men singly against women, only one was marital, a claim of desertion against a second wife. The court ordered the woman to pay compensation. Despite the small sample available here, I suggest there is evidence that women are not disadvantaged in Konedobu village court, compared to men.

Table 9.2. Dispute outcomes by sex of plaintiffs and respondents in thirty-six cases monitored at Konedobu Village Court, 1994 and 1999

Disputant Number/ sexPl'tiff	Resp'nt	Number of disputes	Decision in favour of Pl'tiff	Decision in favour of Resp'nt	Other outcome
1 M	1 M	5	2	0	3
1 M	1 F	3	3	0	0
1 M	2< F/M	5	5	0	0
1 F	1 M	9	7	0	2
1 F	1 F	6	1	0	5
1 F	2< F/M	4	2	0	2
2< F&M	2<F&M	4	3	0	1
Total		36	23	0	13

Pari

Complaints from single plaintiffs are few in Pari. Table 9.3 indicates that male single plaintiffs brought a total of eleven complaints to full court, and women eight. Of the single male complaints three were against women, none were marital issues. One was an accusation of abuse, settled with a public apology, one was a compensation claim for garden damage, which the court ordered the woman to pay. The third was a dispute between a mother and son, which was adjourned and subsequently settled out of court. Of the female complaints five were against a male, and three were marital. Of the latter, one involved a charge of neglect and an issue of child custody and was referred to the district court. One involved the non-payment of a brideprice and an accusation of assault. This was adjourned pending witness testimony, but the disputants did not subsequently attend the court and the dispute was later withdrawn. In the third case an elderly woman complained that her husband had hit her on the head during an argument. Evidence revealed that he had done this in an effort to make her relinquish her grip on his testicles. The couple were lectured by the court on the need for mature behaviour, and the affair was settled with a handshake.

The main disruptive problem in Pari is weekend drunkenness by young men who disturb the peace, swear loudly and make obscene comments to passing women (see chapter 6). Complaints from the

Table 9.3. Dispute outcomes by sex of plaintiffs and respondents in fifty cases monitored at Pari Village Court, 1994 and 1999

Disputant Number/ sexPl'tiff	Resp'nt	Number of disputes	Decision in favour of Pl'tiff	Decision in favour of Resp't	Other outcome
1 M	1 M	5	3	0	2
1 M	1 F	3	2	0	1
1 M	2< F/M	3	2	0	1
1 F	1 M	5	2	0	3
1 F	1 F	1	1	0	0
1 F	2< F/M	2	2	0	0
2< F/M	1 M	20	19	0	1
2< F/M	2<M	9	9	0	0
2< F&M	2<F/M	2	2	0	0
Total		50	42	0	8

community at large, including outraged women, against young men are reflected in table 9.3, with twenty complaints against single males and nine against groups of males. The young men are usually given a nominal fine (if they are fined at all) and ritually shake hands with the aggrieved women. I think these brief details indicate that women are not discriminated against in Pari village court.

The findings from Erima, Konedobu and Pari village courts resonate singly and collectively with the earlier findings of Scaglion, Whittingham and Westermark that women were confident and relatively successful users of the village courts they observed. Under the terms of reference I have adopted I cannot, of course, generalise from this to all village courts. Each of the 1,100-or-so courts would have to be monitored carefully to the same ends. While exercises of this kind can provide us with a quantitative measure of disputants' fortunes in court by gender or other criteria (for example youth, employment status, financial status and so on), there are a number of issues which are ignored, such as whether women are more likely than men to bring certain kinds of dispute to village court (or not), whether alternative dispute-settlement strategies are preferred on a gender basis, and so on. Beyond the observation that women appear to be treated no less fairly than men in the three village courts, I venture no further judgments on the subject of gender and village courts.

Of Human Rights and Individualism

The implication of the discussion in the foregoing sections is that individualism and relationalism are dialectically related in village courts. While they are obliged to subscribe to the discourse of legal individualism in their regulations, and 'locate legal identity and accountability in the person' (Tuzin 1997: 44), village court magistrates' consideration of cases is 'relationalist', or at least, takes account of relationships within and between groups as well as other matters of local sociality. While Tuzin argues that there has been a conversion to legal individualism among the Ilahita Arapesh (1997: 45), my own observation has been that village court practice has not liberated the individual from legal dependency on the group. However, the balance of individualism and relationalism in village court practice may change under the impetus of human rights advocacy which has recently been explicitly introduced into the village court system.

UNESCO initiatives have brought them into coalition with AusAID in respect of the incorporation of community resources into 'law and order' and human rights programs in PNG. Using not only foreign consultants but also local, educated, men and women who have been policy-indoctrinated, organisations such as UNESCO are increasingly using community-level institutions such as the village courts to raise awareness of human rights issues. An example is the employment of Sarah Garap, previously a published critic of village courts (see chapter 3 and above this chapter) as a human rights program designer for the courts in 2005 under a UNESCO program. Garap's specific responsibility was to incorporate human rights awareness into village court officials' training, particularly in relation to the rights of women. In contrast to her comments on village courts in a previously cited article (2000), material written under the terms of reference of her UNESCO employment positioned village courts as an ideal vehicle for the promotion and guardianship of women's rights (2005a, 2005b). Garap's programmatic statements reflected UNESCO concerns for sensitivity to culture while promoting human rights, and consequently a policy that the organisation should ideally facilitate changes that came from within society, rather than impose changes from without. In this respect, on the question of the relationship between 'community/kinship rights' and 'individual rights', she stated:

> In order to establish a legitimate rule of law any system of justice must resonate [sic] the values of the community it serves. The traditional PNG kinship system of dispute resolution is based on collective rights, making it difficult to reconcile with the individual's rights based on contemporary western systems. This rights-based conflict impacts on the legitimacy of the formal justice system in PNG and poses a threat to the rule of law. This context presents a significant challenge for the protection of human rights. Traditional responses to crime often include a breach of human rights and in PNG it is necessary to identify and target responses to the value base that supports these values. (2005b: 9).

The UNESCO program regarded village courts as the 'closest government presence in rural PNG communities' (3), and intended human rights training to contribute to the development of 'models for conflict resolution that manage the dilemma between collective and individual rights' (4). It could be argued, incidentally, that village courts have actually been negotiating the 'dilemma' quite well for most of their existence.

Initiatives such as the UNESCO program portend pressure to shift village court practice towards formal legal practice, as the indented quotation above implies with its references to the 'rule of law'. This legalism, combined with UN human rights policy initiatives, may have significant effects on the way the 'dilemma between collective and individual rights' is managed. The discourse of human rights has become increasingly sophisticated since the adoption in 1948 of the Universal Declaration of

Human Rights, and nowadays attempts to be cognisant of culturally different views of personhood and humanity (á propos of questions such as what it is to be a 'human' with rights) and of the political consequences of the way individual and collective rights are understood in different societies and states (see, for example, Messer 2002: 322–30). Nevertheless, fundamental problems remain, such as the conceptualisation of 'culture' (for the purposes of clarifying issues both of rights *to* culture and of rights *according to* culture), and the relative merits of individual rights and collective rights. Thomas Eriksen (2001) has argued that UNESCO's attempts to acknowledge cultural difference and take account of rights of minorities have not significantly advanced the prospects of negotiating between collective and individual rights. He points out that at several points in the 1995 UNESCO policy document *Our Creative Diversity*, group rights are defended, yet 'it is also committed to the Universal Declaration of Human Rights, which is unanimous in according rights to individuals, not groups. The obvious dilemma in this dual position—the inevitable conflict between collective minority rights and individual rights—is not discussed' (2001: 135).

Eriksen argues that in UNESCO's attempt to accommodate notions of group rights and an outdated concept of culture (as a bounded entity with a specific set of values and practices) it contradicts its 'basic commitment to individual human rights, universal education and global modernity' (2001: 141). Further, Cowan, Dembour and Wilson contextualise formulations such as those used by UNESCO in a discourse of 'human rights culture'—rights talk, rights thinking, rights practices—entailing 'certain constructions of self and sociality, and specific modes of agency' (2001: 11–12). They observe that 'many analysts already talk about the human rights culture as a core aspect of a new global, transnational culture, a *sui generis* phenomenon of modernity. . . . To name a few of its structuring ideas: it is individualistic in conception; it addresses suffering through a legal/technical, rather than an ethical, framework; and it emphasises certain aspects of human coexistence (an individual's rights) over others (an individual's duties or needs)' (12).

In the light of the anomalies of human rights discourse, initiatives like those of UNESCO have the potential to increase the regulation of village court practice in favour of a legalistic concern with human rights, reflecting state policy and practice (since the state is charged with implementing human rights initiatives) rather than the values and rights defined by the diverse societies served by the courts. Inevitably, the drive to uniform practice would result in an emphasis on individual, rather than collective, rights, and a more rigid application of legal principles of individual responsibility and liability. Whether a development of this kind, obliging village courts to be less cognisant of the social context of cases and thus their relationist aspects, would lead to greater community acceptance of legal individualist principles is hard to predict. In the first instance, the more likely result will be the loosening of the intimate relationship between the practice and deliberations of village courts and the sociality of the communities they serve, as magistrates increasingly adhere to a jurisprudence which is alien to the relationalist understanding of justice which continues to prevail in Melanesian societies overall. Many of the decisions I have witnessed in village courts, and which have been regarded as good and just by the community (and generally also by myself as an outsider, albeit after considerable explanation and education by magistrates), would not be possible if the legal model of human rights implied in the UNESCO initiatives were strictly adhered to.

Notes

1. I refer to the stereotype as implied, for example in Sahlins' influential, but now superseded, discussion of political types (1963). The stereotype persists in popular representations, despite being all but destroyed in academic anthropological discourse by subsequent critique (for example, Feil 1987; Godelier 1986; Godelier and Strathern 1991). The closest 'fit' to the stereotype is probably found in what is now the Western Highlands Province in the general area of Mt Hagen.
2. Leenhardt distinguished between three kinds of human beings, which he designated, in French, *personnage*, *personne* and *individu* (1998). In the standard English translation of Leenhardt's *Do Kamo*, Gulati renders *personnage* as 'personage' (1979: xxxii and passim), but I prefer to use the term 'persona'. The persona is constituted by and dependent upon relationships, intrinsic to a mythopoeic experience of the world, and cannot exist outside of these conditions (Leenhardt 1998: 248–51). *Individu* can be translated as 'individual'. For Leenhardt the *individu* was an autonomous, ego-oriented entity, imbued with temporal continuity (1998: 264, 270–71), as conventionally understood in Western society. Between the two, for Leenhardt, is the *personne*, or 'person', neither mythopoeically structured, nor fully individuated.
3. This was not always the case, however, and the names of a handful of in-marrying foreigners of the late nineteenth century (such as Solien, Sariman, Bellem, Kassman) are carried by a significant number of Papua New Guineans today.
4. The others were Idibana Laurina and Idibana Rarua Mase. Later, in 1995–96, a new *iduhu*, Idibana Etau Laio, was created when some lineages broke away from Idibana Taulamiri.
5. The case incidentally demonstrates a number of things about the flexibility of 'rules' of Motu kinship and the limits to that flexibility which I have not elaborated here. I have discusssed the same case elsewhere (Goddard 2001) in relation to kinship and the nature of descent groups.
6. It was unusual for women to complain of physical violence by husbands, even though violence (by both partners) was common in these marriages. The degree

of tolerance of personal violence was related to the social distance of the perpetrator: affinal violence was less tolerated than spousal violence, and women were quick to take action over violence from people other than husbands or kin.
7. The controversial nature of Strathern's argument in the contemporary climate of development aid and human rights endeavours can be indicated by contrasting it with the views of Martha Macintyre (2005). The latter is an anthropologist who has spent recent years heavily involved in consultancy work, experiencing the various attitudes and expectations of development agencies, business ventures and local groups, while investigating the social impact of mining projects in PNG. She has written in particular of the personal effects of her observation of the gender politics involved in local attempts to gain access to jobs, money and other resources and to negotiate social change: 'The most obvious dilemmas arise when basic human rights are denied to women and children.' She has, she writes, become unavoidably judgmental of violence by men towards women in PNG, and her work on 'law and order' issues 'has compromised any anthropological moral relativism I might have embraced intellectually, beyond redemption' (2005: 137).

Conclusion

The Local and the Global

This book has been grounded anthropologically in a close study of three village courts, showing the degree to which they reflect the sociality of the communities they serve. I believe the intimate relation between individual courts and their local communities to be a major factor in the success of the village court system overall over the past three decades. When the courts were first introduced, they were intended to be 'strongly influenced by the customs of the area and by local attitudes and mores' (Desailly and Iramu 1972: 8), and their magistrates were not intended to be trained in law. Rather, they would be selected by the local community on the criteria of their adjudicatory integrity and good knowledge of local customs. They were to be people who could be relied upon to make 'fair decisions' (Village Court Secretariat 1975: 1). While they have been accused since of imposing undesirable custom, the village courts in practice have not actually fulfilled their originally intended 'customary' function. Customary problems in village societies are still being dealt with in customary ways. As the new village courts began to spread in the late 1970s, villagers showed by their responses that they wanted them to be part of the introduced legal system, not 'customary' courts, and village court officials see themselves as being at the foot of the hierarchy of courts in PNG. For villagers the village court is an arena of justice to be utilised when custom fails or is inapplicable.

Nevertheless, something which could loosely be called 'custom' (though not in the sense implied by critics) does come into play in village courts, sometimes as simple common sense or as a nuanced perception of the wider implications of disputes. In the earlier days of the village courts their magistrates had no law books and no recourse to recorded precedent. They did, though, have a nuanced understanding of the social and historical background of the disputes they heard, being themselves members of the local communities they served. Largely neglected and under-resourced by the state, they nevertheless became a popular community-level institution across the country. The growth and resilience of the village courts system over the years has been remarkable, given the administrative and financial uncertainties its magistrates and other officials experienced.

The practice of the three courts used as examples in this book was largely determined by their intimate relationship to the particular sociality of the communities they served (chapters 4, 6, 7 and 8). The village court in Pari, for example, was situated in a village which was missionised a century and a quarter ago and which had absorbed an ideation of Christian morality into its identity. The village's attempts to maintain integrity relied partly on the promotion of harmony through their village court proceedings, in which offenders were only nominally 'punished'. The most important project for Pari's court was the re-integration of offenders into the self-consciously moralistic community. In Konedobu village court, serving an insular settlement community apprehensive of officialdom and living in an atmosphere of jealousy and suspicion, the magistrates attempted to reconcile disputants with each other and with the social exigencies of settlement life, requiring caution and reflection in everyday behaviour. Erima village court reflected a different kind of sociality, a settlement community made up of regional groups from many parts of the country, whose diversity and inevitable frictions had to be managed carefully by village court magistrates. Each village court, then, had a different 'style', and dealt with offenders in a different manner. Not only were the hearings and decisions attuned to local sociality, but the magistrates themselves needed to be able to negotiate local politics if they were to do their job adequately, as we saw in chapter 5.

I have presented the institutional progress of the village courts as a dialectic between ideals and practice. Ideally, informality, wise mediation and pastoral judgment informed by the integrity of 'customary law' were intended to typify village court practice. In practice, they have been burdened by their legislative origins: they were placed at the bottom of a hierarchy of legal courts and made answerable to fundamental demands of state law. These standardising influences were in tension with the social diversity which the village courts negotiated in their everyday practice. A lack of resources and a high degree of neglect by the state over two decades resulted in a synthesis of ideals and practice driven mostly by the desires and needs of local communities whose perceptions of courts, 'law' and 'justice' had been shaped by the colonial encounter.

Local experience of colonial courts generated a desire in their communities for village courts to reproduce the trappings of *kiap*, local and district courts in the form of regular hearings, permanent or semi-permanent buildings or sites for hearings, the spatial relationships of magistrates, disputants and witnesses, opening prayers and so on. These formalities had not been the intention of the system's planners and legislators, who wanted the courts to convene 'from time to time' and 'from place to place' in response to the occurrence of individual disputes which were not expected to be frequent. At the same time as village courts partially reproduced colonially introduced courts, disputes between individuals were understood and handled by the magistrates according to a commonsense understanding of the social dynamics of the community, rather than a rigorous application of technical law based on the rights of individuals.

Ethnographically, and in the cultural relativist tradition, the description of village court practice and their immediate social context reveals a successful adaptation by local societies of a legislatively introduced grassroots justice institution. However, as sections of chapter 9 showed, interventions have recently been made in the interests of a more universally understood model of justice. Necessarily, an anthropology of village courts, while grounded in traditional, localised fieldwork, must be contemporaneously cognisant of global influences. This requires more than a conventional acknowledgement of colonial history. Chapter 1 described historical processes stretching back to the beginnings of colonial control in PNG in the late nineteenth century when the idea that Melanesians were capable of administering justice among themselves was considered equivocal. The administrator of German New Guinea was more confident than his counterpart in British New Guinea in the ability of Melanesians to administer justice at a parochial level. The Australian Administration which succeeded both regimes negated, for a long period, the German initiative before gradually moving towards the idea of a grassroots indigenous-staffed court system in the final decade of colonialism. But the village court system which emerged from century-long transitions in colonial political and juridical thinking and practice could not be the relatively insular postcolonial Melanesian institution that many of its initial supporters wanted.

Village Courts and the Post-Colonial State

Three decades ago, the internationalisation of Western law and human rights and the expansion of the development-aid industry were barely recognised by Papua New Guinean leaders as they celebrated the end of colonialism. In the 1970s indigenous politicians were signalling the advent of the village court system as an emancipation of community justice processes from Western influences. They declared optimistically that there would be no 'European technicalities' or interference from welfare officers and patrol officers (Chalmers 1978a: 267), and that the system would give indigenous communities control over their own affairs. In 1975 some white officials who challenged decisions of one of the first village courts on the grounds that oppressive 'custom' was being applied were told to stop interfering by the Department of Justice and the Department of District Administration (Paliwala 1982: 204). However, the village courts were already legislatively encompassed by a Western legal system which had been introduced almost a century earlier, and at the same time as 'Western influences' were being derogated, the Independent State of PNG was being constitutionally declared a Christian nation 'under the guiding hand of God'.[1]

It should be acknowledged, though, that institutions and ideas introduced by their colonisers have been creatively appropriated into Melanesian praxis since the beginnings of colonial intrusion, and that these appropriations are as transformative of the institutions and ideas as they are of the lives of the indigenes. Thus, the late colonial state of the 1970s is reproduced in the contemporary PNG state only partially, and in its ostensible structure rather than its substantive functions. In this respect its organs appear to a conventional European gaze to be only nominally equivalent to those of a Western state. Discussion of the engagement of the state and society in Melanesia has drawn recently on what has been called the 'state-in-society' model developed by Joel Migdal. Some constituent themes of Migdal's model are that states are almost never autonomous from social forces and have to be viewed in their social contexts (Migdal, Kohli and Shue 1994: 2–3). Migdal's observations destabilise the inference sometimes taken from conventional references to 'the state' that the latter is an entity above and beyond the society it seeks to govern. Further, he argues that the overall role of the state in society 'hinges on the numerous junctures between its diffuse parts and and other social organizations' (3). He adds that the relative position of a social group within the overall social structure is not a simple determinant of the power of that group (3–4), and that 'states and other social forces may be mutually empowering' (4).

Migdal's overall approach, then, challenges monolithic conceptions of 'the state', and thereby has thematic similarities with recent independently developed representations of Melanesian states which see the state as fragmentary or diffuse and socially contextualised (see, for example,

Filer 1992; Gordon and Meggitt 1985; Standish 1981), sometimes in relation to nationhood (see, for example, Hirsch 1997; Wanek 1996). In this respect Migdal's representation of his model as being intended to correct 'an unfortunate tendency in social science to treat the state as an organic, undifferentiated actor' (Migdal 1994: 17) might overstate the tendency. Perhaps the pertinent function of Migdal's model, as far as Melanesia is concerned, is that it tidily encapsulates the kinds of indeterminacies explored by social scientists in particular local settings where the weakness of the state is a political given. The compactness of the model has made it a handy resource in a number of recent discussions of governance and, especially, social control in Melanesia (see, for example, Claxton 2000; Dinnen 2001a; Dauverne 1998).

A question could be raised as to whether the application of Migdal's model in the Papua New Guinean context helps us understand the way the appropriation of colonially and neo-colonially introduced institutions—such as the village court system—into the praxis of local communities results in transformations both of the institutions and the social life of those communities. Migdal comments that the engagement between the state and social forces may be mutually empowering in some instances and a struggle for agency in others, often marked by mutually exclusive goals (1994: 24). To this we could append the anthropological observation that the outcomes of these kinds of engagement in specific local communities are often reflective of the social permeability of localised elements of state, whose employees are likely to come from the communities they serve. This is an important contributing factor in the mutually transformative relationship between state institutions in Melanesia and local groups whose praxis is informed by exigencies of kinship and community.

If we conceptualise the socially embedded state according to Migdal's model, then the village court system can be viewed as an element of state. Conventional political representations of the village court system invite an interpretation that it is a grassroots justice system blending custom and law while, as we have seen, historical investigation lends weight to a more political understanding that it is a state institution whose planners intended it to serve the parochial judicial needs of villagers and rural homesteaders (see, for example, Chalmers 1978b; Gordon and Meggitt 1985: 210–36). My description of village courts in operation certainly fits with Migdal's observation that the engagement between the state and social forces may be mutually empowering in some instances and a struggle for agency in others, involving mutually exclusive goals. Village courts make the justice system accessible to grassroots communities, and simultaneously bring some (but certainly not all) unofficial dispute settlement procedures into the centralised system, as state planners intended. Serving as a village court official offers an opportunity in local communities for individuals to acquire some status and for the authoritative management of community problems, to the advantage of the grassroots communities the courts serve. Yet mutually exclusive goals are certainly evident in the contradiction between the state justice system's imperative of justice for disputants, and magistrates' attempts to weigh matters of individual guilt and punishment against wider communal issues. And in my discussion of 'little big men' in chapter 5, where Andrew's benevolent intent as a magistrate exemplified the ideals of 'grassroots justice' embedded in the original model of the village court system, a very different goal was evident in Reto's ruthless lack of concern with the same ideals in his own quest for status. At the same time, in such examples as the exploitation by Reto of the NCDC's financial dysfunction, we saw the effects within the community of the village court system's administrative connection with other elements of state. Village courts serve as a handy example of Migdal's basic argument about the lack of autonomy of the state from social forces, and the need to view states in their social contexts.

Importantly though, we have also seen that the village court, an element of state, has been transformed in the dialectical relationship with community praxis, a matter which Migdal's model does not appear to address. The transformation is partly due to the village court system's social permeability, staffed as it is by members of the community it serves which enables its political appropriation into the sociality of the community. In the context of a long history of creative appropriation of introduced institutions into Melanesian praxis since the late nineteenth century this last observation is unremarkable, at least in social anthropological terms. Indeed, in observing the village court in relation to both state and local community praxis we simply serve a contemporary imperative for anthropology to contextualise its traditionally localised research in wider social, economic and political processes (preferably without sacrificing the central place of ethnography in our endeavour). Certainly, we should not conceive of the state analytically as autonomous from social forces, and Migdal's model—gathering in themes already explored by social scientists—has heuristic value, particularly in respect of Melanesian societies. At the same time, we should be careful to employ such models in a way which admits the dynamism and creativity of social life and the ongoing transformations both in the state in all its aspects and the local communities with which it is intimately engaged.

There are, however, more forces in play than the interaction of community politics and elements of state. Having gained freedom from direct

Australian rule, the post-colonial state of PNG has become encompassed and colonised by more global, or at least international, interests. Michael Hardt and Antonio Negri (2000) have gone so far as to argue that a new form of 'empire' has arisen, which will only be overcome by a new transnational solidarity. The model developed by Hardt and Negri lacks anthropological nuance, and has drawn criticism for its totalising, Eurocentric and teleological tendencies (see, for example, Wilson 2007: 241–42; Rofel 2002). However, the authors do, importantly, draw attention to what they call the genealogy of 'juridical forms that led to, and now leads beyond, the supranational role of the United Nations and its various affiliated institutions' (2000: 4). The constitution of the contemporary imperial order, they argue, is such that 'the U.N. organizations, along with the great multi- and transnational finance and trade agencies (the IMF, the World Bank, the GATT, and so forth), all become relevant in the perspective of the supranational juridical constitution only when they are considered within the dynamic of the biopolitical production of world order' (31). Hardt and Negri identify important dynamics at work in the global process they call imperial constitution: it transforms international law and also brings about changes in the administrative law of individual societies and nation states: it penetrates and reconfigures the domestic law of nation states and thus 'supranational law powerfully overdetermines domestic law' (17). Here they identify a process which anthropologists of law have also been recently observing, although the latter use differing terms of reference and demonstrate a more nuanced appreciation of local effects (see, for example, Nader 2006; Merry 2003).

It should not be surprising, then, that the rhetorical anticipation by PNG politicians that village courts would be free from Western influences would be negated within a few decades, and 'European technicalities' and 'welfare officers' (in the new clothing of human rights advocates) would reimpose themselves on the courts. The courts nowadays open with Christian prayers before administering forms of justice scrutinised by foreigners concerned, just as they were in the twilight of colonialism, that oppressive 'custom' might be applied or legal and human rights principles traduced. The attention village courts are receiving is a measure of the particular position they occupy in the integration of PNG into contemporary global dynamics.

Village Courts and Global Processes

In the changing international political and economic climate PNG's geographical position, its economic needs, and questions about its political stability have brought it under scrutiny in the regional manoeuvrings of more powerful interests. States perceived as 'weak', 'fragile' or 'failing' give cause for concern among 'strong' nations in a 'globalised' world, according to conventional political analysis. Policy-oriented commentaries expose the common legitimating argument behind such concerns:

> Whereas the failure of some states to carry out their basic functions—controlling their territory, protecting their citizens and delivering basic services to them—was once viewed as a problem mostly for their citizens, it is now viewed as a global concern. Some of the world's weakest states are now given the greatest attention. This concern is largely a product of globalisation. Weak states represent gaps in the international order and frustrate efforts to regulate the malevolent dimensions of globalisation such as transnational crime, terrorism, and infectious disease. (Scott 2005: 7)

Potential economic benefits are of course a major factor in international preoccupations with PNG's survival as a state, though they are not always expressed in ways that nakedly indicate exploitative aims. In the policy-related discussion cited above, for example, concern for the state's wellbeing makes reference to the vulnerability of failed states to mercenary Others, for whom PNG's 'natural resource wealth—its abundant forests, fisheries, minerals and hydrocarbons—is the main magnet' (Scott 2005: 7). Regardless of the phraseology used to express the interests of foreign powers the perceived economic value of PNG makes it important in global politicking, to which it is linked by interventions directed largely through its former coloniser, Australia. Law and order issues are seen as threats to economic stability and the country's attractiveness to foreign investors. Recent development strategies include the 'strengthening' of community-based organisations, to give impetus to grassroots involvement in improving 'law and order' as well as economic development. Christian church organisations have also been drawn into these initiatives as carriers and teachers of moral standards and values, given the high incidence of church attendance by Papua New Guineans of whom, according to development-related literature, roughly 95 per cent identify themselves as Christians (see, for example, Gibbs 2004; Hauck, Mandie-Filer and Bolger 2005).

After a period of relative government neglect and intermittent vilification of village courts, a wider community of economic stakeholders has recognised in them a potential to contribute to the 'law and order' effort. The recognition has manifested itself in positive attempts to make the village courts' practice compatible with development policy and to draw them into the coalition of community-based institutions supported by the development-aid industry. The mostly censorious attitudes towards their alleged shortcomings—their application of oppressive custom, their traducement of law, their misogyny—are being supplanted by new interventions aimed at educating them about (Western) jurisprudence and human rights and encouraging their application of Christian moral principles. The contemporary convergence of human rights discourse, Western legalism and Christianity on village courts portends a situation resonant with Laura Nader's prediction about the ongoing influence of Western ideologies:

> Anthropologists have made strong advances in demonstrating that law and politics are not isolatable, and we are now reaching the understanding that religion and law are not separable. The morality of disputing processes is now everywhere heavily influenced by ideologies of a religious nature. Law and religion may have been officially separated in Western legal systems, but in former colonies of the Western world they are not. It follows from these observations that a new range of questions will center on contemporary disputing as an epiphenomenon of controlling processes that will continue to cycle into the next century. (1990: 322)

The pedagogic introduction of 'alternative dispute resolution' and 'restorative justice' into training courses for village court officials along with the encouragement of Christian moral ideation manifests a current reinforcement of the harmony ideology which Nader saw in Mexico as having evolved as a consequence of colonial political and religious policies (Nader 1990). As I said in the introduction to this book, not every society was successfully implanted with ideas of harmony in PNG, or employed them in local dispute settlement during the colonial era. Some societies did absorb mission-introduced harmony ideation, as we saw in the case of the Motu-Koita (chapters 4 and 6), but others, such as the eastern highland Yagwoia, accept violence as a concomitant of everyday life and have remained relatively impervious in post-colonial times to ideas of peaceful coexistence (see Mimica 2003: 261). However, the development-aid initiatives represent a new wave of harmony ideology which endeavours, through the village courts, to bring disputing in PNG into alignment with a universalised model. Nader has described the universal attributes of harmony ideology as an emphasis on conciliation, a recognition that resolution of conflict is inherently good, a view of harmonious behaviour as more civilised than disputing behaviour, and the belief that consensus is of greater survival value than controversy. 'Harmony ideology can be powerful even when it contradicts the common realities of disputing' (Nader 1990: 2).

The ethnographic content of this book resonates with what Comaroff and Roberts (1986) called the 'processual' paradigm in that it indicates the degree to which village court magistrates are engaged with the particular politics of local communities. An understanding of social process is analytically important here, and conflict is treated as endemic in social life. As Comaroff and Roberts pointed out, in the ideal case an adequate account of a single dispute requires a description of its total historical social context, involving 'a shift in focus *away* from judge- (and judgment-) oriented accounts of the character and function of dispute settlement' (1986: 13–14). While I do not claim to have achieved this ideal, the noticeable differences in the types of disputes, handling of disputes, and attitudes to punishment among Erima, Konedobu and Pari village courts indicate the value of the processual perspective.

The differences among village courts and their communities should serve to warn us of the dangers of generalisation, and the consequent dangers of assuming that in 'training' village court magistrates for their task a single pedagogical paradigm could produce a system which would satisfy local understandings of injustice and its remedies throughout a nation as socially diverse as PNG. However, when Western notions of human rights are added to ADR initiatives and the institutionalisation of Christian moral ideation, the ability of village courts to deliver justice, as originally intended, in a way 'strongly influenced by the customs of the area and by local attitudes and mores' (Desailly and Iramu 1972: 8) is increasingly challenged. Nader considered that ADR tended to shift dispute resolution away from public institutions into private networks 'where essential ingredients, such as transparency, precedent, and social context, are often omitted' (2006: 95). In the case of village courts, in comparison, the addition of human rights doctrine to ADR initiatives shifts village courts towards an internationalised juridical practice where Western precedent is likely to be prioritised over rationales guided by social context.

In chapter 9 I described the UNESCO initiative to incorporate human rights awareness into village court officials' training, particularly in relation to the rights of women. In human rights discourse this involves acknowledgement of the need for sensitivity to culture and an ideal that rather than imposing changes on society the organisation should facilitate changes that came from *within* society. However, these sentiments are qualified by a caution that 'traditional responses' to crime are likely to breach human rights, and that 'values' underlying such responses need attention (see Garap 2005b: 9). Here we see a variant of the demonisation of 'culture' (conceived as a bounded and static set of values) which Sally Engle Merry (2003: 60–64) says accompanies human rights assessments globally at the same time as cultural difference is positively acknowledged. Despite attempts to heed cultural diversity, conformity to universal standards is inevitably demanded (68). Concatenated with human rights discourse, harmony ideology, while proposing 'alternative' dispute resolution and 'restorative' justice, necessarily seeks to shift village court practice closer to formal legalism. The controlling processes being brought to bear on the village courts show little concern for the social diversity of PNG.

At the time of writing, village courts still reflect, in their workings and decisions, the sociality of the particular community each of them serves. Local notions of justice are not yet homogenised by the interventions which, while acknowledging 'cultural diversity' unavoidably seek conformity to a standardising set of juridical views informing the interventions of development-aid organisations and reflecting internationalised sets of values driven by interests far beyond local dispute settling. Adopting the wide vision advocated by Sally Falk Moore of the political milieu in which law is imbricated, an anthropological study of village courts serves to reinforce her point that 'nothing is merely local in its formation or in its repercussions' (2001: 109–10). Certainly, the influences brought to bear on village courts exemplify Nader's representation of the international processes at work: the connections between national legal systems and transnational legal powerbrokers, interwoven with Western approaches to human rights, women's rights, and the need to attract foreign investors (2006: 104). It remains to be seen how village courts will manage to continue to settle disputes in a way that satisfies the sensibilities of local communities under the increasing influence of these global processes and their implicit demands for uniformity.

The Future of Substantial Justice

Inasmuch as the term 'substantial justice' refers to the administration of justice in a way that satisfies a community's sense of fairness while not necessarily adhering strictly to legal technicalities, village courts in PNG generally seem to fulfil their obligation admirably. But, problematically for legalist observers, Melanesian communities' sense of fairness is not attended by a highly developed individualism and consequently they lack the degree of commitment to individualised justice that Western law intends. We have seen repeatedly in the course of this book that—despite a capitulation to introduced notions of 'custom' and 'customary law'—village court magistrates are guided in practice not by definable folk-rules used in a legalistic way towards individuals, but by a sophisticated understanding of local communities' ideas of what is just. Further, they attempt to control incipient conflict in the community—often manifest in disputes between individuals—sometimes at the expense of what we might narrowly define as individual rights according to law.

Historically, the practical dialectic in the work of village courts has involved the contradictory relationship between the application of individualistic state law (discursively complemented by 'custom' or 'customary law') and an understanding of justice informed by the group-oriented rationality to which I applied the currently popular term 'relationalism' in chapter 9. The continuing development of 'training' programs for village court magistrates—incorporating such concepts as 'restorative justice'—in pursuit of the education of magistrates into a simplified application of state law (through which a more universal legalism is refracted) will arguably work increasingly against village courts' ability to achieve substantial justice in the Melanesian sense. Ironically, village court magistrates are contributing to this end, identifying themselves as a substratum in the hierarchy of formal law courts and becoming increasingly persuaded that their lack of understanding of 'law' is an obstacle to good practice. Younger generations of magistrates are voluntarily submitting to education programs negating the original vision of the planners of the village court system that they would be untrained in law.

The recent stage of development in the trend to formal legalism was implicit in an episode in August 2006 which began with a newspaper report of the unfair imprisonment of a woman. The item in *The National*, 'Court orders mum's release' (1 August 2006), evoked the derogatory commentary which had been generated by the reportage of unfair imprisonment of women by village courts fifteen years earlier. In this recent case the National Court had ordered the release of a woman whom the Kimbe (West New Britain) urban area village court was said to have 'imprisoned' for five months with hard labour. The harsh penalty was allegedly for failure to pay K200 compensation as ordered by the court for not repaying a debt of K1.50 to another woman. Justice Canning declared the imprisonment 'harsh and oppressive', and called for the certification of the Village Courts (Amendment) Act 2000 which should have removed the power of the village courts to imprison people. The issue raised in *The National* was very similar to that raised a decade and a half earlier about wrongfully imprisoned women (see chapter 3), and the newspaper's editorial on the following day (2 August),'Correcting the unacceptable', criticised the village courts in the same vein as media commentary on the earlier occasions: 'How widespread are cases of this kind? . . . Are there other victims of ill-judged village court decisions to be found tucked away in our overflowing jails?' The editorial castigated 'many' village courts for their failure to achieve the aims of 'bringing justice to the people' and making the operations of the law more comprehensible to the public, and claimed one of the good outcomes of the case was 'the realisation that our judges are alert to ignorance and misinterpretation of the law and to the infringement of human rights'.

Up to this point the media discourse was similar to that of the early 1990s. But within days of the initial report one newspaper published a letter from a lecturer responsible for training village court officers for a Diploma in Justice at the Catholic Church-funded Divine Word University in Madang. The lecturer condemned the reported behaviour of the Kimbe village court (without questioning the adequacy or accuracy of the report), and proceeded to distance village court magistrates in general from the alleged misdeed: 'Speaking to [diploma trainees] it is my belief that most Village Court magistrates are doing a good job and are just as ashamed of this behaviour as you and I are.' The letter continued with praise for village court magistrates in general, representing them as underpaid, underfunded servants of the people doing a difficult job in spite of threats and violence towards them, including occasional murder (Howley 2006). It was the first public defence for many years of village courts in the popular media against generalisations about human rights abuses, and it catalogued (though not always with strict accuracy) a number of the administrative problems and lack of institutional support faced by village courts in general.

In 1972, investigating the need for village courts, Neil Desailly and Francis Iramu had recommended that the courts would not apply 'strict customary rules,' though they would be 'strongly influenced' by customs, local attitudes and mores (1972: 8). This sensible approximation of the nature of local influences was obscured by the subsequent legislative imposition of notional 'custom', and its corollate 'customary law'. Village courts were rendered vulnerable to accusations that they applied invented or anachronistic customs. Conversely, as we have seen, when village courts attempted to compensate for the unreasonableness of 'custom' by strict application of the (handbook) 'law', they were vulnerable to accusations of excessive zeal. Village court magistrates increasingly believe they need legal training, and they share this belief with many jurists and other interested parties who subscribe to a dichotomous view of law and custom and see the former as a better guarantor of human rights and individual justice.

The 'diploma in justice' course lectured by the letter writer cited above was a recent addition to the educational programs made available for village court magistrates, nowadays employing the philosophy of 'restorative justice' and reinforcing the UN-derived concept of human rights. Training courses emphasise the development of mediation skills, but are also driven by magistrates' desire for better skills in adjudication, a juridical concern to limit *ultra vires* actions, and a bureaucratic concern for accountability. Mock courts and practical exercises in adjudication are now a common feature of village court training programs. Cumulatively, in the course of a decade or two, these influences are likely to produce a form of 'substantial justice' which Justice Pratt might have found more palatable.

Notes

1. This phrase appears on the first page of the preamble to the Constitution of PNG, effective from 1975. The same page contains a pledge by 'the people of Papua New Guinea' to 'guard and pass on to those who come after us our noble traditions and the Christian principles that are ours now'.

Appendix

The Official Range of Offences Heard by Village Courts

Below are the offences which village courts are officially permitted to deal with, as described for village courts magistrates' reference. The descriptions were amended in the Village Court Manual 2004, which was intended to replace the original village court handbook issued in 1976. Both sets of descriptions are given below as rendered in the two documents. Punctuation and emphasis is as in the original.

Village Court Handbook 1976

1. 'If somebody takes money or things from somebody up to value of K100 without consent of owner.'
2. 'If somebody hits someone else.'
3. 'If somebody insults or threatens or uses offensive language to someone else.'
4. 'If somebody intentionally damages someone else's trees, crops or property.'
5. 'If somebody says something bad *and* untrue about someone else.'
6. 'If somebody has spread untrue stories *and* those stories upset other people.'
7. 'If somebody disturbs the peace in the village.'
8. 'If somebody is drunk in the village court area.'
9. 'If somebody carries weapons *and* this makes other people frightened.'

10. 'If somebody does not obey the Order of a Village Magistrate that tells him to do something that he should do under native custom.'
11. 'If somebody does not obey the Order of a Village Magistrate to do something about making the area clean or stopping sickness.'
12. 'Sorcery: (i) If somebody is making sorcery or pretending to make sorcery; or (ii) If somebody threatens someone else that sorcery will be made against them by another person; or (iii) If somebody gets or tries to get, someone else to make or pretend to make sorcery; or (iv) If somebody has or owns some things that can be used to make sorcery; or (v) If somebody pays or tries to pay someone else to make sorcery for them.'
13. 'If somebody breaks a Council Rule which provides that it can be heard by a Village Court.'
14. 'If somebody is ordered to appear before a Village Court or to bring something to the court and does not appear or bring that thing, *and he does not have a reasonable excuse.*'
15. 'If a Preventive Order is made against a person or a group *and they do not obey that Order.*'
16. 'If a Settlement Order or other Order is made against a person or group *and they do not obey that Order.*'
17. 'If a Village Peace Officer orders a person or a group not to fight or not to do something which will lead to fighting or make the fighting worse *and a person does not obey that Order.*'
18. '(i) If a person interrupts or disturbs a Village Court when it is hearing a court. (ii) If a person stops or tries to stop a Village Court Officer doing his job.'

Village Court Manual 2004

(a) 'Stealing something worth less than K100.00.'
(b) 'Striking another person without reasonable cause.'
(c) 'Using insulting, offensive or threatening words.'
(d) 'Intentional damage to trees, plants or crops belonging to another person.'
(e) 'Intentional damage to any other property belonging to another person.'
(f) 'Making a false statement concerning another person that offends or upsets him.'
(g) 'Spreading false reports that are liable to cause alarm, fear or discontent in the Village Community.'

(h) 'Conduct that disturbs the peace, quiet and good order of the Village or of a resident of the Village.'
(i) 'Drunkenness in the Village Court area.'
(j) 'Carrying weapon so as to cause alarm to others in the Village Court area.'
(k) 'Failure to perform customary duties to meet customary obligations after having been informed of them by a Village Magistrate.'
(l) 'Failure to comply with the direction of a Village Magistrate with regard to hygiene or cleanliness within a Village Court area'
(m) 'Sorcery, including: practicing or pretending to practice sorcery; or threatening any person with sorcery practiced by another; or procuring or attempting to procure a person to practice or pretend to practice, or to assist in, sorcery; or the possession of implements or charms used in practicing sorcery; or paying or offering to pay a person to perform acts of sorcery.'
(n) 'Failure to comply with the Court Order to appear or to produce evidence before a Village Court.'
(o) 'Failure to comply with the terms of the Agreement in the Settlement Order.'
(p) 'Causing trouble to the Village Court or trying to stop a Village Court Magistrate or Peace Officer or Clerk from doing his job.'
(q) 'Not performing work which has been ordered by the Village Court and not having a reasonable excuse.'
(r) 'Not obeying an order of a Village Peace Officer to stop fighting.'
(s) 'Not obeying the order of a Village Court about custody of children, or use of land.'
(t) 'Not obeying the order of a Village Court to attend the court.'

REFERENCES

Ainsworth, J. 1924. *Report on the Administrative Arrangements and Matters Affecting the Interests of the Natives in the Territory of New Guinea*, Paper No. 109, Canberra: Commonwealth of Australia Parliamentary.
Aleck, J. 1986. *Law Reform as Development Policy: Customary Law and the Modern Legal System in Papua New Guinea*, Masters thesis, University of Oregon.
———. 1992. 'The Village Court System of Papua New Guinea', *Research in Melanesia* 16: 101–28.
———. 1993. 'Mismeasuring The Law: Some Misconceptions Concerning the Nature of Law and Custom in Papua New Guinea Today', *Timeline* 1(1): 93–109.
Asea, M. 1986. 'Iki, Western Highlands Province', in S. Toft (ed.), *Marriage in Papua New Guinea*, Monograph No. 4, Waigani: Law Reform Commission of Papua New Guinea, pp. 76–84.
Banks, C. 1993. *Women in Transition: Social Control in Papua New Guinea*, Canberra: Australian Institute of Criminology.
Banks, G., and C. Ballard (eds.). 1997. *The Ok Tedi Settlement: Issues, Outcomes and Implications*, National Centre for Development Studies, Pacific Policy Paper No. 27, Canberra: Australian National University.
Barnes, J. A. 1954. *Politics in a Changing Society: A Political History of the Fort Jameson Ngoni*, London: Oxford University Press.
Barth, F. 1975. *Ritual and Knowledge Among the Baktaman of New Guinea*, New Haven: Yale University Press.
Baxter, M. 1973. *Migration and the Orokaiva*, Dept. of Geography Occasional Paper No. 3, Port Moresby: University of Papua New Guinea.
Bayne, P. 1975a. 'Legal Development in Papua New Guinea: The Place of the Common law', *Melanesian Law Journal* 3(1): 9–39.

———. 1975b. 'The Village Courts Debate', in J. Zorn and P. Bayne (eds.), *Lo Bilong Ol Manmeri: Crime, Compensation and Village Courts*, Port Moresby: University of Papua New Guinea, pp. 40–41.

Beals, A. R. 1964. *Gopalpur: A South Indian Village*, New York: Holt, Rinehart and Winston.

Belshaw, C. 1957. *The Great Village*, London: Routledge and Kegan Paul.

Benedict, R. 1946. *The Chrysanthemum and the Sword: Patterns of Japanese Culture*, Boston: Houghton Mifflin.

Berndt, R. M. 1962. *Excess and Restraint: Social Control Among a New Guinea Mountain People*, Chicago: University of Chicago Press.

Bettison, D. G., C. A. Hughes and P. W. van der Veur (eds.). 1965. *The Papua-New Guinea Elections 1964*, Canberra: Australian National University Press.

Biddulph, J. 1970. 'Longitudinal Survey of Children Born in a Periurban Papuan Village—A Preliminary Report', *Papua New Guinea Medical Journal* 13(1): 23–27.

Bohannan, P. 1957. *Justice and Judgment Among the Tiv*, London: Oxford University Press.

Bonnemère, P. (ed.). 2004. *Women as Unseen Characters: Male Ritual in Papua New Guinea*, Philadelphia: University of Pennsylvania Press.

Bowers, N. 1968. *The Ascending Grasslands*, PhD dissertation, Columbia University.

Bradley, C. 1998. 'Changing a "Bad Old Tradition": Wife-Beating and the Work of the Papua New Guinea Law Reform Commission', in L. Zimmer-Tamakoshi (ed.), *Modern Papua New Guinea*, Kirksville, MO: Thomas Jefferson University Press, pp. 351–64.

Braithwaite, J. 1999. 'Restorative Justice: Assessing Optimistic and Pessimistic Accounts', in M. Tonry (ed.), *Crime and Justice, A Review of Research*, 25, Chicago: University of Chicago Press, pp. 1–127.

Braithwaite, J., and H. Strang. 2001. 'Introduction: Restorative Justice and Civil Society', in H. Strang and J. Braithwaite (eds.), *Restorative Justice and Civil Society*, Cambridge: Cambridge University Press, pp. 1–13.

Brison, K. J. 1992. *Just Talk: Gossip, Meetings, and Power in A Papua New Guinea Village*, Berkeley: University of California Press.

Brouwer, E. C., B. M. Harris and S. Tanaka. 1998. *Gender Analysis in Papua New Guinea*, Washington, DC: World Bank Publications.

Brown, P. 1995. *Beyond a Mountain Valley: The Simbu of Papua New Guinea*, Honolulu: University of Hawai'i Press.

Brown, P., and G. Buchbinder. 1976. *Man and Woman in the New Guinea Highlands*, Special Publication No. 8, Washington, DC: American Anthropological Association.

Brown Glick, P. 1987. 'From Birth Hut to Disco: Changing Simbu Lives', *Bikmaus* 7(1): 15–24.

Buck, T. 2005. *Administrative Justice and Alternative Dispute Resolution: The Australian Experience*, DCA research series 8/05, Dept for Constitutional Affairs, London: UK Government.

Bulmer, S. 1971. 'Prehistoric Settlement Patterns and Pottery in the Port Moresby Area', *Journal of the Papua and New Guinea Society* 5(2): 29–91.

––––––. 1982. 'West of Bootless Inlet: Archaeological Evidence for Prehistoric Trade in the Port Moresby Area and the Origins of the *hiri*', in T. Dutton (ed.), *The Hiri in History: Further Aspects of Long Distance Motu Trade in Central Papua*, Pacific Research Monograph No. 8, Canberra: Australian National University, pp. 117–30.

Caplan, P. 1995. 'Introduction: Anthropology and the Study of Disputes', in P. Caplan (ed.), *Understanding Disputes: The Politics of Argument*, Oxford: Berg, pp. 1–10.

Chalmers, D. 1978a. *Full Circle: A History of the Courts of Papua New Guinea*, Master of Laws thesis, University of Papua New Guinea.

––––––. 1978b. 'The Village Courts of Papua New Guinea: Their Introduction, History and Operation Until 1976', *Melanesian Law Journal* 6(1/2): 56–78.

Chanock, Martin. 1998. *Law, Custom, and Social Order: The Colonial Experience in Malawi and Zambia*, Portsmouth, NH: Heinemann.

Chao, M. J. P. 1989. 'A New Sense of Community: Perspectives from a Squatter Settlement', in C. Thirlwall and P. J. Hughes (eds.), *The Ethics of Development: In Search of Justice*, Port Moresby: University of Papua New Guinea Press, pp. 88–106.

Chinnery, E. W. P. 1925. *Anthropological Reports Nos 1 and 2*, Melbourne: Australian Government Printer.

Claxton, K. 2000. 'Violence, Internal Security and Security Stakeholders in Papua New Guinea', in S. Dinnen and A. Ley (eds.), *Reflections on Violence in Melanesia*, Canberra: Hawkins Press/Asia Pacific Press, pp. 263–76.

Cohn, B. 1965. 'Anthropological Notes on Disputes and Law in India', in L. Nader (ed.) *The Ethnography of Law*, Special publication, *American Anthropologist* 67(6), part 2, pp. 82–122.

––––––. 1967. 'Some Notes on Law and Change in North India', in P. Bohannan (ed.) *Law and Warfare: Studies in the Anthropology of Conflict*, New York: Natural History Press, pp. 139–59.

Collier, J. 1973. *Law and Social Change in Zinacantan*, Stanford: Stanford University Press.

Colson, E. 1953. 'Social Control and Vengeance in Plateau Tonga Society', *Africa* 23: 199–212.

––––––. 1971. 'The Impact of the Colonial Period on the Definition of Land Rights', in V. Turner (ed.), *Profiles of Change: African Society and Colonial Rule*, Vol. 3 of L. H. Gann (comp) *Colonialism in Africa*, Cambridge: Cambridge University Press. pp. 193–215.

––––––. 1995. 'The Contentiousness of Disputes', in P. Caplan (ed.), *Understanding Disputes: The Politics of Argument*, Oxford: Berg, pp. 65–82.

Comaroff, J. L., and S. Roberts. 1986. *Rules and Processes: The Cultural Logic of Dispute in an African Context*, Chicago: University of Chicago Press.

Cowan, J. K., M. B. Dembour and R. A. Wilson. 2001. 'Introduction', in J. K. Cowan, M. B. Dembour and R. A. Wilson (eds.), *Culture and Rights: Anthropological Perspectives*, Cambridge: Cambridge University Press, pp. 1–26.

Curtis, L. J., and J. H. Greenwell. 1971. *Joint Review of the Lower Courts Systems*, Canberra: Department of External Territories.

Dauverne, P. (ed.). 1998. *Weak and Strong States in Asia-Pacific Societies*, Sydney: Allen and Unwin in Association with the Department of International Relations, Research School of Pacific and Asian Studies, Australian National University.

Demian, M. 2003. 'Custom in the Courtroom, Law in the Village: Legal Transformations in Papua New Guinea', *Journal of the Royal Anthropological Institute* 9(1): 97–115.

Derham, D. 1960. *Report On The System For The Administration Of Justice In The Territory Of Papua New Guinea*, Melbourne: University of Melbourne.

Desailly, R. N., and F. Iramu. 1972. *Inquiry into the Need for Village Courts and Village Constables*, mimeo, Port Moresby: Department of Attorney General Libary.

Dinnen, S. 2001a. *Law and Order in a Weak State: Crime and Politics in Papua New Guinea*, Honolulu: University of Hawai'i Press.

———. 2001b. 'Restorative Justice and Civil Society in Melanesia: The Case of Papua New Guinea', in H. Strang and J. Braithwaite (eds.), *Restorative Justice and Civil Society*, Cambridge: Cambridge University Press, pp. 99–113.

———. 2006. 'Restorative Justice and the Governance of Security in the Southwest Pacific', in D. Sullivan and L. Tifft (eds.), *Handbook of Restorative Justice: A Global Perspective*, London: Routledge, pp. 401–21.

Dinnen, S., A. Jowett and T. Newton (eds.). 2003. *A Kind of Mending: Restorative Justice in the Pacific Islands*, Canberra: Pandanus Press.

[DJ&AG] Department of Justice and Attorney General, Govt of PNG. 2001. 'Village Court Policy 2001', Policy Statement.

Doherty, T. A. 1992. 'Does the Justice System Work for Women?—The PNG Case', paper presented to the Workshop against Violence against Women, Suva, Fiji, August 1992.

Dumont, L. 1986. *Essays on Individualism: Modern Ideology in Anthropological Perspective*, Chicago: University of Chicago Press.

Dutton, T. 1985. *Police Motu: Iena Sivarai*, Port Moresby: University of Papua New Guinea Press.

Epstein, A. L. 1969. *Matupit: Land, Politics, and Change Among the Tolai of New Britain*, Canberra: Australian National University Press.

——— (ed.). 1974a. *Contention and Dispute: Aspects of Law and Social Control in Melanesia*, Canberra: Australian National University Press.

———. 1974b. 'Introduction', in A.L. Epstein (ed.), *Contention and Dispute: Aspects of Law and Social Control in Melanesia*, Canberra: Australian National University Press, pp. 1–39.

Eriksen, A. 2005. 'The Gender of the Church: Conflicts and Social Wholes on Ambrym', *Oceania* 74(1/2): 284–300.

Eriksen, T. H. 2001. 'Between Universalism and Relativism: A Critique of the UNESCO Concept of Culture', in J. K. Cowan, M. B. Dembour and R. A. Wilson (eds.), *Culture and Rights: Anthropological Perspectives*, Cambridge: Cambridge University Press, pp. 127–48.

Evans-Pritchard, E. E. 1976. *Witchcraft, Oracles and Magic Among the Azande*, Oxford: Clarendon Press.

Eyford, H., et al. 1992. *Evaluation and Development of Village Court Officers Training: Stage One Report*, Port Moresby: University of Papua New Guinea and Department of the Attorney General.
Fallers, L. 1969. *Law without Precedent*, Chicago: Aldine.
Feil, D. K. 1987. *The Evolution of Highland Papua New Guinea Societies*, Cambridge: Cambridge University Press.
Fenbury, D. M. 1978. *Practice Without Policy: Genesis of Local Government in Papua New Guinea*, Canberra: Australian National University.
Filer, C. 1985. 'What is this Thing Called Brideprice?', *Mankind* 15: 163–83.
———. 1992. 'The Escalation of Disintegration and the Reinvention of Authority', in M. Spriggs and D. Denoon (eds.), *The Bougainville Crisis—1991 Update*, Canberra: Research School of Pacific and Asian Studies, Australian National University, pp. 112–40.
———. 2006. 'Custom, Law and Ideology in Papua New Guinea', *Asia Pacific Journal of Anthropology* 7(1): 65–84.
Firth, S. 1986. *New Guinea Under the Germans*, Port Moresby: Web Books.
Fitzpatrick, P. 1980. *Law and State in Papua New Guinea*, Academic Press, London.
Galanter, M. 1981. 'Justice in Many Rooms: Courts, Private Ordering and Indigenous Law', *Journal of Legal Pluralism* 19: 1–47.
Garap, S. 2000. 'Struggles of Women and Girls—Simbu Province, Papua New Guinea', in S. Dinnen and A. Ley (eds.), *Reflections on Violence in Melanesia*, Canberra: Hawkins Press/Asia Pacific Press, pp. 159–71.
———. 2005a. 'Human Rights Program in Village Court Services', mimeo, Port Moresby: Department of Attorney General.
———. 2005b. 'Human Rights in Village Courts: The Challenges and Opportunities of Working with Village Courts', paper presented at Convention on Discrimination Against Women, Port Moresby, Papua New Guinea, 24 November 2005.
Gardner, R. 1968. *Gardens of War: Life and Death in the New Guinea Stone Age*, New York: Random House.
Garo, K. 1977. 'Village Courts in Papua New Guinea', *Pacific Courts and Justice*, Port Moresby: Commonwealth Magistrates Association and Institute of Papua New Guinea Studies.
———. 1979. 'Village Court Secretariat Annual Report, 1979', Port Moresby: Papua New Guinea Department of Justice.
———. 1980. 'Village Court Secretariat Annual Report, 1980', Port Moresby: Papua New Guinea Department of Justice.
Garrett, J. 1985. *To Live Among the Stars: Christian Origins in Oceania*, Suva: World Council of Churches and University of the South Pacific.
Gibbs, J. L. 1963. 'The Kpelle Moot: A Therapeutic Model for the Informal Settlement of Disputes', *Africa* 33(1): 1–11.
Gibbs, P. 2004. 'Politics, Religion and the Churches: The 2002 Election in Papua New Guinea', State Society and Governance in Melanesia Working Paper No. 2, Goroka: Melanesian Institute.
Gluckman, M. 1955. *The Judicial Process Among the Barotse of Northern Rhodesia*, Manchester: Manchester University Press.

Goava, S. 1979. 'Kori Taboro's Story', *Oral History* 7(3): 65–94.
Goddard, M. 1992. 'Of Handcuffs and Foodbaskets: Theory and Practice in Papua New Guinea's Village Courts', *Research in Melanesia* 16: 79–94.
———. 1996. 'The Snake Bone Case: Law, Custom and Justice in a Papua New Guinea Village Court', *Oceania* 67(1): 50–63.
———. 1998. 'What Makes Hari Run? The Social Construction of Madness in a Highland Papua New Guinea Society', *Critique of Anthropology* 18(1): 61–81.
———. 2000. 'Three Urban Village Courts in Papua New Guinea: Some Comparative Observations on Dispute Settlement', in S. Dinnen and A. Ley (eds.), *Reflections on Violence in Melanesia*, Canberra: Hawkins Press/Asia Pacific Press, pp. 241–53.
———. 2001. 'Rethinking Motu Descent Groups', *Oceania* 71(1): 313–33.
———. 2002. 'Reto's Chance', *Oceania* 73(1): 1–16.
———. 2003. 'The Age of Steam: Constructed Identity and Recalcitrant Youth in a Papua New Guinea Village', in S. Dinnen, A. Jowett and T. Newton Cain (eds.), *A Kind of Mending: Restorative Justice in the Pacific Islands*, Canberra: Pandanus Press, pp. 45–72.
———. 2005. *The Unseen City: Anthropological Perspectives on Port Moresby, Papua New Guinea*, Canberra: Pandanus Books.
Godelier, M. 1986. *The Making of Great Men: Male Domination and Power among the New Guinea Baruya*, Cambridge: Cambridge University Press.
Godelier, M., and M. Strathern (eds.). 1991. *Big Men and Great Men: Personifications of Power in Melanesia*, Cambridge: Cambridge University Press.
Gordon, R. 2007. 'Popular Justice', in D. Nugent and J. Vincent (eds.), *A Companion to the Anthropology of Politics*, Oxford: Blackwell Publishing, pp. 349–66.
Gordon, R. J., and M. J. Meggitt. 1985. *Law and Order in The New Guinea Highlands: Encounters with Enga*, Hanover: University Press of New England.
Gore, R. T. 1965. *Justice versus Sorcery*, Brisbane: The Jaranda Press.
Gregory, C. A. 1982. *Gifts and Commodities*, London: Academic Press.
Griffin, H. L. n.d. *An Official in British New Guinea*, London: Cecil Palmer.
Griffiths, J. 1986. 'What is Legal Pluralism?', *Journal of Legal Pluralism* 24(1): 1–55.
Groves, M. 1954. 'Dancing in Poreporena', *Journal of the Royal Anthropological Institute of Great Britain and Ireland* 84: 75–90.
———. 1955. 'Motu Morality', *Annual Report and Proceedings 1955, Papua and New Guinea Scientific Society*, pp. 10–12.
———. 1963. 'Western Motu Descent Groups', *Ethnology* 2(1): 15–30.
Gulliver, P. H. 1963. *Social Control in an African Society*, London: Routledge and Kegan Paul.
Hahl, A. 1980. *Governor in New Guinea*, Canberra: Australian National University Press.
Hardt, M., and A. Negri. 2000. *Empire*, Cambridge, MA: Harvard University Press.
Harris, N. 2001. 'Shaming and Shame: Regulating Drink-Driving', in E. Ahmed, N. Harris, J. Braithwaite and V. Braithwaite, *Shame Management Through Reintegration*, Cambridge: Cambridge University Press, pp. 73–207.

Hasluck, P. 1976. *A Time For Building: Australian Administration in Papua New Guinea 1951–1963*, Melbourne: Melbourne University Press.

Hastrup, K. 2001. 'Accommodating Diversity in a Global Culture of Rights: An Introduction', in K. Hastrup (ed.), *2001 Legal Cultures and Human Rights: The Challenge of Diversity*, The Hague: Kluwer Law International, pp. 1–23.

Hauck, V., A. Mandie-Filer and J. Bolger. 2005. 'Ringing the Church Bell: The Role of Churches in Governance and Public Performance in Papua New Guinea', Discussion Paper No. 57E, Maastricht: European Centre for Development Policy Management.

Healy, A. M. 1967. 'Paternalism and Consultation in Papua, 1880–1960', *A.N.U. Historical Journal*, 4: 19–28.

———. 1986. 'Colonial Paternalism as Metropolitan Defence: The Australian Shaping of Papua New Guinea', seminar paper, Centre of S.E. Asian Studies, School of Oriental and African Studies, University of London.

Heider, K. G. 1979. *Grand Valley Dani: Peaceful Warriors*, New York: Holt, Rinehart and Winston.

Heller, A. 1987. *Beyond Justice*, Oxford: Basil Blackwell.

Herdt, G. H. (ed.). 1982. *Rituals of Manhood: Male Initiation in Papua New Guinea*, Berkeley: University of California Press.

Herdt, G. H., and F. J. P. Poole (eds.). 1982. *Sexual Antagonism, Gender and Social Change in Papua New Guinea*, Social Analysis 12, Special Issue.

Hirsch, E. 1997. 'Local Persons, Metropolitan Names: Contending Forms of Simultaneity Among the Fuyuge, Port Moresby,' in R. J. Foster (ed.), *Nation Making: Emergent Identities in Postcolonial Melanesia*, Ann Arbor: University of Michigan Press, pp. 185–206.

Hitchcock, N. E., and N. D. Oram. 1967. *Rabia Camp: A Port Moresby Migrant Settlement*, New Guinea Research Bulletin No. 14, Canberra: Australian National University.

Hobsbawm, E., and T. Ranger (eds.). 1983. *The Invention of Tradition*, Cambridge: Cambridge University Press.

Hoebel, E. A. 1968. *The Law of Primitive Man: A Study in Comparative Legal Dynamics*, New York: Atheneum.

Hogbin, H. I. 1946. 'Local Government for New Guinea', *Oceania* 17(1): 38–67.

Howard, M. 1991. *Fiji: Race and Politics in an Island State*, Vancouver: University of British Columbia Press.

Howley, P. 2006 'Village Courts Shine', letter to the editor, *The National*, Papua New Guinea daily newspaper, 4 September 2006, p. 10.

Hughes, C. A. 1965. 'The Moresby Open and Central Special Elections', in D. G. Bettison, C. A. Hughes and P. W. van der Veur (eds.), *The Papua-New Guinea Elections 1964*, Canberra: Australian National University, pp. 341–73.

Hughes, H. 2004. 'Can Papua New Guinea Come Back From the Brink?' *Issue Analysis* 49: 1–12.

Hyndman, D. 1988. 'Ok Tedi: New Guinea's Disaster Mine', *The Ecologist* 18(1): 24–29.

———. 1994. *Ancestral Rain Forests and the Mountain of Gold: Indigenous Peoples in Mining in New Guinea*, Boulder: Westview Press.

———. 2001. 'Academic Responsibilities and Representation of the Ok Tedi Crisis in Postcolonial Papua New Guinea', *The Contemporary Pacific* 13(1): 33–54.

Ikupu, O. 1930. 'Story About Kidukidu', *Papuan Villager* 2(12): 7.

Independent State of Papua New Guinea. 1990. 'Annual Report by the Judges', mimeo, Port Moresby: Department of Attorney General.

Inglis, A. 1982. *Karo: The Life and Fate of a Papuan*, Canberra: Australian National University Press.

Inglis, C. 1972. 'Chinese', in P. Ryan (ed.), *Encyclopedia of Papua and New Guinea*, Carlton: Melbourne University Press, pp. 170–74.

Iopa, M. 1988. *The Settlement Communities in the National Capital District*, Port Moresby: National Capital District Interim Commission.

Iramu, F. 1975. 'Local and Village Courts', in J. Zorn and P. Bayne (eds.), *Lo Bilong Ol Manmeri: Crime, Compensation and Village Courts*, Port Moresby: University of Papua New Guinea, pp. 42–47.

Jessep, O. 1991. 'Customary Family Law, Women's Rights, and Village Courts in Papua New Guinea', *Melanesian Law Journal* 19: 65–77.

Jessep, O., and J. Luluaki. 1994. *Principles of Family Law in Papua New Guinea*, Port Moresby: University of Papua New Guinea Press.

Jinks, B., P. Biskup and H. Nelson. 1973. *Readings in New Guinea History*, Brisbane: Angus and Robertson.

Jolly, M. 1992. 'Specters of Inauthenticity', *The Contemporary Pacific* 4(1): 49–72.

———. 2000. 'Epilogue: Further Reflections on Violence in Melanesia', in S. Dinnen and A. Ley (eds.), *Reflections on Violence in Melanesia*, Canberra: Hawkins Press/Asia Pacific Press, pp. 305–24.

———. 2003. 'Epilogue—Some Thoughts on Restorative Justice and Gender', in S. Dinnen, A. Jowitt and T. Newton Cain (eds.), *A Kind of Mending: Restorative Justice in the Pacific Islands*, Canberra: Pandanus Books, pp. 265–74.

Jorgensen, D. 1993. 'Money and Marriage in Telefolmin: From Sister Exchange to Daughter as Trade Store', in R. Marksbury (ed.), *The Business of Marriage: Transformations in Oceanic Matrimony*, Pittsburgh: University of Pittsburgh Press, pp. 57–82.

Joyce, R. B. 1971. *Sir William MacGregor*, Melbourne: Oxford University Press.

Kakaboi, N. 1986. 'Ku: Chimbu Province', in S. Toft (ed.), *Marriage in Papua New Guinea*, Monograph No. 4, Port Moresby: Law Reform Commission of Papua New Guinea, pp. 85–95.

Kaputin, J. 1975. 'The Law: A Colonial Fraud?' *New Guinea* 10(1): 4–15.

Keesing, R. M. 1989. 'Creating the Past: Custom and Identity in the Contemporary Pacific', *The Contemporary Pacific* 1: 19–42.

Keesing, R. M., and R. Tonkinson (eds.). 1982. *Reinventing Traditional Culture: The Politics of Kastom in Island Melanesia, Mankind* 13: Special Issue.

Kelly, R. C. 1977. *Etoro Social Structure: A Study in Structural Contradiction*, Ann Arbor: University of Michigan Press.

———. 1994. *Constructing Inequality: The Fabrication of a Hierarchy of Virtue Among the Etoro*, Ann Arbor: University of Michigan Press.

Keris, P. 1985. 'Village Court Secretariat Annual Report 1985', Port Moresby: Government Printer.
———. 1986. 'The Role of Village Courts', in L. Morauta (ed.), *Law and Order in a Changing Society*, Canberra: Australian National University, pp. 70–75.
———. 1988. 'Village Court Secretariat Annual Report 1988', Port Moresby: Government Printer.
Kidu, B. 1976. 'The Kidu of Pari', *Oral History* 4(2): 92–97.
Kidu, C. 2002. *A Remarkable Journey*, Sydney: Longman.
Kiki, A. M. 1968. *Kiki: Ten Thousand Years in a Lifetime*, Melbourne: Cheshire.
King, J. 1909. *W. G. Lawes of Savage Island and New Guinea*, London: Religious Tract Society.
Kirsch, S. 2001. 'Lost Worlds: Environmental Disaster, "Culture Loss" and the Law', *Current Anthropology* 42: 167–98.
———. 2004. 'Changing Views of Place and Time Along the Ok Tedi', in A. Rumsey and J. Weiner (eds.), *Mining and Indigenous Lifeworlds in Australia and New Zealand*, Adelaide: Crawford House Publishing, pp. 182–207.
———. 2006 *Reverse Anthropology: Indigenous Analysis of Social and Environmental Relations in New Guinea*, Stanford: Stanford University Press.
Koch, K-F. 1975. *War and Peace in Jalémó: The Management of Conflict in Highland New Guinea*, Cambridge, MA: Harvard University Press.
Kopi, S. 1979. 'Babalau and Vada: Religion, Disease and Social Control Among the Motu', *Oral History* 7(3): 8–64.
Kumugl, K. 2001. 'Highlands village courts victimise women', *The National*, Papua New Guinea daily newspaper, 13 December 2001, p. 6.
Kyakas, A., and P. Weissner. 1992. *From Inside the Women's House: Enga Women's Lives and Traditions*, Buranda: Robert Brown and Associates.
Landtman, G. 1927. *The Kiwai Papuans Of British New Guinea*, London: Macmillan and Co.
Law Reform Commission of Papua New Guinea. 1977. *The Role Of Customary Law In The Legal System*, Port Moresby: Government Printer.
———. 1987. *Interim Report On Domestic Violence*, Port Moresby: Government Printer.
Lawrence, P. 1970. 'Law and Anthropology: The Need for Collaboration', *Melanesian Law Journal* 1(1): 40–50.
Leenhardt, M. 1979. *Do Kamo: Person and Myth in the Melanesian World*, trans. B. M. Gulati, Chicago: University of Chicago Press.
———. 1998. *Do Kamo: La Personne et le Mythe dans le Monde Mélanésien*, Paris: Gallimard.
Lipset, D. 2004. '"The Trial": A Parody of the Law Amid the Mockery of Men in Post-Colonial Papua New Guinea', *Journal of the Royal Anthropological Institute* 10(1): 63–89.
Llewellyn, K. N., and E. A. Hoebel. 1941. *The Cheyenne Way: Conflict and Case Law in Primitive Jurisprudence*, Norman: University of Oklahoma Press.
Lohia, R. R. 1982. 'Impact of Regional Bride-price on the Economy of Eastern Motu Villages', in P. A. S. Dahanayake (ed.), *Post-Independence Economic*

Development of Papua New Guinea, Monograph No. 19, Boroko: IASER, pp. 105–10.
Lutkehaus, N. 1995. 'Gender Metaphors: Female Rituals as Cultural Models in Manam', in N. C. Lutkehaus and P. B. Roscoe (eds.), *Gender Rituals: Female Initiation in Melanesia*, New York: Routledge, pp. 183–204.
Lynch, C. J. 1965. 'Aspects of Popular Participation in 'Grass-Roots' Courts in Papua and New Guinea', mimeo, Port Moresby: Department of Attorney General.
———. 1978. 'Letter to the Editor', *Melanesian Law Journal* 6(1/2): 114–17.
Macintyre, M. 1998. 'The Persistence of Inequality', in L. Zimmer-Tamakoshi (ed.), *Modern Papua New Guinea*, Kirksville, MO: Thomas Jefferson University Press, pp. 211–28.
———. 2005. 'Taking Care of Culture: Consultancy, Anthropology, and Gender Issues', in P. J. Stewart and A. Strathern (eds.), *Anthropology and Consultancy: Issues and Debates*, New York: Berghahn Books, pp. 124–38.
Maddocks, D. L., and I. Maddocks. 1972. 'Pari Village Study: Results and Prospects 1971', *Papua New Guinea Medical Journal* 15(4): 225–33.
———. 1977. 'The Health of Young Adults in Pari Village', *Papua New Guinea Medical Journal* 20(3): 110–16.
Maddocks, I. 1971. 'Udumu A-Hagaia', mimeo, inaugural lecture, Port Moresby: University of Papua New Guinea.
———. 1974. *Pari Hanua Lada-Torena*, Port Moresby: University of Papua New Guinea.
Malinowski, B. 1959. *Crime and Custom in Savage Society*, New Jersey: Littlefield, Adams and Company.
———. 1966. *Argonauts of the Western Pacific*, New York: Dutton.
Marksbury, R. A. (ed.). 1993. *The Business of Marriage: Transformations in Oceanic Matrimony*, Pittsburgh: University of Pittsburgh Press.
Martin, J. 1975. 'Some Notes on the Village Courts Based on a Visit to the Mendi Sub-district 10th July 1975', mimeo, Port Moresby: University of Papua New Guinea.
Marx, K. 1974. *Economic and Philosophic Manuscripts of 1844*, Moscow: Progress Publishers.
May, R., and M. Spriggs (eds.). 1990. *The Bougainville Crisis*, Bathurst: Crawford House Press.
McDonald, J., and D. Moore. 2001. 'Community Conferencing as a Special Case of Conflict Transformation', in H. Strang and J. Braithwaite (eds.), *Restorative Justice and Civil Society*, Cambridge: Cambridge University Press, pp. 130–48.
McGavin, P. A. 1993. 'The 1992 Minimum Wages Board Determination: implications for employment and growth', *The Papua New Guinea Economy: Prospects for Sectoral Development & Broad Based Growth*, Canberra: AIDAB International Development Issues No. 30.
Mead, M. 1937. *Cooperation and Competition among Primitive Peoples*, New York: McGraw Hill.
———. 1963. *Sex and Temperament*, New York: Morrow.

Meggitt, M. 1964. 'Male Female Relations in the Highlands of Australian New Guinea', *American Anthropologist* 66: 204–24.
———. 1965. *The Lineage System of the Mae-Enga of New Guinea*, New York: Barnes and Noble.
Merry, S. E. 1988. 'Legal Pluralism', *Law and Society Review* 22(5): 869–96.
———. 1999. *Colonizing Hawai'i: The Cultural Power of Law*, Princeton: Princeton University Press.
———. 2003. 'Human Rights Law and the Demonization of Culture (and Anthropology Along the Way)', *Polar: Political and Legal Anthropology Review* 26(1): 55–77.
Messer, E. 2002. 'Anthropologists in a World With and Without Human Rights', in J. MacClancy (ed.), *Exotic No More: Anthropology on the Front Lines*, Chicago: University of Chicago Press, pp. 319–37.
Migdal, J. 1994. 'The State in Society: An Approach to Struggles for Domination', in J. Migdal, A. Kohli and V. Shue (eds.), *State Power and Social Forces: Domination and transformation in the Third World*, Cambridge: Cambridge University Press, pp. 7–34.
Migdal, J., A. Kohli and V. Shue (eds.). 1994. *State Power and Social Forces: Domination and Transformation in the Third World*, Cambridge: Cambridge University Press.
Mimica, J. 2003. 'The Death of a Strong, Great, Bad Man: An Ethnography of Soul Incorporation', *Oceania* 73(4): 260–77.
Mitchell, B. H. 1985. 'Family Law in Village Courts: The Woman's Position', in P. King, W. Lee and V. Warakai (eds.), *From Rhetoric to Reality?* Waigani: University of Papua New Guinea Press, pp. 81–91.
Monckton, C. A. W. n.d. *Further Adventures of a New Guinea Resident Magistrate*, London: Newnes.
Moore, H. L. 1988. *Feminism and Anthropology*, Cambridge: Polity Press.
———. 1994. *A Passion for Difference: Essays in Anthropology and Gender*, Bloomington: Indiana University Press.
Moore, S. F. 1973. 'Law and Social Change: The Semi-Autonomous Social Field as an Appropriate Subject of Study', *Law and Society Review* 7(4): 719–45.
———. 1977. 'Individual Interests and Organisational Structures: Dispute Settlements as "Events of Articulation"', in I. Hamnett (ed.), *Social Anthropology and Law*, London: Academic Press, pp. 159–88.
———. 1986. *Social Facts and Fabrications: Customary Law on Kilimanjaro, 1880–1980*, New York: Cambridge University Press.
———. 2001. 'Certainties Undone: Fifty Turbulent Years of Legal Anthropology, 1949–1999', *Journal of the Royal Anthropological Institute* 7: 95–116.
Morauta, L. 1984. *Left Behind in the Village*, Monograph No. 25, Port Moresby: Institute of Applied Social and Economic Research.
Murray, H. 1925. *Papua of Today*, London: P. S. King and Son.
———. 1926. 'Native Custom and the Government of Primitive Races with Especial Reference to Papua', paper read to 3rd Pan-Pacific Science Congress in Tokyo, Port Moresby: Government Printer.

———. 1928. 'Indirect Rule in Papua', paper read to Australasian Association for the Advancement of Science, Hobart, Port Moresby: Government Printer.

Murray, J. K. 1949. *The Provisional Administration of the Territory of Papua-New Guinea: Its Policy and its Problems*, Brisbane: University of Queensland.

Mytinger, C. 1947. *New Guinea Headhunt*, New York: Macmillan.

Nader, L. 1965. 'The Anthropological Study of Law', in L. Nader (ed.), *The Ethnography of Law*, Special publication, *American Anthropologist* 67(6), part 2, pp. 3–32.

———. 1990. *Harmony Ideology: Justice and Control in a Mountain Zapotec Village*, Stanford: Stanford University Press.

———. 1999. 'The Globalization of Law: ADR as 'Soft' Technology', *Proceedings of the 93rd Annual Meeting, American Society of International Law*, Washington, DC: ASIL, pp. 1–9.

———. 2002. *The Life of the Law: Anthropological Projects*, Berkeley: University of California Press.

———. 2006. 'Promise or Plunder? A Past and Present Look at Law and Development', *The World Bank Legal Review: Law, Equity and Development*, Vol. 2, The World Bank & Martinus Nijhoff, pp. 87–111.

Narokobi, B. 1977. 'Adoption of Western Law in Papua New Guinea', *Melanesian Law Journal* 5(1): 51–69.

———. 1986. 'In Search of a Melanesian Jurisprudence', in P. Sack and E. Minchin (eds.), *Legal Pluralism: Proceedings of the Canberra Law Workshop VII*, Canberra: Law Department, Research School of Social Sciences, Australian National University.

[NCPNG] National Court of Papua New Guinea. 1980. 'Re Village Courts Act 1974; Re WW (An Infant) Presently in Custody PNGNC 37', Unreported National Court Decisions. Retrieved 7 November 2006 from http://www.paclii.org/pg/cases/PGNC/1980/37.html.

Nelson, H. N. 1976. 'The Swinging Index: Capital punishment and British and Australian Administrations in Papua and New Guinea, 1888–1945', seminar paper, Canberra: Australian National University.

———. 1990. *Taim Bilong Masta: The Australian Involvement With Papua New Guinea*, Sydney: Australian Broadcasting Corporation.

Norwood, H. 1984. *Port Moresby Urban Villages and Squatter Areas*, Port Moresby: University of Papua New Guinea.

O'Collins, M. 2000. *Law and Order in Papua New Guinea: Perceptions and Management Strategies*, State, Society and Governance in Melanesia Project, Working paper 00/1, Canberra: Research School of Pacific and Asia Studies, Australian National University.

Oram, N. D. 1964. 'Urbanization—Port Moresby', *South Pacific Bulletin* 14(4): 37–43.

———. 1975. 'Village Courts: The Arguments Answered', in J. Zorn and P. Bayne (eds.), *Lo Bilong Ol Manmeri: Crime, Compensation and Village Courts*, Port Moresby: University of Papua New Guinea, pp. 66–68.

———. 1976. *Colonial Town to Melanesian City*, Canberra: Australian National University Press.

———. 1979. 'Grass Roots Justice: Village Courts in Papua New Guinea', in W. Clifford and S. D. Gorkhale (eds.), *Innovations in Criminal Justice in Asia and the Pacific*, Canberra: Australian Institute of Criminology, pp. 49–80.

———. 1981. 'The History of the Motu-Speaking and Koita-Speaking Peoples According to Their Own Traditions', in D. Denoon and R. Lacey (eds.), *Oral Tradition in Melanesia*, Port Moresby: University of Papua New Guinea and Institute of Papua New Guinea Studies, pp. 207–29.

———. 1989. 'The Western Motu Area and the European Impact: 1872–1942', in S. Latukefu (ed.), *Papua New Guinea: A Century of Colonial Impact 1884–1984*, Port Moresby: National Research Institute and University of Papua New Guinea, pp. 49–74.

———. n.d. 'Towards a Study of the London Missionary Society in Hula 1875–1968', mimeo, Port Moresby: University of Papua New Guinea.

Orr, R. 1991. 'Provincial Government and Customary Law', *Melanesian Law Journal*, Special Issue, 71–89.

Ottley, B. L. 1992. 'Custom and Introduced Criminal Justice,' in R. W. James and I. Fraser (eds.), *Legal Issues in a Developing Country*, Port Moresby: Faculty of Law, University of PNG Press, pp. 128–45.

Otto, T., and A. Borsboom (eds.). 1997. *Cultural Dynamics of Religious Change in Oceania*, Leiden: KITLV Press.

Otto, T., and P. Pedersen (eds.). 2005. *Tradition and Agency: Tracing Cultural Continuity and Invention*, Oxford: Aarhus University Press.

Paliwala, A. 1982. 'Law and Order in the Village: Papua New Guinea's Village Courts', in C. Sumner (ed.), *Crime, Justice and Underdevelopment*, London: Heinemann, pp. 192–227.

Paney, P., et al. 1973. *Report of the Committee Investigating Tribal Fighting in the Highlands*, Port Moresby: Government Printer.

Papua New Guinea House of Assembly Debates. 1972. Vol. 3, pp. 1163–68.

Papua New Guinea Law Reports. 1992. Port Moresby: Faculty of Law, University of Papua New Guinea.

Parker, L. 2002. 'Possibilities for Restorative Justice in Papua New Guinea', Restorative Justice Online. Retrieved 3 September 2005 from http://www.restorativejustice.org/rj3/Feature/August02/png1.htm.

Pflanz-Cook, S. M. 1993. 'Manga Marriage in Transition, From 1961–1981', in R. Marksbury (ed.), *The Business of Marriage: Transformations in Oceanic Matrimony*, Pittsburgh: University of Pittsburgh Press, pp. 105–26.

Poole, F. J. P. 1981. 'Transforming "Natural" Woman: Female Ritual Leaders and Gender Ideology among Bimin-Kuskusmin', in S. Ortner and H. Whitehead (eds.), *Sexual Meanings*, Cambridge: Cambridge University Press, pp. 116–65.

Pospisil, L. 1958. *Kapauku Papuans and their Law*, New Haven: Yale University Publications in Anthropology No. 54.

Premdas, R. R., and J. S. Steeves. 1978. *Electoral Politics in a Third World City: Port Moresby 1977*, Port Moresby, University of Papua New Guinea.

Pulsford, R. L. 1975. 'Ceremonial Fishing for Tuna by the Motu of Pari', *Oceania* 46(2): 107–13.

Quinlivan, P. J. 1965. 'Handbook of the Law of the Territory of Papua and New Guinea', mimeo, Port Moresby: Department of Attorney General.

———. 1975. 'Local Courts in Papua New Guinea: Bringing Justice to the Villagers', in J. Zorn and P. Bayne (eds.), *Lo Bilong Ol Manmeri: Crime, Compensation and Village Courts*, Port Moresby: University of Papua New Guinea, pp. 59–65.

———. n.d. 'Those Crippling Criminal Circuits', mimeo, Port Moresby: Department of Attorney General.

Radcliffe-Brown, A. R. 1952. *Structure and Function in Primitive Society*, London: Cohen and West.

Reay, M. 1974. 'Changing Conventions of Dispute Settlement in the Minj Area', in A. L. Epstein (ed.), *Contention and Dispute: Aspects of Law and Social Control in Melanesia*, Canberra: Australian National University Press, pp. 199–239.

Reiter, R. R. (ed.). 1975. *Toward an Anthropology of Women*, New York: Monthly Review Press.

Robbins, J. 2004. *Becoming Sinners: Christianity and Moral Torment in a Papua New Guinea Society*, Berkeley: University of California Press.

Roberts, S. 2002. 'Law and Dispute Processes', in T. Ingold (ed.), *Companion Encyclopedia of Anthropology*, London: Routledge, pp. 962–82.

Robinson, N. K. 1979. *Villagers At War: Some Papua New Guinean Experiences in World War II*, Pacific Research Monograph No. 2, Canberra: Australian National University.

Rofel, L. 2002. 'Modernity's Masculine Fantasies', in B. M. Knauft (ed.), *Critically Modern: Alternatives, Alterities, Anthropologies*, Bloomington: Indiana University Press, pp. 175–93.

Rosi, P., and L. Zimmer-Tamakoshi. 1993. 'Love and Marriage Among the Educated Elite in Port Moresby', in R. A. Marksbury (ed.), *The Business of Marriage: Transformations in Oceanic Matrimony*, Pittsburgh: University of Pittsburgh Press, pp. 175–204.

Rowley, C. D. 1965. *The New Guinea Villager: A Retrospect From 1964*, Sydney: F. W. Cheshire.

Ryan, D. 1965. *Social Change among the Toaripi, Papua*, Masters thesis, University of Sydney.

———. 1970. *Rural and Urban Villagers: A Bi-Local Social System in Papua*, PhD dissertation, University of Hawai'i.

Sack, P. 1989. 'Law, Custom and Good Government: The Derham Report in its Historical Context', in S. Latukefu (ed.), *Papua New Guinea: A Century of Colonial Impact 1884–1984*, Port Moresby: National Research Institute, pp. 377–97.

Sahlins, M. 1963. 'Poor Man, Rich Man, Big Man, Chief', *Comparative Studies in Society and History* 5: 285–303.

Salisbury, R. F. 1970. *Vunamami: Economic Transformation in a Traditional Society*, Melbourne: Melbourne University Press.

Sam, P., B. Passingan and W. Kanawai. 1975. 'Bringing the Law to the People', in J. Zorn and P. Bayne (eds.), *Lo Bilong Ol Manmeri: Crime, Compensation and Village Courts*, Port Moresby: University of Papua New Guinea, pp. 161–67.

Scaglion, R. 1981. 'Samukundi Abelam Conflict Management: Implications for Legal Planning in Papua New Guinea', *Oceania* 52(1): 28–38.
——. 1985. 'The Role of Custom in Law Reform', in Ross De Vere, Duncan Colquhoun-Kerr and John Kaburise (eds.), *Essays on the Constitution of Papua New Guinea*, Port Moresby: Government Printer, pp. 31–38.
——. 1990. 'Legal Adaptation in a Papua New Guinea Village Court', *Ethnology*, 29(1): 17–33.
——. 2005. 'From Anthropologist to Government Officer and Back Again', in P. J. Stewart and A. Strathern (eds.), *Anthropology and Consultancy: Issues and Debates*, New York: Berghahn Books, pp. 46–62.
Scaglion, R., and R. Whittingham. 1985. 'Female Plaintiffs and Sex-Related Disputes in Rural Papua New Guinea', in S. Toft (ed.), *Domestic Violence in Papua New Guinea*, Monograph No. 3, Port Moresby: Law Reform Commission, pp. 121–33.
Schapera, I. 1943. *Tribal Legislation Among the Tswana of the Bechuanaland Protectorate*, London: Lund, Humphries.
Schieffelin, E. L. 1977. *The Sorrow of the Lonely and the Burning of the Dancers*, St Lucia: University of Queensland Press.
Scott, B. 2005. *Re-Imagining PNG: Culture, Democracy and Australia's Role*, Sydney: Lowy Institute for International Policy.
Seligmann, C. G. 1910. *The Melanesians of British New Guinea*, Cambridge: Cambridge University Press.
Senge, E. T., et al. 1992. 'Women in Village Courts', *Research in Melanesia* 16: 95–99.
Sexton, L. 1995. 'Marriage as the Model for a New Initiation Ritual', in N. C. Lutkehaus and P. B. Roscoe (eds.), *Gender Rituals: Female Initiation in Melanesia*, New York: Routledge, pp. 205–16.
Smith, P. 1989. 'Education Policy in Australian New Guinea: A Classic Case', in S. Latukefu (ed.), *Papua New Guinea: A Century of Colonial Impact*, Port Moresby: National Research Institute, pp. 291–315.
Snyder, F. G. 1981. *Capitalism and Legal Change: An African Transformation*, New York: Academic Press.
——. 1988. 'Rethinking African Customary Law', *The Modern Law Review* 51(2): 252–58.
Souter, G. 1964: *New Guinea: The Last Unknown*, Sydney: Angus and Robertson.
Srinivas, M. N. (ed.). 1962. *Caste in Modern India and Other Essays*, New York: Asia Publishing House.
Standish, W. 1975. 'Warfare, Leadership and Law in the Highlands', in J. Zorn and P. Bayne (eds.), *Lo Bilong Ol Manmeri: Crime, Compensation and Village Courts*, Port Moresby: University of Papua New Guinea, pp. 104–25.
——. 1981. 'The Fat Men: Conflict and Continuity in Simbu Provincial Politics', paper presented to conference on 'Papua New Guinea, the Recent Past and Immediate Future', May 1980, revised manuscript, Canberra: Research School of Pacific Studies, Australian National University.
Stanner, W. E. H. 1953. *The South Seas in Transition*, Sydney: Australian Publishing Co.

Stephen, M. 1989. 'Constructing Sacred Worlds and Autonomous Imagining in New Guinea' in G. Herdt and M. Stephen (eds.), *The Religious Imagination in New Guinea*, New Brunswick: Rutgers University Press, pp. 211–36.
———. 1995. *A'aisa's Gifts: A study of Magic and the Self*, Berkeley: University of California Press.
Strang, H., and J. Braithwaite (eds.). 2001. *Restorative Justice and Civil Society*, Cambridge: Cambridge University Press.
Strathern, A. 1974. 'When Dispute Procedures Fail', in A. L. Epstein (ed.), *Contention and Dispute: Aspects of Law and Social Control in Melanesia*, Canberra: Australian National University Press, pp. 240–70.
Strathern, M. 1972. *Official and Unofficial Courts: Legal Assumptions and Expectations in a Highlands Community*, New Guinea Research Bulletin No. 47, Canberra: New Guinea Research Unit, Australian National University.
———. 1974. 'Managing Information: The Problems of a Dispute Settler (Mount Hagen)', in A. L. Epstein (ed.), *Contention and Dispute: Aspects of Law and Social Control in Melanesia*, Canberra: Australian National University Press, pp. 271–316.
———. 1975. 'Sanctions and the Problem of Corruption in Village Courts', in J. Zorn and P. Bayne (eds.), *Lo Bilong Ol Manmeri: Crime, Compensation and Village Courts*, Port Moresby: University of Papua New Guinea, pp. 48–58.
———. 1988. *The Gender of the Gift*, Berkeley: University of California Press.
Stuart, I. 1970. *Port Moresby Yesterday and Today*, Sydney: Pacific Publications.
Swadling, P. 1982. 'Shellfishing and Management in Papua New Guinea', in L. Morauta, J. Pernetta and W. Heaney (eds.), *Traditional Conservation in Papua New Guinea: Implications for Today*, Monograph No. 16, Port Moresby: Institute of Applied Social Science and Economic Research, pp. 307–10.
Tarr, J. 1973. 'Vabukori and Pari—The Years of War', *Oral History* 1(7): 13–22.
Taylor, G. 1985. *Pride, Shame and Guilt: Emotions of Self-Assessment*, Oxford: Clarendon Press.
Trompf, G. W. 1994. *Payback: The Logic of Retribution in Melanesian Religions*, Cambridge: Cambridge University Press.
Tua, E. 1986. 'Rakamanda, Enga Province', in S. Toft (ed.), *Marriage in Papua New Guinea*, Monograph No. 4, Port Moresby: Law Reform Commission of Papua New Guinea, pp. 63–75.
Turner, J. W. 1997. 'Continuity and Constraint: Reconstructing the Concept of Tradition from a Pacific Perspective', *The Contemporary Pacific* 9(2): 345–81.
Turner, V. W. 1957. *Schism and Continuity in an African Society: A Study of Ndembu Village Life*, Manchester: Manchester University Press.
Turner, W. Y. 1878. 'The Ethnology of the Motu', *Journal of the Anthropological Institute of Great Britain and Ireland* 7: 470–99.
Tuzin, D. 1997. *The Cassowary's Revenge*, Chicago: Chicago University Press.
United Nations. 1993. 'Vienna Declaration and Programme of Action', United Nations General Assembly: World Conference on Human Rights, Vienna, 14–25 June, 1993, Geneva: United Nations High Commission.
[UPNG] University of Papua New Guinea. 1973. 'Ranuguri Migrant Settlement: A Draft Copy of a Submission to the Housing Commission by Students

and Staff of the Geography Department, University of Papua New Guinea', mimeo, Port Moresby: University of Papua New Guinea.

Van Heekeren, D. 2004. *Being Hula: The Appropriation of Christianity in Irupara Village, Papua New Guinea*, PhD dissertation, University of Newcastle, Australia.

Van Velsen, J. 1964. *The Politics of Kinship: A Study in Social Manipulation Among the Lakeside Tonga of Nyasaland*, Manchester: Manchester University Press.

Village Court Secretariat. 1975. 'Selection of Village Court Officials', mimeo, Port Moresby: Village Court Secretariat.

———. 1976. 'Handbook for Village Court Officials 1976', mimeo, Port Moresby: Village Court Secretariat.

———. n.d. 'Village Court Costs', mimeo, Port Moresby: Village Court Secretariat.

von Benda-Beckmann, F. 1984. 'Law Out of Context: A Comment on the Creation of Traditional Law', *Journal of African Law* 28(1/2): 28–33.

Waiko, J. D. 1993. *A Short History of Papua New Guinea*, Melbourne: Oxford University Press.

Wain, W. 1986. 'Birop, Southern Highlands Province', in S. Toft (ed.), *Marriage in Papua New Guinea*, Monograph No. 4, Port Moresby: Law Reform Commission of Papua New Guinea, pp. 41–46.

Wanek, A. 1996. *The State and its Enemies In Papua New Guinea*, Surrey: Curzon Press.

Warus, J. 1986. 'Uma, Southern Highlands Province', in S. Toft (ed.), *Marriage in Papua New Guinea*, Monograph No. 4, Port Moresby: Law Reform Commission of Papua New Guinea, pp. 47–62.

Weiner, A. B. 1992. *Inalienable Possessions: The Paradox of Keeping-While-Giving*, Berkeley: University of California Press.

Weisbrot, D. 1988. 'Papua New Guinea's Indigenous Jurisprudence and the Legacy of Colonialism', *University of Hawaii Law Review* 10(1): 1–45.

West, F. (ed.). 1970. *Selected Letters of Hubert Murray*, Melbourne: Oxford University Press.

Westermark, G. 1978. 'Village Courts in Question: The Nature of Court Procedure', in *Melanesian Law Journal* 6(1/2): 79–96.

———. 1985. 'Family Disputes and Village Courts in the Eastern Highlands', in S. Toft (ed.), *Domestic Violence in Papua New Guinea*, Monograph No. 3, Port Moresby: Law Reform Commission, pp. 104–19.

———. 1986. 'Court is an Arrow: Legal Pluralism in Papua New Guinea', *Ethnology* 25: 131–49.

Wetherell, D. 1996. *Charles Abel and the Kwato Mission of Papua New Guinea 1891—1975*, Melbourne: Melbourne University Press.

Whiting, J. W. M. 1951. *Becoming a Kwoma: Teaching and Learning in a New Guinea Tribe*, New Haven: Yale University Press.

Williams, F. E. 1969. *Drama of Orokolo: The Social and Ceremonial Life of the Elema*, Oxford: Clarendon Press.

———. 1976. *'The Vailala Madness' and Other Essays*, London: C. Hurst and Co.

Wilson, R. A. 2007. 'Human Rights', in D. Nugent and J. Vincent (eds.), *A Companion to the Anthropology of Politics*, Oxford: Blackwell Publishing, pp. 231–47.

Wolfers, E. P. 1975. *Race Relations and Colonial Rule in Papua New Guinea*, Sydney: Australia & New Zealand Book Co.

Young, D. W. 1992. 'Grassroots Justice: Where the National Justice System is the "Alternative": The Village Court System of Papua New Guinea', *Australian Dispute Resolution Journal* 3(1): 31–46.

Zimmer-Tamakoshi, L. 1993. 'Bachelors, Spinsters and *Pamuk Meris*', in R. A. Marksbury (ed.), *The Business of Marriage: Transformations in Oceanic Matrimony*, Pittsburgh: University of Pittsburgh Press, pp. 83–104,

Zorn, J. G. 1990. 'Customary Law in the Papua New Guinea Village Courts', *The Contemporary Pacific* 2(2): 279–312.

———. 1991. 'Making Law in Papua New Guinea: The Influence of Customary Law on the Common Law', *Pacific Studies* 14(4): 1–35.

———. 1992. 'Graun Bilong Mipela: Local Courts and the Changing Customary Law of Papua New Guinea', *Pacific Studies* 15(2): 1–38.

Zorn, J., and P. Bayne (eds.). 1975. *Lo Bilong Ol Manmeri: Crime, compensation and village courts*, Port Moresby: University of Papua New Guinea.

Index

A
Abel, Charles, 35
Aboriginal Australians, 8
adultery, 29, 40, 140, 171, 197, 205, 220, 221, 253–4
Africa, 6, 10, 15, 16, 19, 44
Ainsworth, Colonel J., 37–38, 42
alternative dispute resolution (ADR), 8–9, 65, 72–73, 76n18, 275, 276. *See also* restorative justice
American Anthropological Association, 10
anthropology of law. *See* law
assault, 29, 56, 90, 101, 102, 108, 136, 138, 169, 197, 217–8, 219, 220–21, 224–7, 245–7, 250, 259, 261
Attorney General's Department, 22, 66, 68, 72–74; Institutional Strengthening Project(ISP) of, 73; changing names of, 73
Australia, 2, 8–9, 25n4, 29, 30, 34–5, 37, 41, 71–2, 249, 274. *See also* colonial administration in PNG
Australian Agency for International Development (AusAID), 72–74, 85, 262

B
Baing, Andrew, 68
Baisu gaol, 80–81, 84
Barnes, J. A., 17
Barotse (Africa), 15
Bergin, Trevor, 55
Berndt, Ronald, 7, 17
big-men, 42, 118, 153, 157, 242, 272
bi-locality, 113–14, 127
Bohannan, Paul, 15, 16, 157
Bougainville Island, 9, 73
Braithwaite, John, 215
brideprice, 32, 33, 80, 81, 89, 99, 140, 171, 213, 221–2, 229–31, 234, 253–4, 258–61

C
Caplan, Pat, 2
Central Court, 34, 43
Central Province, 22, 51n7, 55, 68, 132, 138
Chagga (Africa), 16
Chalmers, D., 46, 49, 55
Chalmers, James, 34, 35, 126
Chanock, Martin, 6, 19
Cheyenne. *See* Native Americans

chiefs, 28, 30, 33, 35, 51n3, 147, 152–3
Chinese people, 189, 194n2
Chinnery, E. P. W., 40
Christianity, 2, 4, 6–7, 33, 119–23, 131, 151, 169, 171, 181, 185, 193, 242, 270, 274, 280n1; and development aid, 274–6; and individualism, 242; church-related activity, 4, 6–7, 40–41, 94, 118–21, 127, 131, 146, 147, 151, 153, 170, 184; London Missionary Society (LMS), 6, 116, 118, 126, 131, 142n3, 169; Catholic Church, 279; United Church, 116, 118, 120, 127, 131, 169; Seventh Day Adventist (SDA), 131; missionaries, 4, 5, 6–7, 19, 28, 32–35, 119, 126 142n3, 191, 275. *See also* harmony
colonial administration in PNG, British, 27–28, 29–31, 33–34; German, 27–29, 32–33, 37, 269; Australian 2, 7, 34, 37–51, 59n1, 269;
Colson, Elizabeth, 5, 16
Comaroff, John, 16, 17, 275–6
Community Courts Administration Unit (CCAU). *See* Village Court Secretariat
Constitutional Planning Committee, 55
Courts for Native Affairs, 39, 43; for Native Matters, 35, 39, 43
Courts of Petty Sessions, 34, 43
cultural relativism, 10, 269
culture: notion of, 11, 12, 15, 264, 276; demonisation of, 12, 276; 'invention' of, 12 (*see also* custom; tradition); juridical effects of, 15, 150, 161, 166 (*see also* relationalism); culture loss, 20
Curtis-Greenwell report, 48
custom: contrasted with law, 14, 15, 39–40, 43, 50, 89, 94–96, 100–10; problematic conception of, 18, 32, 34, 43–45, 74, 89, 91, 96–97, 107, 110; colonial attitudes towards, 15, 30, 32–34, 36, 38–40, 42–51, 53, 96, 107; viewed as oppressive, 56, 78–88, 96–97, 109, 270, 273–4; 'invention' of, 12, 279 (*see also* culture; tradition); in village courts (*see* village courts)
customary law: problematic conception of, 17, 18, 19, 21, 96–100; colonial creation of, 6, 19, 98; in village courts (*see* village courts)

D

Dani people, 5, 25n2
deacons courts, 6, 40–41, 94
Dead Birds documentary, 5, 25n2
Decentralisation Department, 58, 60, 62
Demian, Melissa, 98
Department of District Administration, 56, 270
Department of Justice, 54, 56, 60–61, 72, 79, 270
Department of Provincial Affairs (DPA), 62, 63
dependency theory, 79
Derham, David, 43–48
Desailly-Iramu report, 48–49, 90, 279
development aid, 2–4, 8–11, 13, 24, 65, 71–73, 85, 255, 262–3, 274–5, 277
Doriga, Lohia, 128, 129, 132, 133, 143n15
dispute settlement, 2, 4–6, 7, 16–17, 24, 28, 32, 37, 40, 48–50, 72, 92–94, 98, 147; mediation and, 50, 67, 73–74, 93–94, 156, 161–6, 195, 213–14, 219, 279; anthropological interest in, 2, 14, 15–17, 21, 98. *See also* alternative dispute resolution; restorative justice; processual paradigm; rule-centred paradigm; village courts

Index

District Courts, 12, 43, 46, 57, 79, 82; relations with village courts (*see* village courts)
Divine Word University, 279
Doherty, Judge Theresa, 82, 84, 86
drunkenness, 56, 102, 120–23, 169–71, 173, 180–86, 189–90, 191, 193, 197, 221, 232–4, 261, 281, 283
Dukduk dancers, 32–33

E

Eastern Highlands Province, 22, 55, 68–69, 82, 83, 85, 87, 91, 92, 103–4, 111n6, 133, 252
East New Britain Province, 22, 28–29, 46, 60, 83, 148
Enga people, 243
Enga Province, 22, 55, 61, 62, 82, 87, 90, 148.
Epstein, A. L., 17, 21
Eriksen, T. H., 11, 264
Erima settlement, 137, 138–9, 155, 218, 227
Erima village court, 102, 136, 139–40, 141, 148, 154–5, 157, 158, 159, 160, 167, 171, 217–39, 241, 251, 253, 258–60, 268
evidence. *See* village courts

F

feminism, 10, 85,
Fenbury, David, 42, 44–45, 49
Filer, Colin, 222
First World War, 23, 25n4, 29, 37, 50
Fyfe Bay, 36

G

Gamada (*Piper Methysticum*), 39, 52n11
Garap, Sarah, 86, 255–6, 263
Gardner, Robert, 5, 25n2
Garo, Kila, 57, 58, 62, 69, 94

Gazelle Peninsula, 46
gender relations, 10, 11, 25n3, 85, 87, 97, 146–7, 242, 255, 257, 266n7; in village courts (*see* village courts). *See also* marriage
gift economy, 5, 118, 140, 156, 158, 242, 254, 256. *See also* reciprocity
Ginigini settlement. *See* Vainakomu settlement
globalisation, 3, 4, 9, 10, 20, 21, 264, 273–4, 276–7. *See also* law
Gluckman, Max, 15, 16,
Goaribi people, 34–35
Gordon, Robert, 8, 52n14, 61, 243
Gordons market, 139, 207, 218
Gore, Justice, 15, 18, 19
gossip, 102, 121, 134, 135, 141, 189, 198–208, 220, 259
Gregory, Christopher, 118, 242
Groves, Murray, 119, 191
Guise, John, 49,
Gulf of Papua, 34, 35, 116, 124–6, 130, 138, 142nn1,8, 152. *See also* Gulf Province
Gulf Province, 40, 114, 117, 129–30, 132, 134, 139, 149, 150, 175, 198, 208–9. *See also* 'Kerema' people
Gumine, 229, 231

H

Hahl, Albert, 23, 28–29, 31–33, 34, 37, 38, 50, 51n1
Hanuabada village complex, 40, 114–5, 118, 119, 128, 130, 135, 142n9, 143n15, 195, 248
Hardt, Michael, 273
harmony, 4–10, 50, 53, 73, 123, 188, 190, 191, 194, 251, 268, 275; and Christianity, 4, 6–8, 123, 169, 268; 'harmony ideology', 4, 6–8, 10, 123, 169, 275, 276
Hasluck, Sir Paul, 42–43
Hastrup, Kirsten, 9–10
Hawai'i, 19

Hiri, 52n7, 116, 142n5, 152
Hiri Motu, 51n7, 74, 95, 101, 103, 118–9, 134, 142n5, 162, 181, 199. *See also* Motu language
Hobbes, Thomas, 14
Hoebel, E. A., 15
Hogbin, Ian, 42
Holloway, Barry, 49
Holmes, Ian, 55, 57
House of Assembly, 49, 52n16, 55, 67–68
Hula people, 40, 150
human rights, 2–3, 8, 9–13, 20, 21, 24, 27, 262–5, 266n6; Universal Declaration of, 10, 263–4; Vienna Declaration on, 10–11; in village courts (*see* village courts)

I
iduhu, 115, 116–19, 122, 152, 241, 247–51
Ilahita Arapesh people, 244, 256, 262
independence, 1, 13, 18, 25n4, 41, 48, 49, 96, 97, 115
independence Constitution, 74, 80–82, 84, 95–97, 107, 270, 280n1
individualism, 11, 24, 242–5, 251, 262–5, 277. *See also* relationalism
insult, 14, 56, 102, 122, 134–5, 172, 181–5, 196, 197–205, 220, 227–8, 232, 259–60, 281, 282

H
Jalé people, 5
Jessep, Owen, 82, 84
Judges Report of 1990, 81–82, 84, 86

K
Kadeullo, Andrew (a.k.a. 'chairman Andrew'), 102–6, 155–160, 218–9, 221, 223, 225–8, 232–8, 239, 252, 253–4, 272

Kainantu, 55, 75n8, 91–92
Kakoli people, 7–8
Kaputin, John, 49, 54, 114
Kaugel Valley, 22, 99
kaunsel, 93, 94
'Kerema' people, 117, 125, 128, 136, 140, 160, 162, 166–7, 175, 238
Keris, Peni, 62–63, 65, 72, 74, 95
kiaps, 17, 37, 38, 39, 43–44, 46, 49, 50–51, 52n5, 58, 61, 90, 243, 269
Kidu, Dame Carol, 68, 150–51
Kidu, Sir Buri, 81, 150–51
Kimbe (town), 278–9
kinship, 16, 38, 91, 103–6, 114, 118, 121, 126, 140, 141, 152, 161, 180, 215, 222, 228–31, 238, 251, 252, 263, 265n5, 271. *See also* relationism, wantokism
Kiwai (area), 30, 52n11
Koch, Klaus-Friedrich, 5
Koiari people, 138
Koita people. *See* Motu-Koita people
Konedobu suburb, 124, 128, 130, 131, 142n9, 143n15
Konedobu village court, 124, 129, 133–6, 149–50, 160–66, 195–216, 238, 241, 260, 260

L
Lakwaharu people, 115–16
land disputes, 29, 39, 57, 143n13, 170, 171, 176–80, 193–4, 246, 249
law: anthropology of, 2, 3, 13–21, 100; and colonialism, 6, 19, 21, 23, 27–38, 43–44, 49, 50, 53, 98, 269; and globalisation, 3, 11, 13, 273–4, 277; and religion, 275; and order, 2, 9, 50, 58–59, 61, 62, 68–70, 72–74, 75n8, 88, 94, 124, 128, 130, 142n10, 274; rule of, 3, 8, 11, 20, 32, 40, 263; Melanesian understandings of, 21, 243; substantive and

procedural, 98; and custom (*see* custom; customary law); in village courts (*see* village courts). *See also* legal centralism, legal pluralism
Law Reform Commission, 18, 65, 97–98
Lawrence, Peter, 141, 215, 251
League of Nations, 25n4, 37
Leenhardt, Maurice, 244, 265n2
legal centralism, 17, 18, 79
legal pluralism, 15, 18–19, 21, 47, 72, 100
Le Hunte, Sir George, 34
Local Courts, 45, 46–47, 48, 56, 58, 64, 79, 83–84
Local Courts Act, (1963), 46–47
Local Government Councils, 46, 57, 58, 60–62, 89
Locke, John, 14
Lohia, Dirona, 129, 132, 143nn12,15, 199–205, 209–13
London Missionary Society (LMS). *See* Christianity
luluais, 28–29, 31, 32, 33, 37–38, 41–42, 43, 46, 50, 51n2, 52n8, 93, 154
Lynch, C. J., 47, 49

M
MacGregor, Sir William, 29–31, 33–34, 35, 39, 51n4
Macintyre, Martha, 85–86, 266n7
Madang Province, 22, 83, 91, 279
Magisterial Services Commission, 54–55, 63; renamed Magisterial Service, 55, 59
Maino, Andrew, 57
Mair, Lucy, 42
Malalaua district. *See* 'Kerema' people
Malawi (Africa), 6
Malinowski, Bronislaw, 5, 14, 17, 18, 21
Maniti, Josephine, 143n1, 149–50, 160–67

Mann, Justice Alan, 43–44
Manumanu village, 191
Marai, Tati, 149–50, 160–67
marriage, 33, 39, 80, 105, 108, 140–41, 221–2, 228–31, 234–5, 238, 245–50, 252–4, 259–61, 265n6. *See also* gender relations
Marxism, 10
mediation. *See* dispute settlement; village courts
Meggitt, M. J., 61, 243
Mendi (town and district), 55, 56, 75n8, 78, 79, 86, 111n1
Merry, Sally, 11, 12, 18–19, 100, 276
Migdal, Joel, 270–72
migration, 52n15, 70, 84, 113–4, 115, 117, 118, 124, 126–7, 129, 138–40, 154, 217
Milne Bay Province, 22, 36, 90, 138, 148, 155
Mimica, Jadran, 5
Minj people, 7
missionaries. *See* Christianity
Mitchell, Barbara, 80, 82, 84, 85, 96, 97, 146
Monckton, C. A. W., 31, 51n5
Moore, Sally Falk, 3, 16, 92, 277
Morata suburb, 154
Moripi. *See* 'Kerema' people
Motu-Koita people, 22, 40, 56, 114–20, 123, 124–6, 128, 130, 134, 135, 142nn6,9, 143n13, 149, 150–53, 169, 181, 191, 194n1, 249
Motu language, 36, 51n7, 101, 119, 174, 181, 182
Motu people. *See* Motu-Koita people
Mount Hagen (town and district), 81, 103, 234–5, 265n1
Mount Hagen people, 244
Moveave. *See* 'Kerema' people
Murray, Sir Hubert, 35–36, 37, 38–39, 40
Murray, Colonel J. K., 41–42, 49
Mytinger, Carol, 40

N

Nader, Laura, 3, 4, 6–9, 15, 19, 20, 123, 169, 275, 276, 277
Narokobi, Bernard, 243
National Capital District (NCD), 65, 68, 70, 113, 134, 148, 150, 194n1
National Capital District Commission (NCDC), 65, 68, 150, 158–9, 160–61, 194n1, 218, 272
National Court, 1, 12, 72, 79, 81–82, 84, 88, 95, 97, 278
National Planning Commission, 60, 61
Native Administration Ordinance of 1921, 38
Native Americans, 8; Cheyenne, 15
Native Board Regulations of 1889, 29, 34, 35. *See also* Native Regulations Ordinance
Native Customs Recognition Act of 1963, 45, 47, 50, 53, 77, 89, 96; retitled Customs Recognition Act, 75n2
native magistrates (colonial era), 29, 30, 47
Native Magistrates Courts, 29, 30, 34, 35. *See also* Courts for Native Matters
Native Regulations, 29, 30, 31, 36, 38–39; Ordinance of 1908, 35
Native Regulations Ordinance. *See* Native Regulations
natural justice, 42, 81, 111n4
Ndembu (Africa), 16
Negri, Antonio, 273
New Caledonia, 244
Neu Guinea Kompagnie, 28, 32, 51n1
New Guinea Act of 1921, 37

O

O'Collins, Maev, 86
Ok Tedi mine, 20
Operation *Mekim Save*, 62
Oram, Nigel, 40, 78, 79, 118, 143n11
Organic Law of 1995, 64, 65, 67, 69. *See also* provincial government

P

Paga settlement, 124, 131–3, 135, 143nn14,15, 208
Paliwala, Abdul, 79, 85, 89, 96
Papua and New Guinea Act of 1949, 41
Pari village, 7, 114–23, 141nn1, 2, 151, 245, 247–50
Pari village court, 121–3, 150, 169–94, 245–51, 261–2
Pidgin. *See* Tokpisin
police, 7, 31, 34, 48, 51n7, 88, 94, 170, 195, 196; village courts and, *see* village courts
Police Motu. *See* Hiri Motu
polygamy. *See* marriage
Poreporena Highway, 128, 131, 136
Port Moresby, 7, 22, 40, 42, 47, 52n15, 56, 64, 84, 95, 101, 102, 104, 114–5, 117–8, 120, 122, 124, 126–33, 136–9, 143n15, 154, 155, 181, 186, 193, 194n2, 195, 198, 206, 229, 233, 234, 236, 245–6, 247–8; map of, xix
Port Vila (Vanuatu), 9
Pound, Roscoe, 14
Pratt, Justice, 1, 2, 17, 19, 24, 79–80, 280
processual paradigm, 16–17, 275–6
provincial government, 58, 60–62, 64–65, 67–68, 69–71, 73–74, 87. *See also* Organic Law
Provincial Village Court Acts, 61, 70, 73–74, 87. *See also* Organic Law
Pryke, Tony, 55–56, 57, 59–60, 75n5

Q

Quinlivan, Judge P. J., 44, 46–47

R

Ranuguri settlement, 124–32, 135, 136, 143n11, 149, 160, 198
Radcliffe-Brown, A. R., 14
Reay, Marie, 7

reciprocity, 5, 8, 14, 140, 154, 158, 160, 191, 222, 242. *See also* gift economy
relationalism, 241–3, 251–2, 254–7, 262, 265, 278. *See also* individualism
religion. *See* Christianity
Resident Magistrates, 30, 36, 38, 46, 50. *See also* kiaps
restorative justice, 9, 65, 73, 74, 215, 275, 277, 278, 279
Rigo district, 55, 75n8
Roberts, Simon, 16, 17, 275–6
Robinson, C. S., 35
Rowley, C. D., 31, 38
rule-centered paradigm, 17

S
Sanguma. *See* sorcery
Scaglion, Richard, 85, 97–98, 256
Schapera, Ian, 17
Second World War, 25n4, 39, 40, 41, 52n15, 96, 115, 117, 118, 125, 126, 127, 132, 142n8, 143n15
settlements, 22, 24, 47, 52n15, 93, 94, 124–33, 136, 137–9, 142n10, 143n16, 146, 149, 155, 160, 161, 193, 195, 196, 216, 217, 218, 224; committees in, 94, 133, 134, 140, 155, 227, 238–9; media representations of, 124, 224. *See also* Erima settlement; Ranuguri settlement; Paga settlement; Vanama settlement; Vainakomu settlement
shame, 122, 123, 183, 191, 202, 205, 212, 227–8; and guilt, 191–2
Simbu Province, 22, 86, 103, 132, 132, 138, 148, 229, 232, 255
Small Debts Courts, 34, 43
sorcery, 29, 30, 34, 36, 39, 40, 57, 101–8, 119–20, 123, 125, 134, 142n1, 149, 152, 160, 171, 173, 191, 196, 197, 213, 220, 227–8, 232, 234, 252, 282–3

state, 2, 7, 8, 10–11, 12, 13, 20–21, 23, 79, 85, 89, 110, 264, 268, 269–74; 'weak' or 'failing', 2, 274; 'state in society' model; 270–72 (*see also* Migdal, Joel)
Strang, Heather, 215
Strathern, Marilyn, 17, 110, 242, 244, 251, 252, 256–7, 266n7
substantial justice, 1, 13, 17, 21, 24, 50, 53, 79, 161, 277–8, 280
Supreme Court, 43, 81, 95

T
Talea Zapotec (Mexico), 4–5, 7, 19
Tammur, Oscar, 49
Taurama (site and suburb), 116, 119, 249
Taylor, Gabriele, 192
theft, 29, 56, 57, 102, 108, 123, 140, 159, 170–72, 174–80, 191, 193, 220, 231–4, 236–7, 281–2
Tiv (Africa), 15
Toaripi: language, 134, 162, 165, 167; people, 125–6 (*see also* 'Kerema people')
Tokpisin (lingua franca), 29, 62, 66, 74, 83, 93, 95, 103, 118–9, 181–2, 198–9, 200–01, 202–3, 223, 229, 231, 240n2
Tolai people, 32
Tonga (Africa), 16
tradition: notion of, 9, 18, 33, 39–40, 59, 72, 76n8, 86, 91, 98, 114, 119–20, 170, 193; 'invention' of, 12. *See also* culture; custom
Trobriand Islanders, 5, 14
tultuls, 28, 37, 52n8, 93
Turner, Victor, 16
Turner, William, 152, 153, 191
Tuzin, Donald, 244–5, 251, 256, 262

U
UNESCO. *See* United Nations
United Church. *See* Christianity

United Nations, 10–11, 13, 48, 273, 279; Conference on Women, Beijing (1995), 10; UNESCO, 13, 85, 262–5, 276
United States, 8
Universal Declaration of Human Rights (1948). *See* human rights
University of Papua New Guinea, 21–22, 80, 107, 111n6, 126
unofficial courts, 17, 21, 37, 39, 46, 48, 49, 93, 100, 110, 243

V

Vanama settlement, 124, 125, 127, 128–30, 132, 135, 143nn11, 12, 149, 160, 209
Vainakomu settlement, 124, 125, 130–31, 135, 136, 149, 160
Vani, Molly, 150, 166
Vienna Declaration on Human Rights (1993). *See* human rights
village constables, 20, 29, 30–32, 34, 35, 36–37, 41, 46, 48
village courts: proposals for, 41–42, 48–49; planning of, 50–54; administrative problems of, 54–65, 67–68, 70–75 (*see also* Village Court Secretariat); jurisdiction of, 56–57, 72, 77, 82, 110, 170, 171, 214, 223, 254, 255–6, 281–3; relations with district courts, 57, 62, 63, 67, 69, 71, 79, 82, 83, 87, 88, 89, 90, 106, 109, 121, 123, 139, 141, 156, 194, 205, 214, 222, 230, 231, 239, 269; mimicking of district court procedure by, 53–54, 89, 90, 121, 134, 139, 141, 231; villagers' respect for, 63, 69, 71, 91, 155, 160–67; types of offences heard in, 56–57, 102, 122, 134–5, 140–41, 170–73, 196–7, 219–22 (*see also* assault; drunkenness; gossip; insult; sorcery; theft); mediation in, 14, 23, 50, 54, 63, 67, 73, 74, 93–94, 136, 150, 155–6, 158, 161–6, 195, 213–15, 219, 244, 279; evidence in, 82, 103, 106, 196, 231, 236–7, 238, 243, 253, 259, 283; *ultra vires* practice of, 62, 67, 71, 72, 78–9, 86, 87, 88, 255, 279; criticisms of, 1, 2, 12, 23, 56, 65–66, 68–69, 77–91, 96, 109, 146, 147–8, 251, 255–7, 270, 278–9; gender of officials in, 146–51, 166; treatment of women by, 78, 80–87, 111nn1,2,3,8, 255–62; and human rights, 13, 74, 81–82, 86, 87, 97, 255, 273, 275, 276, 279; issues of custom and customary law in, 23, 47, 49–51, 53–4, 73, 75, 77–96, 100–10, 122, 141, 166, 194, 210–11, 229, 256, 267–8, 271, 277–9, 282–3; issues of law in, 1, 4, 13, 21, 23, 53, 54, 56, 64, 66, 77–78, 83–84, 88–95, 100–01, 106–10, 134, 156, 162–6, 238–9, 267–8, 274–5, 278–9; remuneration issues of, 54, 57, 59, 60, 61, 62, 63 64–65, 67–69, 71, 74, 87, 110, 147, 150, 158–9, 160; relations with police, 58–59, 61, 62, 63, 67, 69, 84, 87, 88, 139, 161, 188–9, 214; handbook for, 56, 57, 66, 71, 74, 77, 79, 83, 89, 102, 103, 108, 134, 141, 154, 156, 171, 173, 239, 281–3; training for officials of, 13, 55, 57, 59, 60, 62, 63–68, 71, 72–73, 81, 84, 95, 154, 263, 275, 276, 278, 279–80. *See also* Erima village court; Konedobu village court; Pari village court; Village Courts Act; Village Court Secretariat.
Village Courts Act of 1973, 4, 50, 53, 54, 55, 58, 62, 77, 79, 80, 81, 82, 88–89, 91, 93, 106; replacement of by Village Courts Act of 1989, 64, 75n2; Village Courts

Administration Act of 1980, 60; Village Courts (Amendment) Act of 1986, 62, 75n2. *See also* provincial government; Provincial Village Courts Acts
Village Court Secretariat (VCS), 55, 57–67, 69–72, 94, 154, 159, 173, 213, 218; renamed Community Courts Administration Unit, 72–73

W

Wabag (town and district), 55, 75n8, 111n6
wantokism, 154, 164, 234. *See also* kinship
Wardens Courts, 34, 43
Weiner, Annette, 256
Welsh, Bob, 55, 58, 59

Westermark, George, 85, 92–93, 262
Western Highlands Province, 7, 22, 80, 82, 83–84, 103, 148, 265n1
Whittingham, Rose, 85, 262
witchcraft. *See* sorcery
Williams, F. E., 40, 142n8
Winters, Sir Francis, 34–35
Wilson, Richard, 3, 10, 20
women's rights, 3, 10, 11–13, 27; village courts and (*see* village courts)
World Bank, 10, 273

Y

Yagwoia people, 5, 275

Z

Zambia (Africa), 6